EAT RIGHT, LIVE LONGER

Also by Dr. Barnard

The Power of Your Plate
A Physician's Slimming Guide
Live Longer, Live Better (Cassette)
Food for Life

EAT RIGHT, LIVE LONGER

USING THE NATURAL POWER OF FOODS TO AGE-PROOF YOUR BODY

NEAL BARNARD, M.D.

HARMONY BOOKS NEW YORK

*To the reader seeking to temper the effects of
time and to the thousands of individuals
in clinical studies who helped us
learn how to go about it.*

Copyright © 1995 by Neal Barnard, M.D.
Menus and recipes copyright © 1995 by Jennifer Raymond

Published by Harmony Books, a division of Crown Publishers, Inc.,
201 East 50th Street, New York, New York 10022.
Member of the Crown Publishing Group.

Random House, Inc.   New York, Toronto, London, Sydney, Auckland

HARMONY and colophon are trademarks of Crown Publishers, Inc.

Manufactured in the United States of America

Design by M. Kristen Bearse

Library of Congress Cataloging-in-Publication Data

Barnard, Neal D., 1953–
Eat right, live longer : using the natural power of foods to
age-proof your body / Neal Barnard.
Includes bibliographical references and index.
1. Nutrition.   2. Longevity—Nuritional aspects.   I. Title.
RA784.B317   1995
613.2—dc20   95-2519
                                                     CIP

ISBN 0-517-79950-2

10   9   8   7   6   5   4   3   2   1

First Edition

CONTENTS

ACKNOWLEDGMENTS

I owe a great debt to many people who helped to bring this volume to fruition.

Jennifer Raymond has translated powerful nutritional concepts into recipes that treat the senses, yet are familiar and simple to prepare.

T. Colin Campbell, Ph.D., provided innumerable insights into the ways that plant-based diets promote optimal human health. His work in the China Diet and Health Study continues to represent the state of the art in research.

The late Dr. Linus Pauling kindly responded to my many requests for detailed information on the role of vitamin C in human health.

Paul Talalay, M.D., of the Johns Hopkins University, and Chithan Kandaswami, Ph.D., of the State University of New York at Buffalo, furnished detailed information on how foods bolster the body's detoxification machinery.

David Kritchevsky, Ph.D., of the Wistar Institute, provided many new insights on the roles of cholesterol and stress in heart disease.

John McDougall, M.D., David Perlmutter, M.D., and Joel Fuhrman, M.D., shared their knowledge of new clinical approaches to arthritis, prostate disease, and other problems.

John R. Lee, M.D., and Jesse Hanley, M.D., are breaking new ground in the use of natural preparations to restore hormone balance and kindly shared their experience.

Albert M. Kligman, M.D., Ph.D., of the University of Pennsylvania, and Michael T. Goldfarb, M.D., of the University of Michigan, supplied invaluable information on strategies for protecting and rejuvenating the skin.

The librarians at Himmelfarb Medical Library of the George Washington University Medical Center—George Ball, Ann Linton, Sally Winthrop, Mary Ryan, Karyn Pomerantz, Nancy Terry, and Daisy Espinosa—responded quickly and thoroughly to my endless requests for information. This book would have been impossible without their help.

A very special thank you to all who provided a palette to color this work: Marjorie Shelley of the Metropolitan Museum of Art, Lesley Stevenson of the National Gallery of Art, Edward S. Van Vleet, Ph.D., of the University of South Florida, Ron Protas, artistic director of the Martha Graham Dance Company, Formula One and Indycar champion Emerson Fittipaldi, Gary Smith of the Aspen Wellness Group, and John Zimmerman of *Racer* magazine.

Deepest appreciation goes to Patti Breitman, whose clarity of purpose, endless good sense, and critical eye add to her enormous talents as a literary agent.

Shaye Areheart made an author's job wonderfully easy. Her skillful editing and enthusiastic support made it a pleasure. This book would have been impossible without the support of Peter Guzzardi, a good friend, editor, and publisher. Karin Wood and Heather Julius have been wonderful to work with, carefully speeding along the editorial process.

Special thanks to Penny Simon, Nancy Maloney, and Brian Belfiglio, without whose tireless efforts my words would have simply gathered dust on bookshelves.

I owe a continuing debt to the staff of the Physicians Committee for Responsible Medicine, particularly Christine Bartlett, who spent her weekends critically reviewing the manuscript while her husband, Dale, mowed the lawn. Thanks also to Nabila Abdulwahab, Peggy Carlson, M.D., Sossena Dagne, Claudia Delman, Doug Hall, Peggy Hilden, Louise Holton, Suzanne McCaffrey, Andrew Nicholson, M.D., Dave Wasser, and Rod Weaver for taking over innumerable tasks while I ensconced myself in research and writing.

A NOTE TO THE READER

My goal is to provide you with information on the power of foods to affect many aspects of your health. However, neither this nor any other book can take the place of individualized medical care or advice. If you have any medical condition, are overweight, or are on medication, please talk with your doctor about how dietary changes will affect your health. Sometimes changes in eating habits can change your need for medication or have other important effects. Also please see your doctor before any substantial increase in your physical activity if you are over forty or have any medical condition. All readers should consult the guidelines on pages 231 to 232.

The science of nutrition grows gradually as time goes on, so I encourage you to consult other sources of information, including the references listed in this volume.

Most of all, if you are currently following the eating habits that are typical of North America and Western Europe, please read this volume and consider changing to a more healthful and powerful way of eating. You will not regret it.

INTRODUCTION

It's Not the Clock; It's Chemistry

A Stradivarius, if it has been well cared for, plays more beautifully than a violin crafted ten or fifteen years ago. Likewise, your body can shine with strength and beauty regardless of your age.

New, revolutionary methods can temper the toll of time and even reverse aspects of aging. You can take their power into your hands and begin to use it right now. Never before have we had such astounding control over the aging process. We now know what attacks the skin and causes wrinkles. We know what pulls calcium out of our bones. We have a new understanding of varicose veins and tremendous new insights on curing weight problems. And you have power you may never have imagined over every one of these and many more.

Imagine how you would like to look. For the moment, throw aside modesty. If you could wave a magic wand and change any aspects of your body at all, what would you do? Make that image as clear in your mind as you can. Picture yourself as you would most like to be. Now, imagine every cell in your body actually working to make that image a reality. Your face, your arms, your legs, your waistline, and all your internal organs are remodeling themselves into exactly the image you have chosen. This is not a new hairstyle or a new pair of shoes. This is a whole new way of thinking about your body.

All the cells in your body have a built-in aptitude for repair and rejuvenation. Some cells specialize in removing chemical pollutants that harm your body tissues. Others burn off fat to keep your waistline slim. Still others reverse damage to the skin. In order to turn these and many other surprising functions on, your cells need the right kinds of nutrients. It is amazingly easy to do. And when you take advantage of certain foods, you begin the process of rejuvenating every part of your body.

In my last book, *Food for Life,* I touched on the power of foods to affect aging, in the context of how they can improve health in many other ways. Since then, I have received innumerable calls and letters from people wanting more information about how to counteract the effects of time. This book is a step-by-step guide. It proceeds in eight steps from the inside of your body outward. When you have finished, you will be amazed at the abilities you will have and astounded as you see other people neglecting to tap these powers for themselves and, regrettably, accepting the consequences as you might otherwise have done.

THE EIGHT STEPS OF AGE-PROOFING

We will begin at your biological core, deep inside your cells. Each day, when you have looked in the mirror at the skin of your forehead or around your eyes, you might have noticed lines gradually forming. What you cannot see is that these lines are the result of destructive chemicals called free radicals forming inside your cells and between them, which damage your skin. Certain nutrients can shield your cells from these attacks, not only in your skin, but in all parts of your body. I am not referring to nutrient supplements from a health food store. The protectors you need are in foods that are probably already in your cupboard or refrigerator or can easily be found at any grocery store. The key is to learn how to use them. They give you enormous power.

But that is only the first step. The next step is to turn on natural enzymes in your body that strengthen your defenses against environmental pollutants that would age you. Some of these pollutants come to us from factories, cigarette smoke, or auto exhaust. Others are hidden in water or food. And given half a chance, they will speed up aging processes. But it turns out that certain protective foods actually help you eliminate pollutants. As amazing as that may be, it has been well established by research at major universities, and you can take advantage of it right now. Moreover, you can take advantage of powerful ways to build your immune system to knock out "living pollutants"—viruses, bacteria, and cancer cells.

These first two steps work hand in hand. The first protects you against the internal threat of free radicals; the second helps you fend off chemicals coming in from the outside.

Step three gives you an ability most people would never have guessed they might have: the ability to control your sex hormones. The issue is not mainly sex drive or sexual potency, although we will have plenty to say about both. Much more important is the ability to control the most fundamental aspects of your body chemistry. Hormones can keep you young and vigorous or they can hand you menstrual or menopausal symptoms, hair loss, prostate problems, and even cancer. Most people have no idea that foods can alter both the amount of sex hormones that are coursing through their blood vessels and also their effect on mind and body. Rather than let your hormones control you and make you look and feel old, you will be able to control them, using foods that are powerful and yet safe, so much so that hormone supplements look crude by comparison. You can even modify hormones that affect the risk of cancer of the breast, uterus, ovary, and prostate. You will be able to use as much or as little of this power as you like.

Step four is to surge-protect your veins and arteries. You will learn how foods can reduce the vein pressures that lead to varicose veins, hemorrhoids, and other problems. There is no need to let your veins go to pot. You can take advantage of these astounding findings within just twenty-four to forty-eight hours. We will also see powerful steps that can keep blood pressure normal. Most people who take blood pressure medications will no longer need them if they follow these simple steps. Let me hasten to add that you should not simply throw your medications away. Let your doctor monitor your progress and taper you off your medications as you progress. I cannot tell you how wonderful it is for people who have been treated with pills of all kinds to be able to get away from them and their side effects and begin to live again. If you thought that could not possibly include you, just wait and see what is in store.

These four steps go a long way toward tackling the supposedly inevitable processes of aging. But there is so much more waiting for you.

If the possibility of slowing or reversing aspects of the aging process is new to you, you are not alone. While some of the principles in this book are becoming more widely known, most are so new that your doctor never learned about them in medical school and health magazines have not yet picked up on them except in the most superficial ways. Nonetheless, the knowledge you will take into your hands is supported by a wealth of research; scientific references are provided for each chapter for those who would like to consult more detailed information.

Step five shows how to rejuvenate your arteries. The blockages that slow the flow of blood and lead to heart attacks, strokes, and even impotence can be prevented and in fact reversed. I will show you the powerful yet simple program that does exactly that. It does not matter how old you are or how long artery blockages have been progressing. They can begin to clear out at any age, without drugs or surgery.

In step six, you will learn about new techniques to keep strong bones that go far beyond the all-too-weak hormone-pills-and-calcium routine. The new methods involve more than slowing bone loss. Amazing as it sounds, there are ways to make your bones denser and stronger, no matter what your age. All of this is done naturally and safely.

I have saved for the seventh step what many people find to be the most delightful part of this program. It is an extraordinary way to get rid of fat by adjusting your metabolism so that you burn calories more quickly. The result is much more powerful than old-fashioned diets, and there is no calorie counting or skimpy meal portions. Best of all, it is permanent. This technique is currently being used by hundreds of thousands of people, and if you have a weight problem—either a big one or a small one—you will be amazed at how you seem to shed years as you shed pounds.

In step eight, we arrive at the surface of your body—your skin and hair. You will learn what causes wrinkles and what you can do about them, taking advantage of the latest scientific methods. We will also look at surprising factors that influence hair loss. No, it is not all genetic, yet even genetic factors can be influenced.

These new methods are not an imaginary fountain of eternal youth.

They are real. After a lecture at a midwestern university, a woman came up to me and said, "I've been following the kind of program you talk about, and it's absolutely marvelous. No one guesses that I'm sixty-three. They think I'm twenty years younger" She fooled me, too. But her experience is not unusual. Many people are finding exactly the same thing.

What could it mean to put all this together? As your bones become stronger, your arteries begin to clean themselves out, your fat layer gradually dissolves, your skin is rejuvenated, and every cell in your body has an extra layer of protection, you can look years younger and feel more energetic than ever before.

It's Not All Genetic

Your body has no expiration date. While many aspects of our biology are coded on our genes, the length of your life, how you feel, and how you look depend to a great degree on choices you can make.

The question is, do you want to take advantage of that power? Surprising as it sounds, not everyone does. Many people still believe that their bodies have a ticking biological clock that cannot be altered. "We're all going to die, sooner or later," they say. "You may as well live it up while you can." They then proceed to eat foods that accelerate aging, weaken their bones, and make them so obese they are unable to go dancing, make love, play tennis, or romp with their children or grandchildren. They "live it up" in doctors' offices, pharmacies, and hospital beds. When they've finally had enough, they end up on long lists of medicines or diets that are tantamount to starvation. As their lives become more and more constricted, applying food to their tongue may be the only pleasure they are physically capable of; their habits have robbed them of all others.

The opposite view—the youthful omnipotence that assumes strength lasts forever—leads to precisely the same result. Greasy food, nicotine, and other poisons go down the hatch day after day until around age forty or fifty we suddenly wake up like a college kid after a tequila-drinking contest, realizing that we have poisoned ourselves.

Most of us assume that aging is simply a matter of genetics: Our skin will gradually wrinkle, our waistlines will expand, our arteries will clog up, and our bones will soften and eventually collapse. If that happened to your parents or grandparents, you might naturally assume that that is what will happen to you. After all, your parents gave you their genes. But there is one vital fact that must not be ignored. Your parents did not only give you DNA. They did not say, "Here you are. This is your genetic endowment. Now your fate is sealed forever." The fact is, your parents also gave you recipes. They gave you tastes for certain foods, culinary traditions, and all sorts of ideas about how you should feel about eating. These things have a profound effect on your body, whether you are aware of them or not. They are passed from parent to child, generation after generation. They make health problems look for all the world as if they are hereditary. When you change the foods you eat, the differences can be astonishing. Characteristics you may have thought were genetic sometimes vanish.

The age to which you live need not be determined by your parents' age. Their experience need not be yours at all. As miraculous as it may sound, you can reshape your destiny, provided you know how to go about it. You can take into your hands strength and beauty that you never dreamed of.

Your success in this enterprise depends on one thing: the willingness to try something new. If you are open to the good things in store for you, you can gain a new level of health and a whole new body to complement the wisdom and experience you have gained and that are now greater than at any time in your life.

A Stradivarius really does play more beautifully than any newer model. So does a Stratocaster, the 1950s-era Fender guitar that was the power of Jimi Hendrix and the soul of Stevie Ray Vaughn. These musical instruments were brilliantly designed and built with precision. But your body is so intricate and so beautifully crafted that it far outshines any human invention. It is waiting to show you its real beauty and strength. Most people never tap even a fraction of their innate biological assets. But for you, things can be very different. Whatever your age, whatever your goals, you can let the natural power hidden in foods work for you.

CHAPTER ONE

PROTECTING EVERY CELL

The light plays gently on the delicate face of Michelangelo's Delphic Sibyl. Her red-brown hair has escaped from its cloth restraint and cascades onto a mantle of pale red and blue. Full of anticipation, her youthful eyes seem to change constantly from wariness to self-assurance to defiance.

You would not know it now, but her eyes had grown dim and her face had become discolored and worn. Michelangelo began the fresco in 1508. Each day he spread his *giornata*, a day's worth of wet plaster, and painted colors that fused with the plaster as it dried. For hundreds of years after the unveiling in 1512, the young prophetess adorned the ceiling of the Sistine Chapel. But candle soot, incense smoke, and dust obscured her beauty so gradually that no one could see what was happening.

Caretakers tried to bring out the colors by adding a layer of varnish but succeeded only in obscuring them even more. Others fumbled with attempts at restoration, sometimes leaving their own marks in the process. Finally, in a carefully planned effort, experts were called in to remove the patina. Even their skilled hands could not eliminate slight areas of permanent damage, but these turned out to be minor. Her magnificent eyes began to emerge from the dark veil that had obscured them for countless decades. When the task was finished, viewers were stunned by the image that had been hidden for so long.

This figure was not damaged by time alone. The damage was done by particles in the air and aggravated by previous treatments that did more harm than good.

The same things that assault a beautiful Renaissance figure also abuse the faces that come to view it. Everyone who walks along the street outside or works in a nearby shop is affected by light, air, and pollutants. And just as time alone did almost nothing to the centuries-old fresco, it cannot account for all that happens to the human body.

The most harmful chemical pollutants do not come from smokestacks in gloomy sections of industrial cities but from biological factories inside our bodies. Manufacturing plants that build bones, skin, hormones, and power plants that turn food into energy to propel our movements are operating every minute of every day. They make their intended products, but they also produce wastes that accumulate within our cells or circulate in the blood, causing all sorts of harm. They are central to the aging process. If you can slow down or stop their effects, you can slow or even reverse important aspects of aging.

You *can* restore your biological artistry. Incredible as it sounds, you can remove the accumulated "soot and grime" from the innermost part of your body to the surface of your skin. Natural, but powerful compounds in foods make that possible. When you have these foods working for you, the protection is automatic.

YOUR CELLULAR ARTISTRY

Not only frescoes are attacked by pollutants. All works of art are vulnerable. The canvas or paper strands that are the foundation of oil paintings were once living and growing cotton or wood. Beneath the painted image, these fibers dry out and crack, and as the years go by, the painting can begin to sag.

Your basic design is held in strands of a different kind. Your hair and eye color, your size and even your shape, all the complicated processes that go on inside your body, and perhaps even aspects of your temperament are coded on the microscopic strands that make up your chromosomes. The molecules of deoxyribonucleic acid—that is, DNA—that make up each chromosome are fragile, too. One small nick in your DNA can destroy the cell. Or it can make it lose control and begin multiplying endlessly, causing cancer. The injury is caused by unstable molecules called free radicals. These aggressive molecules are the equivalent of factory exhaust, forming in your body constantly as your cells carry out their normal functions. While you sleep, free radicals form in your bloodstream. Left to their own devices, they attack your skin, causing the lines and discolorations that many people think are simply due to age. When you wake up in the morning and look at your skin, you cannot see any difference compared to the day before. But over time the result is obvious: wrinkles, lines, and discolorations. They also damage the lenses of your eyes, contributing to cataracts, and attack every other cell in your body. When you think of aging, think about free radicals.

The first step in age-proofing is to protect your cells. You can actually reach every cell from the top of your head to the soles of your feet and surround them in a layer of protection that knocks out free radicals as they form. You can even take steps to stop them from forming in the first place. Let's take a minute to understand these molecular misfits that are trying to obscure your natural beauty and strength.

FREE RADICALS COME FROM OXYGEN

What we are protecting against, believe it or not, is oxygen. We breathe in oxygen every minute of every day. Oxygen is life-giving. But it is also dangerous. If you saw a truck carrying tanks of oxygen down the highway, you would likely give it a wide berth because oxygen is unstable and explosive. As oxygen molecules are used in the body, we think of them as being converted to carbon dioxide and exhaled. But some of them stay in the body. As it happens, they are easily bent out of shape. They take on extra electrons from other molecules or have electrons in unstable orbits. A free radical is nothing more than oxygen that has been altered in these ways. It is no longer a life-giving element that you breathe into your nostrils but a threat. It is ornery, temperamental, and extremely aggressive, ready to take a bite out of any other molecule that happens to be nearby. If that molecule happens to be your DNA, the free radical has scored a direct hit to the heart of one of your cells.

Oxygen can turn into several different types of free radicals, with names like superoxide, singlet oxygen, and hydroxyl radical. The names are not important. What is important is that these molecular kamikazes exist for only a few microseconds before crashing into other molecules. During that lightning-fast interval, much quicker than the blink of an eye, a bit of your body is destroyed. How many nicks can your skin take before it buckles into wrinkles? How many tiny wounds can your joints put up with before they begin to ache and even lose their normal form? Free radicals are trying to age every part of you. It's not the clock that does that—it's chemistry.

When you take control of this process—when you give your cells a protective shield—you can slow down a central part of the aging process.

Your body is already trying to get rid of free radicals. Believe it or not, it turns some free radicals into hydrogen peroxide—the very same stuff that is sold in plastic bottles and used to bleach hair and sterilize cuts. And peroxide is then turned into water.[1] Your cells work that bit of alchemy automatically.* It sounds like a strange and rather pathetic system—taking free radicals and turning them into hydrogen peroxide, of all things. But your body is desperate. It has to get rid of free radicals somehow and this is the best defense it could come up with. And, to an extent, it works. Your cells can use the oxygen they need and the free radicals that inevitably form are turned into peroxide and then water. If the body can turn oxygen-free radicals into water, they can do no harm.

This simple system needs help. It cannot cope with all the free radicals that form. The oxygen hitting your lungs and dissolving into your blood can make enough free radicals to eventually destroy every cell in your body. While your cells have many different defenses against free radicals, their protections are not nearly as strong as they could be. The result is much more harm to your skin, eyes, and internal organs than would otherwise occur. Certain foods come to the rescue. They release protective nutrients into your bloodstream, helping you repel free

---

*For readers interested in technical details, superoxide dismutase is the enzyme that turns superoxide free radicals into hydrogen peroxide in your cells. A second enzyme, called catalase, then turns hydrogen peroxide into water, which is, of course, harmless.

radicals, preserving your cells, and counteracting this aspect of the aging process.

PROTECTING THE SURFACE OF EVERY CELL

Centuries ago, artists could not have predicted what pollutants, smoke, and light would do to their paintings as time crawled by. Perhaps they had not guessed that their works would have an audience many years later. Leonardo da Vinci's *Last Supper* was already delicate when he painted it using an ill-chosen experimental technique in fifteenth-century Milan, and it has seriously eroded over the centuries. Restoration efforts have damaged it even more.

Likewise, the fragility of the Sistine Chapel ceiling became apparent before it was even finished. Water and salts discolored it and cracks formed in the plaster. Early attempts to repair the fresco were crude, to say the least. Stucco was dabbed into cracks. Bronze brackets were fastened in place to stop chunks of masonry from falling to the floor. The most famous detail of the masterpiece, God's and Adam's hands not quite touching, deteriorated to the point that an unknown touch-up artist painted on new fingertips.

Oddest of all were the attempts by a restorer named Lagi to clean the darkened fresco in 1625 by rubbing it with chunks of cheap bread, followed by the Mazzuolis, a father and son, who doused it with Greek wine.[2] It is surprising the whole fresco did not simply dissolve. These failed efforts reinforced the impression that Michelangelo had actually intended the work to be veiled in gloomy darkness.

A serious and comprehensive restoration began in the early 1980s. Modern computers analyzed the fresco in elaborate detail. In an expensive and time-consuming process, precise cleaning techniques restored the arresting radiance of bright colors and dancing brushstrokes.

Cleaning and protecting the microscopic structure of your skin, muscles, or eyes is a much more challenging task. But your body does not rely on cheap bread, Greek wine, or, for that matter, modern computers. It has much more powerful tools.

One place that gets special attention is the thin membrane that surrounds each cell. Cell membranes are what gives your body tissues their shape and substance. When someone kisses your lips, caresses your skin, or admires you from afar, it is the cell membranes of your skin that are getting all that attention. A cell without a membrane is like a cherry or blueberry that has lost its skin; it is fragile and formless and will not last. If free radicals damage even a single molecule in a cell membrane, it can set off a chain reaction that, if not stopped, will destroy the cell. If all your cell membranes were destroyed, you would turn into a pile of Jell-O.

You can protect your cell membranes against damaging free radical attacks if your diet contains generous amounts of foods from four sources: vegetables, fruits, grains (such as breads, cereals, pasta, rice, oats, or corn), and legumes (beans, peas, and lentils). These foods sound very humble and if your diet contains only modest amounts of them, they will not do very much for you. But in more generous amounts, their power reveals itself. They hold natural compounds that actually wedge themselves in the cell membrane and protect it, while other nutrients guard the bloodstream.

Cell Protector Number One: Selenium.   As we saw earlier, one of your cells' defenses is to use enzymes that turn dangerous free radicals into hydrogen peroxide and then water. Unfortunately, some free radicals are so explosively reactive that they attack your cells before they are even spotted by these enzymes. To cope with this problem, cells have other powerful enzymes that watch over the cell membrane, neutralizing free radicals and stopping destructive chain reactions that have started.[3]

One of these enzymes needs a special nutrient, the mineral selenium. Selenium comes from the soil and passes into plants, particularly grains, as they grow. As we break bread and wind spaghetti around our forks, we do not think about the fact that we are tapping a powerful antiaging nutrient. But these grains pass their selenium into your body, where it activates the enzymes that protect your cell membranes.* The amount of

*Another note for the technically minded: The enzyme phospholipase A2 frees damaged molecules from the cell membrane. A second enzyme, glutathione peroxidase, stabilizes them. Selenium is part of the glutathione peroxidase enzyme.

selenium in the soil varies widely from one area to another. You might not get enough selenium if your sources for it were all from the same geographic location, but if your bread comes from Kansas wheat, your spaghetti from North Dakota, and your biscuits from France, there is an averaging effect that was not possible before food shipment became an everyday event, and you are almost certain to get plenty of selenium.

The National Research Council recommends that we get 50 to 200 micrograms of selenium every day. Some people take selenium supplements, but I don't recommend this because selenium is very powerful. A little too much and it becomes poisonous. In the early 1960s, the weathering of high-selenium rock formations in part of China caused an unusual selenium load in the soil. Huge quantities of the mineral ended up in cultivated plants. The average resident got about five milligrams (five thousand micrograms) of selenium per day. The result was an epidemic of hair loss, fingernail changes, and nerve symptoms. Perhaps the world record of selenium consumption was caused by a manufacturer who mistakenly packed 27.3 milligrams of selenium into individual pills. One woman who managed to swallow over two grams' worth (two million micrograms) over a 2½-month period developed nausea and vomiting, fatigue, a peculiar breath odor, and fingernail tenderness and loss, and her hair fell out.[4]

A much better strategy is to be sure that your diet contains generous amounts of bread, rice, pasta, cereals, and other grains. This will provide enough selenium to protect your cell membranes but will avoid excesses.[5] This is very easy to do, of course, but a very powerful first step in age-proofing. If the hands of the clock have become like fists that are pummeling your skin and beating your body out of shape, you have now begun to fight back.

Cell Protector Number Two: Vitamin E.   A second protector is found in the natural vegetable oils inside each grain of wheat that travels to the bakery and then to your kitchen. It is a trace of vitamin E. It is also in the natural oils in beans, vegetables, nuts, and fruits. Vitamin E enters your bloodstream and is delivered to your cells, where it lodges in the cell membrane. There it sits until free radicals come along to threaten the cell.

Vitamin E is a powerful antioxidant—a destroyer of free radicals. The battle against free radicals damages the vitamin E molecule, but it is soon regenerated by vitamin C so it can protect the cell membrane over and over.[6]

The recommended dietary allowance is eight milligrams per day for women and ten milligrams per day for men. Unfortunately, the average American woman gets only about five milligrams and the average American man gets only about seven milligrams.[7] I would recommend that you think of the RDA as a minimum and that you include enough vitamin E–rich foods in your daily menu to meet or exceed it. (Table 1.1, page 15, lists foods rich in vitamin E.)

When supplements are used in research, they often reach doses of four hundred to eight hundred milligrams per day, or even higher. However, such large doses are really used as medications rather than as part of normal nutrition, and they are not a guide to how much your body actually needs. Although benefits have sometimes been shown from these doses, they have generally been in subjects following diets that are otherwise far from ideal or suffering from medical conditions.

My own recommendation is not to rely on supplements but rather to incorporate natural vitamin E–rich foods into an optimal menu, along with the vitamin C that allows vitamin E to be used and reused repeatedly. Shortly you will see exactly how to go about it.

Cell Protector Number Three: Carotenoids.   Carrots, sweet potatoes, pumpkins, and other orange vegetables deliver their pigment, beta-carotene, to your bloodstream where, like vitamin E, it enters the cell membrane to protect it against free radicals. It does its best work in the parts of the body that are remote from oxygen, while vitamin E works best in the oxygen-rich parts of the body such as the lungs and red blood cells.[8]

Food manufacturers use beta-carotene as a natural color. If you were to eat an enormous amount of it, it would color you, too, particularly your palms and soles, which would take on a slight (and harmless) orange tinge. Scientists appreciated it at first only because it can be broken apart to make two molecules of vitamin A, which the body uses for eyesight

TABLE 1.1

Top Foods for Vitamin E (milligrams)

Almonds, 1 ounce, dried	6.7
Avocado, 1 medium	2.3
Brazil nuts, 1 ounce, dried	2.1
Broccoli, 1 cup*	1.0
Brussels sprouts, 1 cup*	1.3
Chickpeas, 1 cup*	5.1
Corn kernels, 1 cup*	9.5
Mango, 1 medium	2.3
Navy beans, 1 cup*	4.1
Brown rice, 1 cup*	4.0
Soybeans, 1 cup*	35.0
Spaghetti, 1 cup*	1.0
Spinach, raw, 1 cup	1.7
Sweet potato, 1 medium*	5.9
Wheat germ, 1 ounce, toasted	4.0

*Figures refer to cooked servings.
Sources: Pennington, J. A. T. 1989. *Bowes and Church's Food Values of Portions Commonly Used.* Philadelphia: J. B. Lippincott; McLaughlin, P. J., and J. L. Weihrauch. 1979. Vitamin E content of foods, *Journal of the American Dietetic Association* 75:647–65.

and other functions. But beta-carotene and its more than six hundred naturally occurring *carotenoid* relatives have eclipsed vitamin A in importance, because they have antioxidant and immune-boosting properties that vitamin A lacks.[9]

This yellow-orange hue appears in Michelangelo's famous fresco. Aptly enough, it is a huge protective cloak wrapped around a man lost in thought, leaning his head against his hand and furrowing his brow. The figure is Michelangelo himself. Perhaps the artist followed a healthy diet because, in spite of the fact that he was never kind in his self-renderings (in the *Last Judgment* on the altar wall, he painted the discarded skin of St. Bartholomew and its dead face was his own), he was healthy, robust, and lived to be nearly ninety.

Beta-carotene cloaks and protects your cells and helps them live longer, too. While carotenoids are particularly concentrated in orange vegetables, they are also in all green and yellow vegetables. You will find lots of them in spinach, squash, kale, and many others.

If your diet contains just two carrots, or a sweet potato and a serving of spinach, or three to four servings of green vegetables every day, you will get twenty to thirty milligrams of beta-carotene, which is the amount shown to be beneficial in research studies (see table 1.2, below), along with the full range of other carotenoids.

Although I am presenting some of the details of how these powerful

TABLE 1.2

Top Foods for Beta-Carotene (milligrams)

Broccoli, 1 cup*	1.3
Butternut squash, 1 cup*	8.6
Carrot, 1 medium	12.0
Collard greens, 1 cup*	2.5
Kale, 1 cup*	5.8
Mustard greens, 1 cup*	2.5
Pumpkin, 1 cup*	1.6
Spinach, 1 cup*	8.8
Spring onions, ½ cup	1.5
Sweet potato, 1 medium*	15.0
Swiss chard, 1 cup*	3.3

*Figures refer to cooked servings.
Source: Pennington, J. A. T. 1989. *Bowes and Church's Food Values of Portions Commonly Used.* Philadelphia: J. B. Lippincott.

allies work for us, let me encourage you not to get so wrapped up in the chemistry that you lose the focus on foods. What we are really doing is exploiting the fact that grains, beans, vegetables, and fruits contain powerful natural protectors that work their way into your tissues to fend off free radicals that would otherwise destroy your cell membranes one by one. When your daily menu is rich in these foods, you have a constant source of protection. Your cells know exactly what to do with antioxidants. You just have to supply generous amounts of them in the foods you eat. In case you are thinking that you have to have one food for vitamin E, another for beta-carotene, and yet another for various other vitamins, let me emphasize that it is actually much easier than that. If your diet is rich in vegetables, fruits, grains, and legumes, you will get a good mix of antioxidants. Foods as simple and delicious as spaghetti with tomato and basil sauce, perhaps with side orders of beans (fagioli) and broccoli with garlic, and fresh fruit for dessert are as appealing to your biochemistry as your palate.

Michelangelo's palette was not simply green, yellow, and orange. He used the full rainbow of hues. Similarly, it is a bit simplistic to speak only of selenium, vitamin E, and beta-carotene. As I noted above, green, yellow, and orange vegetables give you much more than beta-carotene. They supply dozens of other powerful carotenoids and other natural antioxidants, too. Vitamin E likewise exists in several related forms, and these foods will gladly bring them to you. They help insure that your smooth and resilient hands and lips welcome the caresses they have coming.

PROTECTING THE BLOODSTREAM

Protecting your cells is only the beginning. You can also protect your bloodstream because free radicals can form there, too. Happily, vegetables and fruits provide vitamin C, which patrols the bloodstream and steps in and out of the cells of many organs. It enters your joints, your brain and spinal cord, and even your eyes, where it tirelessly removes free radicals.[10]

Rats, mice, dogs, cats, and nearly all other animals make vitamin C right in their own bodies. They do not need any in their diets. Our primate ancestors, however, lost the ability to make vitamin C, as did guinea pigs and the fruit-eating bat, presumably because it was so abundant in all the leaves and fruits around them.[11] If vitamin C–rich fruits and vegetables are not front and center in our diet, we are laying ourselves open to the aging effects of free radicals. (Table 1.3, page 20, lists foods rich in vitamin C.)

Citrus fruits, strawberries, and green vegetables such as broccoli and Brussels sprouts are especially rich in vitamin C. As you eat them, you can almost feel their protection working its way into your blood. It is an extraordinary slayer of free radicals.

Its principal advocate was Nobel laureate Linus Pauling, who demonstrated the vitamin's power against colds. But that was just for starters. Vitamin C helps make the collagen protein that strengthens our muscles, bones, and skin. It is also used to make brain chemicals that regulate moods and other psychological functions.[12] Moreover, people whose diets are rich in vitamin C have less cancer risk, particularly for cancers of the breast, lung, esophagus, mouth, stomach, pancreas, cervix, and rectum.[13]

"At this point, there is little doubt that a higher intake of vitamin C is associated with lower cancer rates," Pauling said. "There is also a role for vitamin C for people who have cancer." Studies have shown improved survival in cancer patients taking large doses of vitamin C. "Dr. Ewan Cameron gave ten grams of vitamin C per day to patients with terminal cancer, and they lived much longer than similar patients in the same hospital who didn't get vitamin C." Dr. Pauling's colleague, Dr. Abram Hoffer, did a similar study using twelve grams of vitamin C per day in cancer patients and found similar results.

That's a lot of vitamin C. If your diet consisted solely of vegetables and fruits, your vitamin C intake could range from three to twelve grams per day, depending on which varieties you chose. If you were to take typical five-hundred-milligram vitamin C tablets, you'd have to swallow twenty-four of them to get twelve grams.

Chimpanzees, gorillas, and other primates get large amounts of vitamin C in the vegetables and fruits they consume throughout the day.

Many humans, however, have developed a taste for chicken and beef, neither one of which contains any vitamin C at all. Our taste buds may relish the dense calories meats contain, but to the extent they are added to the diet, every cell is left with reduced protection. If Mother Nature had known we were going to try to eat like cats and dogs—that is, like true carnivores—she might have kept vitamin C–making machinery in our bodies. "Human beings, as compared with other animals, are being cheated in that they don't get enough vitamin C to keep them in good general health," Pauling said.

"The optimal amount of vitamin C is something I've been trying to determine for years, and my feeling is that it is about twelve grams per day for an adult," Pauling said. His estimate comes from the amount of vitamin C other animals make within their bodies. "They all make about the same amount proportional to their body weight. For an animal about the size of a man, it is about twelve grams per day. They make their own; ours must come from diet or supplements.

"That doesn't mean that to benefit from vitamin C you need to take twelve grams a day," Pauling added. Even modest increases will do some good. After intake reaches three to six grams per day, there are diminishing returns to going higher. Pauling himself took what some would consider a heroic dose, eighteen grams per day, and others have taken even more.

The body pays close attention to how much vitamin C you take in. If your diet contains amounts at or below the recommended dietary allowance of sixty milligrams, the digestive tract absorbs nearly all of it. But if you were to take in one gram per day, only about 75 percent is absorbed. At 1.5 grams, only 50 percent is absorbed. At six grams, only a quarter of the vitamin C (about 1.5 grams) is absorbed and at twelve grams, only 16 percent makes its way into the body. That means that only about two of the twelve grams are actually absorbed. The rest is simply lost in the feces. In addition, your kidneys normally conserve vitamin C, but the more vitamin C you ingest, the more the kidneys let it pass out into the urine.[14] The higher your intake, the less of it your body tries to keep.

Vitamin C can act as a laxative, which tends to limit the amount people can take. However, Pauling did not believe that there was any sub-

TABLE 1.3

Top Foods for Vitamin C (milligrams)

Broccoli, 1 cup*	98
Brussels sprouts, 1 cup*	96
Cantaloupe, 1 cup	68
Cauliflower, 1 cup*	68
Black currants, ½ cup	101
Grapefruit, 1 medium	94
Guava, 1 medium	165
Kale, 1 cup*	54
Orange, 1 medium	80
Orange juice, 1 cup	124
Papaya, 1 medium	188
Pineapple chunks, 1 cup	24
Spinach, raw, 1 cup	16
Strawberries, 1 cup	85
Sweet potato, 1 medium*	28

*Figures refer to cooked servings.
Source: Pennington, J. A. T. 1989. *Bowes and Church's Food Values of Portions Commonly Used.* Philadelphia: J. B. Lippincott.

stantial danger from high doses of vitamin C. "Although one hears of concerns about kidney stones from high doses of vitamin C, there is no case reported in the medical literature of a person getting kidney stones because of a high intake of vitamin C. In studies giving ten to twelve grams a day to thousands of patients over the last forty years, not a single one has had kidney stones. I don't think there is any reason to believe that vitamin C causes stones. So there is little, if any, risk and tremendous potential benefit."

For those who regularly take very high doses, there is a danger in stopping it abruptly. "If a person who has been taking large doses of vitamin C suddenly stops taking it, the level in the blood goes down practically to zero," Pauling said. "The body adjusts to the high dose by making enzymes that change the vitamin C to certain oxidation products. So it takes a week or two for the subject to get back to normal where these enzymes are no longer functioning. During that period, the person is particularly susceptible to illnesses of all kinds. If there is some reason to stop, it should be done gradually over a period of a couple of weeks." Another potential problem is vitamin C's tendency to increase iron absorption, as we will see shortly.

There are continuing hints of other roles for vitamin C beyond colds, cancer, and aging. "Two of my associates carried out an experiment with cells infected with HIV," Pauling said. "They found that vitamin C prevents the virus from multiplying. The amount was equivalent to that which a person gets by taking about ten grams of vitamin C per day. For years I've been recommending that patients with AIDS be given high doses of vitamin C as an adjunct to whatever other treatment they have been getting." Regrettably, researchers have not taken up the challenge of investigating whether the treatment extends survival.

While Pauling advocated the use of supplements, most scientific studies on vitamin C's benefits were based on diets providing vitamin C through vegetables and fruits. Cooking reduces but does not eliminate vitamin C. Some vitamin C can also be lost as it dissolves into cooking water; minimally cooked or raw vegetables and fruits retain more of the vitamin.

A SURPRISING ANTIOXIDANT

Vitamin C is not the only antioxidant guarding the bloodstream. Uric acid is a strong antioxidant that occurs naturally in the body.[15] It is not something you can sprinkle on your breakfast cereal or take as a supplement, and you would not want to attempt to raise the amount of it in your body. But it is an interesting substance because until very recently it was believed to be nothing more than biological garbage. Uric acid is produced as genetic molecules such as DNA are broken down. Excess uric acid in the blood is linked to kidney stones and gout. When doctors put needles into gouty joints, they pull out uric acid crystals, so it has an understandably bad reputation.

Most mammals break down and eliminate uric acid. But the human body guards its uric acid supply. Humans and some other primates have actually turned off—or lost—the genes that would break it apart. As the kidneys filter the blood, they carefully save and return 90 percent of its uric acid, while only 10 percent is lost in the urine. If this is biological garbage, the body is working awfully hard to hold onto it.

This molecule has shown another side. Uric acid is a strong antioxidant. It travels freely in the bloodstream, in the fluids that bathe the joints, the eyes, and even the brain, and passes into the cells that make up various body tissues.[16] It knocks out free radicals and also binds to some particularly reactive forms of iron, reducing their tendency to promote free radical damage. It also protects vitamin C from oxidation. This has led some to speculate that when humans and other primates lost their ability to make vitamin C, they *had* to keep uric acid around to protect the supply of vitamin C they took in from foods.[17]

NATURAL SOURCES OF ANTIOXIDANTS

Membrane Protectors
- Grains provide selenium, which is essential for antioxidant enzymes.
- Beans, vegetables, nuts, and grains provide vitamin E.
- Orange, yellow, and green vegetables are loaded with beta-carotene and other powerful carotenoids.

Bloodstream Protectors
- Citrus fruits and many other fruits and vegetables supply vitamin C to stop free radicals in the bloodstream. Vitamin C also restores vitamin E that has been damaged in the battle against free radicals.
- Uric acid is a powerful antioxidant that forms naturally in the body and is not taken in food.

SHOULD YOU TAKE SUPPLEMENTS?

The restoration of works of art is a touchy subject. The Sistine Chapel ceiling was covered with grime for so long before any of us were born that many believed that the artist had intended a somber, shadowy rendering. In 1987, when Michelangelo's colors emerged from the dark layer, some felt the restorers had gone too far. American contemporary artists Andy Warhol, Robert Rauschenberg, Robert Motherwell, and others sent a joint letter to the Vatican asking that the restoration be suspended. They feared that the gloomy majesty of the chapel ceiling would be turned into Day-Glo colors. As it turned out, Michelangelo's colors were not garish. They were gorgeous. And the restoration revealed subtle details that had been obscured for centuries.

But there were other concerns. What if some of the "soot" being removed was actually shading that had been applied by Michelangelo himself to render depth to figures? The restorers cleaned away a long, dark smudge from under Jonah's left foot. American art historian James Beck studied sketches made of the fresco over the centuries and found that, in those sketches made soon after the fresco's completion, the "smudge" clearly appears as a shadow painted by Michelangelo for dramatic effect.[18] But when the real dirt was removed, so was the shadow. Moreover, critics asked whether removing the layers of varnish and soot might expose the fresco to new assaults by modern pollutants that otherwise would never have touched the painting itself.

Skepticism was fueled by the financial deals that paid for the restoration. The Vatican obtained more than $3 million from Nippon Television Corporation, which got the film, television, and still photography rights in exchange. Was timeless art being destroyed to shoot an exciting documentary?[19]

When people do not age as expected, they provoke controversies, too. When you step aside and let time pass, some may say that you look younger than you are and that maybe you are a little too active and have too much energy for your age. They may say you are having a midlife crisis and that you will eventually learn to wither into a staid, sexless shell. Of course, we have all done damage to ourselves in various ways before we learned better and if other people want to let their bodies go even more, that is their business. But we have the tools for our own restoration and we can use them if we want to.

There is plenty of disagreement over how we should go about dusting off our internal chemistry. Supplements of beta-carotene, selenium, vitamins E and C, and hundreds of other preparations have taken over more and more shelf space in health food stores, drugstores, and convenience markets. Some physicians encourage supplement use and others do not. While the overwhelming weight of evidence supports the safety of most over-the-counter supplements, there has been some cause for concern.

The biggest supplement controversy occurred when vitamin E was given to premature babies. It is understandable that doctors would try it. When oxygen hits a baby's fragile lungs, it sparks the production of free radicals. Babies' lungs are not designed to take in oxygen until they have had nine months in the womb to get ready for it. If they are born too far ahead of schedule, their natural antioxidant enzyme systems are not ready.[20]

To protect the infants, doctors began injecting vitamin E in a preparation called E-Ferol. Instead of getting better, many of the babies became deathly ill. Some developed severe infections. About forty of them died in a six-month period. While some evidence suggests that other ingredients in the E-Ferol preparation were more toxic than the vitamin E, researchers found that vitamin E itself destroyed the infants' ability to fight bacteria.[21]

Although vitamin E is very good at knocking out free radicals, sometimes it is a little too good. As bad as free radicals can be, they also have a vital role in our bodies. White blood cells actually make free radicals to poison bacteria and other undesirables. If they were all neutralized, these important weapons against infections would be lost.

White blood cells are like The Blob, the large, amorphous 1958 B-movie star that swallowed up everything in its path. It indiscriminately ingested innocent people, dogs, cats, a Chevy or two, and possibly even boiled okra. We all have biological B movies taking place in our bodies: Our white blood cells are mini-Blobs that wrap around bacteria. And when they do, they then poison the bacteria with superoxide free radicals. These free radical weapons are not enemies at all but vital defenses against invaders.[22]

White blood cells also use free radicals to make hydrogen peroxide and other antiseptics to kill germs, just as you might use hydrogen peroxide to sterilize a cut or scrape.[23]

It is strange to think of free radicals as friends, but, in this case, that is exactly what they are. If there were no free radicals, we would be easy prey for bacteria. That is what happens to people with an illness called chronic granulomatous disease. Their white blood cells can engulf bacteria or fungi normally but cannot make superoxide or hydrogen peroxide. They have no way to kill the invaders. The result is chronic infections.[24]

On the other hand, some people have a little extra hydrogen peroxide in their cells because they have abnormally low levels of an enzyme that is supposed to remove it. In parts of the world where malaria is common, these individuals are very resistant to it. The tiny disease-causing parasites just cannot get a foothold, apparently because of the higher-than-normal amounts of hydrogen peroxide—made from free radicals—these people have in their cells.[25] So, although we think of free radicals as enemies, sometimes they are the very weapons we need.

The invaders try to fight back. Believe it or not, bacteria carry their own antioxidants to destroy the free radicals our cells aim at them. Staphylococci, for example, make catalase enzymes to break apart the peroxide that our cells are trying to kill them with.[26]

And here is where the supplement controversy starts. If free radicals are sometimes needed to fight infections, maybe massive doses of antioxidants are not such a good idea. High doses of vitamin E do seem to interfere with white blood cells. In an interesting experiment, researchers gave three hundred milligrams of vitamin E each day to a group of teenagers and young men. They then took blood samples from each subject and tested how well their white blood cells could battle *E. coli* bacteria. This is the type of bacteria which has recently begun turning up in hamburger; some strains are deadly. When their white blood cells were tested, it was clear that the high doses of vitamin E impaired their ability to make free radicals and they had a much harder time knocking out the bacteria.[27]

Vitamin E also slows down blood coagulation a bit, making it a little harder for you to stop bleeding when you are cut. People with bleeding disorders or high blood pressure may be advised by their doctors to avoid vitamin E supplements.[28]

It is still an open question whether anyone other than tiny premature infants will be seriously harmed by large doses of vitamin E. But it does seem that huge doses, used essentially as a medicine, act very differently than the vitamin E traces consumed in foods.

Our bodies are designed to extract vitamins and minerals from foods. The tablets of vitamin E, beta-carotene, and the like that are sold in drugstores and health food stores greatly exceed normal quantities. In addition, these single antioxidants do not begin to match what nature offers in vegetables, fruits, and other plants. Beta-carotene tablets, for example, contain lots of beta-carotene, but miss the dozens or even hundreds of related carotenoids that occur naturally in plants. Some of them are probably more important than beta-carotene for protecting the heart, the eyes, and other organs.[29] For example, a research team found that people whose diets were loaded with spinach or collard greens were protected against macular degeneration, an eye problem occurring in older people that may be caused by free radical damage. The protective factors were not beta-carotene, but other carotenoids, called lutein and zeaxanthin.[30] The names are not important. What is important is that dark green, leafy vegetables supply them in natural quantities that pills do not.

Supplements also miss innumerable other healthful compounds in plants, some of which remain to be discovered. Most studies on antioxidants were done with subjects getting them in foods, not in supplements. So some of the benefits attributable to vitamin C, for example, may be due to other parts of vegetables and fruits, such as their other antioxidants, their low fat content, their lack of cholesterol, and so on. Antioxidant tablets are crude formulations compared to the natural sources of these nutrients.

Moreover, concentrated doses of one antioxidant can interfere with others.[31] Beta-carotene supplements can reduce the amount of vitamin E in the blood by as much as 40 percent.[32] A diet rich in vegetables, fruits, legumes, and grains, on the other hand, provides a balance of antioxidant vitamins in exactly the form the body is designed to accept.

Some people argue for supplements, however. Part of their case rests on the fact that most people do not eat the foods their bodies are designed for. Those who center their diets on meat and dairy products are likely to miss out on a broad range of antioxidants. And the continual cultivation of the soil has depleted minerals like selenium. Vitamin C and other antioxidants are fragile and easily lost to some degree during transportation, prolonged storage, and cooking.

My recommendation is to assure that your diet includes vegetables, fruits, grains, and legumes in quantity and in a reasonable variety. Supplements, then, should be reserved for those few situations in which we miss the normal sources of vitamins. For example, those who spend all day in an office or a factory rarely have sunlight touching their skin, which is how vitamin D is normally made. They need a dietary source of vitamin D. Likewise, healthful sources of vitamin B_{12} are uncommon and supplements, as described on pages 231 to 232, are helpful. Also, some doctors now use vitamin and mineral supplements in the treatment of many illnesses. Aside from these uses, I do not normally recommend supplements. If, however, you decide to take them, here are some important suggestions:

- First, supplements cannot make up for a poor diet, so start with an optimal diet (see guidelines in chapter 12).
- Most of the benefits of supplements are gained on lower doses, for example, the quantities provided in a standard multivitamin. Adding more does not necessarily help much more. Higher doses prescribed by physicians have a valid role in the treatment of specific conditions.
- Avoid vitamin A. It can be toxic in even modest overdose and should be avoided unless prescribed by a physician. Beta-carotene provides all the vitamin A the body needs and is much safer. Research studies showing benefits from beta-carotene use doses in the range of twenty to thirty milligrams per day and occasionally higher. This amount is easily obtained from carrots, sweet potatoes, spinach, and other natural foods.

• Infants should receive vitamins only as prescribed by a pediatrician.

• Be careful about selenium. Typical dosages used in research range from fifty to one hundred micrograms. This range is probably safe, but higher doses are potentially toxic.

• If you have been taking vitamin C for several weeks or longer, do not stop it abruptly unless directed by a physician. If you plan to discontinue it, do so gradually over a week or two to allow your body time to adjust to the new lower intake. Doses used safely in research studies range as high as ten to twelve grams per day or even higher.

• If you are pregnant, follow your doctor's advice about supplementation.

• Vitamin B_{12} is safe, even in very large doses, although the body needs only about one microgram per day for healthy blood and healthy nerves. Vegetarians should take a B_{12} supplement unless they are getting the vitamin in fortified foods, such as breakfast cereals.

FOOD'S FALSE FRIENDS

By now, you have a good understanding of the first steps that can protect you against free radicals. If your diet is rich in natural antioxidants, your skin cells can defend themselves against signs of aging, your eyes have better protection, and every other part of your body is strengthened against chemical assaults. However, this is only the beginning. To complete the first step in age-proofing, we must slow down the production of free radicals at the source, which is surprisingly easy to do. It simply requires knowing which foods encourage the production of free radicals.

The first of these turncoats, believe it or not, is iron. Iron encourages free radical damage. Vegetable and fish oils also contribute to the problem. We do need some iron and oil in the diet. But as scientists have recently discovered, even a little too much can mean serious problems.

RUST-PROOFING

A trace of iron is a vital part of hemoglobin, which allows the blood to carry oxygen. Without it, we would never survive. But there is another side of iron, as you have noticed if you have ever left a cast-iron fry pan in the sink too long or left any iron object out in the yard for a day or two. Iron rusts. Oxidation does not just attack fry pans. The same thing happens inside your body. Iron acts as a catalyst, encouraging both the formation of free radicals and all the destruction they cause.

There is no good way for the body to get rid of it. If carbon dioxide were to build up in your bloodstream, your lungs could exhale it. If you were to eat a huge amount of starchy vegetables, your body would have no trouble breaking down the excess carbohydrate. But iron is on a one-way street. It enters the body and just waits, ready to cause damage.

This is surprising to many people. But it is no surprise to your body, which has long been trying to defend itself against the onslaught of iron and the free radicals it generates. Your cells pack iron into special molecular containers to keep it out of harm's way. One of these, called ferritin, can hold up to 4,500 iron atoms inside a protein shell.[33] The more iron that comes into the body, the more ferritin your cells make to store it because your body is trying to see to it that iron does not run free in the blood.

Unfortunately, that does not stop its dangers. People with large amounts of stored iron have many health problems, including weakness, fatigue, arthritis, diabetes, impotence or loss of menstrual periods, shortness of breath, and neurological symptoms. Iron buildup also encourages cancer and heart disease, presumably because of the free radicals that iron encourages.[34]

Children do not normally accumulate excess iron. Their steady growth uses it up. Some very young children can even become iron-deficient, especially if their diets contain dairy products, which can irritate the digestive tract and result in slow, chronic blood loss. Young women are largely protected from iron overload by the monthly loss of blood with menstruation, and they can occasionally develop iron deficiency. Adult men and postmenopausal women, however, rapidly accumulate iron. Surprising as it may sound, iron overload is actually a much more common and often more serious problem than deficiency.

Iron is abundant in legumes, such as beans and lentils, and is also found in vegetables and grains. When the body is low in iron, it absorbs more from foods, and the vitamin C in vegetables and fruits encourages iron absorption. The body can guard against iron overload by reducing its absorption from these sources when it has had enough.

So how would we ever get too much? Well, the culprit is a different form of iron, called heme iron, which is found in red meats, poultry, and fish and defies the body's attempts to regulate its absorption. Even when there is plenty of iron in the body, heme iron barges right through the intestinal wall into the bloodstream like an uninvited guest. This high absorbability was thought to be an advantage back when iron was not known to have potential dangers. If you grew up, as I did, on the roast beef, chicken, fish, and pork chops that are typical in Western countries, you very likely have too much iron in your body. It is ready to aggravate your problems with free radicals.

When people take vitamin C supplements, they can make matters worse. Vitamin C can increase iron absorption and its tendency to cause free radical damage.[35] Perhaps this is the reason that nature provides us vitamin C in the form of leaves and fruits rather than as highly concentrated tablets and why these same foods provide a form of iron whose absorption is more easily regulated.

Iron overload is also encouraged by iron pots and pans. Wine, especially red wine, is also loaded with iron, which may explain why the symptoms of iron excess were first discovered in France. To make matters worse, the alcohol in wine—or in any other alcoholic beverage, for that matter—causes the body to absorb even more iron from the digestive tract. Nearly all multivitamins contain iron, an unfortunate holdover from the days when the metal's dangers were not appreciated. Most people who take multivitamins already have plenty of iron in their diets and loads of stored iron in their bodies.

In addition, some doctors and pharmacists have been overzealous in prescribing iron pills or iron-rich foods to patients complaining of fatigue. Fatigue is much more likely to be caused by stress, depression, or illness than by iron deficiency.

So much for the bad news. The good news is that it is easy to find out how much iron you have in your body and to get rid of any excess. The tests shown below will show if your iron level is too low, too high, or just right and can help you avoid supplements when they will do more harm than good. These tests are far more accurate than standard hemoglobin or hematocrit blood tests, which are not sufficient. Don't be shy about asking your doctor to run a test or two for you. Most doctors welcome such requests because they know that a patient who takes an active interest in his or her health is much more likely to stay healthy over the long run.

How to Check Your Iron Level

Your doctor or clinic can run the following tests. In some states, commercial laboratories will run these tests without a doctor's request. Results should always be interpreted by a physician.

- Serum ferritin (normal values are 12 to 200 mcg/l)
- Serum iron
- Total iron-binding capacity (TIBC)

Serum iron should be checked after an overnight fast. The serum iron measurement is divided by TIBC. The result should be 16 to 50 percent for women and 16 to 62 percent for men.

Results above these norms indicate excess iron. Results below these norms indicate too little iron. If the result suggests iron deficiency, your doctor may request an additional test called a red cell protoporphyrin test for confirmation. A result higher than 70 mcg/dl of red blood cells suggests insufficient iron. To diagnose iron deficiency, at least two of these three values (serum ferritin, serum iron/TIBC, or red cell protoporphyrin) should be abnormal.

If You Have Too Much Iron. If you have excess iron, as most adults in Western countries do, the first step is to stop the influx of even more iron, which means changing your diet. Cut out the meat, poultry, and fish and get your nutrients from the foods your body is designed for: vegetables, fruits, legumes, and grains.

The only way to reduce your iron level reliably and quickly is to donate blood. At the risk of resurrecting images of medical bloodletting, donating a pint of blood lets you off-load more than two hundred milligrams of iron in the form of hemoglobin. If you donate blood regularly, your iron level will gradually drop back to normal. Those who cannot donate blood at regular centers due to a history of infectious illness can usually arrange to have a physician or other health professional assist them. Strange as it may seem, the altruistic act of donating blood is a great way to protect yourself from the free radicals that iron encourages.

Exercise also reduces iron levels by increasing iron losses in sweat as well as through urine and feces.[36]

If You Are Low in Iron. Iron supplements are not justified by a low hemoglobin or hematocrit test; you could end up doing yourself more harm than good. Supplement only if prescribed by your physician, who will run the tests on page 31.

A balanced diet of legumes (beans, peas, and lentils), vegetables, fruits, and grains, as described in chapter 12, provides nonheme iron, the type of iron the body can absorb more of if it needs it and less of if it already has plenty.

Meats, liver, or other animal products are not healthy sources of iron because they contain large amounts of animal fat and cholesterol.

Vitamin C increases iron absorption. People with normal or low iron stores would do well to include fruits and vegetables in their diet. This is not a justification for vitamin C supplements, which can be a problem, especially for people with high levels of stored iron.

If you are using dairy products for calcium, they are extremely low in iron and tend to crowd it out of the diet. You can get both calcium and iron from green vegetables.

WHAT TO DO ABOUT IRON

Most people in Western countries have too much iron in their bodies, which promotes free radical damage. Simple steps for keeping iron in check are:

- First, be choosy where you get your iron. Plant sources of iron, such as beans, vegetables, and grains, allow the body to regulate how much it absorbs.
- Avoid meats completely, as their heme iron tends to enter the body whether you need it or not.
- Avoid iron supplements unless you have a diagnosed iron deficiency.
- Avoid uncoated iron cookware and keep wine consumption modest and intermittent.
- Check your iron level by asking your doctor for the tests listed on page 31.
- Regular blood donation lowers high iron levels.
- Regular exercise helps the body to eliminate excess iron.
- Pregnant women often need more iron, mainly in the second half of the pregnancy. A ferritin test at the beginning and middle of the pregnancy can show whether iron is needed or not. In general, pregnant women with a history of iron deficiency or who are not tested should begin a supplement of about thirty milligrams per day or sixty milligrams for those who are large, anemic, or pregnant with twins. The reason for testing before using iron supplements is that iron supplementation may prolong pregnancy and lead to a slightly increased risk of complications.[37]

FREE RADICALS FROM YOUR FRYER

Let's pop down to a fast-food restaurant for an order of fries. They're cooked in vegetable oil nowadays, so they must be healthy. And while we're at it, how about a fish sandwich? Fish is a health food, right?

These are risky ideas because iron is not the only thing that encourages the production of free radicals. Oils do, too. Probably the worst are fish oils, which, in spite of the health myths they once spawned, are actually very unstable molecules. Fish oils were popular for their omega-3 fatty acids, which can reduce the levels of fats called triglycerides in the blood. The problem is that these unstable oils encourage the production of free radicals.

Fish oils are not the only problem, however. Excessive amounts of any liquid oil are likely to encourage free radical production. This is not a reason to use solid animal fats or shortening because their health consequences are even worse. The key is to reduce consumption of all fats and oils. The only oils your body needs are traces of polyunsaturated oils, and these are naturally part of vegetables, beans, and grains. They supply omega-3s in a more stable form.

FREE RADICALS WITH A TWIST OF LIME

Have you noticed how people with serious alcohol problems often appear to be much older than they are? Their skin sags, their eyes look tired, and their faces are drawn. Alcohol conspires with free radicals. First, the alcohol (ethanol) molecule rearranges itself to make various forms of damaging free radicals. Second, alcohol encourages oxygen to turn into free radicals. Some of them attack brain cells, which is obviously of concern because right now you have all the brain cells you are ever going to have and most of us cannot afford to lose any. It makes sense that alcohol would damage the brain because its desirable effects all relate to turning off brain functions, particularly our inhibitions and awareness of pain. Alcohol-related free radicals also attack the liver, heart, stomach, testes, and other organs.[38]

Iron and alcohol bring out the worst in each other. Alcohol increases iron absorption, which is the last thing most people need. It also helps iron to sneak out of the ferritin safe-storage molecules. In turn, iron accelerates alcohol-related free radical damage.

To make matters even worse, alcohol depletes the antioxidants in your body, particularly vitamin E, selenium, beta-carotene, and glutathione, which we will read about in the next chapter. Alcoholics have markedly low levels of antioxidants in their blood even when their diets are normal.[39]

Nowadays, many people have heard that a little red wine is good for the heart, a theory encouraged by the so-called French paradox—low rates of heart disease in the face of a high-fat diet. It actually turns out that what had wine connoisseurs rejoicing appears to have been a statistical goof. French death certificates record many heart attacks simply as "sudden death," while other nations list them as cardiac deaths. When the same record-keeping methods are used, the French have about the same heart disease risk as other Western nations. If there is a benefit to wine, it is probably not the alcohol, but rather the natural fruit antioxidants, which are as plentiful in grapes and grape juice as in wine.

CELL-PROTECTING FOODS

The cells of your body can be wrapped in a layer of protection when you give them a more generous amount of antioxidants than most of us get these days. The following steps will help you do that and at the same time reduce the production of free radicals:

- Have at least 3 servings of vegetables and 3 servings of fruits each day. See details in chapter 12.
- Orange vegetables, such as sweet potatoes and carrots, are particularly rich in beta-carotene. Just two carrots provide twenty to thirty milligrams of beta-carotene. However, it is important to have a variety, including green, yellow, and orange vegetables.
- Include raw vegetables, such as carrots or leaf spinach, in addition to cooked vegetables.
- Instead of one vegetable serving at meals, try two.
- Start meals with vegetables, rather like an appetizer. A sprinkle of lemon juice makes steamed broccoli or Swiss chard delectable.
- Keep fruit on hand for snacks and dessert.
- Fruits are not the only source of vitamin C. You'll also find it in many green vegetables.

- In addition to vegetables and fruits, round out your menu with grains and legumes (beans, peas, and lentils). Corn, chickpeas, and soy products are loaded with vitamin E.
- Avoid all meats, poultry, fish, dairy products, and eggs. They can undo much of the good your fruits and vegetables provide.
- Avoid fried foods and added vegetable oils.
- Avoid iron supplements unless prescribed by your physician.

As powerful as they are, foods will not avert or reverse every problem. The restoration of the Sistine Chapel ceiling was not perfect either. It revived 335½ human figures. The remaining half was lost in 1797 when a gunpowder explosion caused the midsection of a male nude figure to fall from the ceiling. Likewise, Michelangelo's *Pietà* was damaged, not by an accident, but by a man wielding a hammer.

Even so, foods can be transforming. They can change your future and redesign the effects of your past.

All of Michelangelo's images are full of movement. The Delphic Sybil's eyes seem to dart in anticipation of something about to happen. Her beauty leaps from the fresco's surface, defined not as a static image but by what the future will bring.

Likewise, you are not standing stock-still with a pitchfork in hand, decade after decade, like Grant Wood's dour farm couple. You are moving, changing, anticipating your own future. And you have begun to decide just what that will be.

CHAPTER TWO

CLEAN BLOOD, STRONG IMMUNITY

Leaving Rome on route E35, it is 550 kilometers to Venice, a city not even remotely like any other. The main street is not a street at all, but a waterway flowing past magnificent buildings and palpable history. Along the two-mile winding course of the Grand Canal gondolas carrying visitors are passed by motorboats loaded with food and wine. Smaller side canals wander off on adventures of their own. It is perhaps the most romantic spot on earth.

Venice houses magnificent artistic treasures, each with its own story. Veronese's 1573 painting, *The Last Supper*, covers an entire wall at the Academia. Soon after its unveiling, the Vatican complained about the inclusion of "dogs, buffoons, drunken Germans, dwarfs, and other such absurdities" in the solemn scene. Rather than change his interpretation, Veronese simply renamed it *Feast at the House of Levi*. The two-thousand-year-old bronze horses at St. Mark's Basilica traveled as spoils of war from Rome to Constantinople and Venice, then to Paris with Napoleon, back to Rome, and, for now at least, are back in Venice. Two hundred palaces, some majestic, others crumbling, line the banks of the Grand Canal.

Venice lies in the middle of the Laguna Veneta—the Lagoon of Venice, which empties into the north Adriatic Sea. What started out as a few islands affording the fifth-century Venitii a refuge from invaders has been tirelessly extended and remodeled, using canals as thoroughfares.

You would not want to drink the water. It is rich with oil, pesticides, and sewage. Nearby, at Porto Marghera, oil tankers off-load their cargo for storage. Along with the ever-present motorboats, they leak oil and exhaust into the lagoon, which are met by fertilizers and pesticides trick-ling in from farms. The sediment in the lagoon and canals picks up poly-chlorinated biphenyls (PCBs) from industry. And Venice still has no sewage treatment facility. Untreated human waste goes straight into the water.[1]

The mussels that normally live in the lagoon and canals have had a hard time coping with the pollution, and it shows. Instead of the clean shells and white interior of normal mussels, they are dark and unhealthy and have died out in some areas. The ebbs and flows of the tides help flush out the canals and they are being dredged to remove toxic sediment. Nonetheless, human waste continues to be dumped into the water every day and pollution remains a serious problem.

The mussels cannot climb out of Venice's dirty canals. But if they could, they would hear the sculpted horses and angels complaining about the pollution in the air. After standing proudly for hundreds of years, they have been assaulted by sulfur dioxide and other modern-day pollut-ants, causing more damage in the last few decades than in many previous centuries.

You do not have to live in Venice to be confronted with chemical challenges. A few years ago, I was traveling through Iowa giving a series of lectures. As I drove along, the radio announced that a water alert was in effect for children and pregnant women. Contamination levels were too high and tap water was not to be touched. This is Iowa, not Chernobyl, I thought to myself. But I learned that such alerts occur there regularly. The main reason is livestock: Two out of every three cultivated acres in Iowa are devoted to animal feed crops. Huge loads of agricultural chemi-cals drain into streams and rivers that supply drinking water.

New regulations have reduced some of the pollution in Venice and elsewhere around the world, but whether you live near a toxic waste dump or in the Green Mountains of Vermont, you will be hit with a dose of gas fumes while filling the tank as well as by auto exhaust, pesti-cides on the neighbors' lawn, new food additives, compounds emanating from cleaning products, new carpets, or woodworking chemicals, to name just a few.

Many of these chemicals contribute to the damage to your body that passes for aging. They enter through your lungs or digestive tract and can poison your cells directly. They also stimulate the release of free radicals that can age your skin, attack your arteries, and stress your body in other ways.

Think about people you have known who were heavy smokers. What did their skin look like? Chances are, their faces were wrinkled and drawn. The chemicals in smoke did that to them. Exactly the same thing can happen to nonsmokers, albeit more slowly. Just as free radicals age us from within, toxins we breathe in or swallow in foods can accelerate aging processes as well. We don't notice it. Most of us don't think about trying to fend off the attack. We submit to the chemical insults that add to free radical injuries, wearing us down inside and out.

It does not have to be that way. In the previous chapter, we saw how to protect ourselves against free radicals that arise within the body. In this chapter, we will look at surprising and powerful techniques that can actually eliminate outside toxins before they harm you.

A natural chemical removal system built into your basic biochemistry is powerful enough to eliminate thousands of different chemicals should they ever find their way into your body. It just needs to be turned on, and certain nutrients do exactly that. Whether you are a tourist sitting at a sidewalk café or a busy office worker racing through lunch at your desk, these foods will help you eliminate toxic chemicals from your body before you even knew they were there. In the process, you will sidestep the aging effect of these antagonists. This is the second step in age-proofing.

ENZYMES THAT CLEAN YOUR BLOODSTREAM

Put your hand on your stomach. Just underneath your thumb is the site of one of the most surprising discoveries of modern medicine. It is so tiny it could fit on the head of a pin and have room to spare. But the power under your thumb—inside the cells that make up your liver, to be exact—is something the residents of Venice, Iowa, or just about anywhere else would give their eyeteeth for if they could put it to work in their waterways. It is a set of tiny machines—enzymes, actually—that can take the most powerful and dangerous chemicals and, in an instant, render them totally harmless.

Now, for most people, these masterful enzymes are not quite ready for action. If fact, they might be sound asleep. It takes certain foods to wake them up and get them going. Without these foods, these somnolent enzymes simply let you take one chemical hit after another. Let me show you how this amazing system works and, most importantly, how to turn it on.

Your enzymes are designed to eliminate chemicals in two steps. In phase 1, an enzyme in the liver cell grabs hold of the toxic molecule and attaches oxygen to it, like a policeman slapping one end of a pair of handcuffs onto a criminal's wrist. In phase 2, a second enzyme hooks the "criminal" molecule onto a large carrier molecule, such as glutathione, which drags it away. These captured chemicals are then shipped out in your urine or feces, like crooks going up the river. The whole process is rapid and remarkably effective. Oxygen is attached to the toxic molecule, it is quickly hooked onto a second molecule, and away it goes.

As this arrest is in progress, there is one very dangerous point. When a toxic chemical has had oxygen attached by the phase 1 enzymes, it can be even more active than it was when it entered the body. When it is not yet attached to a carrier molecule that will lead it away, it can be wildly dangerous. In fact, many of the most serious pollutants are not particularly threatening until the phase 1 enzymes attach oxygen "handcuffs" to them. The key is to have plenty of phase 2 enzymes around to grab these activated toxins, attach them to carrier molecules, and get them out.

FOODS THAT TURN ON ENZYME PRODUCTION

All of this depends on food. Certain foods contain powerful enzyme inducers, which cause the body to make more phase 2 enzymes that come in like a new supply of squad cars. Broccoli may not look like power food, but it is one of the very best at turning on the phase 2 enzymes that help drag chemicals away.

"We isolated from broccoli a compound called sulforaphane, which turned out to be an exceedingly potent booster of phase 2 enzymes," said Dr. Paul Talalay of The Johns Hopkins University. This powerful extract causes the liver cells to churn out enormous quantities of phase 2 enzymes to add real muscle to your detoxification team. Many related plants do the same thing. "Cruciferous plants—not just broccoli, but also cabbage, Brussels sprouts, cauliflower, kale, and others—are very rich in natural chemicals that increase the production of phase 2 enzymes."

Broccoli and the other cruciferous vegetables, so named for their cross-shaped flowers, are the sergeants that recruit new cops, give them their orders, and send them out onto the streets. These vegetables are particularly good at raising levels of the phase 2 rather than phase 1 enzymes, which is important, because increasing phase 1 enzymes without an equal or greater increase in phase 2 enzymes can lead to the production of intermediate compounds that are dangerous if not removed.

"The vast majority of cancer-causing chemicals are not carcinogenic in and of themselves," Dr. Talalay said. "But when they enter cells and are acted on by phase 1 enzymes, these relatively innocuous substances are converted to highly reactive compounds that can damage our DNA, setting in motion the process that leads to cancer. If the phase 2 enzymes are high, these reactive chemicals are intercepted and excreted before they do any damage."

Various vegetable juices have been tested for their ability to stimulate the production of liver enzymes that can eliminate cancer-causing chemicals found in beef (yes, certain chemicals in beef can cause cancer). The very best detoxifiers, again, are cruciferous vegetables, with Brussels sprouts and white cabbage at the top of the list. Even an extract made from beans has shown some effect.[2] Beef eaters, take note, however. None of the vegetable juices tested reduced the risk to zero, so steering clear of beef is still the best advice, even while you boost your vegetable intake.

The idea is not to focus only on broccoli or Brussels sprouts, but to take advantage of the full range of enzyme boosters in plants. "Everybody is saying broccoli is terribly good for you, and I'm sure it is," said Dr. Talalay, "but we are also finding similar actions in other edible plants." Soybean products, such as tofu, tempeh, and soy milk, also contain natural compounds that stimulate your body to make more phase 2 enzymes, which may be part of the reason why Asian countries have especially low cancer rates. Green onions are also potent enzyme boosters, as are many other vegetables.[3] Cooking docs not destroy them.

You may find yourself wanting to slip a little extra cabbage in your soup or have steamed broccoli florets sprinkled with lemon as an appetizer. You can almost feel the protection they give your cells as they drag away intruders.

SHOWING CHEMICALS THE DOOR

Phase 1 and phase 2 enzymes are especially known for taking action against polycyclic hydrocarbons, the cancer-causing chemicals that you breathe in when automobile exhaust, factory fumes, or barbecue smoke drifts past your window. This is extremely important. Smokers who stay free of cancer have been shown to have a greater ability to eliminate carcinogens compared to those who develop cancer, and it is enzymes such as these that work that bit of magic.[4] This is not a reason to smoke, of course. But it shows that if you have a good team of enzymes that can kick out carcinogens, wherever they come from, you are better protected.

Smokeborne chemicals are by no means the only undesirables these powerful enzymes can get rid of for you. "These enzymes are able to react with a great many different chemicals," Dr. Talalay said. "This is very important from an evolutionary point of view because they have to deal with a lot of substances they've never seen before."

We are confronted by new chemicals every day, and our natural enzyme systems are busy trying to disarm them. They even try to destroy medications. Researchers at Rockefeller University in New York gave Brussels sprouts and cabbage to research subjects over the course of several days. They then tested their response to phenacetin and antipyrine, two analgesic and anti-inflammatory drugs. They found that when subjects were on the vegetable-rich diet, they tended to eliminate each medicine more rapidly.[5] Tests with many other medications have shown the same result, although the response varies from one person to the next.

Don't let this scare you. It does not mean that medicines do not work on vegetarians. It simply means that plant-based diets make your body more ready and able to knock out chemicals of many types. Overall, that is a great plus, although it may mean that some medicines are ejected a bit faster than they might be otherwise.

Glutathione from Raw Vegetables and Fruits

You can further strengthen your defenses with foods that give you extra glutathione, the carrier molecule that hauls toxins out of the body. There are two rich sources. Fruits, such as oranges, grapefruits, cantaloupe, watermelon, bananas, apples, peaches, pears, tangerines, and strawberries, are loaded with glutathione. Second, vegetables that are commonly eaten raw (carrots, lettuce, cucumbers, tomatoes, cabbage, and green peppers) have the same property. For some reason, cooked vegetables do not seem to be as helpful in this regard. When these fruits and raw vegetables are abundant in your diet, some of their glutathione enters your blood-stream. You can almost hear the squad cars racing in to protect you.[6]

Doctors have long known that one drug can increase or decrease the effects of another or influence how fast it is eliminated from the body. What they may not have known is that foods act like drugs, too, trying to push other chemicals out of the body. Meals are like three-times-a-day compound medicines made up of hundreds of chemicals, with a broad range of effects on your body. Whether those effects are good or bad depends on which foods you have chosen.

If you have built up your antioxidant defenses, as we saw in the last chapter, and then strengthened your antipollutant enzyme systems and have a ready supply of glutathione carrier molecules to eject chemical intruders, you can spare yourself some of the stresses and aging effects that pollutants would have on your body.

You want that protection. Because while you are cruising down the highway enjoying the sunshine, particles of dust, dirt, and smoke are attacking you. They are joined by sulfur dioxide from far-off industries, ozone, and auto exhaust.[7] You may not notice them, but they all want to attack you.

It's no good trying to hold your breath until they are all gone. What you can do is to avoid chemical exposures to the extent possible and to strengthen your body against them. If your meals contained broccoli and Brussels sprouts or other vegetables yesterday, you are better protected today. As rapidly as that, your liver cells are turning on their production of phase 2 enzymes and those enzymes are hard at work pushing toxic chemicals out of your body.

AVOIDING CHEMICALS IN FOOD

As powerful as enzyme inducers are, they do not take the place of avoiding chemicals to begin with. Certain foods are loaded with them. Here are the most common sources of chemical exposures:

Fish and Shellfish.   The streams, rivers, and coastal areas where sewage and pesticide runoff end up are exactly where fish live. As water passes over their gills, chemicals dissolve into their blood and end up in muscle tissue. As larger fish eat smaller fish, the contaminants become more and more concentrated. If you join this food chain by eating fish, their contaminants become part of you.

According to a 1992 *Consumer Reports* survey, half of the flounder sampled in New York contained pesticides. Highly toxic PCBs were found in 43 percent of salmon, 50 percent of whitefish, and 25 percent of swordfish.[8] The National Research Council reports that PCBs are found in virtually every site where fish or shellfish are tested—even in spots as remote as rural Alaska, the Virgin Islands, and Hawaii—and they are not going away. They concentrate in your fat cells and are so potent that a tiny amount can cause cancer or birth defects.

Swordfish and tuna are good places to find mercury, whose brain-damaging effects contribute not only to the fictional Mad Hatter's mental state in *Alice in Wonderland,* but to Parkinson's disease, a disease of abnormal muscle control. Of 145 sites recently sampled for mercury in shellfish, it was found in every single one of them. Avoiding fish eliminates half of all mercury exposure.[9]

Even at their best, inspection practices do not detect any of this. It all goes straight to the consumer. This is an awful-sounding situation, but the fact is that government tests provide no reason for optimism whatsoever. If you were hoping to use fish as a "heart-healthy" food, there are much better ways to be good to your heart, as we will see in chapter 8.

Livestock Products. Poultry and "red meats" get generous amounts of chemicals from medicated feed and various veterinary compounds. Similarly, dairy products carry contaminants from the animals they came from. Antibiotic residues, for example, have been found in as many as one in every three milk cartons at the retail store.[10]

Do these chemicals actually get into your body to a significant degree? Unfortunately, yes. One particularly sensitive measure is to test breast milk because the breast contains fatty tissue where contaminants can easily end up. In a comparison with the general population, women who had adopted vegetarian diets had 98 to 99 percent lower levels of several pesticides as well as lower levels of all other chemicals tested except one.[11] Avoiding animal products helped them avoid the chemicals that meat eaters get three times a day. The one exception, interestingly, was PCBs, for which the vegetarians had levels that were similar to the meat eaters. PCBs remain in the body for many, many years after fish consumption or other exposure, and adopting a vegetarian diet later in life will only reduce existing residues very slowly. It would be interesting to test lifelong vegetarians, but to my knowledge this has not been done.

Chemically Treated Produce. Vegetables and fruits are not given hormone implants, cannot concentrate pesticides as animals do, and are not nearly as much of a problem as animal products are. Nonetheless, they may well be sprayed with pesticides and fungicides. The amount that remains on them varies widely. Happily, organic produce is now widely available. Gone are the days when organic produce was second-rate. If you thought that vegetables and fruits have to be chemically treated to look right, it is time to take another look. Health food markets are bigger than ever and have an impressive and ever-growing organic selection in fresh, frozen, and canned varieties. Many larger grocery stores are also starting to respond to the demand. An increasing number of states as well as retail stores have specific criteria that producers must meet in order to label their products as organic.

METALS

In the last chapter, we looked at iron's ability to promote free radical damage and how to reduce your risk. There is more to the iron story. In Alzheimer's disease, tiny abnormal structures, called plaques and neurofibrillary tangles, disrupt communications between brain cells. Iron may be one of the causes. When Alzheimer's patients were studied with magnetic resonance imaging (MRI), their brains were found to have excess iron, which researchers theorize may damage the brain by encouraging free radical attacks and disrupting brain proteins.[12] They tested the theory by giving special treatments that rapidly remove iron from the blood and, indeed, the disease progression slowed down for the treated patients.[13]

Zinc is under suspicion, too. At first, researchers theorized that zinc would improve alertness and they gave zinc supplements to Alzheimer's patients. The results were disastrous. Within two days, the patients deteriorated dramatically and the study was immediately halted. The researchers retreated to the laboratory, where test-tube tests showed that even modest increases in zinc can cause normal brain proteins to clump into plaques.[14] Zinc excesses are likely to occur only when supplements are used.

Aluminum may be another vandal that delights in sabotaging the brain's intricate switchboard. Several studies have shown that populations consuming more aluminum have a higher risk of Alzheimer's disease, and autopsies reveal concentrations of aluminum in the plaques and tangles. Kidney patients are often exposed to high levels of aluminum during dialysis, and the result can be Alzheimer's-like abnormalities in the brain.[15]

You don't have to be on dialysis to be exposed to aluminum. It is often in drinking water. Some researchers believe that high levels of aluminum in tap water (greater than one milligram per liter) can more than double the risk of Alzheimer's disease.[16] Your local health department can tell you the water quality in your area. Some antacids (e.g., Rolaids, Maalox) are loaded with aluminum. Aluminum cans and cookware also contribute and many deodorants contain aluminum, some of which is absorbed through the skin.[17]

We need a trace of iron and zinc in our diets, but we do not need huge amounts of either one. Supplements of these metals should only be used when medically necessary. Our bodies have no need for aluminum at all.

ELIMINATING CHEMICALS FROM YOUR BODY

- Natural compounds in many vegetables help eliminate toxins that may be inhaled from auto exhaust, industrial pollution, and other sources. They stimulate your liver to make more phase 2 enzymes.
- The strongest enzyme inducers are found in cruciferous vegetables: broccoli, cauliflower, Brussels sprouts, cabbage, and kale.
- Fruits and certain raw vegetables (carrots, lettuce, cucumbers, tomatoes, cabbage, and green peppers) supply glutathione, which helps carry chemicals out of the body.
- A low-fat vegetarian diet may discourage chemicals from entering your body by reducing the amount of cholesterol in your blood. Chemical toxins travel on cholesterol particles.
- Avoiding fish and other animal products reduces your exposure to chemicals that concentrate in their tissues.
- Organic produce is free of the chemicals used in routine agriculture and is found at most health food markets.

THE CHOLESTEROL CONNECTION

There may be another way to keep chemicals out of your body: Keep a very low cholesterol level. When airborne pollutants, such as exhaust or tobacco smoke, try to sneak through your lungs into your blood, the way they do that is by dissolving through your lung tissue into the cholesterol particles in your bloodstream. The cancer-causing chemicals in cigarette smoke, for example, do not just float around in your blood. They ride on your cholesterol particles.[18] It may be that the less cholesterol you have in your blood, the less your lungs become doormats for dangerous chemicals. So the vegetables and fruits that strengthen your enzyme defenses and also tend to be low in chemical contamination compared to animal products also have the advantage of keeping your cholesterol level low. In chapter 8, we will look in more detail at how you can dramatically lower your cholesterol level.

BUILDING STRONG IMMUNITY

So far in this chapter, we have looked at powerful defenses against threats that enter our bodies from the world outside. But not all of these threats are chemical toxins. Some of them are alive. Our defense against them is our immune system.

The mussels in the sewage-laden Venice canals do not look anything like their cousins living in cleaner waters. Their shells are fouled with algae and barnacles and their tissues are dark and discolored. In some of the interior canals, they have simply been wiped out.[19]

Every cell in your body is like a little clam or mussel, filtering the watery environment it lives in. It is not very likely to be attacked by barnacles, but it is constantly exposed to bacteria and viruses. Foods can build your immunity against them and cancer cells that can arise in your own tissues. A strong immune system can help you stay robustly healthy all year long, holding colds and other minor and major illnesses at arm's length. So while everyone else carries around boxes of tissues and cold remedies or comes down with the flu, you'll be on the ski slopes, enjoying a vacation, or doing whatever else you do best. More important, you'll be better protected against other serious illnesses, including cancer, that can cut life short.

Traveling with your red blood cells, which are busy carrying oxygen, are white blood cells—the sentries of the body. Woe to the errant bacterium caught dawdling in the path of a healthy white blood cell! The cell rapidly engulfs the intruder and proceeds to break it apart, molecule by molecule.

If we had no immune sentries, we would not survive the first week of life. David, a boy in Houston, Texas, was born in 1971 without functioning white blood cells. The slightest exposure to bacteria or viruses would have been fatal. He lived for twelve years inside a plastic bubble until he was felled by complications of an attempted bone marrow transplant.[20] The only reason we do not all need airtight bubbles is that we have white blood cells coursing through our arteries and veins, destroying viruses and bacteria.

Some, called B cells, make antibodies, which are protein molecules that coat the surface of bacteria and attract other white blood cells to engulf them the way blood attracts sharks. The B cells' actions are directed by a second type of white blood cell called T cells, some of which turn B cells on, while others turn them off. In addition, natural killer cells look for cancer cells and cells that are infected with viruses, and attack them quickly and efficiently. Their name comes from the fact that they really do shoot first and ask questions later. Other white blood cells—The Blobs we met in chapter 1—swallow up and digest invaders.

White blood cells are extremely clever. They can tell the difference not only between you and a staphylococcus, but also between a cell from the middle of your right kidney and a cell from exactly the same spot in your brother's or sister's right kidney. Given the chance, they would wipe out the impostor. This causes no end of frustration for transplant surgeons, who struggle to suppress the immune system's ability to recognize and destroy anything that is out of place.

As many people get older, their immune functions weaken. The natural killer cells are the first to go, beginning to decline as early as age twenty. By eighty or ninety, most people have almost none of them left.[21] Their B cells stay pretty sharp, making antibodies throughout life, but T cells become less and less effective against invading cells. These less-than-competent T cell soldiers have more trouble attacking the enemy and become more and more likely to attack the body's own cells.[22] As time goes on, more white blood cells turn off immune reactions rather than turning them on.[23]

The result can be that, if there is a cold going around, you are very likely to get it. You can become more susceptible to just about any kind of infection. Bacteria in food become distinctly more dangerous than they were before, and after a while, you will find your doctor pushing the flu vaccine more vigorously, on the theory that your normal defenses are down. Your white blood cells can even lose some of their vigilance against cancer.

You can strengthen your white blood cells. As amazing as it may sound, you can whip this sorry bunch of soldiers into fighting form and gain immune strength that you may never have had before. The key is to change the nutrients that reach them.

One surprising reason for a loss of immune strength may be cholesterol, which interferes with white blood cells. Small amounts are always in the bloodstream. But excess cholesterol clogs arteries, leads to heart attacks, escorts toxins into the body as we saw earlier, and may also help explain why older people are more susceptible to infections.[24]

When scientists have added cholesterol to white blood cells in the test tube, their immune strength is greatly reduced. Some evidence suggests that cholesterol harms the cells' outer membranes, making them less able to function, and the more cholesterol there is in your blood, the more likely it is that this will happen.[25]

Cholesterol is not the only immune system poison. Fat in the foods you eat can also harm your immunity.[26] White blood cells swim through the bloodstream, looking for bacteria and cancer cells. They cannot work in an oil slick. For them, a cheeseburger with fries is like the Exxon *Valdez* tanker disaster.

Researchers in New York asked a group of men to cut their fat intake in half, from about 40 percent of calories to 20 percent. Three months later, a blood sample was drawn from each subject and their white blood cells' ability to knock out cancer cells was tested. On the low-fat diet, their natural killer cells were noticeably better at knocking out the cancer cells. Those who cut their fat intake the most had the strongest natural killer cells.[27]

Researchers have gone so far as to hook intravenous lines into volunteers and slowly drip soybean oil into their veins. Once again, the same theme emerges. Their immune cells did not work very well.[28] All these experiments have shown the same thing: The less fat there is in the blood, the stronger the white blood cells become.

This applies to *all* fats. For your heart, corn oil or olive oil is better than chicken or beef fat, but as far as your immune system is concerned, vegetable oils are every bit as bad as animal fats. Likewise, fish oils and other sources of omega-3 fatty acids can also compromise the immune system.[29] An immune-boosting menu keeps all fats to modest amounts.

IMMUNE-BOOSTING FOODS

To stay strong, your immune cells need to do more than stay away from cholesterol and grease. Their difficult seek-and-destroy missions demand that they receive a broad range of vitamins and minerals. As we get older, many of us do not get the vitamins we need. Sometimes this is because of poorer intestinal absorption. Other times it is due to interference from medications or physical inactivity that leads us to eat less. The problem is aggravated by the diet of meat and dairy products that is common in Western countries. There is no vitamin C in meats, and beta-carotene is scarce as well. Western diets are also often low in vitamin E, vitamin B$_6$, folate, magnesium, and zinc.[30] The combination of the Western diet, reduced absorption, physical inactivity, and medications can starve your white blood cells for the vitamins and minerals they need.[31]

Scientists have tested various nutrients to see if a little more zinc, vitamin E, or beta-carotene will affect immune function. To an extent, they do. But a team of researchers in New Jersey stumbled on an interesting lesson. They wanted to test the effects of zinc. So they gathered together a group of older men and women and divided them into two groups. One group was given zinc supplements and the other group was given placebo pills. And just to make sure that none of the subjects was missing any vitamins or minerals, everyone in both groups was asked to take a standard multivitamin supplement each day. As it turned out, everyone had an improvement in their immune function, whether they were in the zinc group or the placebo group. Without recognizing it, the researchers had corrected a whole range of nutrient deficiencies with a simple multivitamin, and everyone's immune functions improved.[32]

The multivitamin gave them what their diets should have provided but didn't. If your diet is rich in vegetables, fruits, legumes, and grains, you will get a cornucopia of vitamins and minerals.

The New Jersey researchers found that correcting vitamin and mineral deficiencies improved immunity. But they learned another lesson, too. Contrary to what they were expecting, those subjects who took zinc with their multiple vitamins did *worse* than those taking the placebo. It turns out that while a little zinc is needed by the white blood cells, higher amounts *inhibit* immune actions.[33] When an infection occurs, the body reduces zinc levels as a way to trigger the white blood cells into action. Unless a person is grossly deficient, supplements of zinc appear to disrupt this system.[34]

Having said that, certain nutrients in foods are clearly essential for immune strength. One immune supercharger is beta-carotene. We have already seen how beta-carotene from orange, yellow, and green vegetables neutralizes free radicals. This powerful yellow molecule also strengthens white blood cells. When our daily diets contain as little as thirty milligrams of beta-carotene (the amount in two large carrots) we have measurable increases in natural killer cells and T-helper cells.[35] Beta-carotene counteracts supposedly age-related changes in T cells, helping the body maintain an active immune system.[36]

In addition, beta-carotene protects the white blood cells themselves from free radical damage. Like any other part of the body, they are subjected to free radical attacks and to the extent they can be protected, their immune function will be preserved.[37]

Many people think of beta-carotene and vitamin A as equivalent because, as we noted in the previous chapter, beta-carotene consists of two molecules of vitamin A. However, for some reason that has never been quite clear, vitamin A from liver and other animal products or from supplements lacks most of the immune-boosting power of beta-carotene, which comes from plants. Beta-carotene easily produces all the vitamin A the body needs and helps build immunity, too.

Like beta-carotene, vitamins C and E and the mineral selenium act as both antioxidants and immune boosters.[38] Vitamin E helps stimulate the immune system, boosting both B cells and T cells and increasing the ability of white blood cells to engulf bacteria.[39] We saw in the previous chapter that highly concentrated vitamin E supplements can impair white blood cells' ability to make the free radicals they need to poison bacteria. However, diets that are naturally rich in vitamin E from plants seem to improve immunity. A study of French men and women over sixty years of age showed that the more vitamin E they had in their blood, the more immune "muscle" their white blood cells had.[40]

BUILDING IMMUNITY

- Vegetables, fruits, beans, and grains contain beta-carotene, vitamins C and E, and selenium to strengthen the immune system, in addition to their antioxidant actions.
- Reducing your cholesterol level may help your white blood cells. Powerful ways to lower cholesterol are described in chapter 8.
- Avoiding fat—from either animal or vegetable sources—can improve your white blood cells' ability to work.
- The best combination of all these immune boosters is a low-fat, vegetarian diet.

How strong can your immunity get? For example, what if you were to eliminate all animal fats, keep vegetable oils to a minimum, and boost vitamin-rich vegetables and fruits? The immune-strengthening effect can be profound. Researchers at the German Cancer Research Center in Heidelberg have compared the immune strength of vegetarians to that of people on typical omnivorous diets. They took a blood sample from each subject and tested the ability of their white blood cells to destroy standardized samples of cancer cells. It turned out that the vegetarians had an enormous advantage. Compared to the nonvegetarians, they had more than twice the natural killer cell ability to destroy cancer cells.[41] That extra boost can help counteract the loss of natural killer cell activity that often comes with age.[42]

At least part of the vegetarian advantage, presumably, is that their diets contain little or no animal fat and lots of vegetables. The best vegetarian diets keep vegetable oils low, too. There may be other reasons for the vegetarian advantage, such as reduced exposure to animal proteins and to chemicals used on animal feeds.

Strengthening your defenses is easier than you might have guessed. The same vegetables and fruits that are loaded with antioxidants—orange, yellow, and green vegetables; citrus and other fruits; beans; and grains— are also the richest sources of the nutrients that tune up your detoxifying enzymes and your immunity. On the other hand, the meats, poultry, fish, dairy products, and fried foods that are low in antioxidants are also useless as enzyme inducers and can actually interfere with your immunity. If you were to eat what some people think is a healthy meal, say, chicken breast with low-fat yogurt, you would miss important antioxidants. There is no "cruciferous chicken." You would do nothing for your detoxifying enzymes, and you would miss the vitamins that power your immune system. A low-fat, vegetarian meal, on the other hand, is what your body is waiting for. The nutrients we are designed for are packed into plants.

COFFEE AND CAFFEINE

One chemical in the bloodstream deserves special mention. At any given time, the average American has about two milligrams of caffeine in every liter of his or her blood plasma. Health concerns have reduced the number of coffee drinkers from 80 percent of the population a decade or two ago to just over half in 1991, but it remains, by far, the most popular stimulant in Western countries.[43]

Theoretically, coffee ought to turn us to a heap of rubble. When you mix a little caffeine with human cells in a test tube, the chromosomes break.[44] However, when researchers have tried to identify actual risks in human beings drinking coffee, they are fewer than you might imagine.

In fact, for many coffee drinkers, the biggest problem is not having any. Caffeine is clearly addicting, and if a habitual coffee drinker goes for eighteen hours or so without it, withdrawal ensues, with headaches, fatigue, anxiety, nausea, and an intense desire for a cup of java. Part of the pleasure of a morning cup of coffee is that, like a smoker's first cigarette of the day, it stops the withdrawal. Even cola or tea drinkers can have mild withdrawal symptoms if they miss their daily fix.

Surgeons have noticed that many of their patients develop headaches after surgery. Was it the anesthetic? Maybe a medication problem? It turned out that because the patients were not permitted to have any food prior to surgery, they missed their morning coffee and were in caffeine withdrawal. A cup of coffee relieves the headache in minutes.

The amount of caffeine in coffee depends on how you make it. Percolated or drip coffee packs more than than brewed or instant (see table 2.1, below). Tea has about half the caffeine of coffee; oolong and green teas have less than black tea. Colas get caffeine from the cola nuts they are made from and manufacturers add a little extra, too.

Caffeine is not shy. Virtually 100 percent of it goes straight from your digestive tract into your blood. Needless to say, it enters your brain and penetrates all other body tissues as well. To show how well caffeine gets around, sperm cells in men who drink a cup or two of coffee each day actually swim faster than those of non–coffee drinkers.[46] (It does not, however, improve fertility.) Caffeine easily crosses the placenta and addicts the fetus, who may then have caffeine withdrawal at birth unless

---

TABLE 2.1

Caffeine Content (in milligrams)[45]

Percolated or drip coffee, 1 cup	115–180
Brewed coffee, 1 cup	80–135
Instant coffee, 1 cup	65–100
Tea, 1 cup	30–50
Coca-Cola, 12 ounces	46
Pepsi, 12 ounces	38
Chocolate, 1 ounce	6–26

he or she is breast-fed by a coffee-drinking mother, in which case caffeine intake continues uninterrupted.

Smoking causes caffeine to be excreted faster. When smokers quit, their caffeine levels double and the jitters they assume are from tobacco withdrawal can actually be from that extra caffeine jolt.

Caffeine's contribution to aging is a worsening of osteoporosis. It encourages calcium loss in the urine. The higher the caffeine intake, the more calcium is lost, and people who consume more than about two cups per day have a significantly higher risk of hip fracture.[47]

Caffeine has other problems, too. It makes premenstrual symptoms worse, also in a dose-related fashion.[48] It does not matter if the caffeine comes from sodas, tea, or coffee. The more caffeine, the more PMS. Many women report that getting away from caffeine makes a big difference for them.

Coffee also stimulates stomach acid production.[49] However, the cause is not caffeine but an as-yet-unidentified chemical in coffee.

What about its effect on cholesterol? Research studies were in continual disagreement until it was found that what determines coffee's effect is not its caffeine but the method of brewing. Caffeine does not raise cholesterol levels, and drip and instant coffee have little or no effect on cholesterol either. On the other hand, boiled coffee, which is popular in Scandinavia, does raise cholesterol levels. Apparently the protracted boiling process releases cholesterol-raising chemicals from the coffee beans.[50]

Decaf can cause a slight elevation (about 3 percent) in cholesterol levels.[51] The reason might be the methyline chloride or ethyl acetate solvents used to remove caffeine. Because of health concerns about these chemicals, Taster's Choice and Nescafé are decaffeinated with a water purification process.[52] Are they healthier? There is no evidence yet one way or the other. Moderate coffee use does not seem to increase the risk of heart problems, but researchers have not ruled out the possibility of risk from heavy coffee use (greater than 4 cups of coffee per day).

So the main problems from coffee are calcium loss, aggravations of PMS, and stomach acid secretion, along with the insomnia and jitters that most coffee drinkers are familiar with. Decaffeination eliminates its contribution to all of these except acid secretion.

KEEPING SUGAR IN CHECK

Finally, a few words about one last chemical that finds its way into your internal canals. No other part of the diet is so loved, so hated, and so feared as sugar. Some people's taste buds crave sugar to the point where they would almost like to take it intravenously. Yet we feel guilty if we even go near it.

Actually, sugar is not such a villain. At worst, it deserves a mixed verdict. Yes, sugar causes cavities. But contrary to popular belief, it is not particularly fattening. Sugar has less than half the calories that are found in any kind of fat, and, while sugar can attract us to cakes and pies, it is the shortening or butter in pastries that fattens us up, not the sugar itself. More on this in chapter 10.

Sugar's bad side is its effect on moods. In some people, it causes marked irritability and depression. Often they do not recognize the cause. A friend of mine, for example, is in charge of special events in a large art museum. She arranges openings of exhibits and donor receptions. She noticed that after these events, she was often depressed and irritable for a couple of days. At first she thought her feelings were due to stress or minor disagreements that cropped up between staff members. But these stresses were minor and she liked her coworkers. Eventually she came to suspect that there was a link with food. Cakes and other sweet pastries were routinely catered for special events and the sweet leftovers usually lasted for a few days. She tried avoiding sugary foods and discovered that her mood remained fine. If she ventured back into sugarland, she again became depressed and irritable.

Many people find the same thing. Sugar makes them tired or cranky. Their doctors have pretended to believe them, but knew all too well that blood tests did not confirm the patients' theory. The idea was that eating lots of sugar causes the body to release insulin, a hormone that moves sugar out of the blood and into the cells of the body. If insulin does its job a little too well, there is too little sugar left in the blood, a condition known as hypoglycemia, and that has been offered as the explanation for moody episodes. The vast majority of people reporting this effect have perfectly normal blood sugar levels. So their doctors nod sincerely and send the patients off for psychiatric help.

That would have been the end of the story except that the doctors overlooked one thing: Sugar also increases a brain chemical called serotonin, which plays an important role in moods and sleep. The more sugar in a meal, the more the brain makes serotonin. The effect varies enormously from one person to the next. Some people actually feel better after eating sugar. Others feel worse. For very sensitive people, even the sugar in fruit juice, if consumed every day, can trigger depression or irritability.

If you have bouts of moodiness, try avoiding all sugars (even so-called natural sugars and fruit juices) for a while and see if you do not feel better. For most people, the explanation is not hypoglycemia but a change in brain chemistry.

Genuine hypoglycemia does exist. If the blood sugar drops rapidly, the result can be fatigue, confusion, anxiety, palpitations, headache, sweating, and tremulousness. The brain is not getting the sugar it needs. To diagnose hypoglycemia, doctors look for a blood sugar level dropping below sixty milligrams per deciliter after an overnight fast or below fifty milligrams per deciliter after a test dose of glucose.

Some doctors treat hypoglycemia with a low-carbohydrate diet. The theory is that, since carbohydrate is what stimulates the release of insulin, a low-carbohydrate diet would keep insulin in check. The problem is that when carbohydrate is taken out of the diet, you are left with mainly protein and fat (in the form of chicken, fish, beef, and eggs), which cause worse problems. In addition, low-carbohydrate diets may cause the body's ability to handle sugar to deteriorate even more.

A better approach is to increase complex carbohydrates, with generous amounts of beans, rice, potatoes, and pasta, and eliminate simple sugars, such as table sugar, sodas, candies, and fruit sugar. Complex carbohydrates release sugar more gradually. Legumes (beans, peas, and lentils) may be particularly helpful. It may also help to use whole grains, such as brown rice, as opposed to ground-up grain products, such as pasta or bread, and to have frequent small meals. There is a great deal of variation from one person to the next, so you will need to see which foods are your allies and which are not.

DIABETES

The opposite problem—too much sugar—is called diabetes. It gets more and more common as we get older, especially if we gradually gain weight. But the approach to diabetes has been revolutionized. In fact, it is usually preventable and the majority of adult-onset cases are actually reversible. This is wonderful news for those who feel that the disease is "part of getting older" or that they are stuck with it.

Insulin controls the amount of sugar in your blood. If insulin is not doing its job, however, sugar builds up. Over the long run, diabetes causes serious damage to blood vessels and nerves.

The most common form occurs in people who are overweight and on high-fat diets. The fat on their bodies and in their bloodstream gets in insulin's way. There is usually enough insulin in the body; the challenge is to let it do its work. This adult-onset form of diabetes (also called non-insulin-dependent or Type II diabetes) responds wonderfully to changes in eating habits and physical activity. Over a decade ago, researchers found that a low-fat, plant-based diet, combined with regular physical activity such as daily walking or cycling, could get 90 percent of adult-onset diabetics who had been treated with oral medications off their medicines in less than a month. In the same short time frame, 75 percent of adult-onset patients taking insulin no longer needed any at all. This remarkable result continued for most patients when they were checked years later.[53]

Not only can the combination of a plant-based diet and mild exercise get blood sugars under control, it can also dramatically reduce the risk of eye, kidney, or nerve complications.[54] Even when patients are at the point of developing painful or numbing nerve symptoms, it is not too late to change things. A recent California study showed that painful nerve symptoms go away completely in most patients within two weeks when they let a vegetarian diet and mild exercise work for them. To their amazement, most of these patients either no longer needed any medication at all or needed far less to keep their blood sugar under control.[55]

The childhood-onset form of diabetes, technically known as insulin-dependent or Type I diabetes, is different. In this case, the cells that make insulin have been destroyed. Researchers are pointing their fingers at cow's milk proteins, viruses, and genetics as likely culprits.[56] People with insulin-dependent diabetes will need insulin injections regardless of the diet they follow, but most find that a low-fat, vegetarian diet along with regular exercise make the illness much more manageable.

Why does this kind of diet work so dramatically? First of all, it cuts out fats that interfere with insulin.[57] Second, it is a powerful way to lose weight, which greatly improves insulin's action. Third, it is loaded with complex carbohydrates, which help stabilize the blood sugar. Some foods have special effects. Beans, for example, help keep blood sugar stable. Fruits, vegetables, and legumes contain soluble fiber, which also helps control blood sugar.[58]

Physical activity is a powerful part of the treatment, too. Working muscles pull sugar out of the blood, even with very little insulin present.

Let me caution you not to simply throw away your medication and start shopping for pasta. Treatments have to be tailored to your own needs in consultation with your physician. You may need to convince your doctor that this program is worth trying because, although its results are striking and often revolutionary, diabetes organizations have been slow to abandon older, less effective diets. The American Diabetes Association (ADA) diet guidelines use "exchange lists," which divide foods into six categories: milk, fruit, vegetables, starch/bread, meat, and fat. Drawing from these lists, diabetics maintain consistent intakes of fat, protein, and carbohydrate.[59] The problem is that the milk, meat, and fat groups tend to drive up the fat, cholesterol, and protein content of the diet, aggravating insulin resistance and pushing the diabetic toward heart disease, circulatory problems, and kidney damage. This is not nearly as powerful a regimen as low-fat vegetarian menus.

MAKING CHOICES

People are really not so different from the Venetian filter-feeding mussels. In fact, one begins to wonder if humans might have descended not from apes but from clams. Unlike other primates, humans do not wander from tree to tree, picking out just the right fruit to eat. Most of us sit passively in one spot and food is brought to us. We take in the food that comes to us at home, from the office coffee pot, or the fast-food drive-through, letting whatever chemicals they may hold drift into our bodies.

We take in chemicals from the air and water with little intention or choice. We are also psychological filter-feeders, taking much of our stimulation passively in the form of video input.

This is not necessarily good or bad. But it is important to know that, if our foods, air, and water might not be so pristine, we can choose foods that will help us to clean away some of the toxins. We can strengthen our immunity against intruders. And we can control more aspects of our body chemistry than many of us had thought possible.

CHAPTER THREE

HOW TO CALM THE HORMONE STORMS

America has a Venice of its own. In 1904, tobacco tycoon Abbot Kinney laid plans for a new cultural capital of the Western hemisphere, modeled after Italy's original. He laid out his architectural style, dug miles of canals, and aimed to attract intellectuals and celebrities to grace a fleet of gondolas.

It did not quite work out. Wedged between Santa Monica and Marina del Rey, the town of Venice, California, ended up with skateboarders and sunglasses vendors. There are no gondoliers but plenty of surfers. Instead of palaces, there are beachside eateries, and they have no fresh Italian bread, but plenty of hot dog buns. By 1930, most of the canals were paved over and those that remain are so dirty they make their Italian counterparts look like mountain springs.

But like Venice, Italy, chemicals are a problem here, too. The most noticeable ones are not sewage or industrial effluents. The chemicals you notice on Venice Beach are hormones. Groups of young men are working on their tans, hoping to be noticed by nearby young women who are also working on their tans and hoping to be noticed by someone other than these young men. Bodybuilders are pumping iron on the beach. The scene is dedicated to the grooming of the human body in the service of sexuality.

Hormones in this beach town are not gentle waves lapping the shores of human biology. They are surging tidal waves. If you were to measure the sex hormones coursing through the veins of men and women along

Venice Beach—or, in fact, anywhere else in America—you would find that they are higher than in many other countries. The result is puberty that arrives years earlier than it otherwise might, menopause that is more difficult than it should be, and hormone-related cancers that are now epidemics, among many other problems.

Sex hormones don't just affect sex drive. From before puberty through oldest age, they influence how we look and how we feel. They affect moods, our weight, our hair, the strength of our bones, and many other aspects of our biology. When your hormones are working for you instead of against you, you feel good and look good. You are physically healthier and mentally more in tune.

If you could control the amounts of sex hormones you have in your blood, you could control many things. The fact is, you *can* influence them quite easily. Because hormones affect so many things, this third step in age-proofing will be divided into four parts. First, we will see the profound effect that foods can have on our hormones. Second, we will see how hormones and psychological factors affect sexuality. Next, we will look at specific problems that affect women and men. We will look in detail at hormonal preparations and separate the safe ones from the not-so-safe ones. First, let us look at some basic principles that are important for both women and men at all stages of life.

What causes the waves of hormones crashing against Venice Beach and everywhere else in America and other Western countries? The cause of this hormone surge is covered with ketchup and mustard. The hot dogs and fries and the milkshakes that go with them pump up hormones in sunbathers who pick up a quick snack on the way home from the beach. And while the worst of it happens with the hot dogs, burgers, and drumsticks that are standard fast-food fare, every American pulling into a steak house or cutting up a roaster on the kitchen counter is about to get a hormone adjustment he or she does not want.

Foods have a dramatic effect on hormones. While a small part of the issue is the hormones used in livestock production, the main factors are the foods themselves, which may surprise you. But just as certain foods can knock out free radicals or toxic chemicals, their effect on hormones can be profound. Some foods make hormone problems worse; others essentially cure them.

How Hormones Work

Your brain keeps tabs on the amount of sex hormones in your blood. When it senses that there ought to be a bit more, it signals the body to make more. For men, this means that the testes make more testosterone.

Testosterone builds muscles, stimulates sperm production, and causes hair to grow on the chin and chest. It also contributes to some things men could live without: hair loss on the scalp, enlargement of the prostate, and prostate cancer.

In women, the ovaries make estrogens and progesterone. Although their names are similar, they work very differently. "Estrogen" is actually not the name of a single hormone, but a generic term for a group of hormones that control many aspects of a woman's body. The various types of estrogen act similarly, so I will usually refer to them by their group name.

Each month as a woman's menstrual period begins, the ovaries start making more and more estrogen, which causes the lining of the uterus to thicken in anticipation of the possibility of pregnancy. After about two weeks, ovulation occurs. An ovary releases an egg, which heads down the fallopian tube toward the uterus in hopes of meeting a sperm cell. The tiny spot on the ovary where the egg had been starts manufacturing progesterone, a name that means, in essence, "pregnancy-promoter." It takes over where estrogen left off.

Always the optimist, progesterone starts planning for pregnancy. It fills the wall of the uterus with blood vessels to nourish a growing baby. If the egg is fertilized, the ovary keeps making progesterone, which helps sustain the pregnancy. If the egg is not fertilized, the disappointed ovary quits making progesterone and the lining of the uterus is shed (menstruation). The next month, the process starts all over again.

Estrogen is also responsible for the physical changes that occur in girls at puberty and both estrogen and progesterone influence bone strength.

Many people have come to believe that the more hormones they have, the better. Estrogen pills, in particular, are sometimes described as healthy and even "feminizing." Men may imagine that a little extra testosterone can make them more virile. Actually, just the opposite is true.

High hormone levels mean that when estrogen drops during the menstrual cycle, it has a lot further to fall. The profound shift makes menstrual periods much more uncomfortable. And when women with high estrogen levels reach menopause, their estrogens drop violently to a dramatically lower level. That is when hot flashes begin. Under the tumultuous hormone shift, the bones lose their strength, mood changes can occur, and all the other menopausal symptoms take their toll. But evidence strongly suggests that, for women who are adapted to lower levels of estrogen before menopause, the change is much easier, sometimes barely noticeable. A major factor is diet. Women on Western diets have unusually high levels of estrogens during their reproductive years and a dramatic change at menopause. They have a much worse time with menopausal symptoms, including much more aggressive bone loss, than do women on plant-based diets. They also have much more breast cancer and other hormone-related cancers. More on all of these in chapter 5.

Men on Western diets have a far higher risk of prostate problems. It is hard to imagine that the prostate gland in the lower abdomen could be affected by your dinner. But foods do influence hormones very strongly, and hormones have powerful influences on all reproductive organs, including the prostate. There is even evidence that whatever genetic tendency men may have toward baldness will be expressed earlier in those on high-fat diets. As we will see in chapter 11, the dietary hormone boost may increase testosterone's damaging effect on the hair follicle.

But the problems don't start there. Researchers have been watching the age at which puberty occurs, particularly in girls, because an early puberty is linked to a higher risk of breast cancer. The age of puberty is dropping. In Western countries, young women have their first period (menarche) at an average age of 12½ years. It was not always so. World Health Organization records from 1850 show that at that time menarche occurred on average at about seventeen years of age. The age of sexual maturity has slowly but surely dropped in the United States and Western Europe. Of course, girls of twelve or thirteen are not psychologically mature enough to sustain a long-term relationship, let alone raise a child. Why should they be fully reproductively mature? This was not nature's idea. It appears to be the result of the foods we find on the dinner table.

The same phenomenon seems to be occurring in boys, who are reaching sexual maturity earlier and earlier. The effects are evident in both their bodies and behavior, and the cause appears to be the gradual change in what children eat.

Diets have changed dramatically over the decades. Of course, even a century and a half ago, there were some people who had eggs and sausage at breakfast, luncheon meats midday, and roast beef or poultry every night. For wealthy people, that would have been routine. But for most people, the staples of the diet were beans and grains they could keep dried on the floor of their barns, vegetables or fruits they could grow, and coarse breads. Meats and fried foods were in shorter supply.

Very gradually, that has all changed. Meat-based diets are now universal in Western countries. For the past several years, I have spent a few hours each week providing medical care at a homeless shelter in downtown Washington, D.C. There, the most indigent people in America consume high-fat, high-cholesterol diets because local soup kitchens serve the meat, dairy products, and other fatty foods that Americans have become accustomed to. The result is that their indigent clientele develops the diseases of affluence: obesity, high blood pressure, heart disease, and cancer.

The overt effects of high hormone levels begin at puberty and continue throughout life. But it can be like day and night when hormones come under better control and the bothersome problems they cause finally vanish.

Hormones are a part of your body. But you don't need waves of them crashing over you. Foods give you the power to control them.

USING FOODS TO TURN HORMONES ON AND OFF

Here's how to get hormones under control. First, cut the fat. Believe it or not, reducing the amount of fat you eat helps eliminate hormone excesses. Cutting fat intake in half, from the current American average of about 40 percent of calories to 20 percent, lowers estrogen levels by about 17 percent, according to the National Cancer Institute.[1] That is enough to make a very healthy difference and it seems to act similarly on testosterone. Researchers have not been able to figure out exactly why fat affects the body's sex hormone factories so strongly, but it does, quickly and dramatically.[2] There is no shortage of fat in the diet, from beef and poultry (even chicken white meat is about 20 percent fat) to fish, dairy products, and eggs. Vegetable oils and fried foods also contribute their load of grease. The first step in hormone control is to eliminate animal products and to keep vegetable oils to a minimum.

Second, fiber actually helps your body get rid of excess hormones.[3] Although most people think of fiber as part of breakfast cereals and breads, the term just means the part of any plant that resists digestion. Here is how it works: The liver pulls hormones from the bloodstream and sends them to the intestine via a small tube called the bile duct. There fiber soaks them up. If you have been eating vegetables, fruits, beans, and grains, fiber in your digestive tract scoops up your waste hormones and carries them out of your body. If, however, your diet is based on animal products, there will be a lot less fiber in your digestive tract because there is no fiber at all in poultry, fish, meat, dairy products, or eggs. Meat eaters' intestinal tracts contain lots and lots of semidigested protein and fat, but fiber comes only from plants. If there is less fiber to carry sex hormones away, the waste hormones actually pass from the digestive tract back into the bloodstream and become active again. This sort of hormone recycling drives up hormone levels. Switching to a plant-based diet can easily double your fiber intake and assure that waste hormones exit as they should.

A recent Dutch study showed how powerful foods can be. The researchers tracked the eating habits of a group of young girls and took blood samples to measure their hormones. The results were striking: The girls who ate more vegetables and grains had less estrogen in their blood and reached puberty later.[4] The girls may not have noticed much difference, but cancer researchers are thrilled with it because a later puberty can mean lower cancer risk. A little bit of fiber made a big difference. Those Dutch girls who ate the most vegetables got about twenty grams of fiber per day, about two grams more than girls who ate the least vegetables. Vegetarian diets boost fiber considerably further—easily to thirty or forty grams per day—and can rein in hormone effects even more. This does not mean you will have too little in the way of hormones. Rather, it helps your hormones come into much better balance.

A plant-based diet has another surprising effect. It increases the amount of sex hormone binding globulin (SHBG) in the blood.[5] SHBG is a protein molecule that acts like an aircraft carrier that holds the estrogen or testosterone "airplanes" until they are needed. It keeps sex hormones in check. The result is not just a more stable menstrual cycle or reduced cancer risk. The psyche seems to be affected as well. Researchers from the Massachusetts Male Aging Study, a large, ongoing study of middle-aged and older men in the Boston area, have found that those men with more SHBG in their blood are less domineering and aggressive.[6] It may well be that a better diet can make you (or bring you) an easier-to-get-along-with partner.

Some foods have special effects. Soy products, such as tofu, contain phytoestrogens, which are very weak plant estrogens. They attach to microscopic receptors on cells, displacing some of a woman's normal estrogen. The result is less estrogen stimulation and apparently less cancer risk.[7]

If the Venice Beach hot dogs were replaced with the soy hot dogs that are now sold at health food stores, they not only would have less than half the fat, they would also have estrogen-taming phytoestrogens and even a bit of fiber, which is totally absent in the meat variety.

Not surprisingly, vegetarians have lower levels of sex hormones than do nonvegetarians.[8] This does not mean that their sex drives are lower or that their sexual performance is reduced. As we will see, plant-based diets can actually enhance some aspects of sexuality. But it does mean that the untoward effects of sex hormone overproduction can be reduced by cutting the fat and going vegetarian. Women with painful menstrual periods often notice a profound difference. When animal products are eliminated and vegetable oils are kept to a bare minimum, menstrual discomfort can be greatly reduced or eliminated altogether.

Plant-based diets leave out much of the fat that drives hormone levels up and have plenty of fiber to bring them down. In addition, it turns out that the same vegetables that induce the body's detoxification enzymes (see chapter 2) also encourage the conversion of estrogens to harmless by-products.[9] All these factors work together to bring hormonal waves under control.

HORMONES YOU NEVER BARGAINED FOR

Chemicals can drive up hormones. One of the most important is alcohol. Two mixed drinks per day can increase a woman's estrogen levels by 30 percent.[10] This may be part of the reason why even moderate alcohol consumption increases the risk of breast cancer.[11] One drink a day can increase breast cancer risk by up to 50 percent, a fact that remains largely ignored by both doctors and patients because of the emphasis on mammography rather than prevention.

Chlorine and related chemicals can mimic the effects of estrogens. When widespread water chlorination was first proposed, critics, who were widely regarded as crackpots, said it would poison America. It turns out that they had some basis for their concern. Chlorination began in Chicago in 1908. By the mid-1970s, it was clear that chlorine reacts with natural compounds in water to produce trihalomethanes, nasty chemicals that can damage DNA and raise cancer risk.[12] Does that mean that using tap water for drinking or cooking is dangerous? No one knows how much risk there may be, but the U.S. Environmental Protection Agency is concerned enough that it is looking into other methods of water disinfection.

Unless new findings emerge that can set these concerns aside, I suggest using bottled water for drinking and cooking and reserving tap water for other household needs.

Also of concern are organochlorine pesticides and industrial chemicals, the most famous of which is DDT. Not only do organochlorines mimic estrogen, they also cause genetic mutations that lead to cancer and suppress the body's immune strength to fight cancer.[13] Although DDT is now banned, it persists in the environment and is still found in the fatty tissues of livestock. Humans store DDT in their body fat, too, where it remains for the rest of their lives. Researchers at Mt. Sinai School of Medicine in New York City found that women with more DDT breakdown products in their blood have a fourfold increase in breast cancer incidence.[14]

Likewise, women who are exposed to organochlorines in the workplace have more breast cancer.[15] When Israel banned the use of organochlorine pesticides, the incidence of breast cancer fell.[16]

But it is not just huge factories that make chemicals that interfere with our body chemistry. We have hormone "factories" right in our own body fat. Body fat makes estrogen.[17] The more body fat you have, the more estrogen you make. The result is seen in higher cancer rates in overweight women and a worse prognosis when cancer strikes.[18] Similarly, as men gain weight their body fat produces estrogens. As you can see on any beach in America, overweight men often have breast enlargement. While this is partly fat, it is also breast tissue growing under the influence of estrogen coming from their body fat. In extreme cases, this estrogen overload leads to impotence. When the excess weight is lost, estrogen levels wane, the breast enlargement shrinks, and potency returns.

Sex hormones themselves can find their way into foods. If you were to look behind the ear of a steer on just about any American farm, you would find a small implant about the size of the end of a sharp pencil. The implant contains hormones that make cattle grow faster: estradiol, testosterone, progesterone, trenbolone acetate (a synthetic testosterone), and zeranol (a synthetic estrogen). All five are perfectly legal. Do they end up in meat? Sure, but their effect is tiny compared to the animal fat meat gives you and the fiber it is missing.

FOOD CHOICES TO REDUCE HORMONE LEVELS

Reducing the effects of sex hormones on your body can have many benefits, from less painful periods to a smoother experience at menopause and reduced cancer risk, without the loss of any of the normal actions of these hormones. The steps listed below will reduce your fat intake to 10 to 15 percent of calories, increase your fiber intake to thirty to forty grams per day, and exploit special properties of foods to improve hormone balance.

• Eliminate animal products from the diet. Their fat stimulates hormone production in your body, and they lack the fiber your digestive tract needs to carry hormones away. These are a much bigger problem than the hormones used in livestock production.

• Keep vegetable oils to a minimum. Vegetable oils stimulate hormone production, just as animal fats do.

• Whole grains are preferable to refined grains, such as white bread or white rice, and whole fruits are preferable to fruit juice. Beans and vegetables are also good fiber sources.

• Certain plants, particularly soy products, contain helpful phytoestrogens, which reduce the effects of normal estrogens on a woman's body.

• Keep alcohol to a minimum.

• Until more is known about chlorine's effects on hormones, use bottled water for drinking and cooking.

Dairy products contain sex hormones, too.[19] Farmers keep dairy cattle pregnant virtually constantly. This keeps their milk production high. The hormones circulating in a pregnant cow's blood easily pass into her milk. In fact, one of the ways farmers test whether their cows are pregnant or not is to measure estrogens in their milk.[20] You cannot taste them, but they are there. These hormones end up in milk regardless of whether the farmer gives extra hormones to the cow; the cow makes them herself and they go straight into her milk. Several population studies have shown a correlation between dairy product consumption and breast cancer incidence.[21] Is the problem caused by the extra hormones in milk or by the dairy fat, or is it just a statistical fluke? Milk clearly contains hormones, but researchers have not yet sorted out these questions.

The legalization of bovine growth hormone (BGH) injections in the United States in 1993 means that farmers can inject extra hormones into dairy cows. BGH causes cows to make massive amounts of milk. Only a tiny trace of BGH ends up in the milk, but it still causes problems, both for the cow and for people who drink milk. The first is that forcing cows to overproduce milk often leads to mastitis, an infected udder, to which the farmer responds with antibiotics. Before BGH was legalized, antibiotic traces were already found in up to a third of milk cartons sampled.[22] BGH is likely to make the problem even worse as farmers counter this "side-effect" with more and more antibiotics. The resulting overuse of antibiotics encourages the growth of antibiotic-resistant bacteria.

More worrisome is the fact that BGH causes the cow to make more of a compound called IGF-1 (insulinlike growth factor) and traces of it end up in milk.[23] IGF-1 promotes cancer cell growth.[24] BGH proponents point out that cow's milk always contains some IGF-1 anyway, and BGH does not increase IGF-1 levels to more than about double its usual concentration in milk.[25] What they overlook is that milk consumption is only biologically normal during infancy (and then only from one's own species). Extended exposure to milk and its contaminants, including IGF-1, is not something that nature ever had in mind. Perhaps long-term exposure to IGF-1 or other milk constituents is part of the reason that milk drinking is linked to breast cancer risk.

If BGH and IGF-1 end up in milk, will they be broken down in the human digestive tract? Probably not. Proteins and protein fragments in cow's milk easily pass from your digestive tract into your blood. This fact was learned in a rather peculiar way. It has long been known that cow's milk proteins in baby formulas often cause colic. When babies are switched to soy formulas, the colic vanishes. But some children are colicky while they are breast-fed. When researchers tested their mothers' breast milk, they found traces of cow's milk proteins. The mothers had drunk cow's milk, and the milk proteins had passed through their digestive tracts, into their blood, and finally into their breast milk. When breast-feeding mothers stopped drinking cow's milk, their babies' colic disappeared.[26] It was once believed that proteins are thoroughly broken apart in the digestive tract before they are absorbed, but this is now known not to be the case. BGH and IGF-1 from cow's milk can travel right into your blood, along with other undesirable cow proteins.

The degree of risk posed by BGH-tainted milk is not yet known. But one thing is certain. Those doctors and consumers who were already cautious about milk because of its fat, cholesterol, allergenic proteins, lactose, and antibiotic traces are not going to be reassured by the emergence of BGH.

The American Medical Association and the American Dietetic Association both issued press releases on November 5, 1993, supporting BGH use. One might wonder why two health organizations would jump simultaneously to defend a genetically engineered drug that has no health benefit, does not improve milk in any way, and was marketed only to help dairy farmers get more milk per unit of feed. The relationships are at least partly financial. Monsanto Corporation, a major BGH manufacturer, made a grant of $30,000 for an AMA television program "educating" consumers on BGH. Monsanto also kicked in $80,000 to the American Dietetic Association for a consumer hotline giving out positive information on BGH.

This should not be too surprising. The AMA's video program for doctors on the treatment of high cholesterol levels was bankrolled by the Beef Board, Pork Board, and National Livestock and Meat Board. Its program on health risks of alcohol was paid for by the Licensed Beverage Information Council. And the AMA has more than once taken money from tobacco companies. Doctors and consumers are left wondering whether AMA policies are based on medicine or corporate economics.

There is a more direct way that excess hormones are added to the body. That is in the form of hormones themselves. Birth control pills contain estrogens and inexact synthetic copies of progesterone. Estrogens are also prescribed for postmenopausal women to reduce bone loss, heart problems, and menopausal symptoms. Some symptoms get better, while others get worse. Most worrisome is that both oral contraceptives and estrogen "replacement" hormones increase the risk of cancer of the breast and, in some cases, the uterus. The National Cancer Institute estimates that long-term postmenopausal estrogen replacement increases breast cancer risk about 30 percent.[27] There are much safer approaches to menopausal symptoms, as we will see in chapter 5.

The place to start is with a low-fat, vegetarian diet, which smooths out the hormone ups and downs and eliminates many of the problems they can cause. This makes every aspect of hormone function easier.

So while we took our bad example from the hot dogs and burgers of Venice Beach, we can draw a better one from a little further north. At Candlestick Park, where the San Francisco Forty-Niners and Giants butt heads with visiting teams, the concession stand will gladly sell you a veggie hot dog. It tastes exactly like the beef variety but is made from soybeans. With a little ketchup and mustard, even the most food-dissecting child will never know the difference. Across the bay, the Oakland Colosseum serves them, too.

A veggie hot dog is not exactly a culinary revolution, but it is a step in the right direction. When your diet is rich in vegetables, beans, grains, and fruits and animal products and extra oils are eliminated, your hormones start working for you instead of against you.

In the next three chapters, we will look in detail at how foods affect sexuality and at particular concerns of women and men.

CHAPTER FOUR

STAYING YOUNG SEXUALLY

Sex is a lot of trouble for all species. Salmon swim hundreds of miles upstream, defying rapids and fishermen's hooks. The male praying mantis is decapitated by his consort in the act of copulating. Parents are forced by their pubescent children to wait for hours to use the phone. One might ask, who needs this, anyway? How many broken hearts, infectious diseases, crimes of passion, and reams of bad poetry owe their existence solely to the rages of sexuality?

Biologists have struggled for many years to figure out why sensible methods of reproduction, like simply splitting in two as amoebas do, have been replaced by complicated mating rituals, impregnation, and the birth process.

The reason is simple. Sex exists to counteract the effects of free radicals. That's right. If beta-carotene worked a little better and vitamin C were more vigilant, sex would not be necessary.

Sex does not mean copulation. Intercourse is only the brief final scene in an extremely complex play. Getting the eggs and sperm cells ready is the tricky part. When you were conceived, your father's sperm donated twenty-three chromosomes and your mother's egg donated the other twenty-three to give you the normal forty-six, unless you are one of those rare individuals who got one too many or too few. But nature would not dream of allowing your father and mother to give you one of their own chromosomes. They have been banged up over and over again by free radicals, radiation, and who knows what kinds of chemicals. Biologists estimate that your DNA is attacked over a thousand times per day in every cell, sometimes overwhelming the cells' defenses and repair mechanisms.[1] With that as your genetic endowment, you would have been born wrinkled and worn out.

In the process of making up your chromosomes, each of your parents shuffled their genes in a process called meiosis and came up with twenty-three spanking new chromosomes, none of which exactly matched their own. They then combined their two sets, resulting in a whole new person. The reshuffling during meiosis and the combination with chromosomes from another person allows damaged chromosome sections to be repaired, or at least masked by other chromosome segments, like taking parts from two damaged automobiles to make a single intact one.[2] We need this shuffle-and-repair plan so that each generation can start fresh and new. So while you may have been attracted by her blue eyes and quick wit or his gentle looks and tender touch, all nature really wanted was spare parts.

That's the system. Now we're stuck with it. We cannot go back to the amoeba's way of doing things, no matter how efficient it may seem.

Our chromosomes make sure that logic and reason do not affect our sexual choices too much. They make surging hormones to propel men and women into all kinds of foolish and heroic acts. While moralists and psychologists have laid out theories for how the hormonal call for sexual fulfillment is to be answered, they are quickly washed away in the flood of passion that follows the designs of our genes and hormones.

Human sexual feelings are often inhibited, suppressed, and disguised. Mating rituals stretch on for months and years of dinners, movies, and nervous chats with future in-laws. Competition between rival males is disguised as well, taking place on golf links and tennis courts rather than in actual combat.

It would be simpler if humans, like other mammals, went into estrus, episodes of intense hormonal drive sometimes called heat. When animals go into estrus, sexual feelings are clear-cut and profound. There are none of the ambiguities that complicate human sexual function. And when they are over, they are unambiguously over. But human passions are much more subtle and unpredictable. Some people have little interest in sex, while others have sexual feelings that seem nearly constant.

For older people, two myths can create problems. The first is that the sex drive ought to die out as we get older. The second is that it ought not to die out.

For some people sexual feelings remain much the same throughout life. A Michigan study of married couples found that about 80 percent of men and 60 percent of women are sexually active in their sixties. In their seventies, about 55 percent of men and 40 percent of women remain sexually active, and after age eighty, the figures are roughly 25 percent for both sexes. The numbers are lower for women because they are often married to older men.[3] Menopause does not usually make much difference in libido. About half of women find no decrease at all in sexual interest after menopause. When a reduction does occur, it is usually mild.[4] Those who maintain vigorous sex lives at any age are in good company.

But as wrong as it may be to assume that older people have no sexual feelings, an equally oppressive myth is that if the procreative drive has waned, somehow one is not living up to the idea of eternal youthfulness. The fact is, the frequency of sexual activity often declines gradually as people get older. It is less a part of thoughts and dreams and often not the priority it once was. Satisfaction with one's sex life can remain high, however, because sexual activity matches sexual needs.[5] This varies widely from one person to another. So there is no reason to dictate norms but every reason to gratify your natural sexuality to the extent you want to.

YOUR SEX DRIVE

What determines whether the sex drive explodes or wanes? Sex hormones are essential for sexual feelings and their intensity is sparked or damped by psychological factors—romance, caring, and nurturance.

In men, testosterone is the basis for the libido. In most healthy men, testosterone levels stay pretty much the same throughout life,[6] but in some the testes are less vigorous about making testosterone as time goes on. In addition, the protein in the blood that binds testosterone, sex hormone binding globulin, typically increases with age, so testosterone is kept in check a bit more as men get older.[7] Some of this effect is countered by exercise because physical activity increases testosterone levels. Within minutes of beginning exercise, hormone levels rise, which may be part of the reason why exercise builds muscles.[8]

However, minor changes in testosterone levels do not make any difference as far as the sex drive is concerned because a little bit of testosterone goes a long way. As long as men are healthy and testosterone is anywhere in the normal range, sexual interest remains active. This is important because reducing testosterone levels through dietary changes may be beneficial from the standpoint of reducing cancer risk. For those who worry whether that could have a negative effect on sexuality, the answer is no. If anything, dietary improvements will improve sexual functioning as weight problems melt away and health improves.

The impotence that is so common among older men is not usually due to falling testosterone levels, nor is it caused by old age. It is caused by blockages in the genital arteries, aided and abetted by medications, hypertension, and diabetes, among other conditions, as we will see in chapter 6.

Although estrogens are thought of as "feminizing" hormones, they do not do a thing for a woman's sex drive. Falling estrogen levels do not reduce libido, and estrogen pills or patches do not increase it. Estrogens are responsible for breast development, vaginal moisture, and other feminine characteristics that allow sex to occur, but they do not increase desire at all. Estrogens just make the body *able* to have sex. The female sex drive is based on the same thing as the male sex drive: testosterone. Along with estrogen, the ovaries produce a little testosterone, about one-tenth the amount produced by a man's testes. The adrenals also produce chemical precursors that can be converted to testosterone.

Without a touch of testosterone, sexual feelings vanish. This was dramatically shown in a study by Helen Singer Kaplan of New York Hospital-Cornell Medical Center. She studied women who had been treated with anticancer drugs or received other treatments that destroyed their ability to make testosterone. When the hormone was gone, so was sexual desire. Many described their genitals as feeling "dead." Most still enjoyed the closeness of intimacy with their husbands or partners, but sexual feelings were gone. When tiny doses of testosterone were administered, their sexuality reawakened.[9] As in men, a little testosterone is all it takes.

By the way, testosterone treatments are not a cure for a lustless relationship. To avoid side effects, they have to be used carefully and they only work on women who have lost their ability to produce the hormone. If a woman experiences sexual feelings from fantasies or films but not from her husband, the problem is not in her ovaries. In the vast majority of cases, sexual feelings are lost for psychological reasons.

At menopause, the ovaries gradually shut off their production of estrogen. But along with the adrenal glands, they continue to provide testosterone, although it may eventually decline as well for some women.[10]

A significant loss of testosterone is most commonly due to surgery or chemotherapy or occasionally to medications such as tamoxifen, synthetic progestins (inexact copies of progesterone), or oral contraceptives, which can make testosterone less biologically available.

Alcohol raises a woman's testosterone level, particularly if she is ovulating or taking birth control pills. Some have speculated that this is responsible for alcohol's slight aphrodisiac effect. However, alcohol's ability to dissolve inhibitions also gets some credit for any ensuing romantic interludes. Alcohol does not raise testosterone levels in men and, if anything, reduces sexual desire and performance.[11]

Some evidence suggests a role for progesterone in a woman's sex drive. As we will see in more detail in chapters 5 and 9, natural progesterone is a transdermal cream used to treat menstrual symptoms and rebuild bones that have been weakened by osteoporosis. Women who use it often report a noticeable increase in sex drive.[12]

Men and women can remain sexually active at any age if their health is good. But that is a very big "if." In Western countries, obesity and heart disease are epidemics that affect many aspects of sexuality. Thyroid problems reduce sexual feelings. Many drugs wreak havoc with the sex drive. Birth control pills, sedatives (e.g., Valium, Xanax, or Halcion), antidepressants (e.g., Prozac or Elavil), antipsychotics (e.g., Thorazine or Haldol), cimetidine (Tagamet), propranolol (Inderal), diet pills, and even over-the-counter cold remedies can reduce sexual feelings. Drugs used to treat high blood pressure can reduce vaginal lubrication, impair orgasm, and reduce libido.[13] Virtually all recreational drugs (marijuana, cocaine, amphetamines, and narcotics) reduce the interest in sex.

In the first chapter, we looked at the toxic effects of excess iron. One we did not talk about is the loss of sex drive, a common result when the body is severely iron overloaded, perhaps because iron accumulates in the parts of the brain that are responsible for hormone regulation. Whether sexual desire is impaired by the moderately increased iron levels that are extremely common in adult men and postmenopausal women is not yet known.[14]

Coffee increases sexual activity, particularly as you get older, giving a new meaning to the "best part of waking up." Women over sixty who drink coffee are more sexually active and male coffee drinkers have lower rates of impotence compared to those who do not drink coffee.[15] Caffeine stimulates the central nervous system and relaxes smooth muscles, improving both desire and performance.

PSYCHOLOGICAL FACTORS

Gertrude Stein said, "A rose is a rose is a rose." Roses are fragile and need a lot of attention. Given full sunlight, the right amount of water, and protection in winter, even a century-old rosebush will prove Ms. Stein right. Without that care, a rose is a wilted rose is dust is gone.

Sexuality is a rose. It is the most fragile of all human functions. It is the first to go when we are ill or out of sorts. With any kind of stress, the sex drive is altered, usually decreased.

Depression eliminates sexual feelings along with every other spark of life. The problem is obvious when your mood is gloomy or irritable, sleep and appetite are disrupted, and apathy has set in. But depression can be subtle, sometimes masquerading as ordinary fatigue or vague physical symptoms. New short-term psychotherapies are enormously helpful. Medications help, although a few, such as Prozac and Zoloft, can reduce sexual desire even while they improve mood.[16] Dietary changes often help, for reasons that are not quite clear. When people start a low-fat, vegetarian diet, their moods sometimes lift. It may be because they are getting away from fat, which makes blood more viscous and contributes to a feeling of sluggishness. Or it may be that they are avoiding sugar, which, as we saw in chapter 2, leads some people into depression and irritability. It may also be because vitamin C, which is plentiful in a plant-based diet, helps in the manufacture of mood-regulating brain chemicals. Or it may simply be that improving physical health fuels psychological health. Whatever the reason, it helps.

Self-image is an important part of sexuality, and the single biggest determinant of self-image is our health. Remember the last time you had a bad cold or flu? How sexy did you feel? How did you think you looked? If we are in good shape, we feel attractive, and we *are* attractive, because a healthy, strong body radiates with vigor. If we feel unattractive, we are likely to be defensive and withdrawn. On the other hand, when you conquer a chronic weight problem or other health conditions, the insecurities that have restrained your sexuality start to dissolve.

ROMANCE IN YOUR LIFE

New relationships are filled with passion, inflating the attractions of the object of our love and blurring any faults. As time goes on, our mates may have trouble living up to our romantic first blush, but they also have attractions we had not predicted, not the least of which is the caring and affection they offer in spite of our own failings.

If anything predictably restrains relationships, it is the psychological baggage that we carry with us from the past. For example, if our parents were in constant conflict or held strongly negative views of sexuality, these images register permanently in our minds. They cannot help but affect our own relationships later on, not to mention our views of sex.[17]

We inevitably transfer feelings that we had toward our parents to our romantic relationships. When a woman dates a man, she cannot help but attribute to him at least some of the traits of her father, her brothers, or other men she has known. In turn, she will be the recipient of the whole range of pent-up resentments, fears, and expectations that he has developed toward women, starting with his own mother. When these feeling lead to conflicts, sexual feelings wither and die.[18] A man who was afraid of his mother is not likely to be passionate and assertive with his wife. He is more likely to be timid or perhaps defensive. And his wife will wonder what she is doing wrong.

Most of these feelings occur without our understanding where they came from. Of course, we don't necessarily need to know where they came from. What we need to do is to recognize them and try to set them aside. That allows us to blow the dust off our relationships and keep them emotionally alive or, if a new relationship is starting, to prevent misinterpretations from turning it sour.

Healthy relationships grow over time. Rose growers say "a bud is not a bloom"—you cannot begin to judge the merits of a rose until it is half to three-quarters open. Some roses do not reach their full beauty until they are wide open, showing the colors both of their petals and their interior. A bud of a relationship does not reveal its full beauty either. When people really get to know each other, they find more to love than they could have imagined from external appearances. And when they have been through some hard times and come through them together, their bond continues to deepen.

Sexuality is awkward at first, too. As the old joke goes, Niagara Falls is the honeymooners' second biggest disappointment. It needs time to grow and bloom, too. As time passes, sexuality need not fall by the wayside but can mature and improve.

STAYING OPEN TO CHANGE

Friendship, love, and companionship of any kind help us grow and stay flexible. Two people can find more new movies, new books, or new jokes than one can alone and can enrich each other's lives. Unfortunately, many couples simply let their relationships petrify. They rarely try anything new and settle for the least common denominator, doing nothing that lacks unanimous approval. They may make tacit conspiracies, silently agreeing to let each other get out of shape physically and emotionally in a camaraderie of decline.

It need not be so. Being emotionally open to trying new things allows you to enjoy new physical and intellectual experiences, giving you new things to offer each other.

AFFECTION AND INTIMACY

Psychologists have studied malnourished infants and their mothers and have found that these listless children do not elicit the same mothering response as healthy children. In other words, the baby's smile is essential to bringing out the maternal response. If there is no smile, the mother's behavior is noticeably different. The same is true in other relationships. Affection sparks affection.

Rejection sparks withdrawal. Just as we yank our hand back from a hot stove, we pull back emotionally if we are afraid of getting burned. And we retreat just as vigorously when rejection is imagined as when it is real. Some couples sink into a chronic passionless state because over time they have felt burned by each other. For some, trying to understand what has happened is an exercise in futility and can even reopen old wounds. It may be easier to simply offer affection, set aside defensiveness, and stick with it until fears and resentments dissolve.

The primary focus in any relationship should be on intimacy, not intercourse. If the relationship is healthy and intimate, sex will be part of it. If a couple is very uncomfortable with intimacy, all the sex guides in the world will not succeed. Imagine a couple stressed by excessive demands from jobs, kids, and financial problems. Night after night, the husband has a half-dozen cups of coffee while trying to finish a detailed report for work. He has repeatedly snapped at his wife and kids. Very late one night he finally gets the report done. He crawls into bed next to his sound-asleep wife and begins to paw at her. She becomes annoyed. He feels rejected and blames her for her unresponsiveness.

This couple does not have a sexual problem. They have, for the moment, an intimacy problem. With a little time to talk, catch up on things, and maybe an apology or two, their intimacy will build again.

Imagine that man trying to grow a flower the same way. He ignores the seeds for months, then suddenly fills a pot with soil, pokes several seeds into the dirt, and dumps fertilizer into the pot. He waters it over and over for several minutes, wondering why no flower has emerged. Intimacy is to romance as soil is to flowers.

When couples fall in love, they do not simply want to jump in the sack. They want to be important to each other and to be intimate with each other. Psychological intimacy is what allows physical intimacy to follow.

Here are ten intimacy builders:

• Rest. Go to bed early. Take a nap when you need one. The crankiness that overtired babies display so vividly can still hit when you're grown-up. If you are chronically sleep deprived, your emotional palette loses its color.

• Never underestimate the power of privacy. You and your mate need brief periods away from distractions. Walking in the park together after work or sitting together at a restaurant allows you to unwind, talk through the day's mundane events, and sort out what would otherwise continue to play on your mind. Get away for the weekend once in a while—somewhere simple, where you don't have to bother with a lot of packing and driving.

• Listen. Ask your partner about what is going on in his/her life. Give your full attention and ask whatever you are curious about. If he/she clearly does not want to talk about it, don't push. By the way, failure to listen is not necessarily a sign of a bad relationship. It is usually just a sign of familiarity. We no longer notice the walls of our house, not because we are trying to snub them but because we are simply very familiar with them.

• Apologize anytime you have a half a reason. A few sincere words can do a world of good when you've slipped up. The best apologies are prompt, full, and not watered down with hidden barbs, such as "I'll take half the blame." A good apology can totally dissolve angry feelings. And by the way, you can send flowers even if you have not done anything wrong.

• Always side with your partner no matter what. Never take anyone else's side against your him or her in a disagreement or join in poking fun at your mate.

• Touch. A little caress here and there is what separates young love from tired-out relationships.

• Let some things pass. Don't feel that you have to talk through every disagreement. When you were dating, you didn't consider it your business if the toilet seat was up or down, if the toothpaste tube was this way or that, or how he/she drives. It *still* is not your business. Intrusiveness and bossiness always breed resentment, and resentment is incompatible with affection. Remember, you are still dating.

• Keep your faults to yourself. There is no need to point out to your partner that your weight problem is worse, that you feel old, or that you just noticed a new wrinkle or gray hair, unless that is the image you are striving for.

• Never mention past relationships. People are always jealous whether they admit it or not.

• Spend some time all by yourself. Go to the shopping mall, on a walk, or whatever. Time alone prevents you from smothering each other and lets you appreciate your mate.

PSYCHOLOGICAL APHRODISIACS

Intimacy is the foundation for sexuality, but it is only the beginning. There are ways to turn up the heat, if you will.

• Look at your mate. Caress him/her with your eyes. Appreciate the curve of an ear or the color of a cheek, and take as much time as you would take to let a drop of wine fall over your tongue. Don't avert your eyes too soon. Even on black and white celluloid, Lauren Bacall's steady, strong gaze could seduce an entire theater. All you have to work on is one person.

• Notice how your mate is dressed and if you like it, say so. If a particular detail strikes you, point it out.

• Look your best. There is no need to look like you just stepped out of a fashion magazine, but a little attention to hair and clothes is a compliment to your mate. Men are particularly at fault on this one, but women can be, too.

• When you touch your mate, imagine what your touch feels like to him/her. Take your time.

- Give your partner a nice, long back rub to melt away stress. Start at the top of the head and work your way down the back, and down each arm and each leg. Gently squeeze the tension out of each muscle group in a downward direction, as if you were squeezing toothpaste downward and out the feet.
- Do not pressure for intercourse. Let it flow. If the answer is no, give him/her a massage.
- Hygiene is always in vogue. Smelly bodies can be made to sound good in romance novels but do not work out too well in practice.
- In spite of what was taught in health class, vaginal sex is not enough for most women to reach orgasm. Clitoral stimulation is usually necessary. As they say in the restaurant business, location is everything.

If you have had a weight problem or health concerns, you will find that, as you regain your physical well-being, you will enjoy intimacy more. As the weight comes off or your energy improves, you will feel more alive. And as the psychological benefits arrive, they reinforce the lifestyle changes that brought you there.

Special Information for Women

Menopause, Menstrual Symptoms, and Cancer

In chapter 3, we saw the dramatic effects that foods can have on hormones. In this chapter and the next, we will put that power to work, looking at specific problems women and men run into and the surprising power that foods and other factors have to solve them.

This chapter focuses on a new way of thinking about menopause and ways to make this transition smooth and easy. We will also take a fresh look at menstrual symptoms and at the breakthrough approaches to preventing cancer and improving survival for those who have cancer. You can take control of your body in ways that were never before possible.

Understanding Menopause

Some have suggested that menopause is simply the result of women outliving their ovaries. At the turn of the century, the argument goes, the average woman's life expectancy was only forty or fifty years. Today, women are living decades longer, but their ovaries still give out in the late forties or early fifties. The lack of estrogen and all the accompanying symptoms are just the result of women living beyond what nature intended.

That argument is nonsense. It comes from a misunderstanding of human biology and human life span. The fact is, menopause is as much a part of nature as puberty or losing your baby teeth and so is a long, healthy life after menopause.

The forty-good-years-are-all-you-get argument is what they said about dancers, too. Suzanne Farrell, one of the great dancers of this century, is a case in point. After years of pounding her feet into the floor and forcing her hips, knees, and ankles into the demanding positions required by ballet, she needed a hip replacement while she was still in her forties. And her case is hardly unique. For all its seeming delicacy, ballet is like professional football. Dancers' bodies are punished by leaps, twists, and falls on a daily basis, taking abuse that is far beyond what the body was designed for. As dancer and choreographer Agnes de Mille wrote, "Distortion is the very essence of all art and all dancing. Distortion is what saves ordinary rhythmic movement from being bland paddling in the air."[1] The joints and muscles are pushed beyond their limits and a ballet career is indeed a short one.

Isadora Duncan seemed to confirm the tragedy of a dancer's life. She achieved enormous fame for her free-form interpretations that cast aside shoes, corsets, and the conventions of classical technique. But soon her life simply unraveled. Her two children drowned in a car, a blow from which she never recovered. She fell into alcoholism, and by age forty she was out of shape and failing on stage. At forty-nine, her scarf tangled in the wheel of a car in which she was riding, strangling her. Such tragedies breed romantic myths about artists living wild and dying young.

But there is a very different side to dance that breaks through the "forty-year barrier." Ruth St. Denis and Margot Fonteyn had long careers in contemporary dance. Most noteworthy of all, Martha Graham did not quit at forty—or fifty or sixty. She danced professionally until her seventies and choreographed for twenty years more.

Graham did not begin to study dance until she was twenty-two. She was "like a young tornado," according to Ruth St. Denis, her teacher. She was only five feet, two inches tall, with pale skin offset by dark hair and deep-set eyes. She was reckless and uncontrollable as a child and was no less rebellious, temperamental, and fiercely determined as a dancer.

When she started her own dance company, she used every dime she could get her hands on to pay for costumes and to cover the rent on theaters where she performed. She and her dancers sewed their own clothes and managed her embryonic company, with barely enough money left for food. She was poor, but she attracted a lot of attention. Critics were stunned by her jolting raw emotion, carving out entirely new forms and paring away any superfluous movement. Her life offstage was filled with constant practice, and her dance compositions followed rapidly, one after another. Her devoted students worked fanatically, too, to the point that they became known as the "Graham Crackers."

At forty, her career was not winding down. She was only beginning. Her new compositions became enduring masterpieces. Audiences exploded to their feet, and critics described her work as an emotional catharsis, almost a religious experience. President and Mrs. Roosevelt asked her to perform at the White House, and four decades later, President Ford hung the Medal of Freedom around her neck.

Martha Graham was not shy about speaking her mind. She refused to appear at the 1936 Olympics in Germany and personally told a Nazi delegation exactly what they could do with their invitation. She actively opposed segregation, refusing to perform in a segregated hall.[2]

It took even more fortitude to pull herself out of a prolonged crisis in her own life. As she approached sixty, she developed arthritis that began to limit her movement. At the same time, her marriage failed and several lifelong friends died. She began drinking heavily. Cirrhosis and other health problems took their tolls. At age seventy-two, she felt she could no longer give the audience what it came to see and gave her last performance.

Health problems landed her in the hospital and as her health continued to fail, doctors expected her to die. But she did not die. She gradually recovered her strength, got her diet into shape, and came out of the hospital. She swore off alcohol. She got her company back in gear and if she was not going to dance professionally into her eighties and nineties, she would direct and choreograph, taking her dancers to performances in New York, London, and Paris.

Martha Graham did not even think about quitting at forty. She had three decades of dancing and then 2½ more of directing in front of her.

Women and men have lived to ripe old ages for centuries. It is not true that we were all dying out at forty or fifty until recent times. The *average* life span was shorter in the past because, until fairly recently, infant mortality was very high. Contamination of drinking water and food was common and antibiotics were not available, so infections were often fatal in tiny babies. Infant mortality skews life span statistics. If a country were to lose half its children in their first year of life but the remaining people all lived to be eighty, the *average* life span would be calculated as being only forty. If a country lost half its children at birth and the remaining half of the population lived to be one hundred, the average life span would come out to be only fifty. Does that mean that the body is designed by nature to give out at forty or fifty? Hardly. The human body is designed for a long life. Even in countries without advanced medical technology—especially in those countries, in fact—those who get through the rigors of infancy often live to their eighties, nineties, and beyond.[3]

Menopause lets you be done with reproduction and get on with your life. There is at least as much in store for you after menopause as before it.

Menopause Is Not a Diagnosis

Every day, in hundreds of doctors' offices, the same conversation takes place between women going through menopause and their doctors. The doctor writes out a prescription for estrogen pills or patches, saying they will replace the hormones her body ought to be making. They will cure her hot flashes, slow her bone loss, and reduce her risk of a heart attack. The patient asks if the pills cause cancer. The doctor acknowledges that there is an increased risk of uterine and breast cancer but says that the benefits to the heart and bones are worth taking the chance

Other risks enter into the discussion: strokes, blood clots, and water retention, among others. Women who have seen friends or relatives die of cancer or stroke might not find this very reassuring. They may have menopausal symptoms, and they would like a solution. But they are looking for something safe that doesn't cause more problems than it solves.

Take heart: There are dietary steps, other lifestyle changes, and natural hormone preparations that can make menopause much more manageable. They are better for your heart and bones than estrogen prescriptions could ever hope to be, and they accomplish these things without the side effects of estrogens.

Estrogen supplements do reduce menopausal symptoms, but they cause problems of their own. Premarin is a commonly prescribed estrogen preparation from Wyeth-Ayerst Laboratories. Although doctors sometimes describe it as "natural" for women, it is actually a horse estrogen. On farms in North Dakota and Canada, 75,000 mares are impregnated and then confined from the fourth month through the end of their eleven-month pregnancy so their urine can be gathered in a collection harness called a "pee bag." After they give birth, the mares are reimpregnated. Their foals usually end up as horse meat, and the urine estrogens are packed into pills. The trade name Premarin is simply a condensation of the words "pregnant mares' urine"—hardly a natural substance for human beings to swallow. While Premarin contains estradiol and estrone, two types of estrogen made in humans, it also contains an enormous amount of equilin, a horse estrogen that never occurs at all in humans.[4]

Estrogen supplements can have serious side effects. They are particularly risky for women with clotting disorders, undiagnosed vaginal bleeding, liver disease, a past history of breast cancer, or a strong family history of breast cancer.[5]

They increase the risk of uterine and breast cancer and make existing cancers much more aggressive. The risk of uterine cancer is increased four- to eightfold, and the longer you use them, the higher it gets.[6] Breast cancer is of even greater concern because it is already extremely common. Women taking estrogen supplements have 30 to 80 percent more breast cancer risk than other women.[7]

If progesterone is added to the regimen, it removes the increased risk of uterine cancer, although it does not seem to counteract the higher risk of breast cancer.[8] Synthetic progestins have side effects of their own, sometimes causing breast tenderness and fluid retention and making depression worse.[9]

Estrogen supplements increase the risk of blood clots and gallbladder problems and can cause high blood pressure, gallstones, vaginal bleeding, nausea, weight gain, breast tenderness, skin discolorations, headaches, and depression.[10]

So why are so many doctors prescribing them? Partly to treat meno-pausal symptoms. But more of the push for estrogens relates to osteopo-rosis and heart disease. Osteoporosis is very common in Caucasian women, less so among other races. About a quarter of white women over sixty have compression fractures of their vertebrae and many develop hip fractures due to the gradual loss of bone. But estrogens are not nearly as good at protecting the bones as women may be led to believe, and they rarely arrest bone loss. At their best, estrogens simply slow the rate of bone deterioration. As we will see in chapter 9, there are much more ef-fective ways of preserving bone strength. There are even ways to rebuild bones without the dangers of estrogens.

Heart disease is a major killer for older women, as it is for men. The risk of heart disease among estrogen users is decreased by half or more.[11] But that is not nearly as good as lifestyle changes. As we will see in chapter 8, a vegetarian diet, daily modest exercise, smoking cessation, and stress reduction can actually *reverse* existing heart disease. Estrogens have no-where near that power and carry risks that lifestyle changes do not.

If you are considering starting estrogen replacement therapy, please read chapters 8 and 9 first for much more powerful approaches for a healthy heart and strong bones. Some doctors suggest hormone treat-ments for virtually all postmenopausal patients. This knee-jerk prescrib-ing is fostered by physicians' lack of familiarity with nondrug approaches and aggravated by drug manufacturers' aggressive promotions.

In this chapter, we will tackle the other symptoms of menopause.

NATURAL CHANGES

At around age fifty, the ovaries stop producing estrogens. The adrenal glands (small organs on top of each kidney) continue to make estrogens, as does fat tissue. But the ovaries have produced the greatest share of the body's estrogens for decades, and when they quit, the blood levels of es-trogens drop dramatically.

Many women go through this change feeling fine both physically and psychologically.[12] Nonetheless, some women are bothered by symptoms, including hot flashes, depression, irritability, anxiety, shortness of breath, dizziness, fatigue, digestive complaints, painfully sensitive skin, memory lapses, vaginal dryness, muscle and joint pain, and breast tenderness.

Menopause occurs earlier in left-handed women, believe it or not. The difference—about three to five years—has been attributed to alterations in the uterine environment before birth that cause various hormonal changes and influence handedness simply incidentally. Women who took diethylstilbestrol (DES) during pregnancy had a higher-than-normal percentage of left-handed daughters, and premenopausal breast cancer appears to be more common among left-handed women, again suggesting links between hormones and handedness.[13]

THERE IS NO JAPANESE WORD FOR HOT FLASHES

In America and other Western countries, about two-thirds of women have hot flashes as they go through menopause. For many, they continue for five years or more.[14] The heat comes up from the chest, causing perspiration, often followed by a chill.

Stress can make hot flashes more likely. Researchers tracked how frequently hot flashes occurred in a group of women while they exposed them to noise, arithmetic tests, and a shop safety film called *It Didn't Have to Happen,* showing traumatic shop accidents. The stresses did not trigger immediate hot flashes but did increase hot flashes later on in the day.[15]

Diet is a greater contributor. It has long been known that menopause is much easier for Asian women than for most Westerners. In a 1983 study, hot flashes were reported by only about 10 percent of Japanese women at menopause.[16] And not only are hot flashes much rarer than in North America or Europe, but bone strength is not assaulted to the extent it often is among Western women. Broken hips and spinal fractures are much less common.

The most likely explanation is this: Throughout their lives, Western women consume much more meat, about four times as much fat, and only one-quarter to one-half the fiber as do women on Asian rice-based diets. The result is a chronic elevation of estrogen levels. At menopause, the ovaries' production of estrogen comes to a halt, causing a violent drop in estrogen levels. Asian women have lower levels of estrogen both before and after menopause, and the drop appears to be less dramatic. The resulting symptoms are much milder or even nonexistent.

Those who enter menopause on a low-fat, vegetarian diet often breeze right through it. There is no shortage of reasons to get away from meat, dairy products, and vegetable oils, and a smoother transition at menopause is yet another advantage of such a switch. Those on high-fat, meat-based diets are set up for the crashing reduction in hormones at menopause and the hot flashes that result. Of course, the Japanese diet is now changing under Western influences, with an exploding demand for meat and dairy products and fast-food restaurants cropping up like weeds. This may well be followed by a growing market for hormone supplements to counter the menopausal symptoms encouraged by meat-based diets.

More evidence of the diet link comes from a fascinating study by a medical anthropologist from the University of California who interviewed Greek and Mayan women about their experience of menopause.[17] The Greek women lived in a village in the eastern part of Evia, Greece. They were subsistence farmers, using traditional farming methods and plowing with horses and mules. Menopause occurred at an average age of forty-seven for the Greek women, compared to over fifty in the United States. About three-quarters had hot flashes, which they call *exapsi*, and headaches and dizziness were common. These were considered normal events, however, and did not cause women to seek medical treatment.

The Mayan women were also subsistence farmers, living in the southeastern part of Yucatán, Mexico. The dynamic changes occurring throughout Mexico, with new tourist spots being built in the northern Yucatán, had bypassed their homeland. Their clothes, ceremonies, and customs still reflected Mayan traditions. Menopause occurred earlier than in Greece or North America, at an average age of forty-two. Unlike the experience of Greeks and Americans, hot flashes were totally unknown among Mayans and, like the Japanese, they had no word for them. Midwives, medical personnel, and the women themselves reported that hot flashes simply do not occur, nor are they mentioned in books on Mayan botanical medicine. The only sign of menopause was the cessation of periods.

The difference between Americans, Greeks and other Europeans on the one hand, for whom hot flashes are common, and the Mayans and Japanese on the other, for whom they are rare or unknown, appears to be diet. The Mayan diet consists of corn and corn tortillas, beans, tomatoes, squash, sweet potatoes, radishes, and other vegetables, with very little meat and no dairy products. Like the traditional Japanese diet, it is extremely low in animal products and low in fat in general. The Greek diet, while rich in vegetables and legumes, also contains meat, fish, cheese, and milk, as does the cuisine of other countries in Europe and North America. As we saw in chapter 3, animal-based meals affect hormone levels rapidly and strongly and undoubtedly contribute to the range of menopausal problems that are common in Western countries.

This does not mean that women who have menopausal symptoms have somehow failed. But it does indicate the enormous power of food choices to help in the transition.

TREATING HOT FLASHES

For women who are experiencing hot flashes, there are useful steps in addition to the low-fat, vegetarian diet that is strongly recommended for so many reasons. Regular aerobic exercise helps. A vigorous walk every day or so or any equivalent physical activity seems to alleviate hot flashes.

Andrew Weil, M.D., a well-known physician and author, recommends the herbs dong quai, chaparral, and damiana, taking two capsules of each once daily at noon or, if used as a tincture, one dropperful in a cup of warm water. In doses of 400 to 800 IUs per day, vitamin E has also been reported to be helpful. People with high blood pressure should use no more than 100 IUs per day. Jesse Hanley, M.D., a family practitioner in Malibu, California, has found that certain Chinese herbs, called

Changes for Women by Zand Herbal and Menofem by Prevail, are helpful in reducing menopausal symptoms for some women. These supplements are available at most health food stores.

For those women who are considering hormone supplements, some
preparations may be safer than others. Estrogens that are commonly prescribed by physicians contain significant amounts of estradiol, which is
one of the forms of estrogen that has scientists and many postmenopausal
women concerned about cancer risk. A different estrogen, estriol, appears
to be safer. The best evidence indicates that estriol does not increase cancer risk.[18] Plant-derived transdermal creams containing estriol and
smaller amounts of other estrogens are available without a prescription.
The estrogens pass through the skin and enter the bloodstream, reducing
menopausal symptoms. Creams containing pure estriol must be ordered
by doctors, not because they are more dangerous (they are not), but because the process of concentrating them qualifies them as drugs rather
than natural preparations.

Dr. Hanley finds that a mixture of plant-derived estrogens and progesterone is often helpful. Transdermal creams containing estriol, estradiol, estrone, and natural progesterone are very effective in reducing hot
flashes.

"The hardest part of using a transdermal cream," Dr. Hanley said, "is
that, because it comes in a jar and looks like ordinary skin cream, women
may not think of it as a medication. They may not use it regularly or
measure it properly." But it works. "For most women, hot flashes dimin-
ish in one to six weeks after beginning to use the cream."

Regrettably, less research has been done on the use of estriol compared to estradiol. Even though there is no evidence of cancer risk with
estriol, Dr. Hanley recommends that if any estrogen cream, including estriol, is used, it should be accompanied by progesterone to reduce the risk
of uterine cancer and it should be monitored by a physician so it can be
tailored to a woman's individual needs. "Whatever formula is used, it
should have some progesterone in it," Dr. Hanley said. "Also, women
should cycle their hormones. The cream is used from day 1 to day 26 of
the cycle, followed by 4 to 6 days off." If additional natural progesterone

is used, it should be added for the final two weeks (days 13 to 26) and both stopped together.

Natural progesterone alone helps reduce symptoms for some women. Progesterone and estrogen creams are available from Professional Technical Services (800-648-8211), Women's International Pharmacy (800-279-5708), or Klabin Marketing (800-933-9440).

NATURAL SOLUTIONS FOR DRYNESS

Although the word *potency* usually refers to a man's capacity to have sex, the word can relate to women as well. In a man, sexual arousal sends a vigorous blood flow to the genitals. In a woman, the same blood flow causes vaginal lubrication.

At menopause, vaginal blood flow falls and erotic feelings cause less lubrication than before. The change is not caused by age but by hormone shifts.[19] The reduction in secretions also changes the vaginal pH, which is normally slightly acidic. The result can be the growth of bacteria, which then infect the urinary tract. Some medications, especially blood pressure medicines, can aggravate the problem and reduce vaginal lubrication further.[20]

The drop in estrogen can also cause the skin that lines the vagina to become thinner and more sensitive to irritation. The vagina actually becomes a bit shorter and narrower, sometimes making intercourse painful.

What is to be done? First of all, it is important to remember that the body is always producing some estrogen. Even after the ovaries stop, the adrenal glands and the fat tissue continue to contribute to estrogen production after menopause. In addition, phytoestrogens in plants provide weak estrogen effects. Soy products, such as tofu, tempeh, and miso, contain huge amounts of these natural compounds. The concentration of these weak plant estrogens has been measured in the urine of Japanese women and is nearly a thousand times higher than the concentration of normal estrogens.[21] Because their biological effects are extremely weak, however, they serve to blunt the effects of the body's normal estrogens but can provide a bit of an estrogen effect when the hormone is lacking.

Vaginal dryness seems to be caused by the *change* in estrogen levels rather than by the actual estrogen level itself,[22] which is why vaginal dryness can occur after childbirth, when the loss of the placenta reduces estrogen levels, and during lactation, when the hormone prolactin reduces estrogen. It may be that the more modest changes in hormone levels at menopause that result from a low-fat, vegetarian diet can also reduce the changes in the vagina.

The plant-derived estrogen and progesterone creams described above can be helpful. Used on a regular basis, these creams maintain a moist vaginal lining. They should not be used as a sexual lubricant, however, as an older couple learned the hard way. A letter to the editor of the *New England Journal of Medicine*[23] described a seventy-year-old man who developed an enlarging left breast. He went to see his physician, who removed the mass. Several months later, the same thing happened on the right side. It suddenly struck him that his wife was using a vaginal estrogen cream, not only twice a week to treat vaginal dryness, but also as a sexual lubricant two or three times per week. As gratified as his doctor may have been to learn that this older couple was still maintaining frequent conjugal bliss, the doctor had to conclude that the estrogen cream had caused the man's breast enlargement. They switched lubricants and his enlarged breast went away.

Researchers in Gainesville, Florida, were so taken with this report that they asked a group of young male volunteers to smear estrogen cream on their own penises. Lo and behold, it went through their skin within minutes, raised the estrogen levels in their blood, and drove their testosterone levels down.[24] The moral of the story is that vaginal estrogen cream is a medication, not a lubricant, and it goes through any skin it touches.

Many women prefer to avoid hormone creams entirely and use ordinary lubricants or moisturizers instead. Sexual activity itself, including self-stimulation, helps maintain the normal vaginal pH and helps prevent the thinning of the vaginal lining.[25]

THE PSYCHOLOGY OF MENOPAUSE

Menopause affects both body and mind. Although psychoanalysts have devoted considerable attention to the meanings of this change of life, such as the empty nest syndrome and feelings about getting older, some of its psychological complications are nothing more than hormonal changes affecting brain cells. Hormone shifts have a remarkable and varied effect on moods. To the extent that these shifts are smoothed out by dietary steps, psychological effects are more manageable. The most common psychological accompaniments of menopause are anxiety, depression and irritability, and poor memory and concentration.

Anxiety. Women who have never had a problem with anxiety before may become more self-conscious and more worried about minor events. In some cases, panic attacks occur. These are brief periods (usually a half hour or less) in which intense panic comes out of nowhere, causing a sense of helplessness and doom and the full range of physical anxiety symptoms: racing pulse, rapid breathing, sweating, weakness in the legs, faintness or dizziness, trembling, and numbness or tingling sensations.

Mental health professionals have a variety of effective treatments. Many people feel much better just knowing what their condition is. I once was called to the emergency room to see a woman who had experienced brief but intense panic episodes for several months. She had no idea what was going on and feared that the episodes were a sign of some dreaded undiagnosed disease. I opened my diagnostic manual and showed her the definition of panic disorder and she breathed a huge sigh of relief. While we still needed to run some tests to rule out thyroid abnormalities and other conditions that can contribute to anxiety, she was greatly reassured to find her symptoms were common and readily treated.

The most important piece of advice is not to let anxiety restrict your activities. When anxiety or panic disorders cause people to avoid stressful situations, the result can be an ever-tightening leash that keeps them from enjoying life. Anxiety can lead to agoraphobia, in which individuals avoid situations they cannot quickly escape from, which can rule out travel by air or train, movies, elevators, and crowded shopping areas (the term agoraphobia comes from the Greek word *agora,* meaning "marketplace"). Prompt treatment prevents panic episodes from turning into agoraphobia.

Depression and Irritability.   Depression seems to be particularly common when menopause is medically induced, e.g., after removal of the uterus and ovaries because of illness. Natural feelings about the loss of fertility and concerns about recurrent illness mix with mood-mangling hormone shifts.

Irritability is common at menopause. Things that never would have been bothersome before suddenly become intolerable. However, this life transition can also bring on a new assertiveness that comes from a reappraisal of your goals and needs. What may look like irritability may actually be newfound assertiveness.

To the extent that depression, irritability, or anxiety need treatment, it is important to explore the full range of available options. The first step is to get your diet in order and to have regular exercise. This helps stabilize hormone shifts and reduces the physical symptoms that can aggravate mood problems. Psychotherapy can be very useful, and new short-term techniques have demonstrated their effectiveness at considerably less investment than is demanded by traditional therapies. New antidepressants and antianxiety drugs have emerged in the past several years that have fewer side effects than older medications. I prefer to avoid prescribing benzodiazepines (Valium, Librium, Ativan, Xanax, and related compounds) because they are not much help against depression and can even make it worse. While they are very effective for anxiety, it is hard to stop them without the resurgence of anxiety symptoms, leaving many patients effectively stuck on them.

Poor Memory and Concentration.   Some women find that menopause brings occasional memory lapses, often related to reduced ability to concentrate. This can be upsetting and annoying, but happily it seems to go away on its own as time goes on.

MEANINGS OF MENOPAUSE

In the Mayan and Greek cultures, menopause has positive meanings. Older women gain more power and respect, and their wisdom is often sought, for example, in treating sick family members. Also, in both cultures, menopause liberates women from the burdens of the childbearing years.[26]

Mayan women are glad to leave fertility behind. They bear many children, and contraceptives are unknown. In the Mayan culture, it is considered a sin to tell girls anything about menstruation before it happens, so it often begins as an unpleasant surprise. With no sanitary napkins, Mayan women use rags that have to be washed and reused. Menstrual blood is considered a dirty substance of which the body is trying to rid itself, and a menstruating woman is believed to be dangerous to others. She must avoid contact with newborn babies. If she passes too close to an area where men are digging a well, a cave-in could result. At menopause, these taboos fall away. Premenopausal women look forward to the event and its arrival is not associated with any sort of life crisis or anxiety. Nor is it the harbinger of physical problems, such as osteoporosis. Physicians and medical personnel who provide services to the Mayans note that they are remarkably free of physical and psychological problems at menopause. The end of fertility and childbearing is simply a welcome relief.

In the Greek village, a menstruating woman is similarly considered impure, bearing the curse of Eve's original sin. She is not allowed in church or even to light candles or touch religious icons at home. Bread would not rise and wine would be spoiled if she were to go near them as they are being made. At menopause, she is freed from these restrictions and can participate fully in church activities. She can also enjoy sex with her husband free of the risk of pregnancy. Nonetheless, these Greek women have mixed feelings about menopause. It is still associated with getting older and a general decline of life, when bright clothes give way to gray or black.

In general, menopause seems to be viewed more positively when it (1) occurs earlier, (2) is more or less symptom-free, and (3) frees a woman from burdens associated with fertility. In America, menopause usually occurs after age fifty, perhaps due to the abnormal hormone elevations that persist on meat-based diets. It is often accompanied by hot flashes and other symptoms that can make a woman *feel* old. Widely available contraception makes fertility less of a burden than in less developed areas. While Mayans celebrate their liberation from taboos and the burdens of childbearing, North Americans and Europeans often associate menopause with a loss of youth and femininity.

Luckily, the Mayans did not patent their diet or the physical activity that is integral to their lives. In 1932, Martha Graham was awarded a Guggenheim Fellowship, which she used, not to carve out new dance steps in her New York studio, but to study Mayan and Aztec cultures in Mexico. She absorbed everything she could from their traditional dances and incorporated them into compositions of her own. We can take advantage of them, too. And while Japan is trading its traditional plant-based diet for a Westernized, fast-food menu, we have every reason to reverse this process. Replacing animal products and oily foods with pasta, rice, bean dishes, vegetables, and the wide array of delicious foods from the soil can smooth our physical transitions.

Foods for Menstrual Symptoms

While the transition at menopause is a major one, it is certainly not the only one women go through. Hormonal shifts occur every month during the reproductive years, sometimes causing all kinds of physical symptoms. Foods can change that.

A patient called me one day. She had intense menstrual pain and her mother suggested that she ask for a prescription for Demerol, a narcotic painkiller often used in hospitals. I agreed to prescribe strong analgesics, but asked her to try an experiment for the next four weeks. I suggested eliminating all animal products, fried foods, and added oils from her diet. That sounds like a tall order if you are currently following a standard American diet, but it is easier than it sounds.

As you know by now, eliminating animal products and other fatty foods causes estrogen levels to drop. The result is that, over the course of the monthly cycle, estrogen levels shift much more gently and discomfort during periods is greatly reduced. Some women are extremely sensitive to even small amounts of fatty foods, which cause them to have much more difficult periods.

She called me a month later to say that she felt incredible; there was virtually no discomfort at all. She continues to follow a vegetarian diet and to keep vegetable oils to a bare minimum. When she has deviated from this menu, she has felt all too strongly the difference at the end of the month.

This dietary experiment reduces your fat intake dramatically (although there is still a trace of natural oil in vegetables, grains, and legumes) and doubles your fiber intake compared to a standard American diet. To do this right, all animal products have to be eliminated, along with all foods containing any substantial amount of vegetable oil—potato chips, salad oils, donuts, and so on, and this is true throughout the cycle, not just at the end. The effect is profound. Many women notice a dramatic improvement in how they feel.

Most people who try this way of eating come to find it preferable in every way to the grease-laden, typical American diet. Vegetarian low-fat dishes—pasta marinara, bean burritos, veggie chili, and endless others—are delicious. And they also find that these foods begin to "feel right" for their bodies.

PREMENSTRUAL SYNDROME

It took a long time for doctors to take premenstrual syndrome seriously, but hormonal shifts are now clearly recognized as the cause of mood changes and physical symptoms. Fortunately, they can also be controlled to a great extent.

PMS starts a week to ten days before a period. The symptoms can include headaches, abdominal bloating, breast swelling, fluid retention, thirst, increased appetite, cravings for sweet or salty foods, anxiety, irritability, and mood swings. If you felt there was nothing you could do about it, try these steps:

1. Try a low-fat, vegetarian diet for one or two cycles and you will be sold. The key is to keep animal products out of the diet and vegetable oils to an absolute minimum, too, to reduce hormone shifts.

2. You may find that avoiding sugar helps tremendously. As we saw in chapter 2, sugar often causes irritability and depression. The reason seems to be sugar's ability to increase serotonin, a brain chemical involved in mood regulation. While this makes some people feel better, it makes others cranky. Sodas and sweets are obvious offenders, but even fruit juices can affect moods for sensitive people.

Unfortunately, premenstrual days are just when chocolate may be calling out to you the loudest. The easiest way to deal with this is to build up a little momentum. If you have managed to stay away from sugar for the past week or so, you'll find it much easier to resist today. But if you had sugar each of the last couple of days, the temptation today will be strong.

3. Avoid caffeine. As we saw in chapter 2, caffeine aggravates premenstrual symptoms in a dose-related fashion and also worsens the symptoms of fibrocystic breasts. Getting away from all caffeine sources—coffee, tea, sodas, chocolate, and caffeinated medications—makes a real difference.[27]

4. The antidepressant Prozac (fluoxetine) has been shown to help. It is usually taken every morning throughout the cycle, but some women have found relief using it just during the last two weeks before a period.

5. Consider the use of natural progesterone cream. Here's why it works for PMS. Many women go through an entire monthly cycle without ovulating. No one knows exactly why, but stress, dietary factors, and even chemical exposures may contribute. You will not be aware that ovulation did not occur, but your body knows it. If neither ovary releases an egg, the ovary does not step up progesterone production, as described in chapter 3. Without progesterone, estrogen dominates the entire menstrual cycle instead of just its first half, as nature intended. The resulting "estrogen dominance" encourages PMS, painful fibrocystic breasts, and fibroid tumors in the uterus.

Natural progesterone cream is applied to the skin and gradually enters the bloodstream, countering estrogen's actions. In carefully controlled tests, progesterone has been shown to improve both mood and physical symptoms of PMS.[28] It also helps fibrocystic breasts, fibroids, ovarian cysts, and endometriosis, a painful disease in which clusters of uterine cells have become lodged in the abdomen.[29]

Natural progesterone is a plant-derived compound that is an exact match for the hormone produced by the body. Available evidence shows that it has no untoward effects and does not increase cancer risk. For treatment of PMS, a two-ounce jar of progesterone cream is gradually applied to the skin over ten days, using up the jar just before the period is expected to begin. For some, smaller doses are effective. More details on its use are on pages 172 to 176 or in a short, technical book called *Natural Progesterone*, by John R. Lee, M.D., available from BLL Publishing, P.O. Box 2068, Sebastopol, California 95473. Synthetic progestins, such as Provera, are commonly prescribed by gynecologists, but they are not the same as natural progesterone. They cause many side effects and, in my opinion, should not be used.

Women who suspect they do not ovulate regularly can confirm this with a progesterone blood test taken four to five days after ovulation should have occurred. However, because natural progesterone is available without a prescription and appears to have no adverse effects, most women try it without testing.

PREVENTING BREAST CANCER

One of the greatest health concerns women have, particularly as they get older, is cancer. Breast cancer is frighteningly common. When I started medical school in 1976, breast cancer attacked one in every fourteen women. During my residency in the early 1980s, the rate was one in ten. It is now one in eight. At the same time, however, there has been a revolution in our understanding of ways to prevent cancer and to improve survival when it is diagnosed.

As we have seen, foods exert a powerful influence over hormones and hormones play a decisive role in breast cancer. Asian countries, such as Japan, which have traditionally followed diets based on rice and vegetables, with little meat or dairy products, have had very low breast cancer rates. The disease is common in North America and Europe, where diets are largely based on animal products. But as the Japanese diet has westernized, breast cancer rates are climbing fast. Affluent women who eat meat every day have nearly nine times the breast cancer risk compared to women who rarely or never eat meat.[30] Those who continue to base their diets on rice and vegetables have much lower cancer rates.

While avoiding fatty foods in general is good advice, steering clear of animal products seems to be particularly important. In a study of Italian women, those with breast cancer were similar to other women in the amounts of olive oil and carbohydrates they consumed. But they had habitually eaten more meat, cheese, butter, and milk, contributing to a significantly higher cancer risk.[31]

Modest changes in the diet, such as switching from beef to turkey breast, taking the skin off the turkey, or changing from whole milk to skim, are largely a waste of time, according to the best evidence. They simply do not change the diet enough. Americans get about 37 percent of their calories from fat. Switching from beef to poultry and fish is often suggested as a way to lower this figure to around 30 percent. But in the 1950s, when Japan's cancer rates were very low, their fat intake was only about seven percent of calories. As westernization has driven that figure up to about 25 percent, cancer rates have steadily climbed. Those Westerners who are dabbling with "lean meat" and poultry are not even close to a cancer prevention diet. A Harvard study showed that a 30 percent fat diet leads to no lower breast cancer rates than an unrestricted American diet.[32]

Similar evidence comes from China. In some Chinese provinces, the diet consists almost entirely of rice, vegetables, beans, and other plant products. In others, meat makes up somewhat more of the diet, although still a small percentage by Western standards. As the various provinces are compared, it turns out that the more animal products there are in the diet, the higher their cancer rates.

To really do your breast cells a favor, there is nothing like the low-fat, vegetarian diet that our bodies were designed for. It easily reduces fat intake to around 10 percent of calories and provides the antioxidant-rich vegetables and fruits that help keep cancer at bay.[33] As we saw earlier, soy products contain natural compounds called phytoestrogens, which can mute the effects of normal estrogens and may be part of the reason why Japanese women have low cancer rates.[34]

Holding alcohol at arm's length can help, too. Even one drink a day can increase breast cancer risk by up to 50 percent compared to non-drinkers.[35] As we saw earlier in this chapter, estrogen supplements raise cancer risk, and that is true both for birth control pills[36] and estrogen treatments used after menopause. Avoiding obesity helps protect against breast cancer after menopause.[37]

Radiation is also a factor. Breast cells are extremely sensitive to it and can become cancerous after radiation exposure.[38] This is why many doctors are reluctant to overuse mammography. While it can detect cancer, it also contributes to the body's radiation dose. Current guidelines recommend routine mammography only after age fifty, with the proviso that mammography equipment be new and well-maintained to keep radiation doses minimal.

Heredity alone causes about 5 percent of breast cancers[39] and genes probably also have subtle effects on cancer susceptibility, for example, by influencing the strength of your immune system. Those with a known genetic predisposition to cancer have all the more reason to follow a healthful diet and minimize known risks.

Avoiding industrial chemicals also helps. Toxins in the air or food tend to concentrate in the breast and other fatty tissues, where they can damage your genes. They also encourage the growth of cancers once they have formed, like fertilizer on weeds. This is not just a theoretical problem. Women who live near toxic waste sites do in fact have higher rates of breast cancer.[40] As we saw in chapter 2, we can not only try to minimize these exposures but can select foods that help remove carcinogens before they do any harm.

Those who have a briefer interval between puberty and their first pregnancy have lower breast cancer risk. While scientists have advanced various explanations for this, it may simply be that the low-fat high-fiber diet, which allows puberty to occur a bit later, as we saw in chapter 3, also reduces cancer risk.

In addition to improving the diet, minimizing alcohol use, and avoiding radiation and chemical exposures to the extent possible, exercise also adds a measure of protection. Researchers at the University of Southern California found that one to three hours of exercise per week during the reproductive years cuts breast cancer risk by 30 percent. Four or more hours of exercise each week cuts risk by fully 60 percent.[41]

Regrettably, one still hears reporters and health advocates say that the cause of breast cancer remains unknown. The suggestion is that, aside from using mammography and self-examination to find cancer at as early a stage as possible, women are helpless in the face of the disease. It is true that, like heart disease and many other conditions, there are gaps in our knowledge about breast cancer risk factors. It is also important to avoid any implication that cancer victims are somehow to blame for their illness. But it is essential that women and their families have information about more than cancer screening techniques. Diet and all the other factors you have just read about are vitally important ways to reduce the risk that cancer will ever start.

BETTER SURVIVAL

Foods not only help prevent cancer, they can also improve survival for those who have cancer. The more the diet is plant-based and the lower its fat content, the better the odds.[42] Researchers in Buffalo, New York, found that for a woman with breast cancer that has spread to other organs, her risk of dying at any point in time increases 40 percent for every thousand grams of fat she consumes per month.[43] That is a powerful statistic that can be put to work by building a healthful diet.

In general, vegetable-rich plant-based diets improve survival while alcohol reduces the survival odds.[44] Reducing body weight also helps. Several studies have shown that slimmer women live longer with cancer than women with more body fat.[45]

PREVENTING CANCERS OF THE
UTERUS AND OVARY

Cancers of the uterus or ovary bear many similarities to breast cancer. All three organs are strongly influenced by sex hormones and so are affected by foods that change hormone levels. Like breast cancer, uterine cancer is rarer among those who follow low-fat, plant-based diets. Women who avoid overweight are also at lower risk.[46] As we saw earlier, hormone supplements can increase the risk of uterine cancer, depending on how they are used.

Foods play an important role in preventing cancer of the ovary, too.[47] Yale University researchers recently found that two small vegetable servings per day can lower risk by 20 percent. On the other hand, every ten grams of saturated fat in the daily diet *increases* a woman's risk of ovarian cancer by 20 percent. That is the amount of saturated fat in just two ounces of cheddar cheese, four ounces of pot roast, or two glasses of whole milk.[48] There is no need to measure your saturated fat intake or count your vegetable servings, however, if your diet is vegetarian and without added fat. There is almost no saturated fat in such a diet.

Dairy products may be a particular culprit because, in addition to whatever fat they hold, they also contain lactose sugar. Harvard researchers have found that when the diets of women with ovarian cancer are examined, they tend to be higher in dairy products.[49] The lactose sugar in milk breaks down in the body to another sugar called galactose, which is believed to be able to damage a woman's ovaries, reducing fertility and increasing cancer risk.[50]

EMBRACING CHANGE

Martha Graham took everything she could from life—artistic fulfillment, fame, and a tremendous influence on those who followed her. She was also a passionate woman. She fell deeply in love, although she never remained happily attached. "I was never promiscuous," she said. "I always had only one boyfriend at a time. I didn't have time for lovers or love affairs—with some delightful exceptions." Graham was fond of Ingrid Bergman's secret of a happy life: "Good health and a bad memory."

She knew that to live and be productive, she had to have a healthy body. "Our body is our glory, our hazard, and our care," she said.[51] Not surprisingly, she was a vegetarian. Partly this was for health but also because of a deep reverence for animals. "It is one of the reasons I am a vegetarian today," she said. "As a child, however, I enjoyed meat, potatoes, and all vegetables. But today no meat, no fish, nothing of the kind. Animals exist as a power, as an entity in themselves. Animals deserve to live."[52]

She welcomed new knowledge, new experiences, new opportunities, and the changes life brings. She lived in the instant, not in the past or the future. "When you put your foot in a stream of water, you can't put it in the same stream twice, because that's gone. You're in a new place in the stream. I believe in . . . constant growth. Constant rebirth."[53]

SPECIAL INFORMATION FOR MEN

Impotence and Prostate Problems

Many men do not think about their health very often. We are not too concerned about our coronary arteries. We don't worry about future heart attacks or high blood pressure. For a lot of us, the only health problems we worry about are pulled hamstrings on our favorite quarterback.

But there is one aspect of health that men do worry about, and that is virility. As men get older, their virility is threatened. By age sixty, one in four American men is impotent. The older they get, the more common it is. Every year impotent men schedule 400,000 doctor visits and 30,000 hospitalizations, and pay close to $150 million to treat it.[1] It may surprise them to learn that foods play a vital role in potency. Foods are not aphrodisiacs or fertility enhancers. Rather, the right foods can help keep a man's sexual apparatus in working order and can help get things in order if they have gone a bit askew.

Impotence is not caused by old age. In fact, there is no reason why sexual functioning should be lost at any age. Impotence is preventable in the vast majority of cases and often reversible.

Erections depend on blood flow. Just as blockages in the arteries to the heart can cause a heart attack and choked off blood flow to the brain can lead to a stroke, when the arteries to the genitals are blocked, that part of the body will not work so well either. Other factors, including medications, diabetes, and psychological factors, can add to the problem.

The anatomy is simple. The arteries to the penis empty into spongy channels, called the *corpora cavernosa*. Like any reservoir, if the inflow is faster than the outflow, they expand. If the veins do not drain blood out too quickly, an erection will occur.

That is the system nature came up with. Regrettably, it is easy for things to go wrong. Blockages can form where the aorta branches into smaller arteries that supply the genitals and legs, or further downstream. Doctors can actually measure the loss of blood flow by taking the blood pressure in the arm and the penis simultaneously, using a special monitor. If your arm is getting a lot more blood flow than your genitals, you may be a great arm wrestler, but your lovemaking will suffer.

When the arteries are blocked only slightly, it takes longer to get an erection. Sometimes blood flow stays normal until sexual thrusting begins and the muscles of the legs and buttocks drain blood from the arteries. The annoying result of this "pelvic steal" syndrome is an erection that disappears just when it is needed most.[2] As the blockage worsens, complete impotence occurs.

Researchers have long known that there was a link between artery problems and impotence. Men who have heart attacks very often have difficulty getting an erection.[3] At first, this was thought to be an emotional response to the heart attack or some type of physical incapacitation that the heart attack caused. However, it is now clear that impotence *precedes* the heart attack in 40 to 70 percent of cases.[4] The reason, of course, is that blocked arteries in one part of the body often mean blocked arteries elsewhere.

Impotence can actually predict heart attacks. Older men who have reduced genital blood flow have about a one-in-four chance of a heart attack or stroke within the next twenty-four to thirty-six months.[5]

Blockages in the arteries are strongly linked to meat-based diets, smoking, hypertension, and diabetes and all of these are major contributors to impotence.[6] As you might expect, impotence is linked to cholesterol levels. A large Massachusetts study found that men with lower levels of the "good cholesterol" (high density lipoprotein) are more likely to be impotent.[7] In chapter 8, we will see how to keep HDL levels up while keeping total cholesterol levels way down. Changes in diet and lifestyle can prevent artery blockages and even reverse them in most men. But we are getting ahead of ourselves. First, let us look at more of the causes.

Diabetes contributes to impotence by encouraging artery blockages to form very aggressively. Diabetes can also damage the nerves that control blood flow to the genitals. But as we saw in chapter 2, diabetes is by no means a one-way street.

Overweight is another big contributor. Fat tissue is a factory for making estrogens, which can ultimately lead to impotence. Here again, dietary changes can usually solve the problem, as we will see in chapter 10. As weight problems melt away, sexual function often returns.

GETTING OFF MEDICINES

When I was in medical school, I was taught something that has proven true over and over again. In assessing any medical problem, whatever it might be, it always pays to check whether it might have been caused by medications. For all the good they can do, medications cause many side effects, and sexual functioning is often disrupted. Doctors at an impotence clinic at Jefferson Medical College in Philadelphia found that two-thirds of their new patients had been on at least one medication. Half were on two or more and 16 percent were on at least four different drugs.[8] Those medications are often the cause of the problem.

Blood pressure medications are the commonest offenders. Men with high blood pressure are more likely to be impotent to start with and when they are put on drugs the impotence rate goes up still higher.[9] Partly, this is because they do their job a bit too well. When the arteries are partially blocked, a little extra blood pressure may be needed for blood to squeeze through. Medications that reduce blood pressure can make it more difficult for blood to get past arterial blockages.

Thiazide diuretics are among the most commonly prescribed blood pressure medicines, and impotence is the number-one reason that men stop taking them.[10] Some evidence suggests that thiazides can not only interfere with blood flow to the genitals[11]; they can also cause testosterone to fall to unusually low levels,[12] apparently as a result of reducing the amount of zinc in the blood. When zinc levels are greatly reduced, potency is lost, and zinc supplements can restore it.[13] Zinc can be toxic, however, and should not be used unless specifically prescribed.

Other blood pressure medications, including methyldopa, pro-pranolol, clonidine, guanethidine, and reserpine, can all reduce po-tency.[14] This does not mean that medications are not useful and even life-saving. But it does mean that it is sometimes necessary to change pre-scriptions and, most importantly, to begin lifestyle changes that allow your doctor to reduce and hopefully eventually eliminate medications.

As we will see in the next chapter, most people taking medicines for high blood pressure can get off them with a vegetarian diet and regular walking. You cannot feel the change in your blood pressure, but you might notice the improvement in your sexual function—in addition to the drop in your prescription charges.

Blood pressure pills are not the only medications that can cause im-potence. The cholesterol-lowering drugs clofibrate and gemfibrozil, along with cimetidine (Tagamet, which is commonly prescribed for ulcers), di-goxin, corticosteroids, various sedatives, methotrexate, and even timolol (Timoptic) eyedrops cause impotence in some patients. Antidepressant and antipsychotic medications occasionally contribute to impotence, al-though the conditions they treat can be far worse in this regard.[15]

Tobacco joins the conspiracy by increasing the impotence-inducing effects of medications, encouraging artery blockages, and reducing blood flow to the genitals.[16] The old image of smoking as sexy is certainly not supported in reality. Similarly, researchers have found that alcohol is di-rectly toxic to the testes and to the nerves that control sexual function[17], supporting Shakespeare's often-quoted observation (in *Macbeth*) that al-cohol "invokes the desire, but takes away the performance."

When doctors evaluate impotence, they check for neurological prob-lems, thyroid diseases, kidney problems, cirrhosis, and depression because they can all contribute. Surgery on the prostate, bladder, or colon causes impotence if the nerves to the genitals are disrupted, as they often are.

How about plain old performance anxiety? It is a big factor early in life but less so later on—that is, until physical factors cause just enough difficulty with erections that anxiety returns and adds to the problem.[18]

Impotence is often caused by several factors at the same time. A man with artery blockages may also be overweight, with high blood pressure and a trace of diabetes. This gang of health problems knocks out normal blood flow. And even the slightest loss of sexual function can generate enough anxiety to inhibit the very nerve impulses that are needed for potency.

To a man facing artery problems, diabetes, or high blood pressure, the treatments are often complicated, not to mention expensive. For most men, though, there is a much easier way. It costs nothing and is usually much more effective than drugs or surgery. The only problem is, it is so simple, men may not try it because they cannot imagine that it really works.

The combination of four factors—a vegetarian diet, mild exercise, smoking cessation, and reducing stress—has a powerful effect on all of these conditions. Blood pressure usually begins to fall very soon and doctors often decide to discontinue blood pressure medications. Diabetes becomes better controlled and often disappears. Cholesterol levels fall and plaques begin to reverse. Within just a few weeks, men feel like their body is beginning to transform itself, which is exactly what is happening.

Of course, the usual treatments for impotence are very different, ranging from penile injections to various prosthetic implants, some of which are reminiscent of the flying machines in the pre–Wright Brothers era.

CURRENT TREATMENTS FOR IMPOTENCE

Once on a trip to New York, I got off the train at Penn Station and hailed a cab. The driver asked why I had come to the Big Apple and I mentioned that I was in town to do a television interview on nutrition. "Oh, I don't go for any of that," he said. "I've got a high cholesterol, but I eat whatever I want and the pills bring it down." He also had high blood pressure. "But I've got pills for that, too, and they fix it pretty well. They say I've got a touch of diabetes, but so what? There are treatments for that, aren't there?"

Driving a cab in New York is tough on the body. Meals are usually on the run and often at fast-food restaurants that offer even deadlier fare than the average high-fat Western diet. Physical movement is minimal and dull, constant stress is routine. His cholesterol level and blood pressure problems were the predictable results.

"Changing your diet would help you," I said. "Because even if pills do reduce your cholesterol level and blood pressure, they won't do anything to prevent the other problems like colon cancer or weight problems that can come from a meat-based diet." I could tell these meant nothing to him. So I played my trump card. "High-fat diets can even make men impotent. It comes from artery blockages or from the drugs you can end up on."

"Oh, I got that, too," he said. "But I take injections for it." Better living through chemistry!

Many other impotent men do the same thing. Using the same syringes and tiny needles that diabetics use for insulin, injections with papaverine, sometimes in combination with phentolamine or prostaglandin E_1, increase blood flow to the penis, provided arterial blockages are not too severe. The injections are not usually very painful, although bruising and scarring can occur. One major side effect: Once in a while, the erection refuses to go away and medical attention is necessary. The medical term for this condition, priapism, comes from Priapus, the Greco-Roman god of procreation, although when this painful condition occurs that will be the last thing the sufferer is interested in.

Surgeons can treat impotence by inserting semirigid or inflatable prostheses in a fairly simple procedure. Most patients report success with them, although infection or erosion through the skin can occur.

Some impotence clinics recommend vacuum devices consisting of a cylinder into which the penis is inserted. A suction pump draws blood into the penis, after which a rubber band is placed around the base of the penis to keep blood from leaving too quickly. With an understanding partner, these devices are well accepted. Don't forget to take the rubber band off promptly or damage to the skin and blood vessels can occur.

Yohimbine is a natural substance derived from the bark of the African Rubaceae tree. Occasionally doctors prescribe it for impotence, and about a third of patients, mainly those with mild impotence, report some benefit from it. Side effects are not common but include headaches, dizziness, sweaty palms, nervousness, and nausea. Men with kidney disease should avoid yohimbine.

REVERSAL OF IMPOTENCE

It may be that injections, prostheses, and vacuum devices could be relegated to medical museums if diet and lifestyle changes were used to their full potential. It has been known for more than fifty years that arterial blockages can cause impotence and that removing them can restore sexual function[19] (although this type of surgery is strictly experimental). The question now is whether the same thing can be achieved without surgery, using diet and lifestyle changes alone.

Blockages in the coronary arteries can be reversed in the vast majority of patients if they take full advantage of diet and lifestyle changes. It is very likely that, for some patients at least, the same return of arterial flow will happen in the genital arteries. Hypertension, of course, can also be greatly improved with lifestyle changes and most patients with high blood pressure will be able to stop medication use if they follow a vegetarian diet and take a half-hour walk daily.

Of course, none of this means that impotence has to be treated. Some men who have lost sexual function do not want to be treated. Their sexual desire has waned and they may not be up to the heroic-sounding nature of most available treatments. However, changing the menu is much easier. And its benefits are so dramatic and so numerous that, one day, it may eclipse all other treatments in popularity.

Many men have never tried a vegetarian diet. They may find it hard to imagine how good they'll feel when they are in a healthy and strong body. But the program described in detail in chapter 12 has the power to help every aspect of your body stay in peak form year after year after year.

The New Approach to Prostate Problems

The prostate is an organ that sits snuggled up under the bladder. In spite of decades of research, we still have no idea what it is doing there. We do know that prostate secretions end up in semen. But sperm are perfectly capable of fertilizing an egg without the prostate's contributions. When the prostate is removed, men live without it quite happily. The only health problems are caused by the surgery itself.[20]

One might wonder if the main purpose of the prostate is to aggravate older men. As time goes on, many men have an enlargement of their prostates, causing annoying and sometimes painful urinary problems. The prostate is also the number-one cancer spot in a man's body.

These problems are not inevitable. They depend in part on what men eat. Like so many other parts of our biology, the mixture of nutrients we choose every day can encourage prostate cells to grow into an aggravating mass or can help them stay put.

The bladder empties into a tube called the urethra, which passes through the prostate gland, where it is joined by another tube carrying sperm from the testes. Starting at about age thirty, the prostate cells alongside the urethra start to multiply. If this continues, they can pinch off the urethra, causing a poor urinary stream, dribbling, pressure, and ultimately infection and kidney damage. Irritation of the urethra causes the urge to urinate and repeated nighttime trips to the bathroom. It does not take much prostate growth before the urinary symptoms begin. The technical term for an enlarged prostate is "benign prostatic hyperplasia." It is not cancer because these cells will not invade neighboring tissues or spread to other organs.

By age eighty, some cell multiplication has occurred in most men. Only about half of them actually have significant enlargement of the gland and only a quarter have any urinary symptoms. In many men, the prostate actually shrinks as they get older.[21]

Mild prostate symptoms sometimes improve with no treatment at all. In one study, men with mild prostate enlargement were followed for five years, by which time a quarter of them had improved without treatment. About half stayed the same and another quarter had gotten worse.[22] However, men with difficulty urinating should not defer medical treatment because they can end up with serious kidney problems, not to mention continued discomfort.

Doctors sometimes prescribe drugs to relax the pressure in the prostate or to block the hormones that lead to enlargement. Finasteride (Proscar) is in the latter category. It shrinks the prostate and is well tolerated. In more severe cases, urologists remove a bit of prostate tissue, which, with modern techniques, can be done through the penis. The operation is called a TURP, or transurethral resection of the prostate, and is very commonly done.[23] In some cases, a simpler procedure works, making only small incisions in the prostate (transurethral incision of the prostate, or TUIP). A researcher named Burhenne developed a balloon device for dilating the prostate (transurethral balloon dilation of the prostate, TUDP) and actually tried it on himself. Similarly, some researchers are trying out a transurethral laser-induced prostatectomy (TULIP). Balloon and laser procedures are still experimental.[24]

Although male readers have undoubtedly crossed their legs by this point in the discussion, a TURP is actually a fairly easy procedure, particularly compared to treatments used in times past. The main downside of the TURP is that, by eight years after the operation, up to 16 percent have to be repeated.[25]

YOUR PROSTATE WOULD RATHER BE A VEGETARIAN

Changing your eating habits can help prevent prostate problems. The reason is not hard to imagine. The prostate is under hormonal control. In the prostate cells, testosterone is turned into a powerful hormone called DHT (dihydrotestosterone), and DHT is what drives prostate enlargement. This is the conversion that finasteride blocks.

As we saw in chapter 3, foods can strongly influence sex hormones, including testosterone. Could it be that cutting out meats and dairy products and adding more vegetables to our plate could turn down the hormonal stimulation of the prostate and prevent prostate problems? That is, in fact, exactly what researchers have found. Daily meat consumption triples the risk of prostate enlargement. Regular milk consumption doubles the risk and failing to consume vegetables regularly nearly quadruples the risk.[26] Prostate hyperplasia is reportedly increasing in Asian countries, paralleling the westernization of the diet that has occurred in recent decades.[27]

The meat-based diet that has become routine in Western countries and is now spreading to other parts of the world encourages many hormone-related conditions, and prostate enlargement is no exception. Even if you grew up as a meat eater, your prostate would rather be a vegetarian.

By the way, the enzyme that turns testosterone into DHT (5–alpha-reductase) is also found in the scalp,[28] where it works mischief of a different sort. DHT plays a critical role in baldness. Without it, men will not lose their hair, no matter what their genetics may dictate. DHT activity in the scalp may be subject to dietary manipulation, too, as we will see in chapter 11.

Nutritional treatments for prostate enlargement are being explored by an increasing number of practitioners. The first step is a low-fat vegetarian diet. Physician and medical author David Perlmutter, M.D., has reported success in reducing prostate symptoms using the following regimen (all listed supplements can be found at health food stores) in addition to a vigorous program of dietary changes:

1. Saw palmetto (*Serenoa repens*), a natural plant extract, taken in a dose of 160 milligrams twice a day.
2. Cold-pressed flaxseed oil, two tablespoons per day. If this causes loosening of the stool, the problem usually abates after a week or so.
3. Vitamin E (Carlson brand), 400 IUs per day with food. Reduce to 100 IUs per day if you have high blood pressure.
4. Vitamin B_6, 100 milligrams per day.
5. Avoid caffeine and keep alcohol consumption to a minimum.

Saw palmetto is extracted from a type of palm tree and has been shown to prevent the conversion of testosterone to DHT and to reduce prostate symptoms in clinical tests.[29] The flax oil provides essential fatty acids and vitamin E is used to protect the flax oil against oxidation.

PROSTATE CANCER

Prostate cancer differs from prostate enlargement in that cancer cells can invade neighboring tissues and spread to other parts of the body. If cancer cells would simply stay put, the disease would be little more than an inconvenience.

Researchers have examined the prostates of men who have died from accidents or other causes and have found something you might not have expected. Among thirty- to forty-year-old American men, 30 percent have cancer cells in their prostates.[30] By age fifty, this figure rises to about 40 percent.[31] This is a shockingly high percentage. But in most cases, these are *latent* cancer cells. While they are clearly abnormal, they are not yet at the stage where they rapidly multiply and spread. In many cases, they never will be. Again, foods can make the difference.

A comparison of different countries is revealing. In Asia and Latin America, latent cancers are much rarer than they are in the United States or Western Europe. Moreover, the risk of these cells growing into invasive or spreading tumors varies in precisely the same way. A man in Hong Kong has a 16 percent likelihood of having latent cancer cells in his prostate after age forty-five, while a Swede's risk is double that figure, at 32 percent. And compared to a man in Hong Kong, the Swede is eight times more likely to die of the disease.[32]

Cancers are like weeds whose seeds blow from place to place. On moist, fertile soil, they take root and grow uncontrollably. But if the soil is not watered or fertilized, they lie dormant or even whither away. The Swedish diet makes the male body fertile soil for cancer. Asian diets do not provide such welcoming ground for cancer growth. No country has a perfect diet, but the trend is clear. Countries with fatty, meaty diets have much higher cancer rates than countries that use rice, other grains, beans, or vegetables as their staples.

Testosterone and related hormones stimulate prostate cancer cells like fertilizer on weeds. The high-fat, meat-based diet boosts testosterone's effects and has been linked in many studies to high rates of prostate cancer.[33]

Vegetarians and populations whose culinary traditions are based on rice, soy products, or vegetables not only have lower cancer rates; they also have far lower risk of progression should cancer cells gain a foothold.[34] The possibility that survival for cancer patients may be improved to the extent that they adopt a plant-based diet is bolstered further by the findings that vegetables and fruits strengthen the immune cells that seek out and destroy cancer cells and inhibit their spread.

For the patient contemplating surgery, doctors are often less aggressive than for other cancers. This is partly because prostate surgery can cause a lot of problems, at least in the short term. Incontinence can last for weeks and is permanent in a small percentage of cases.[35] Damage to nerves and arteries during surgery often causes impotence, although in some cases the nerves and arteries can be spared.[36] Doctors realize that prostate cancer often advances very slowly. Most patients live many years whether they have surgery or not, and some researchers believe that surgery does not always change the long-term odds very much.[37]

It is essential to tailor your treatment to your specific condition, taking advantage of a second opinion if necessary. Doctors may recommend observation alone, particularly for older men whose tumors are small and less aggressive, as determined by biopsy results.[38] If surgery is deferred, the physician can periodically monitor levels of PSA, prostate-specific antigen, which indicates changes in the tumor.

PROSTATE-SPECIFIC ANTIGEN

PSA, a protein made within the prostate and secreted into semen, shows what the prostate is doing. If the gland is disrupted for any reason—surgery, biopsy, trauma, or cancer—PSA leaks into the bloodstream and easily shows up on a simple blood test. A low level of PSA is present in the blood of any man with a functioning prostate; higher levels alert physicians that a change of some type has occurred in the prostate.

PSA levels vary greatly from one person to the next. For cancer patients, doctors are less interested in the exact PSA level than in changes over time. If the prostate is surgically removed and there has been no spread of the tumor elsewhere in the body, the PSA will fall to zero within three weeks after the operation. Radiation treatments cause a slower drop.[39] A PSA increase may be a sign that further treatment is needed.

Increased PSA levels do not necessarily mean cancer. They can also be caused by benign prostate enlargement, infection, or surgical manipulation.

If your diet is right, you may never know you even have a prostate except when your doctor asks to check it. The very same low-fat vegetarian diet that is so good for you in many other ways is by far the best diet for preventing prostate problems.

CHAPTER SEVEN

SURGE-PROTECTING YOUR VEINS AND ARTERIES

E arlier in this book, we looked at the remarkable ability of certain foods to help eliminate dangerous chemicals from the body, drawing an analogy from Venice's struggle against toxins in its canals. But as the residents of Venice learned long ago, chemicals in water are only half the problem. Clean water is a problem too if there is too much of it—like four feet of water covering St. Mark's Square, as happened on November 4, 1966. The canals were inundated and the city was paralyzed.

It may well happen again because the majestic buildings and squares are settling a tiny bit each year. In 1950, the water table that props up the city like a cushion started to be aggressively tapped to supply the needs of industry, and the city sank faster. When the wells were replaced with aqueducts, the descent was again slowed.

But meanwhile, the seas are rising. The daily tides rise two to three feet and a hot southerly wind, called the sirocco, can push another three feet of Adriatric seawater northward toward Venice. In addition, the sea pitches back and forth in the long narrow Adriatic, like the seesaw of water in a bathtub, adding yet another two feet at its peak. Throw in an extra 3½ inches from the melting of the polar ice caps during the last century and there is an easy eight feet of water just waiting to spill over the city. On that November day in 1966, a rise of about 6½ feet pushed water in and over Venice.[1]

We fare no better when our veins or arteries are overwhelmed by flows for which they are not prepared. Varicose veins, hemorrhoids, and high blood pressure are all caused by too much blood in too little space.

But vein and artery problems do not have to be part of getting older. Believe it or not, foods can help prevent those spidery tattoos from showing up on your ankles and calves and can avert other vein disorders, too. They can go a long way toward keeping your blood pressure right where it should be and can even get you off blood pressure medications.

People who have computers or other delicate electronic equipment plug them into surge-protectors, which stop electrical surges from doing any damage. In this chapter we will see how to protect against fluid surges that can destroy your veins and tax your arteries. Getting and keeping your blood vessels in good shape is the fourth step in age-proofing your body. In the next chapter, we will see how foods can help clean your arteries to prevent and even reverse the blockages that could otherwise result in heart attacks, strokes, impotence, and other problems.

PREVENTING VARICOSE VEINS

Varicose veins have been the subject of more medical myths than just about any other condition. Authoritative treatises have attributed them to the evolution of upright posture in the human species, even though in countries where varicose veins are rare people stand just as upright as they do in countries where varicose veins are common. Other authorities have held that the condition is a result of pregnancy, even though the countries with the highest birthrates have low rates of varicose veins. The confusion ultimately results from the fact that for many years researchers focused their efforts on devising ever more heroic treatments for varicose veins and have simply not paid much attention to what caused them.

In the mid-1970s Dr. Denis Burkitt offered a radically different way of thinking about the problem. While practicing surgery in Africa for twenty years Dr. Burkitt found that doctors in Africa and Asia rarely saw varicose veins. The average hospital treated only two cases per year.[2] The reason was not that Africans or Asians are reluctant to seek treatment for varicose veins because more serious vein conditions, such as vein ulcerations and blood clots, which demand medical treatment, were similarly rare. In contrast, these were everyday problems in doctors' offices in Western countries and still are.

Dr. Burkitt's answer to varicose veins was surprising, even disconcerting. As it gradually came to be accepted, medical texts had to be rewritten. What Burkitt discovered gives people a way to protect their veins from the punishment they might otherwise endure.

The arteries carry blood from the heart down to the feet. The veins have the challenge of carrying it back up again. To keep blood from flowing back downward with gravity, the veins have a series of valves that close if blood shifts backward. They work like double doors, swinging to the side to let blood pass and closing together to stop the backflow. These valves are fragile. If a wave of blood were to flow backward down the veins, the valves would try to stop it. But if the wave were too strong, it could expand the veins to the point where the "doors" are no longer able to close properly. When that happens, blood flows backward right through the valves. The veins swell with blood, becoming visible in the lower leg and sometimes even breaking open at the surface. The valves will eventually be destroyed by the pressure.

Varicose veins—dilated, tortuous leg veins—can start early in life. In one study, 12 percent of children had incompetent valves in their leg veins and nearly 4 percent already had varicose veins by age sixteen.[3]

Dr. Burkitt hypothesized that the problem starts not in the veins but in the digestive tract, and the weight of evidence supports his findings. While the explanation is a bit graphic, it is offered here so the reader can take advantage of it.

For many years, people in Western countries have not gotten the fiber their bodies need. Fiber is what used to be called natural plant roughage. There is plenty of fiber in vegetables, cereals, whole grain bread, beans, and fruits. But Westerners have had quite a taste for meats and dairy products, none of which contain any fiber at all. Similarly, ever-popular white bread and white rice have had most of their fiber removed.

Fiber is essential for regularity because it holds water in the intestinal tract like a sponge. Without it, the wastes harden, resulting in varying degrees of constipation. It is no surprise that grocery stores in Western nations sell dozens of laxatives, some of which contain essentially the same fiber that had been taken out of bread, and that Westerners often keep magazine racks in their bathrooms.

The daily pushing and straining to evacuate the wastes that results from a fiber-depleted diet forces everything in the abdomen downward, including the blood that is trying to make its way up out of the legs. If this occurs with any frequency, the backward flow of blood can force open the valves of the legs. From the top of the leg on down, the valves lose their ability to hold blood. The backward flow damages the veins themselves and causes them to enlarge like overflowing rivers. The results show up on your ankles or calves.

Countries with traditional plant-based diets get lots of fiber, and a doctor who tried to set up a vein clinic there would have trouble finding any customers.

Heredity might play some role in varicose veins. They do occur more commonly in individuals whose parents had the same condition.[4] While this may simply reflect the fact that dietary habits are passed from parent to child, it may also mean that some families may tend toward weaker veins that are more susceptible to damage. For those individuals, putting the fiber back in the diet is all the more important.

Like heredity, prolonged standing and pregnancy might contribute to the problem, but they do not appear to be primary causes.[5] Diet is both the most decisive factor and the easiest one to change.[6]

REGAINING HEALTHY VEINS

Venice has minor flooding so often that merchants construct makeshift walkways so patrons can wend their way to shops or restaurants. The *acqua alta* (high water) is an inconvenience, but the major floods are something else: They threaten the city's survival. Many remedies have been proposed, and some are ambitious, to say the least. One firm tried injecting mud and cement under buildings to see if they could be raised. It works, but to do it for the entire city would be a monumental task. The city agreed to a different plan—constructing a series of floodgates that shut out the sea when storms arise, hopefully preventing the major flooding that inundated St. Mark's Square.

This is exactly the system that your veins use. The key is to protect the floodgates, rather than pummel them on a daily basis. While putting the fiber back in the diet sounds much too simple, it works. Dr. Burkitt was particularly fond of the fiber in whole grains, but beans, vegetables, and fruits also help. The best diets exclude meat, dairy products, and overly refined grains because they displace the fiber-rich foods your body needs. The very first day that you begin a vegetarian diet that is generous in whole grain breads, brown rice, baked beans, broccoli, spinach, fresh fruit, and all the other foods your body was designed for, your digestive tract begins to change. Straining is no longer necessary and valves that are not irreparably damaged can recover when they finally have the pressure off. Chapter 12 will show you how to start.

Combine this dietary change with regular walking. Like the menu change, it sounds too simple. But walking reduces vein pressures dramatically as the leg muscles pump blood back up to the heart. In 1949, researchers in Minnesota passed a pressure monitor into the ankle veins of volunteers. When the subjects were lying down, the vein pressure was very low, as you would expect, averaging about twelve millimeters of mercury. When the subjects sat up, the pressure increased to fifty-six. Standing sent the pressure in the ankle veins up to ninety in about twenty seconds. But when a subject started to walk, the contraction of the calf and thigh muscles pumped the blood up and out of the legs, lowering the pressure in the ankle vein back down to about twenty-two. When the subject stopped walking and stood still, the leg vein pressure shot back up to near ninety.[7]

This is why doctors like their varicose vein patients to keep walking—especially if they find themselves outside a steak house or chicken restaurant.

If treatment is needed for existing varicose veins, minor cases can be treated with injections of sclerosing agents or cryosurgery (freezing). More advanced cases usually require removal of a portion of the vein, as lesser treatments often lead to recurrence.[8] Some doctors are reluctant to remove the leg veins, since these are the veins that are commonly used to replace the coronary arteries in heart bypass surgery.[9] Of course, a healthy diet and regular walking makes both vein problems and heart troubles a lot less likely.

Throughout this book, we have seen the extraordinary power of plant-based diets. They bolster our defenses against free radicals, they turn on the enzyme systems that eliminate cancer-causing toxins, and they help us conquer hormone swings and many other problems. But an additional and surprising benefit of a lentil curry, a whole grain muffin, or a side of broccoli is that your veins are better able to keep their strength and resilience.

PREVENTING BLOOD CLOTS

Varicose veins are not the only sign of damaged valves in the leg veins. When blood pools in the deep veins of the legs, it has a tendency to clot. This blocks blood flow even more and leads to inflammation called thrombophlebitis. (The prefix *thrombo* means "clot," *phleb* refers to veins, and *itis* means "inflammation.") The leg becomes swollen, red, warm, and painful. Doctors worry about blood clots in the legs. If a piece of the clot breaks free and travels up to the heart, it can lodge in the arteries to the lungs, which is a very dangerous condition indeed.

Studies of cultures consuming high-fiber diets show that not only are varicose veins rare but blood clots are too.[10] The reason is not only that fiber helps take the pressure off veins. Evidence suggests that meat-based diets encourage the growth of intestinal bacteria that produce compounds that promote more rapid clotting. Meat also contains a type of fat, called stearic acid, that encourages clotting.[11] Plant-based diets help return the digestive tract to normal. Some surgeons have prescribed fiber for patients on the days leading up to surgery in order to reduce the risk of dangerous clots in the leg veins.[12]

Your taste buds love it when you have an apple or an orange, some split pea soup or minestrone, a bean burrito or vegetable curry. And your veins are delighted, too.

FOODS THAT STOP HEMORRHOIDS

Since the publication of *Food for Life*, I have received many letters reporting success using foods to conquer health problems. But one problem in particular has generated a degree of enthusiasm I had not expected. A letter from a fifty-year-old man told how he had started a low-fat vegetarian diet after hearing a lecture I had given. His weight, which had always been a problem, finally came down and stayed down. His cholesterol level dropped dramatically. Those results were very gratifying but not surprising because those benefits are now widely known. What he really appreciated was something different: His hemorrhoids had gone away. These hemorrhoids had bothered him for years and led to all kinds of marginally helpful treatments but no end to his misery. But they suddenly went away within a few weeks of changing his diet.

I recently received another letter that read:

> I heard you on the radio about two months ago. Just from what you said in that interview, I concluded that (1) you were on to something important and (2) that you knew what you were talking about. I, therefore, that very day, completely stopped eating meat, poultry, fish, animal products, and dairy products. My wife thought I had lost my mind, but she is coming around.
>
> One of the most impressive consequences was that I seem to have had a total, immediate, and miraculous cure of my recurring problem with bleeding hemorrhoids. Hardly a week went by that I did not see bright red blood in my toilet, and now, without meat or dairy products in my diet, the problem has *vanished*.
>
> I also lost about seven pounds, without even trying to lose weight. I feel so much more alert. Thanks for making such an important improvement and change in my life.

People do not often discuss hemorrhoids with their physicians or friends and, if they do, they are not likely to learn about the dietary approach.

But hemorrhoids are really not much different from varicose veins.

The veins surrounding the anus have a purpose. Just as the soft red cushions we call lips close and seal the mouth so that we can chew and swallow, the normal venous cushions around the anus close the other end of the digestive tract. Pushing and straining causes these veins to fill with blood. As hard stools are passed, the engorged veins can be pushed downward and out through the anus.

Countries that abandon plant-based diets in favor of westernized diets often see large increases in the prevalence of hemorrhoids and that happens even sooner than the increase in varicose veins.[13] Conversely, when people who have been suffering with hemorrhoids begin plant-based diets, the result is much softer stools and no more straining, and the engorged hemorrhoidal vessels often begin to shrink within a few days.

Other types of abdominal straining, such as lifting heavy boxes, are not likely to contribute to hemorrhoids. Although pressure is generated within the abdomen during lifting, the contracted anal sphincter blocks the flow of blood into the hemorrhoidal vessels.[14]

Sometimes women find that pregnancy and delivery trigger their hemorrhoids.[15] However, studies of different countries show that if plant-based diets are followed, pregnancy does not seem to lead to a high rate of chronic hemorrhoids.

Any rectal bleeding should be checked by a physician. More serious conditions, such as rectal cancer, are much rarer than hemorrhoids, but it is impossible for an individual to tell the source of the problem.

Doctors treat hemorrhoids with surgery, lasers, freezing, rubber bands, and injections. Sometimes these treatments cannot be avoided.[16] But a healthy diet can help shrink minor hemorrhoids and help prevent recurrence after treatment. Chapter 12 will show you how to put fiber easily and naturally in your diet.

KEEPING OR RESTORING
A HEALTHY BLOOD PRESSURE

Even if our bloodstream is as clean as a mountain spring, we are not built to withstand repeated waves of high blood pressure. High pressure in the arteries stresses the artery wall and increases the likelihood of artery damage, heart attack, and stroke.

It is surprising how many people develop high blood pressure. Over sixty million Americans have it, and almost half do not know it. Those who do—believe it or not—pay $12.5 billion every year to treat it.[17] But medicines have never been an entirely satisfactory solution. Thiazide diuretics have been most doctors' first line of defense but are enough of a nuisance that one in five patients stops taking them. High blood pressure itself has no symptoms, so patients are not likely to put up with the shortness of breath, fatigue, lethargy, and impotence these drugs sometimes cause. At the same time, thiazides have very little effect on the risk of heart disease and can actually cause cholesterol levels to rise.[18]

Although some people need medications, most people can lower their pressure with diet and lifestyle changes alone. In fact, studies show that the majority of patients taking medication to control their blood pressure can get off all medications and can actually have a lower blood pressure than when they were on medication, provided that their diet and lifestyle changes go far enough. If you are on blood pressure medications currently, keep your doctor involved as you begin your diet and lifestyle changes, as it is very likely that your prescriptions will need to be adjusted.

When a doctor takes your blood pressure, he or she inflates a cuff around your arm and then gradually reduces the pressure in the cuff while listening for your pulse through a stethoscope. The point at which the pulse is first heard is the systolic blood pressure, the surge of pressure from the heartbeat. The doctor then continues to reduce the cuff pressure until the pulse is no longer audible. This point is the diastolic pressure, that is, the pressure in the arteries between beats. A blood pressure of

120/80 means that your blood pressure rises to a peak of 120 millimeters of mercury with each heartbeat and falls to 80 millimeters of mercury between beats. Blood pressures over 140/90 are considered high.

If a doctor checks your blood pressure and finds it a bit high, he or she will usually want to check it again before prescribing medications because just the sight of a white coat can stress people enough to raise their blood pressures substantially. (The effect of seeing a doctor's bill has not yet been tested.) If it stays high on retesting, it is time to do something about it. The first step is to improve the diet.

Most people are aware that lowering sodium intake can help reduce blood pressure. It is by no means all that you can do, but it is nonetheless important. Sodium draws water into the blood vessels, and too much water in the artery can lead to too much pressure.[19] Reducing salt intake is really quite easy, and we will go into that in more detail in chapter 9.

The same vegetarian diet that protects your veins has a powerful effect on blood pressure. Vegetarians have only about one-third the prevalence of high blood pressure compared to non-vegetarians.[20] This holds true even when other lifestyle factors are taken into account. For example, virtually all Seventh-Day Adventists avoid tobacco and alcohol. But about half of them are also vegetarians. When the vegetarian and nonvegetarian Adventists are compared, they are similar in lifestyle factors other than diet, yet the vegetarians have only about one-third the prevalence of hypertension. There is something about vegetarian foods that is almost like magic for your blood vessels.

Of course, a vegetarian diet helps people lose weight, which, in turn, reduces blood pressure. But there is more to it than that. When people begin a vegetarian diet, their blood pressures drop *before* they lose any weight.[21] They even drop a little if their blood pressure was normal to start with.[22] No one knows why it works so well. It is not just because vegetarian diets are lower in salt and higher in potassium, although those are good features.[23] Vitamin C, which abounds in plant-based diets, also helps lower blood pressure.[24]

The fact that there is not much fat in these foods is a big plus. Low-fat diets make the blood "thinner" (less viscous).[25] Imagine drinking water through a straw. Simple, right? Now imagine that the water was replaced with oil. You would have a tougher time getting it through the straw. So does your heart when it has to push fat-laden blood through your arteries.

Whatever the reason, a vegetarian diet lowers both systolic and diastolic blood pressure so quickly that the difference is obvious within a few weeks. The combination of a pure vegetarian (vegan) diet and a daily half-hour walk is particularly powerful. One fascinating study involved twenty-six patients with high blood pressure. All of them were taking medications to bring it under control. They were asked to begin a vegan diet and take a walk every day. One year later, their blood pressures were checked. Of the twenty-six patients, twenty had stopped their blood pressure medications completely. Yet the average blood pressure of the group was actually *lower than when they were using medications*.[26] In other words, lifestyle changes, if they go far enough, can be more powerful than pharmaceuticals.

The vast majority of patients with high blood pressure can be managed without medications if their diet and lifestyle changes are sufficient. Keep in mind, however, that very high blood pressure can be extremely dangerous. Let your doctor guide you on your need for medication. But watch the look on your doctor's face when a good diet helps bring your blood pressure under control on its own. No, it's not a faulty blood pressure cuff. It's the power of healthy foods.

Our arteries and veins are normally among the most resilient parts of our bodies. There is no theoretical limit to their ability to remain open and ready to carry life-giving blood to all parts of the body and to bring it back to the heart and lungs to be filled again with oxygen.

Age is not to blame for the damage to our blood vessels any more than time alone is responsible for water spilling over St. Mark's Square. The Venetians now know where that water comes from and have taken steps to stop it. We know where vein and artery damage comes from, too. While we cannot undo all of our past contributions to the problem, there is a lot we can do to repair it and prevent further overflows. No matter how old you may be, you can keep your blood vessels in great shape.

CLEANING YOUR ARTERIES

As a child in Italy, Mario Andretti dreamed of becoming a racer, winning at Monza against the legends of Formula One. Emigrating to the United States as a teenager, his dream soon came true. Between 1965 and 1969, he won thirty races and three national championships. In the 1970s, he took the checkered flag in Spain, France, Italy, Holland, Belgium, Germany, Argentina, and the United States. Two decades later, Andretti had still not slowed down. He set a new closed-course world speed record at 234 miles per hour in 1993. His longtime rival, Emerson Fittipaldi, has not slowed down either. He won the Formula One world championship back in 1972 and still left the entire field in the dust as he blasted past the finish line at the 1993 Indianapolis 500, while his nephew Christian was getting started in Europe's racing circuit.

As these champions have shown, 90 percent of winning is staying in the race. Take the Monaco Grand Prix. Just two dozen drivers take the world's fastest cars through the streets of Monte Carlo in the pinnacle of Formula One. They zoom up and around the old Casino, down to the port, and around the Rascasse restaurant, where diners grip their drinks almost to the breaking point as the racers fly straight toward them. Most of the starters never make it to the finish line. In the intense pressure of the race, they fly off the track, burn, or break down. Damon Hill crashed into Mika Hakkinen at the start of the 1994 race. Katayama and Blundell had engine problems. Christian Fittipaldi's gear box went bad. Karl Wendlinger was already in the hospital, having crashed into the wall during the time trials. The winner was Germany's Michael Schumacher. Other cars were arguably faster down the straightaway, but Schumacher knew how to take the turns and stay out of trouble while he flew down the course.

Most people crash and burn driving nothing more than their knives and forks around their dinner plates. They make dangerous choices that exact a terrible price down the road. With the right foods, however, you have incredible power to prevent and even reverse serious problems.

Of course, we often romanticize about characters who, James Dean–style, live fast and die young. But the fact is, James Dean and every other fallen hero would much rather be in the race. It was his air of defiance that people liked, not his demise.

Cleaning Your Arteries

Your arteries carry oxygen and other nutrients to power the muscles of your arms and legs as well as keep your mind sharp and your heart beating strong. As time goes on, however, blockages tend to form in these passageways so that blood has trouble getting through. As blockages grow in the arteries to the heart, less and less blood gets through to bring oxygen to the heart muscle. This is called atherosclerosis, or common heart disease, and it causes bouts of chest pain (angina). Initially, chest pain only occurs when exercise or excitement gets the heart beating faster. If the blood supply becomes completely blocked, however, a part of the heart muscle dies (heart attack or myocardial infarction). Every day in the United States, about four thousand people have heart attacks. These same blockages can cause a stroke in the arteries to the brain. They can cause impotence in the arteries to the genitals.

The bad news is that old-fashioned cholesterol-lowering diets (switching from beef to chicken breast, for example) are nearly worthless. To be effective, much more vigorous dietary changes are necessary. Moreover, while cutting fat from the diet is very important, it has overshadowed other powerful steps that people can also take.

The good news is that there are powerful approaches that can not only prevent those blockages from forming, they can actually *reverse* them. It does not matter how old you are or how long your blockages have been developing. You can take steps to reverse them, starting today. It is much easier than you might imagine. In this chapter, we will look at an extraordinary program that was pioneered by Dean Ornish, M.D., and has since been used by many, many people. It can rejuvenate your arteries and give you a new level of health and well-being you may not have dreamed possible.

To take advantage of this incredible breakthrough that cleans away years of artery damage, let's take a detailed look at how the process begins.

If you could look inside your own arteries, you would see, among the red and white blood cells, tiny particles flowing to your arms and legs, coursing up toward your brain, and drifting along to every other part of your body. They are much smaller than blood cells and there are a lot of them. These particles are racing along to make sure all parts of your body have enough of a certain raw material that is needed to strengthen cell membranes and to build hormones. The material these particles are so diligently carrying is, believe it or not, cholesterol. That very stuff that has earned the worst possible reputation—and deservedly so—is delivered around the body like a valuable substance. Cholesterol has a vital function. It is the cement that holds cell membranes together. When a load of cholesterol arrives at its destination, it is placed into cell membranes like cement poured into the foundation of a building. It is also used to build estrogens, testosterone, progesterone, digestive secretions, and other parts of the body.

Now, as important as cholesterol is, the body only wants a very limited amount of it in the blood. And just as we don't want cement dumped just anywhere on our roadways, the body is similarly choosy about where and how cholesterol is delivered. It is manufactured in the liver and is carefully transported in special protein particles.

So far, so good. But when people ingest cholesterol in foods or eat foods that cause the liver to make more cholesterol than normal, suddenly there is too much of it in the body—loads of "cement" being carried around in the blood with nowhere to go.

When you know how to control the cholesterol in your blood, you gain real power over what happens in your arteries.

There are two main cholesterol particles in the blood that you should know about. The first is called LDL, low-density lipoprotein. LDL is busily delivering cholesterol to your body tissues. There is also a particle the body uses to remove cholesterol from cells, a tight little package called HDL, high-density lipoprotein, sometimes called the "good cholesterol," because it takes cholesterol away. When doctors measure cholesterol levels, they want to see less LDL and more HDL.

When an LDL particle gets damaged, the cholesterol it carries can act like an irritant, setting in motion a deadly series of events. Special cells mop up the damaged cholesterol and sequester it in the artery wall. In turn, these cells are damaged by the cholesterol they have taken in. The muscle cells that normally reinforce the wall of the artery, like the steel bands in a tire, respond by multiplying like a tumor. The result is a mass of cholesterol, cells, and biological debris growing in the artery wall, called a plaque. As the plaque grows, it closes off the passage for blood. Arteries are not enormous pipelines. They are small passageways, and it does not take an especially big plaque to reduce the flow.

A look into the arteries of an average twenty-three-year-old man is shocking. You would not know it from his healthy exterior, but his arteries are diseased. At various points in the arteries, plaques slow blood flow as surely as cement would slow a drain. Plaques start growing in childhood and by age twenty-three they are already present in three out of four young men in Western countries. Often there is no sign of what has been happening until a heart attack, stroke, impotence, or other impairment strikes.

Our bodies try to prevent this. First, the liver normally makes only a modest amount of cholesterol—enough for the body's needs but not an excess, so it is less likely that any LDL particles will be damaged and trigger the plaque-building process. Second, the body has built-in methods to protect LDL against damage. Whether this system works or not depends to a large extent on what you eat.

Protecting Cholesterol

What damage the LDL particle and trigger the whole plaque-forming process are free radicals—the same free radicals we read about in chapter 1. And there is a lot you can do to stop them.

As each LDL particle is built, vitamin E molecules are strategically packed into its surface to fend off free radicals, about six vitamin E molecules per LDL particle. The richer the diet is in vitamin E, the more of it gets packed into LDL.[1] LDL is also protected by the other antioxidants described in chapter 1: vitamin C and uric acid in the blood and beta-carotene joining vitamin E on the LDL itself. As long as these protectors are in place, LDL is not harmed by free radicals.[2]

By now, you know where these lifesaving antioxidants come from. Carrots and sweet potatoes are gold mines of beta-carotene, but it is also found in all other green, yellow, and orange vegetables. Fruits are particularly rich in vitamin C, but many vegetables pack a lot of it, too. Vitamin E is found in a variety of beans, nuts, grains, and vegetables. Different vegetables, fruits, grains, and legumes have different antioxidant profiles and, taken together, they are powerhouses of protection.

More Protection Against Free Radicals

A healthful diet does not just mop up free radicals after they are formed. It also slows down their production in the first place.

As we saw in chapter 1, it helps to avoid fish and fish oils. Of course, many people still seem to think fish is better for your heart than beef, in the same sense that low-tar cigarettes might be slightly better than regular brands. But fish products are not health foods by any stretch of the imagination. They can encourage the production of free radicals. By skipping fish, you not only avoid the cholesterol and fat they hold—yes, all fish contain both cholesterol and fat, as we will see in more detail below—but you also avoid a potential contributor to free radical production. If you were eating fish or fish oil capsules as a source of essential fatty acids (omega-3s), these compounds are available in a more stable form in vegetables such as broccoli, spinach, lettuce, and beans.[3]

An additional advantage of plant-based diets is that they allow the body to regulate how much iron it takes in. Too much iron can be a serious problem because iron encourages free radical damage, as we saw in chapter 1. In a study of nearly two thousand Finnish men, researchers found that having too much iron in the body increases the risk of heart attacks.[4] A recent Harvard study showed that, although a higher intake of iron from plant sources does not increase the risk of heart disease, a higher intake of iron from meat does.[5] The heme iron from meat just seems to barge in through the digestive tract wall whether it is needed or not, adding to iron overload and the risk of free radical damage. Test tube experiments show that heme directly attacks (oxidizes) LDL, which is exactly what free radicals do in your bloodstream. When your diet is loaded with antioxidants, you are able to fend off some of the damage,[6] and eliminating animal products is an important way to get overly absorbable iron off the plate.

THE 150 CHOLESTEROL GOAL

Perhaps the most important way to prevent damage to cholesterol particles is not to have too many of them in your blood. The fewer targets there are, the less likely it is that any will be hit.

But what is a safe amount of cholesterol in the blood? When doctors measure cholesterol, they first look at the total cholesterol level, which combines all the different types of cholesterol in the bloodstream: LDL, HDL, and other forms. Many health authorities hold that total cholesterol levels should be two hundred milligrams per deciliter (mg/dl) or less (equivalent to 5.2 millimoles per liter, the unit used in most countries other than the United States). That is a nearly useless goal. Every day, people with cholesterol levels around 200 mg/dl have heart attacks. However, if you reduce your cholesterol level to lower levels—to 190, 180, 170, and lower—your risk of having a heart attack continues to drop until you reach about 150. The Framingham Heart Study, named for the Massachusetts town where it has been conducted since 1949, found that for more than three decades running, not a single person with a cholesterol level below 150 mg/dl had a heart attack. That does not mean that it is impossible to have a heart attack with a very low cholesterol level; it is just very unlikely. The goal worth remembering is 150. Whatever cholesterol level you start with, every 1 percent that you reduce it reduces your risk of having a heart attack by 2 percent or more.[7]

THE "GOOD CHOLESTEROL"

While LDL (the "bad cholesterol") can be thought of as cholesterol on its way in, HDL is the "good cholesterol" that is on its way out. Higher HDL levels are desirable. Doctors normally do not have a specific target for HDL. Rather, they look for the ratio of total cholesterol to HDL, which ideally should be about three to one. Unfortunately, most Americans have ratios around five to one. For example, if your total cholesterol level were two hundred and your HDL level were forty, your ratio works out to be five to one. While that is about average for Americans, when it comes to cholesterol you don't want to be anywhere near average because most American adults have substantial heart blockages and half will die of a heart attack.

Vegetarian diets reduce all forms of cholesterol, including HDL, but usually improve the ratio of total cholesterol to HDL. For people with very low total cholesterol levels (below 150, for example), HDL is usually disregarded because the risk of heart attack is very low.

HDL levels can be increased slightly by exercise and vitamin C–rich foods and tend to fall when people smoke or are overweight.[8]

How to Read Your Cholesterol Test

U.S. authorities measure cholesterol levels in milligrams per deciliter. Most other countries use a different unit, millimoles per liter, which is listed in parentheses.

Although you can have your cholesterol tested at commercial laboratories without a doctor's order in some locations, the results should be interpreted by your doctor. Here are guidelines to help you discuss your test results with your physician.

Total Cholesterol
- Above 240 mg/dl (6.2 mmol/L): High risk
- 200 to 240 mg/dl (5.2 to 6.2 mmol/L): Above-average risk
- 205 mg/dl (5.3 mmol/L): Average for U.S. adults
- 150 mg/dl (3.9 mmol/L) or less: Very low risk

High-Density Lipoprotein (HDL)

HDL values are interpreted by using the ratio of total cholesterol to HDL. In general, the lower your ratio, the better. If total cholesterol is below 150, most authorities disregard HDL. The Framingham Heart Study[9] reported the following ratios:

- 5.8 to 1—average male with heart disease
- 5.3 to 1—average female with heart disease
- 5.1 to 1—average male without heart disease
- 4.4 to 1—average female without heart disease
- 3.5 to 1—average Boston Marathon runner
- 3.0 to 1—ideal
- 2.9 to 1—average vegetarian

Triglycerides should be checked after an overnight fast. Levels above 200 mg/dl are generally considered abnormal.

TRIGLYCERIDES

If a blood test shows you have too much fat in your blood, your doctor words this more politely by saying your triglycerides are elevated. Triglycerides are special molecules the body uses to transport fat in the blood and to store it. However, health authorities are not yet sure just how much risk triglycerides pose.

Triglycerides are built in the liver from the foods you eat. They are packed into particles called very low-density lipoprotein (VLDL), which carry them to your body fat.

Triglyceride levels above 200 mg/dl are usually considered high and those that are extremely high (greater than 1000 mg/dl) can inflame the pancreas and cause other serious problems. Doctors are uncertain, however, about triglyceride levels between those two extremes. Some studies have linked triglyceride levels above 200 mg/dl to increased risk of heart disease, particularly for women,[10] but some researchers believe that this only applies to people who also have high cholesterol levels.

When people switch from meat-based diets to plant-based diets, their cholesterol levels fall dramatically and triglycerides often fall as well. However, for some, triglyceride levels rise a bit. What is apparently happening is that some of the carbohydrate in the diet is simply being converted to triglycerides for transport in the body. This does not increase the risk of heart disease.[11]

Fruits, juices, simple sugars, and alcohol can sometimes raise triglycerides. Beans and other legumes have been shown to lower them, as do exercise and weight loss.[12]

NEW FINDINGS ON THE HORIZON

Before researchers had finished scratching their heads about triglycerides, other discoveries were made that they are now trying to sort out. Most doctors do not yet use these findings in practice, but they and you will soon be hearing more about them so I will summarize them below for those who are interested. Otherwise, feel free to skip ahead to the next section.

Homocysteine.   Proteins are made of building blocks called amino acids. One amino acid called homocysteine tends to build up in the blood of some people and when it does it encourages artery blockages, apparently by increasing the likelihood of blood clots or damaging the artery lining.[13] A study of American physicians found that those in the top 5 percent of homocysteine levels had triple the risk of a heart attack compared to those with lower levels.[14] Homocysteine levels above fourteen micromoles per liter should be considered high, although no clear dividing line has yet been drawn between normal and high levels.[15]

Homocysteine is made in the body from another amino acid called methionine, which is particularly common in animal products. Vegetarian foods, which have so many other advantages, also have the benefit of being lower in methionine.

Some cases of elevated homocysteine are genetic. Others are due to a lack of certain B vitamins—B_6, B_{12}, and folate—which are needed to break down homocysteine and its relatives. Beans, vegetables, and fruits give you plenty of folate and B_6. The best sources of vitamin B_{12} are discussed in chapter 12. Standard multivitamins can also correct these deficiencies. Meats and dairy products are very low in folate, and although they do contain B_6 and B_{12}, their load of fat and cholesterol causes them to do much more harm than good.

Lipoprotein(a).   One newly discovered cholesterol-containing particle in the blood is named lipoprotein(a). It is very similar to LDL (the "bad cholesterol") and some research suggests that people with extra lipoprotein(a) in their blood have a higher heart disease risk. It is not yet clear to what extent lipoprotein(a) levels are controlled by heredity as opposed to diet or environment, and health authorities do not yet have specific recommendations for physicians or patients for lipoprotein(a).[16] Stay tuned.

Small LDL. There are also different types of LDL. Some LDL particles are a bit smaller than others and these small ones seem to be more aggressive than the larger ones in promoting plaques. Researchers are now beginning to test individuals to see if they have more big or small particles. About 30 percent of people tend to have the more dangerous small LDL particles, while about 60 percent have more large LDL particles. The remaining people have a more even mix of the two.[17] For the moment, this is simply a research tool. Diet and lifestyle guidelines are the same for all groups.

Different Types of HDL. There are also several different types of HDL in the blood and it is not certain that they all reduce heart disease risk. The importance of this was demonstrated when it was found that alcohol raises HDL levels. A glass of wine is good for your heart, some thought. Well, it turns out that alcohol raises a type of HDL that may not help against heart problems.[18]

GETTING—AND KEEPING—A LOW CHOLESTEROL LEVEL

Many people have been disappointed to find that switching from beef to chicken or fish did not improve their cholesterol levels very much. Researchers have had plenty of time to study poultry and fish diets and it is now clear that they are almost useless, only lowering cholesterol levels by about 5 percent. But take heart. Newer dietary approaches have a much more powerful effect on cholesterol levels and are lifesavers for your blood vessels.

It is easy to take control of the two parts of foods that drive cholesterol levels up and very effective when you do. There are also special foods that can drive cholesterol down, as we will see shortly. The first cholesterol booster is cholesterol itself. The second is saturated fat.

CHOLESTEROL:
ALWAYS IN ANIMAL PRODUCTS, NEVER IN PLANTS

As we saw earlier, cholesterol is made in the liver. Cows have livers, too. So do pigs, chickens, turkeys, and fish. All their lives they have been making cholesterol and packing it into their muscles and other organs just as humans do. If you were to eat any part of an animal or an animal product such as milk or eggs, some of the animal's cholesterol will make its way into your bloodstream. Plants do not have livers, so grains, vegetables, fruits, and all other plant foods never have any cholesterol at all.

Cholesterol in foods has two bad aspects. First, it adds to your own cholesterol, raising the level of cholesterol in your blood.[19] Everyone is different, but, as an overall rule of thumb, every hundred milligrams of cholesterol in the daily routine adds about five points to your total cholesterol level. What does that look like on your plate? A four-ounce serving of beef contains one hundred milligrams of cholesterol. Four ounces of chicken contains exactly the same amount of cholesterol as beef—one hundred milligrams, a fact many people find surprising, since chicken is sometimes mischaracterized as a healthier food. Chicken is slightly lower in fat, and we will shortly see just how slight the difference is. But chicken is not at all lower in cholesterol.

Fish vary. A four-ounce serving of tuna has forty milligrams of cholesterol, while haddock or rainbow trout has more than eighty milligrams. None are even close to being cholesterol-free and some are extremely high—mobile shellfish like shrimp, lobster, and crayfish, for example. Ounce for ounce, shrimp have about double the cholesterol of beef.

Milk and eggs are animal products, so they contain cholesterol, too. Three cups of whole milk contains one hundred milligrams of cholesterol. A single egg contains 213 milligrams.

Although our bodies use cholesterol, we do not need any in our diet. The liver makes plenty for all our needs. If we add cholesterol by including animal products in our diet, cholesterol levels climb unnecessarily.

Cholesterol in foods has a second effect, completely separate from its ability to raise your blood cholesterol level. The more cholesterol you ingest, the higher your risk of artery blockages, *even if you do not have a particularly high level of cholesterol in your blood.* Although this is news to many people, it is not news to researchers. Numerous studies have shown the effect. For example, men working at the Western Electric Company near Chicago were examined in 1957 and 1958. Their diets were assessed and numerous blood tests were run. For the next twenty-five years, researchers tracked what happened to them. It turned out that those whose meals contained more cholesterol were much more likely to die of heart disease, regardless of their blood cholesterol level.[20]

This is very important. Many people mistakenly feel that, if dietary indiscretions have not increased their cholesterol levels, they must not be at risk for heart problems. The fact is, less cholesterol on the plate means less risk—as much as 50 percent less—whether or not it lowers blood cholesterol.[21]

Cholesterol-containing foods should be avoided completely. A recent international conference of leading heart researchers, including Michael DeBakey, M.D., Dean Ornish, M.D., and many others, addressed the question of how much cholesterol a person should eat. They concluded that "the optimal intake of cholesterol in the adult is probably zero,"[22] echoing the same conclusion reached by Harvard researchers.[23] Zero cholesterol means a diet of plant foods. A diet that contains any chicken, fish, beef, eggs, or dairy products at all is not a zero-cholesterol diet.

HOW TO SPOT SATURATED FATS

Saturated fat is even worse than cholesterol in foods because it stimulates your liver to manufacture more cholesterol. The term "saturated" simply means that the fat molecule is completely covered with hydrogen atoms. Saturated fats are easy to recognize. They are solid at room temperature, while unsaturated fats are liquids. You will find them in three places: animal products, baked goods, and fried foods. When I was growing up in

North Dakota, my mother used to save bacon drippings in a jar. It was liquid in the fry pan, but as it cooled it became waxy. That is a clue that it is loaded with saturated fat.

Animal fat is a solid, waxy substance you want to avoid completely because it will turn on the cholesterol-making machinery in your cells. But it is not just the outer, visible fat that is a problem. Fat is marbled throughout meats, and the only way to avoid animal fat is to avoid meats. Yes, even chicken breast has loads of fat. When the skin is removed before cooking, about 20 percent of its calories still come from the animal fat lurking in the chicken muscle.

POULTRY AND FISH ARE NOT HEALTH FOODS

Let's set aside a dangerous myth. Many people have come to believe that if they switch from red meat to chicken and fish, they are following a diet that will keep their arteries clear. The fact is, the chicken and fish diet does almost no good at all.

The April 29, 1993, *New England Journal of Medicine* reported a carefully done study of what happens when people follow a diet emphasizing poultry and fish, called the National Cholesterol Education Program Step II Diet. It recommends modest portions of fish and skinless poultry and nonfat cooking methods and is essentially the type of diet that most doctors and the popular press currently promote for heart patients. But when its effects on cholesterol levels were checked, the results were dismal. Even among patients with good adherence, the cholesterol lowering was only about 5 percent.[24] That means that for those starting out with a cholesterol level of 250 mg/dl (6.5 mmol/L), a 5 percent drop would bring them to about 235 mg/dl (6.1 mmol/L), which is still far too high for safety. Many other studies have shown the same thing.

The reason is no great mystery. Chicken and fish muscles contain plenty of cholesterol and fat, just as cow muscles do. Chicken's cholesterol content is the same as for beef and its fat content is almost as bad. The leanest cuts of beef are 29 percent fat (as a percentage of calories). Even without the skin, white chicken meat is still about 20 percent fat.

Compare that to beans (4 percent), rice (1 to 5 percent, depending on the variety), or potatoes (less than 1 percent), all with no cholesterol at all.

Fish vary, but like all other animals, fish contain cholesterol and fat. Of the fat in fish, about 15 to 30 percent is saturated fat. This is lower than beef and chicken, but still a problem.

Cholesterol and fat are not the only reasons to cut out animal products. Animal protein itself is part of the cholesterol problem. When researchers test various diets in which fat and cholesterol are kept constant but plant protein is used instead of animal protein, cholesterol levels fall. Soy protein in particular lowers cholesterol levels, independent of the effect of fat or cholesterol.[25] Many years ago, animal protein was thought to be advantageous, but it is now believed to be part of the problem, not part of the solution. Poultry, fish, and other meats contain whopping doses of cholesterol, fat, and protein and not much else.

When doctors track what happens inside the arteries, diets based on chicken and fish do not reverse arterial blockages. In fact, the blockages continue to get worse for most patients following such diets. Vegetarian diets are entirely different, and actually promote *reversal* of blockages.[26]

It is tragic to see millions of people bringing chicken and turkey packages home from the store believing them to be "heart-healthy" foods. They have been repeatedly tested, and they simply do not work. A vegetarian diet is what your heart is looking for.

TROPICAL AND HYDROGENATED OILS

Animal products are easy to spot and avoid. The saturated fats in baked goods and fried foods can be trickier. Two different forms of artery-clogging fat are often stuffed into pastries, donuts, french fries, and onion rings. Tropical oils include coconut oil, palm oil, and palm kernel oil. Hydrogenated oils are liquid oils that have been chemically hardened. Unlike other vegetable oils, these two villains are loaded with saturated fat. Most people never cook with them, but large commercial bakers use them because they are cheap, have a long shelf life, and impart a smooth texture to foods.

These oils are more common than you might guess. Snack pastries, potato chips, cookies, fried foods, and processed foods of all kinds contain hefty doses of tropical and hydrogenated oils. And just like butter or chicken fat, they will raise your cholesterol.

TRANS FATS

One variant of hydrogenated oils, the so-called trans fats, deserves some special mention. You've read the headlines: "Doctors Find That Margarine Is as Bad as Butter." The accompanying news stories said that trans fats, which are found in supposedly healthful margarine, could push your cholesterol level through the roof. Appropriately concerned consumers started to check the labels on margarine and other foods. But they never found the words *trans fats* on any of them, either in the ingredient lists or on the government-required nutrition labels. What's going on here?

From a chemistry standpoint, it's very simple. Certain oil molecules are curved. Those curly little molecules make the oil stay liquid. When manufacturers hydrogenate oils, however, the hydrogen atoms often attach on opposite sides of the carbon chain in what is called the trans configuration, which straightens the molecule out. When that happens, the oil becomes solid. Food chemists found that this is an easy way to turn liquid vegetable oil into spreadable margarine. But the resulting trans fats increase LDL and reduce HDL—just the opposite of what you want—and promote heart disease in the process.[27]

So why are the words *trans fats* never on food labels? Because they are simply a form of partially hydrogenated vegetable oil. When you see those words on a label, think trans fats. You can almost hear your coronary arteries snapping closed as you pick up the package.

Around 1990, fast-food chains took the beef fat out of their deep fryers. That was a good move. But they began using partially hydrogenated vegetable oils instead, which are about as bad. If you were to analyze the fat used to cook french fries or onion rings at leading fast-food chains, between a quarter and a third of it would be pure trans fats.[28]

Did you ever wonder what happens to all that used cooking oil when fast-food restaurants are finished with it? They use gallons and gallons of it and they do not just pour it into the dumpster out back or bury it in a landfill. They have found a market for their used cooking oil, believe it or not, in the poultry industry. The poultry business is highly competitive, and the winners are those farmers who can fatten up chickens quickly and cheaply. Used cooking oil fattens chickens as quickly as any more expensive fat,[29] and if it's chock full of trans fats, the chickens are none the wiser and neither is the consumer. Used cooking oil is mixed with feed grains, sometimes along with fat left over from slaughtered animals, and fed to tens of thousands of birds simultaneously in huge factorylike operations. The National Research Council described the kinds of grease fed to poultry:

> Fats used for feeding poultry are of three general sources: animal or poultry fats obtained from the rendering industry, restaurant greases, acidulated soapstocks from the vegetable oil industry, and/or mixtures thereof.[30]

Sounds appetizing, doesn't it? Another surprising place to find trans fats is in cow's milk. Cows are ruminant animals, which means that they regurgitate partially digested food from their four-compartment stomachs, chew it a while, and swallow it again. Bacteria in their stomachs produce trans fats, which end up in milk fat. The amount of trans fats produced varies over the year and is higher in the summer than the winter.[31]

Consumption of trans fats in the United States tripled from the early 1900s until the mid-1960s, when it began to decline.[32] As bad as trans fats are, they are not a reason to switch from margarine back to butter. Butter is over 60 percent saturated fat. Trans fats *add* to the problems posed by animal fats, and the only solution is to steer clear of dangerous products, whatever their source. It pays to avoid animal products and fried foods completely and check the labels on unfamiliar baked goods.

One last point about fat: Even though liquid oils are much better than other sources of fats, all oils contain at least some saturated fat. Olive oil is 13 percent saturated fat, canola oil is 12 percent saturated fat, and other oils are similar. While those figures are better than animal fats, the best advice is to keep vegetable oils to a minimum, too. Learning to cook without adding oil is easier than you might guess, as you will see in the delicious recipes at the end of this book.

SPECIAL EFFECTS

Foods from plants are loaded with natural antioxidants, never contain potentially dangerous heme iron, are always zero cholesterol, and are usually very low in fat. As if that were not enough, certain plants have special cholesterol-lowering properties.

Oat bran made a name for itself because of its soluble fiber. Fiber simply means the residue of plants that resists digestion and the term "soluble" means that it dissolves in water as opposed to, say, wheat bran, which does not. Soluble fiber lowers cholesterol levels. It takes advantage of the fact that some of the cholesterol in the body is converted into digestive juices called bile acids. Fiber in the digestive tract absorbs these bile acids the way a sponge soaks up water and carries them out with the wastes.[33] This is a handy way to get rid of some of the body's cholesterol. As we saw in chapter 3, the body gets rid of estrogens and testosterone in the same way. If there is not much fiber in the intestinal tract, bile acids are broken back down into cholesterol, which is reabsorbed into the blood. In addition, fiber may actually cause the liver to turn down its cholesterol production.[34]

In spite of what television commercials might suggest, oat bran is only one of many good sources of soluble fiber. Beans also contain soluble fiber. If beans had a lobby group as strong as the dairy or meat industries, everyone would know that beans are not only calcium-rich, zero-cholesterol, extremely low-fat protein powerhouses, and a good source of omega-3 fatty acids but also contain lots of soluble fiber. Many different beans and bean extracts have been tested and have shown the ability to lower cholesterol levels.[35] It does not take a huge serving. Just a four-ounce serving of beans daily cuts both cholesterol and triglycerides.[36]

Fruits contain a type of soluble fiber called pectins, which are best known for their use in making jams and jellies and which, like other kinds of soluble fiber, lower cholesterol levels significantly.[37] Barley, a grain often used in soups, also contains soluble fiber and has the same great benefit.

So there is no need to look for oat bran–covered donuts. Soluble fiber is in many grains, vegetables, fruits, and legumes. Conversely, meats, poultry, fish, eggs, and dairy products, which always contain cholesterol, never contain even a scrap of fiber. It is a feature of plants only.

Walnuts should be added to the special effects team. Like other nuts, they are loaded with fat (about 81 percent of calories). But researchers in California found that when they are used to replace the fats in meats, butter, margarine, and other fatty foods, cholesterol levels drop more than 20 mg/dl (0.58 mmol/L). The amount tested was three ounces a day for four weeks.[38]

Garlic has long been a popular folk remedy and has gotten more and more attention from medical researchers. As little as ½ to one clove per day lowers both cholesterol and triglyceride levels and does so in people with both normal and high cholesterol levels.[39]

TOBACCO

Tobacco accelerates artery damage. In the Framingham Heart Study, smokers had 1½ times the risk of heart problems compared to nonsmokers. But when smokers quit, the heart risk drops back to normal very rapidly, within one year of quitting.[40]

If you are a smoker, you have undoubtedly tried to quit and have found it difficult. I smoked for a couple of years while in medical school. Medical students, physicians who trained us, and any patient who wandered downstairs could buy cigarettes at the hospital gift shop, just as the hospital cafeteria sold fried chicken and endless other meat dishes. It was a peculiar thing to be caring for heart disease and cancer patients and then to light up on the way home, but many of us did exactly that. I tried to quit many times and soon learned how addicting nicotine can be. The key is to keep trying. Whether you use a nicotine patch or some other quit-smoking aid is not as important as simply trying again. Sooner or later you will succeed, as I and millions of others have.

PHYSICAL ACTIVITY

Your body loves to move. We all have different feelings about how much physical activity we want, and some of us are rather reluctant athletes. But whether you know it or not, every cell in your body is like a puppy ready for a run down the block. When your muscles get a chance to get off the couch and get moving, every part of your body is rewarded and that includes your arteries.

I am not talking about exercise in the usual sense. Forget the "no pain, no gain" attitude unless you actually enjoy pumping iron. Your cells are puppies, not masochists. They want to play and run, not be tortured.

Other primates play all their lives. They do not hesitate to roll on the ground and frolic with their children or nieces and nephews. Humans are very physical, too, until about age twenty, when, for some reason, they suddenly become reluctant to do anything other than stand up and sit down. Our bodies become as miserable as a dog left chained up in the backyard.

A little physical activity is great for your arteries. If you were to include a walk or run in your daily schedule and measure the amount of HDL (the "good cholesterol") in your blood, you would find that it gradually goes up. At the same time, triglyceride levels start falling.[41] You do not have to exercise especially vigorously or aim for a target pulse rate. Your arteries benefit from light physical activity, such as daily walking.

Physical activity works *with* a healthful diet; it cannot replace it. Even trained athletes can have severe artery disease if they follow meaty diets. In the Korean War, doctors examined the arteries of young men who were killed in battle. These soldiers were physically fit and active every day. But when doctors examined the coronary arteries of three hundred American soldiers whose average age was just twenty-three, 77 percent had significant blockages, sometimes blocking off entire arteries.[42]

People who believe that physical activity will undo the effects of a poor diet are in for a rude awakening. Often athletes run more risk than other people because they mistakenly believe they need meat or dairy proteins to build muscle, forgetting that bulls, stallions, gorillas, and other muscular animals build their muscles from plants, not from meat. Exercise burns calories but cannot burn off cholesterol or other aspects of an unhealthful diet.

A simple way to take advantage of the benefits of exercise is with a half-hour walk each day or an hour three times a week. That is the amount of exercise that has been used in programs to reverse heart disease, and although it sounds very simple, it is all you need.

CONTROLLING STRESS

At work and at home you might have to cope with a mountain of stress. It can drive your blood pressure up and wreak havoc with your arteries.[43] In the Framingham study, impatient, workaholic men and women had double the risk of heart attacks,[44] apparently due to stress.

In the *fight-or-flight* response to stress, which is programmed into your body, hormones prepare the muscles for quick action. Unfortunately, running away or fighting is not helpful in dealing with your boss, a tax audit, or an approaching deadline. And while our hormones gear us up to run or fight, they raise cholesterol levels and add to artery damage.

Whether stress is damaging or not may depend on control. If you are teetering on the edge of a mountaintop with racing skis on your feet and a two-thousand-foot vertical drop in front of you, you might be under stress. But the stress is entirely different if someone pushes you over the edge or if you have chosen to be there. Control makes all the difference. If an avalanche of work is dumped in your lap, your stress level is likely to be higher than if you are voluntarily tackling a huge challenge.

Uncontrolled stress can be deadly. During the battles in Lebanon in the 1980s, those who were directly exposed to skirmishes had more rapid growth of blockages in their coronary arteries.[45] Even minor stresses, such as public speaking or solving arithmetic problems, cause our hormones to respond, speeding the heartbeat, increasing the blood pressure, and changing body chemistry in many ways.[46] "Stress has been shown in a number of experiments to raise serum cholesterol levels," says Dr. David Kritchevsky of Philadelphia's Wistar Institute. "If you are going to have your cholesterol checked, and you have a car accident on the way to the clinic, chances are it will be higher. Medical students' cholesterol levels peak the week of any exam. As income tax deadlines approach, accountants' cholesterol levels go up, and after they mail off their returns, their cholesterol levels go down again. The fluctuations in cholesterol levels can be as high as 20–30 percent."

If we respond to stress by getting extra help, taking time to plan, and getting a little more sleep, our anxiety levels drop. If, on the other hand, we dose ourselves with increasing amounts of coffee or alcohol and start cutting back on sleep, we lose more control and become victims, not only of the original stresses, but of our Band-Aid response to them.

Before You Blame Genetics

When people have high cholesterol levels that persist even after they have changed their diet, their doctors often tell them that their problem is genetic—a conclusion that is especially likely if many family members had heart disease at early ages. True enough, for about 5 percent of people with high cholesterol levels, genetics really are responsible. But many people falsely conclude that their problems were genetic because a chicken and fish diet did not help them very much. As we have seen, such a diet only lowers cholesterol levels about 5 percent. Heart disease that runs in families may be due to genetics, but it can also be due to recipes, tastes, and eating habits that are passed from one generation to the next.

Before you conclude that your problem is genetic, give a low-fat, pure vegetarian (vegan) diet a chance for a couple of months. Avoid cigarettes completely, take a half-hour walk every day or an hour three times a week, and reduce stress in your life. Then check your cholesterol level. Most people are astounded by the results. If you are one of the few people whose cholesterol levels remain high, you may decide with your doctor to consider cholesterol-lowering medications. But if you truly do have a genetic cholesterol problem, you will want to be especially sure to have all the lifestyle factors working for you. Whatever genetic hand you have been dealt, these steps can be enormously helpful.

ARTERY BLOCKAGES ARE REVERSIBLE

Arterial blockages can be reversed. It does not matter how old you are; arterial plaques can shrink at any age. However, reversal will not occur for most people if they simply switch from red meat to poultry and fish. But if you are willing to go a step further, the results can be extraordinary.

Dean Ornish, M.D., is a Harvard-trained physician, now on the faculty of the University of California at San Francisco. In a ground-breaking study he took patients who had arterial plaques clearly demonstrated on angiograms and separated them into two groups. The control group followed their own doctors' orders, which generally meant avoiding tobacco and following American Heart Association guidelines to eat meats in modest portions and to favor chicken and fish. You can predict the results. After a year, when their blockages were again measured on angiograms, they were actually worse than when they started. Regrettably, several other studies have shown exactly the same thing: The American Heart Association guidelines and similar weak diets do not reverse heart disease; they actually contribute to it as it gets worse and worse.[47] That is not to say such diets are as bad as completely unrestricted diets, but they are simply too high in saturated fat and cholesterol to arrest or reverse the growth of arterial plaques for most patients.

Dr. Ornish's other patients got a very different prescription. They were asked to follow a low-fat vegetarian diet, take a half-hour walk daily or an hour walk three times per week, avoid tobacco, and learn to manage stress. When their blockages were measured a year later, they not only were not getting worse, they were actually starting to shrink in 82 percent of patients. That remarkable result was achieved without surgery or medications—not even cholesterol-lowering drugs.[48] As time went on, the patients continued to improve. The blockages that had been growing in their arteries for decades were finally beginning to dissolve and go away.

At least five different studies have clearly demonstrated that artery blockages can be reversed.[49] But doing so requires eliminating the factors that caused them in the first place. A low-fat vegetarian diet is the only way to get cholesterol, animal fat, and heme iron off your plate and to boost soluble fiber and antioxidant vitamins. Not so many years ago doctors believed it was not possible to restore your arteries to health without surgery. We now know that the knife and fork are more powerful than the scalpel.

PREVENTING STROKES
AND OTHER ARTERY DISORDERS

The brain is fed by arteries that pass up through the neck. Plaques can form there, just as they do in the other major arteries, and when an artery is blocked, the brain cells will die, just as the heart muscle dies in a heart attack. This is called a stroke. It generally costs its victim whatever function those brain cells had been performing. Often the parts of the brain responsible for movement or language are damaged, leading to paralysis or a loss of speech. If several small strokes progressively wipe out portions of the brain, the result can be dementia that masquerades as Alzheimer's disease.

Half a million Americans have strokes every year. A third of them die and, for the remainder, the rehabilitation process can be tediously slow.

Strokes do not have to occur. The same factors that prevent and reverse blockages in the arteries to the heart—a vegetarian diet, avoiding tobacco, managing stress, regular physical activity, and keeping blood pressure under control—go a long way toward keeping the arteries to the brain working right.

Avoiding tobacco is essential. A large study of nurses showed that those who smoked twenty-five or more cigarettes per day had ten times the risk of bleeding in the brain compared to nonsmokers; other forms of stroke are also much more common among smokers.[50]

Aspirin and fish oils, which some people take in hopes of reducing their risk of a heart attack, increase the risk of bleeding into the brain because they reduce the blood's ability to clot. While that may prevent a blood clot from lodging in an artery narrowed by plaques, sometimes you want your blood vessels to be able to stop bleeding promptly. Fish oils interfere with that process. People who consume large amounts of fish have a higher risk of bleeding strokes.

The arteries to the legs are also easy targets for the formation of plaques. Walking any distance then causes severe leg pains, called claudication, and the loss of blood supply to the legs becomes an ever-shortening tether.

Plaques also form in the arteries to the genitals, a leading cause of impotence in older men, as we saw in detail in chapter 6.

Artery blockages were once believed to be treatable only by surgery, which is risky, expensive, and—sadly—only temporary in its effects. Bypass surgery and angioplasties must be repeated within several years in the vast majority of cases. Diet and lifestyle changes provide a revolutionary approach that is powerful and proven.

Before the Indianapolis 500 begins each May, doctors test the drivers to make sure that they can take the two-hundred-plus-miles-per-hour speeds. Although Emerson Fittipaldi has been racing at a championship level for over twenty years, age and enormous stress have not done him in. In fact, his medical tests keep getting better every year.

Not only is his car head and shoulders over what he has driven in past years, the fuel he puts in his body is more carefully chosen, too. He grew up on a Western-style diet of meat and dairy products, but traded them for rice, pasta, oatmeal, and other grains, as well as a variety of vegetables and beans. Working with Gary Smith of the Aspen Wellness Group, which provides nutritional advice to many top athletes and celebrities, he has tuned up his body. And while others fall by the wayside, Fittipaldi and his team keep on winning.

You may never be called upon to veer through a field of competitors at two hundred miles per hour. But you want to keep the best edge you can in the race you are in. The foods that help you do that are ready and waiting for you.

CHAPTER NINE

Strong Bones and Healthy Joints

The first thing you notice about a person—whether it is on a blind date, at a job interview, or just passing on the street—is their bones. You don't see the bones themselves, unless you have X-ray vision, but the very first impressions people give you are whether they are tall or short, broad-shouldered or petite, and whether their posture is straight and confident or slumped and weary. A beautiful body on a worn-out skeleton is like a well-cut suit dangling from a broken hanger.

All of your life, your bones can remain strong and resilient. And research shows that, if they have been weakened by osteoporosis, you can actually strengthen them again. As surprising as that may be to people who have come to believe that bone loss is forever, you may find it even more surprising that keeping or regaining strong bones has little to do with how much calcium you consume and nothing whatsoever to do with milk. There are much more powerful ways to keep your bones healthy. This is step six. First, we will look at how to keep bones strong. Then we will see how you can actually restore bones that have been weakened by osteoporosis. Finally, we will look at new approaches to arthritis with power that bottles of medicines don't have.

PROTECTING YOUR BONES

As people get older, many tend to lose bone tissue. Weaker bones are more likely to fracture, and repeated small breaks gradually cause the spine to collapse and bend forward. The condition is called osteoporosis and the result is the hunched-over posture common among older people and, even worse, hip fractures that are extremely debilitating.

The cause of osteoporosis is not ordinarily an inadequate calcium intake but calcium loss. People on Western diets tend to lose calcium from their bones surprisingly fast. For women the situation gets even worse after menopause: The more calcium they lose, the weaker their bones get.

The solution to the problem has been obscured by commercial pressures. It is hard to turn on the television without hearing commercials suggesting that milk promotes strong bones. The commercials do not point out that only 30 percent of milk's calcium is absorbed by the body or that osteoporosis is common among milk drinkers. Nor do they help you correct the real causes of bone loss. Trying to cope with bone loss with dairy products or calcium supplements is like trying to make up for money that falls through a hole in your pocket by taking a second job. It is better to sew up the hole.

Drug companies have their own solution, pushing estrogen supplements for postmenopausal women in spite of their dangers and in spite of the fact that, if supplemental hormones are needed, a simple, over-the-counter preparation is safer and much more effective than prescription hormones, as we will see shortly.

You can gain extraordinary power over the strength of your bones by avoiding calcium depleters and taking advantage of bone builders. Using them is easy, and the effects are striking.

SURPRISING FINDINGS ON PROTEIN

A group of Yale University researchers looked at hip fracture rates in sixteen different countries. Because osteoporosis is particularly aggressive in women after menopause, they focused on women over fifty. They expected to find that countries with a higher calcium intake would have fewer hip fractures. But that was not what they found at all. To their surprise, just the opposite was true. Countries with greater calcium consumption actually had *more* hip fractures, not fewer.[1]

Calcium was not causing the fractures. The countries with a high calcium intake happened to be those where Western diets—meat and dairy products—were popular. When the researchers looked at how much meat these populations ate and their incidence of hip fractures, they found their culprit. The more meat people ate, the more fractures they had. The problem was apparently something in the meat, and the high calcium intake was not able to stop the fractures.

YOUR BONES ARE VEGETARIANS

If you want to weaken your bones, have a chicken salad sandwich. When researchers feed animal protein to volunteers and then test their urine a little later, it is loaded with calcium. That calcium comes from their bones. When the subjects stop eating animal protein, they save calcium much more easily.

Here's why: A protein molecule is like a string of beads, and each "bead" is an amino acid. When protein is digested, these "beads" come apart and pass into the blood, making the blood slightly acidic. However, the body is extremely finicky about how acidic the blood gets because even a tiny change in acid levels can derange body chemistry. In the process of neutralizing that acidity, calcium is pulled from the bones. It ends up being lost in the urine. The more protein you consume, the more amino acids pour into your bloodstream and the more calcium you lose.

Meat, eggs, and other animal products have far more protein than the body needs. Back in the 1950s and 1960s, this was thought to be an advantage. We now know that these protein-dense products do much more harm than good. The more protein in your diet, the more acidic molecules your body has to cope with.[2]

A meat-based diet is disastrous for bones. Switching from beef to chicken or fish does not help because these products have as much animal protein as beef or even a bit more. Bodybuilders and others who take protein supplements have even greater calcium losses. The problem is not just the amount of protein in meats but also the type. Meats are loaded with what are called sulfur-containing amino acids, which are especially aggressive at causing calcium to be lost in the urine.

So instead of meat sauce on spaghetti, if you were to top your pasta with chunks of vegetables in a tomato sauce, the antioxidants in those veggies are only part of the edge they bring you. Grains, beans, vegetables, and fruits easily provide enough protein for your body's needs but avoid the excess. They are powerful calcium savers that help keep bones strong and calcium dense. A recent report in the *American Journal of Clinical Nutrition* showed that when research subjects eliminated meats, cheese, and eggs from their diets, they cut their urinary calcium losses in half.[3]

Meats have another problem, and that is phosphorus. Poultry and beef have about fifteen times as much phosphorus as calcium and this tremendous phosphorus excess encourages calcium loss.[4] Vegetables tend to have roughly equal amounts of the two and help keep calcium where it belongs.

Meats are not the only problem. An old term for sodas was "phosphates," referring to their longtime recipe: water, flavorings and colorings, caffeine, and phosphoric acid, as you will see on any Pepsi or Coke label. The popularity of colas is another reason for the prevalence of osteoporosis.

When Caffeine Goes In, Calcium Goes Out

Another advantage of avoiding sodas is that you will avoid the caffeine that is in many of them. Caffeine is a weak diuretic that causes calcium loss via the kidneys. And, of course, there is even more caffeine in coffee and tea. You can adjust to caffeine's effect on your sleep, but you cannot adjust to its effect on bone. The more caffeine that goes in, the more calcium goes out. For men and premenopausal women, the effect on bone density is negligible. But for women after menopause, the effect is significant.[5]

The bottles of spring water that are now edging their way into convenience store coolers next to Coke and Pepsi have a big advantage for your bones. They quench your thirst and leave your calcium where it belongs. The same is true of decaffeinated coffees and teas.

SALT DISSOLVES BONES

Another very powerful step is to choose low-salt foods. That's right—if you throw salt on a slippery sidewalk, it dissolves the ice; if you sprinkle it on your food, it can dissolve your bones, albeit by a different mechanism. For an average person, cutting sodium intake in half reduces the daily calcium requirement by about 160 milligrams.[6] That is a sizable amount of the eight hundred milligrams that some authorities recommend.

The reason is this: Just as your body carefully controls the acidity of your blood, it also tries to keep the amount of sodium in the bloodstream fairly constant, neither too high nor too low. If you take in extra sodium, your kidneys have to get rid of it, and when that happens, they end up sending calcium along with it.[7]

The effect of sodium on bones is well-known to scientists. Unfortunately, it is virtually unknown to the public. If there were an American Salt Reduction Council, you would have seen television commercials about it, but, of course, no industry benefits directly from reductions in salt (sodium chloride) intake. When health organizations make diet recommendations, they prefer to emphasize what people can *add* to their diets rather than what people might omit because industry groups complain vigorously when their products are criticized.

Sometimes they complain very loudly. An advertising agency in New England made an ad for a large American health organization that read: "Last year 2 million Americans left the same suicide note." The accompanying picture was a shopping list: butter, eggs, mayo, potato chips, ham, and bacon. A major potato chip manufacturer complained, and the ad was quickly withdrawn. My organization, the Physicians Committee for Responsible Medicine, subsequently acquired the rights to the ad and ran it again in spite of the company's objection.

What are the low-sodium foods? Actually, the healthiest foods— grains, vegetables, fruits, and beans—contain almost no sodium unless it is added in cooking. Dairy products and meat contain much more sodium, as shown in table 9.1, page 165. It is interesting to note that human breast milk, which, of course, is designed by nature for human babies, has much less sodium (forty milligrams per cup) than the milk nature designed for baby cows (120 milligrams) or goats (122 milligrams), another reminder that Mother Nature continues to scratch her head when the dairy industry pushes cow's milk as "natural" for people.

Dairy products and meats are not the worst offenders, however. Foods with added salt can push sodium levels much higher. Two ounces of potato chips have 240 milligrams of sodium. Some canned foods are practically off the scale. Happily, reduced-salt versions of many foods are now available, and you'll see the difference on the label. A half cup of

---

TABLE 9.1

Sodium and Potassium in Foods (milligrams)

Plant Products	Sodium	Potassium	Animal Products	Sodium	Potassium
Apple, 1 medium	1	159	Whole milk, 1 cup	120	370
Banana, 1 medium	1	451	Skim milk, 1 cup	126	406
Black beans, 1 cup*	6	801	Goat's milk, 1 cup	122	499
Broccoli, 1 cup*	16	254	Human milk, 1 cup	40	128
Cauliflower, 1 cup	8	400	Yogurt, 1 cup	105	351
Cream of wheat, 1 cup*	7	48	Cheddar cheese, 2 ounces	352	56
Grapefruit, 1 medium	0	316	Ground beef, 4 ounces*	88	344
Navy beans, 1 cup*	2	669	Roast beef, 4 ounces*	72	255
Orange, 1 medium	1	250	Chicken breast, 4 ounces (no skin)*	82	286
Potato, 1 medium*	16	844	Haddock, 4 ounces*	99	452
Rice, 1 cup*	0	57	Swordfish, 4 ounces*	130	419

*Figures refer to cooked servings.
Source: Pennington, J. A. T. 1989. *Bowes and Church's Food Values of Portions Commonly Used.* Philadelphia: J. B. Lippincott.

---

ordinary canned green beans has 360 milligrams of sodium. The no-salt version has only ten. An ounce of Original Wheat Thins has 170 milli-grams of sodium, while the low-salt variety has only seventy-five. A cup of regular canned black beans holds eight hundred milligrams of sodium, while the low-salt variety has only seventy. The difference is simply in how much the manufacturer decides to add.

A reasonable—and easily achievable—limit for sodium intake is one thousand to two thousand milligrams per day. As you can see, grains, vegetables, fruits, and beans are far below that level. You could eat a gal-lon of bananas, broccoli, or black beans and never come even close to a thousand milligrams of sodium. But it is easy to go way over that amount if you draw your menu from meats, dairy products, snack foods, and canned products with added salt.

Your taste buds are used to the amount of salt you're now using. But if you reduce it gradually, the change is almost imperceptible. It is easy to cut down on salt used in cooking, and salt shakers from the table can be hidden in potted plants or replaced with salt substitutes, which come in many varieties.

Plant products are high in potassium rather than sodium, and potas-sium's effect is just the opposite of sodium's. It helps keep calcium in the bone, apparently by reducing calcium loss via the kidneys. If you are get-ting the potassium your body needs, you are better able to keep calcium in your bones.[8] There is no need to go out of your way in search of high-potassium foods. A vegetarian diet is loaded with it.

LETTING YOUR BONES BREATHE EASIER

When smokers quit, their whole body breathes a sigh of relief, and the bones are no exception. Smoking is tough on bones. Australian scientists rounded up forty-one sets of identical twins, all of whom were adult women. They found that if one twin smoked and the other did not, the smoker's bones were about 10 percent less dense in the spine and about 5 percent less dense in the hip and thigh bones, even though their genes were, of course, identical.[9] A 10 percent loss of bone density may not sound like much, but it can mean a 44 percent increase in the risk of a hip fracture.

Smokers can even calculate their losses. Every ten pack-years of smoking causes about a 2 percent bone loss at the spine and 1 percent bone loss at the hip and thigh. Ten pack-years means one pack per day for ten years, two packs per day for five years, and so on.

As you can see, there are lots of reasons why people in Western countries lose calcium from their bones. Their diet is loaded with animal protein, phosphorus, sodium, and caffeine. A chicken salad sandwich and cola pack an ugly dose of all four. The answer is simple. Shift your menu from animal products to plant foods and you will leave animal protein and sodium behind while keeping potassium high, which helps your bones stay strong. If you avoid caffeine and tobacco, you skip two more calcium depleters.

CALCIUM DEPLETERS

- Animal protein
- Caffeine
- Excess phosphorus (sodas, animal products)
- Sodium (animal products, canned or snack foods)
- Tobacco
- Sedentary lifestyle

HEALTHY CALCIUM SOURCES

Some health organizations have promoted high calcium intakes in recent years, typically eight hundred milligrams per day or more. They are trying to make up for the extraordinary calcium losses caused by animal protein, phosphorus, caffeine, sodium, tobacco, and other factors. It does not work very well. Many research studies have shown that calcium intake has little effect on osteoporosis, particularly at the hip and spine.[10] Ironically, countries with a high calcium intake actually have far more hip fractures than countries with more modest calcium intakes.[11] Calcium is simply not able to counteract the profound bone loss caused by all the factors described above. On the other hand, you can keep strong bones with a much lower calcium intake when you avoid the calcium depleters.

This does not mean that you do not need calcium in the diet. If you get very little, say, less than four hundred milligrams per day, you may not be giving your body the calcium it needs.[12]

Dairy products are not the healthiest source. They do contain calcium, but only about 30 percent of it is absorbed. The remaining 70 percent never makes it past the intestinal wall and is simply excreted with the feces. Dairy products have many other undesirable features, including animal proteins that contribute to some cases of arthritis and respiratory problems, lactose sugar that is linked to cataracts, frequent traces of antibiotics, and other problems that lead many doctors to suggest that we avoid them and get calcium from healthier sources.

The healthiest calcium sources are "greens and beans." Green leafy vegetables are loaded with calcium. One cup of broccoli has 178 milligrams of calcium. What's more, the calcium in broccoli and most other green leafy vegetables is more absorbable than the calcium in milk.[13] An exception is spinach, which has a form of calcium that is not well absorbed.

Beans, lentils, and other legumes are also loaded with calcium. We think of beans as a humble food, but they are an extraordinary source of nutrition. They have calcium, omega-3 fatty acids, the cholesterol-lowering soluble fiber that many people thought was only in oat bran, and healthy complex carbohydrates. If you make green vegetables and beans regular parts of your diet, you'll get two excellent sources of calcium.

You don't need to eat six cups of broccoli or huge servings of beans to get enough calcium. A varied menu of vegetables and legumes can easily give you all you need, and the amount your body needs is far less when you steer clear of meats and the other calcium depleters. The World Health Organization recommends a daily calcium intake of just four hundred to five hundred milligrams per day.

The same foods that provide a healthy source of calcium also provide boron, an element that helps keep calcium in the bones. Fruits, vegetables, legumes, and nuts are loaded with boron, while meats and dairy products have little or none. Table 9.2, page 170, lists sources of healthy calcium.

Calcium supplements are not usually necessary. If you decide to add extra calcium, calcium-fortified orange juice is a good choice. It contains more calcium than milk, and it is in the form of calcium citrate, which is much more readily absorbed than that in milk or in calcium carbonate supplements.[14]

EXERCISE

Just about every part of your body loves to get some physical activity, and that's certainly true of your bones.[15] Bones that have nothing to do lose their strength. When you walk, play tennis, take the stairs, or engage in other activities, your spine, hips, and thighs get a good workout. No special exercises are needed. The key is simply to have a brisk walk daily or every other day.

This may be one reason why overweight people have stronger bones than those at normal weight. Their bones are doing extra work simply in the daily routine of getting around.

SUNLIGHT

Your bones like a little sun. As sunlight touches the skin, it turns on the natural production of vitamin D, which helps your digestive tract absorb calcium from foods and makes your kidneys hold onto it as well. You do not need to bake under the sun for hours. Brief periods of sun exposure can give your body all the vitamin D it needs, although the amount generated depends on the sun's intensity and how much pigment is in your skin. For example, a Caucasian in the northern United States would get more than enough vitamin D from just ten minutes of summer sun on the face, hands, and arms two or three times per week.[16] Blacks produce vitamin D more slowly than do whites, but generally have significantly stronger bones, apparently due to genetic factors.

TABLE 9.2

Healthful Calcium Sources (milligrams)

Black turtle beans, 1 cup, boiled	103
Broccoli, 1 cup, boiled	178
Brussels sprouts, 8 sprouts	56
Butternut squash, 1 cup, boiled	84
Celery, 1 cup, boiled	54
Chickpeas, 1 cup, canned	78
Collard greens, 1 cup, boiled	148
Cornbread, a 2-ounce piece	133
English muffin	92
Figs, dried, 10 medium	269
Great Northern beans, 1 cup, boiled	121
Green beans, 1 cup, boiled	58
Kale, 1 cup, boiled	94
Kidney beans, 1 cup, boiled	50
Lentils, 1 cup, boiled	37
Lima beans, 1 cup, boiled	52
Navel orange, 1 medium	56
Navy beans, 1 cup, boiled	128
Onions, 1 cup, boiled	58
Orange juice, calcium-fortified, 1 cup	300*
Pancake mix, ¼ cup, 3 pancakes	140
Pinto beans, 1 cup, boiled	82
Raisins, ⅔ cup	53
Soybeans, 1 cup, boiled	175
Sweet potato, 1 cup, boiled	70
Tofu, ½ cup	258
Vegetarian baked beans, 1 cup	128
Wax beans, 1 cup, canned	174
Wheat flour, calcium enriched, 1 cup	238
White beans, 1 cup, boiled	161

*Package information
Source: Pennington, J. A. T. 1989. *Bowes and Church's Food Values of Portions Commonly Used.* Philadelphia. J. B. Lippincott.

In the skin, sunlight forms a compound called previtamin D_3, which gradually turns into vitamin D over the next several days and weeks. Vitamin D is then stored in body fat and muscle,[17] giving you a good supply for a rainy day or a whole string of rainy days.

People who rarely go out in the sun risk vitamin D insufficiency. This happened during the Industrial Revolution, when many people migrated to crowded urban areas. Those who lived in narrow dark streets and spent most of the day indoors had abnormal bone growth. Similarly, people who are confined indoors for prolonged periods or who live at extreme north or south latitudes will not get the sun exposure that is normal for their body chemistry. Window glass and sunscreens block the ultraviolet sun rays that make vitamin D.

If you get no sun exposure, you need supplemental vitamin D,[18] which is why it is in all multiple vitamins. It is also commonly added to milk, although dairies have not been as careful as pharmaceutical houses at measuring how much they put in. A study of vitamin D supplementation in milk was conducted after several people became ill from vitamin D overdose. Of the milk samples tested, nearly all had either significantly more or significantly less vitamin D than the dairy was trying to add. Only 12 percent had the intended amount.[19] The same problem has been found in infant formulas.[20]

The sun is nature's intended source. For those who get infrequent sun exposure, any common multivitamin containing five micrograms (200 IUs), taken daily, provides adequate vitamin D. For people who never go outdoors due to chronic illness, ten micrograms (400 IUs) is recommended.[21] Higher doses of vitamin D are potentially toxic and should be avoided.

RESTORING STRENGTH TO BONES

After menopause, many women are given estrogen supplements in order to slow down osteoporosis. But as we saw in chapter 5, supplemental hormones can increase the risk of cancer of the breast and uterus and cause many other problems.

Estrogens do not build bone. The best they can usually do is to slow bone loss, and recent studies have thrown more cold water on doctors' enthusiasm for estrogen supplements. Researchers have found that even if postmenopausal women take estrogens religiously, most will still lose bone, albeit at a slower rate. And as they approach their seventies and eighties, the effects of estrogen replacement wane and many women have fractures in spite of hormone use.[22] Estrogen has not provided the protection many had hoped it would.

As we have seen, changing your diet and adding exercise can help preserve bone strength without the risks of hormone treatments. And the only "side effects" are positive ones: weight loss and reduced risk of heart disease and cancer, among many others. But there is much more you can do.

The hormonal changes at menopause can encourage the loss of calcium from bones. However, as we saw in chapter 3, these hormonal shifts are strongly influenced by foods. When women are on meat-based diets, the amount of estrogen in their blood is artificially elevated. At menopause, it comes crashing down to a much lower level. Women on low-fat plant-based diets, on the other hand, have slightly lower levels of estrogens in their blood before menopause, are adapted to those levels, and have less of a change at menopause. This is probably why, just as Asian doctors report that menopausal symptoms are less common there, hip fractures are also much rarer in Asia than in the West. Women who follow low-fat vegetarian diets going into menopause are more likely to keep strong bones.

In chapter 5, we briefly looked at natural progesterone, which is an exact copy of the progesterone made by the body, derived from various plants, most notably wild yams and soybeans. Applied to the skin, it releases a bit of progesterone into the fat layer. From there, it is gradually released into the blood.

Progesterone has an amazing property. It does not just slow bone loss; it actually builds bone. It apparently stimulates tiny cells, called osteoblasts, to build bone in areas where it has been lost. This is a remarkable effect that does not occur with estrogens. It also eases many other menopausal symptoms. Best of all, unlike estrogens, it does not appear to increase cancer risk. In fact, it apparently has no side effects at all. For post-menopausal women who have feared advancing osteoporosis, natural progesterone actually *builds* bone.

So why do we not see drug company advertisements for it? Progesterone is a natural compound, so drug companies cannot patent it, and there is not much money to be made by selling it. Drug companies do take progesterone from plants, but they alter it in various ways to make it chemically unique and therefore patentable. The altered forms, called progestins (e.g., Provera), are heavily promoted by drug companies and are commonly prescribed by doctors. But these unnatural chemicals do not quite fit into the body's systems for using and eliminating progesterone. They are the biological equivalent of using the wrong replacement part in your car's engine. While the pharmaceutical companies' financial machinery hums along just fine, your biological machinery can have a multitude of side effects, ranging from facial hair growth and depression to heart disease, liver problems, and even breast cancer. The body was built to use natural progesterone, not inexact copies.

John R. Lee, M.D., is the leading advocate of natural progesterone in the medical community. After graduating from Harvard University, the University of Minnesota medical school, and graduate medical training at Minneapolis General Hospital, Dr. Lee opened his office in California. As the years of clinical practice went by, he found that many of his patients had advancing bone loss. They were taking calcium pills and vitamin D, but their bones kept getting weaker, as they do for many American women. Although estrogen supplements were the standard medical treatment, many of his patients could not take estrogens for various medical reasons.

Dr. Lee tried a transdermal progesterone cream on his patients and measured their bone density as the treatment continued. The results were surprising. Not only did their bone loss stop; their weakened bones actually started to rebuild. One after another had a steady *increase* in bone density.

Every patient who used the progesterone cream improved in bone density. Where bones had lost their strength, progesterone encouraged the development of new bone. "The effect can be quite striking," Dr. Lee said. "One of my patients had a pathological arm fracture at age seventy-two. Now at eighty-four, her bone density has increased 40 percent and she has no fractures." Other practitioners began to find the same thing in their patients.

In a study of one hundred postmenopausal women, the average patient had a 15 percent increase in bone density after three years of treatment.[23] What makes this so remarkable is that doctors have been looking for ways to slow the rate of bone loss, and most never dreamed it would be possible to actually build bone. But an increasing number of clinicians are finding exactly that.[24]

One patient did not improve initially. It turned out that she had such low stomach acid production that she could not absorb calcium normally. With supplements of hydrochloric acid, she improved.

Dr. Lee's patients not only built new bone, which was like insurance against hip and spine fractures; they also felt better. If they had painful fibrocystic breasts, they gradually improved. Hot flashes were often reduced. Many hypothyroid patients no longer needed thyroid supplementation because progesterone seems to improve thyroid hormone's actions in the body. People with weight problems began to lose weight more easily.

As powerful as natural progesterone is, it also seems to be surprisingly safe. It is sold without a prescription, and there are no side effects reported in the medical literature. "The only 'side effect,' " Dr. Lee said, "is that the guy across the room will get a little better looking." Progesterone can increase the sex drive in women, which makes biological sense since it is normally produced by the ovary just after it releases an egg. "Presumably this is nature's way of assuring a meeting of the egg with a sperm after ovulation," Dr. Lee said. This can be a relief for women who have lost their sex drive as a side effect of estrogen supplements or premenopausal women who have a reduced sex drive due to a relative dominance of estrogen over progesterone.

Progesterone cream is sold without a prescription in health food stores and by mail order. Sources are listed on page 97. Dr. Lee initially advises that a two-ounce jar be used up each month. Later the dosage may be reduced to one ounce per month. In postmenopausal women, the cream is usually used each month for two to three weeks, then stopped until the beginning of the next month. In women who have not yet stopped menstruating, Dr. Lee suggests using the cream from about day 13 to day 26 of the menstrual cycle. To maintain its effect, it is discontinued for at least five to seven days each month.

It is spread on areas of thin skin, such as the insides of the arms or legs, the neck, upper chest, and abdomen, covering as wide an area as possible and varying the areas to which it is applied. It takes a while for progesterone to build up in the fat tissue, so it may take two or three months before effects are seen.

Because progesterone facilitates the effects of thyroid hormone, women taking thyroid medications may need to reduce or discontinue their thyroid medications after beginning progesterone, which should be done in consultation with their doctors.

A two-ounce-per-month dosage provides about fifteen to twenty milligrams of progesterone per day, which is about the same as is produced naturally in premenopausal women. For comparison, the body makes up to three hundred to four hundred milligrams of progesterone per day during pregnancy.

Postmenopausal women who are taking estrogens are often advised to cut their estrogen dose in half when starting progesterone because progesterone temporarily increases the body's sensitivity to estrogen. Many women find that they no longer need estrogen at all after a few months using the progesterone cream.

Women who are currently using an artificial progestin, such as Provera, can easily switch to natural progesterone, but should taper off the progestin gradually. A typical regimen would be to cut the progestin dose in half for the first month that progesterone cream is used. In the second month, it should be cut in half again, using it every other day, if necessary. By the third month, the progestin can be safely discontinued.

PROTECTING YOUR BONES

- Avoid calcium depleters: animal products, caffeinated coffee or tea, sodas containing caffeine or phosphoric acid, high-salt canned or snack foods, and tobacco.
- Choose healthy calcium sources: green leafy vegetables, beans, and lentils.
- If you miss normal sunlight, vitamin D (5 micrograms) should be taken daily.
- Do weight-bearing exercise daily.
- Natural progesterone can safely rebuild bones.

All of this raises the question as to why anyone should need hormone supplements at all. Doesn't nature provide the hormones the body needs?

"I don't think nature is to blame," Dr. Lee said. "Many plants contain progesterone and natural estrogens, which help maintain health in people who consume them. In the Trobriand Islands off New Guinea, for example, the yam is a dietary staple. It is also a totem signifying good health and good life. Yams, of course, contain a source of progesterone, and, not surprisingly, the Trobriand Islanders enjoy good health and vigorous sex lives. In modern America, we tend to neglect the healthful foods nature offers and we pay a price for that."

Just as many plant foods, particularly soy products, contain weak estrogens, it may be that plants containing progesterone or other natural hormones were a part of the human diet for most of our history, only to be displaced by refined foods and animal products that contribute to the hormonal imbalances that bother so many Westerners.

ARTHRITIS AND GOUT

There is great news, not just for your bones, but for your joints, too. New research has shown how to use nutrients that can cool down painful joints and how to eliminate foods that trigger arthritis.

Rheumatoid arthritis is an autoimmune disease, meaning that your white blood cells attack your own joints, leading to pain and inflammation. Exactly why this happens is poorly understood. Just as many diet-related conditions are more common in Western countries and rarer in Asia and other countries that follow a plant-based diet, rheumatoid arthritis and related diseases follow a similar pattern. They are somewhat less common in Asia and are usually milder when they do occur.[25]

For many years, doctors doubted the links between diet and arthritis. But a stream of research reports has shown that foods do indeed play a role in both the cause and treatment of arthritis for many people. For some, specific foods spark arthritis and steering clear of those foods can relieve their symptoms.

A forty-five-year-old woman from Michigan was working as a school administrator and, along with her husband, raising two children. She was very busy and rarely took a day off. From an almost imperceptible start, the joints in her hands started to ache. The pain gradually increased, and her joints became warm and swollen. Anti-inflammatory medicines relieved the pain somewhat, but did not stop the arthritis as it spread to other joints. Her doctor made a diagnosis of rheumatoid arthritis and told her that symptomatic treatment was all medical science could offer.

She and her husband attended a lecture I gave at a university near their home. They had come for information on how he could reduce his high cholesterol level. After a long discussion about cholesterol, they asked about how diet might affect arthritis.

The fact is, researchers have studied a wide range of dietary treatments. Diets rich in animal products either do nothing or make the symptoms worse.[26] A number of studies have shown that supervised fasting is very helpful.[27] Fasting, of course, eliminates essentially all foods, including any that might trigger arthritis.

A team of Scandinavian researchers found a particularly helpful approach. They put arthritis patients on a supervised fast using only herbal teas, vegetable broths, and vegetable juice extracts. No fruit juices were used. After seven to ten days, foods were reintroduced one at a time every other day until the patients were consuming a varied vegan (pure vegetarian) diet. After 3½ months on the vegan diet, other foods were introduced and their effects noted. If any newly introduced food caused the arthritis to return, the dietary trigger was eliminated again. The result was a substantial reduction in morning stiffness and joint swelling and tenderness. Grip strength also improved, although damage already done to joints did not reverse.[28]

Based on this and other studies, many doctors now treat arthritis by eliminating dietary triggers.[29] Among the common offenders are dairy products. The culprit is not the dairy fat, however, but the protein, so skim and nonfat products are just as problematic as whole milk. Dairy proteins are now under investigation for their role in triggering other autoimmune conditions, such as insulin-dependent diabetes.

Other foods can contribute: Corn, wheat, citrus fruits, and eggs are common triggers. Patients have also blamed red meat, sugar, fats, salt, caffeine, and nightshade plants (e.g., tomatoes, eggplant).[30] This does not mean that an affected individual is necessarily allergic to the problem food. The nature of the sensitivity is not entirely known and may not be an allergy, but what is clear is that avoiding the offending food can eliminate the problem.

Here is a common way in which the dietary treatment is done.

Four-Week Partial Elimination Diet. The first step is a partial elimination diet. For four weeks, the following foods are eliminated completely:

Dairy products (regular, skim, and nonfat versions)
Meats (beef, pork, poultry, fish, and so on)
Eggs
Wheat, oats, and rye
Corn
Citrus fruits
Caffeine
Alcohol
Vegetable oils
Refined sugar
Nightshades (tomatoes, eggplant, potatoes, peppers)

Chocolate

Nuts

This will take some doing, but this test only has to be done once if it is done carefully. If at four weeks your symptoms have cleared up, you can then add back vegetable, fruit, and grain products one at a time every two days. As you do so, have a generous amount of each newly added food over a two-day period to see whether symptoms recur. It may take a few days for the effect to show. I do not recommend adding meat, dairy, eggs, or more than a trace of vegetable oils back to the diet because of their many adverse health effects.

One-Week Full Elimination Diet.   If symptoms continue unabated after four weeks, a full elimination diet is the next step for identifying other dietary triggers. A full elimination diet only lasts about a week but is a considerably stricter test. During the test week, the diet is limited to the following foods:

1. Brown rice
2. Cooked noncitrus fruits
3. Cooked green and yellow vegetables (e.g., asparagus, green beans, lettuce, spinach, squash, sweet potatoes)

Condiments other than salt are also omitted during the weeklong test. The remaining foods are well tolerated by just about all arthritis patients. Once symptoms are gone, foods can be added back one at a time as described above.

If that regimen sounds difficult, it may be easier than a traditional Chinese treatment called snake wine, which is made by soaking one hundred dead snakes in five liters of red wine with various herbs for three months and adjusting the final alcohol content to 40 percent. The resulting liquid is drunk three times a day for six to twelve weeks. A Chinese physician gave his opinion of the treatment at an arthritis conference: "I would say it is of no use."[31]

Many patients improve simply with a low-fat, pure vegetarian diet because it eliminates dairy products, one of the most common triggers. A vegetable-rich diet also increases antioxidants. As we saw in chapter 1, free radicals are the direct cause of many forms of tissue damage and arthritis is no exception. It is likely that the joint damage of arthritis is done by free radicals released by cells, perhaps in response to dietary triggers. A plant-based diet also helps prevent iron overload. As we have seen, iron increases free radical damage. This is particularly important in joints that are already inflamed. As you take a step or clench your fist, blood flow to your joints can be momentarily cut off. When blood rushes in again, the oxygen it brings turns even more readily to free radicals. Iron aggravates this process, accelerating the production of free radicals and the damage they do.[32] Guidelines for keeping iron in check are found on page 33.

The couple from Michigan decided to try a change in their diet. They omitted all animal products and built their diet from vegetables, legumes, grains, and fruits. I suggested that she also initially avoid citrus fruits, wheat, and corn and reintroduce them later to see if they were tolerated.

The effect was rapid and dramatic. Her joint symptoms ended within several days. The pain, stiffness, and swelling were totally gone. She was able to grip her tennis racquet without pain and to play the piano without the feeling of awkwardness that her arthritis had caused. She found, however, that if she had yogurt or other dairy products, the symptoms started again. Not everyone benefits from dietary changes, but many do. And, by the way, his cholesterol level dropped, too.

Essential Fatty Acids. An additional step, favored by many clinicians, is the use of essential fatty acid supplements. These natural oils alter the balance of prostaglandins, which are chemicals in the body that control inflammation. A common regimen would include all of the following taken each day, usually with the evening meal:

1. Flax oil, one tablespoon (or four capsules)
2. Either borage oil or blackcurrant oil (1000 milligrams, usually taken as two 500-milligram capsules) or evening primrose oil (three 1300-milligram capsules)
3. Vitamin E, 400 IUs, or 100 IUs for people with high blood pressure

It usually takes several weeks for benefits to be seen. Flax oil may cause loose stools, which usually abate after a few days. These natural oils reduce inflammation, while animal fats and frying oils sometimes aggravate inflammation and should be eliminated.

Glucosamine sulfate, five hundred milligrams three times a day, has helped many people and appears to be much safer than the usual anti-inflammatory medications. The herb feverfew is also sometimes found to be helpful. Typically, one capsule is taken two to three times per day. Feverfew should not be taken if you are pregnant. Both of these products are available in health food stores.

OSTEOARTHRITIS

Osteoarthritis is very common, but what causes it is still largely unknown. Inside the joints, especially the spine, hands, wrists, hips, knees, feet, and shoulders, cartilage deteriorates and bony spurs develop. The joints hurt and motion becomes more difficult. It has been suggested that these changes come, not from damage per se, but from the joint's attempts to repair itself.[33]

The first step in guarding against osteoarthritis is to stay slim. Every ten extra pounds you carry can increase your risk of developing knee osteoarthritis by about 30 percent.[34] Surprisingly enough, excess weight even increases the risk of osteoarthritis of the hands.[35] It is easy to see why excess weight would strain the knees, but harder to see why chubby fingers would harm the finger joints.

Some researchers believe that the reason is estrogens. Women do have more osteoarthritis than men,[36] and those who have had symptoms of estrogen excess, such as uterine fibroids or abnormal uterine bleeding necessitating hysterectomy, have more frequent osteoarthritis.[37] Estrogens are produced in fat tissue and may encourage joint damage. Researchers are still debating this theory, however, particularly since hormone supplements do not seem to increase the risk.[38]

Joint injuries can increase the likelihood of osteoarthritis,[39] and doing the same motion at work day after day can encourage osteoarthritis of the hands.[40] After all, your hands were designed to do a million different tasks, not to stick to exactly the same movements day in and day out like a ticking clock. Similarly, people whose jobs involve knee bending over and over again are more likely to develop osteoarthritis of the knees.[41] Studies of runners have not shown a higher risk of osteoarthritis.[42]

While weight loss and avoiding joint injuries are important, there is not enough evidence to show whether the essential fatty acid supplements described above are of any use in osteoarthritis. Regrettably, they simply have not been tested to any significant degree.

GOUT

In chapter 1, we saw the good side of uric acid. It is a strong antioxidant, able to neutralize free radicals in the bloodstream. However, uric acid also has its not-so-good side. It is the central player in gout.

The patient usually arrives at the emergency room in misery. Pain starts in the big toe for reasons that no one understands. It can also affect other joints. Doctors draw a small amount of fluid from an affected joint and find crystals of uric acid.

Gout is often described as a disease of the wealthy because it is associated with a diet rich in animal products and alcohol. As the genetic material from the cells of the food are broken down, uric acid is released. The worst culprits are sardines, anchovies, and organ meats, such as liver, kidneys, and brains, although other animal products contribute as well. Alcohol, especially beer, is near the top of the list, too.[43] Humans lost their ability to break down uric acid long ago, a characteristic that puts us in the company of insects, birds, and reptiles. So chalky deposits of uric acid crystals end up, not only in the joints, but also in the skin of the ear, the forearm, the elbow, or the Achilles tendon.

Three centuries ago, Anton van Leeuwenhoek, the inventor of the microscope, obtained some of these crystals from a stricken relative. He could describe the crystals, but did not recognize them as uric acid. In the early 1960s, a young researcher named Daniel J. McCarty became convinced that uric acid depositing in the joints was the cause of gout. To test his theory, he and a colleague injected uric acid crystals into each other's knees. At first nothing happened, and they began to wonder if their theory might be wrong. But after about six hours, the pain set in. It soon became excruciating. They could not move the affected leg, let alone walk. They eventually hobbled home on crutches with a supply of narcotic painkillers.[44]

Gout is not caused by uric acid alone. The problem starts when white blood cells take in the crystals, triggering inflammation, which leads to pain and joint damage.

A vegetarian diet is an excellent prescription for gout patients. For reasons that are not entirely clear, getting meat off the plate makes gout less likely, and avoiding alcohol helps, too. However, people with a tendency to develop gout are particularly vulnerable at times of dietary change and should continue on their medication throughout the dietary transition. Some may continue to need medication thereafter.

HEALTHY JOINTS

- Follow a low-fat vegetarian diet.
- If symptoms persist, use a partial or full elimination diet to identify dietary triggers.
- Consider essential fatty acid supplements.
- Check your iron status (see page 31).
- Keep alcohol use moderate and intermittent.

FOODS FOR HEALTHY BONES AND JOINTS

We have better tools than ever before against bone loss and joint damage. A menu drawn from plants, rather than animal products, supplies the calcium that the bones need while avoiding the animal proteins, phosphorus imbalance, sodium excess, and other factors that weaken bones. At the same time, it is an important step in soothing and often curing painful joints.

CHAPTER TEN

HOW TO DISSOLVE FAT PERMANENTLY

Breakthroughs have occurred in so many areas of health, from shielding the body against the assaults of chemicals and stopping the hormone rampages that are caused by foods, to cleaning the arteries after decades of abuse and slowing the aging process itself. But no advance has been more exciting than the dramatic revolution in weight loss. If there was ever an area that needed a breakthrough, this was it. Because in no other area has there been more frustration.

So many people have thought that extra weight is an inescapable part of getting older. It is not. You can turn it around starting right now. Some may imagine that weight problems are simply genetic. The fact is, heredity is not always the decisive factor many people believe it to be. Old-fashioned diets made us believe that beating a weight problem demands tremendous self-discipline. But when you try the surprisingly easy methods described in this chapter, you will find that you do not need a fraction of your willpower to slim down.

The solution is simple. It makes biological sense, takes the pounds off, and gives lasting results. This is step seven in the process of rejuvenating your body.

THE NEGATIVE CALORIE EFFECT

The first part of the solution is a remarkable property of certain foods. When you learn how to take advantage of it, you can forget diets forever and eat normal portions at every meal. You will increase your metabolism and reduce the tendency of foods to go to fat because you will know which foods turn on the calorie-burning power of your cells and which foods encourage weight gain.

It is called the negative calorie effect. The basic principle is that certain foods have the power to increase your body's calorie-burning ability while other foods encourage fat storage. By knowing which ones are which, weight control becomes easy. It also becomes permanent.

Until very recently, it was believed that whether foods were fattening or not depended on just one thing: the number of calories they held. A calorie was a calorie. It did not matter if they came from rice or bacon grease; all calories were equally fattening. The body was treated like a bank account. The calories coming in would be saved up as fat if they were not spent by an equal amount of exercise.

But researchers began to find that different foods had very different effects. Certain kinds of meals made research subjects feel warm. Careful measurements showed that, in fact, they were producing slightly more body heat because they were burning calories faster than usual. Other foods lacked this thermogenic effect. In addition, some foods go to fat quite easily while others do not. And different foods have very different effects on your appetite. The idea that all that matters is the calorie content of foods has had to be thrown out in favor of a completely new understanding that lets you choose foods that speed up your metabolism and that cannot add directly to body fat.

Let me give you a few examples of how the new approach works. Each one is real and I have changed only the identifying details.

Bobbie worked at a television station in Memphis. She had been on diet after diet. She had lost weight, only to gain it back over and over again, and ended up unhappy and much heavier than she wanted to be.

After her next diet, when her weight had yo-yoed down to its fleeting low point, she learned about the program you will read about here. And when she started it, it was surprisingly easy. She ate delicious food and did not limit how much she ate. It worked wonderfully. She stayed at the weight she wanted, more than one hundred pounds below her peak. The weight gain that she had suffered time and time again never came back. And she did it without counting a single calorie. It was a bit of a switch for her to stop worrying about *how much* she ate and to focus instead on the *type* of food she ate, but it worked and her weight problem was finally solved.

Mike lived in St. Louis, Missouri. He not only had a weight problem; his cholesterol level was up and he had been on insulin for diabetes. His daughter brought him to one of my lectures and he decided to see if the system works. He lost seventy pounds, his cholesterol dropped more than eighty points, his triglycerides plummeted back to normal, and his doctor stopped his insulin. He did not need it anymore. More importantly, the improvements stayed with him.

Susan lived in Topeka. She had seen an interview I had done on television and called my office to say that she could hardly believe her success. She had battled a weight problem all of her life. "I've been on every diet there is," she said, "and the weight kept coming back and then some. It just kept getting worse and worse." She finally found the solution. In Susan's case, weight loss was very rapid—actually much faster than I would normally recommend. "I lost 183 pounds in about six months and I've kept it off. And I've finally figured out why those diets I had been on kept letting the weight come back." She tested herself with the foods she had come to discover were responsible for her weight problem. Every time, the results were the same. The weight started returning. But by simply avoiding these foods and enjoying the full range of fat-burning foods, her weight problem resolved itself naturally.

With a few principles of food selection, your eating patterns can be totally normal. The foods themselves help you burn fat. Here is how to dissolve your fat layer:

1. Choose foods that step up your metabolism.
2. Use modest physical activity to accelerate your metabolism further unless a medical condition precludes it.

3. Learn to identify weight-promoting foods and steer clear of them.

4. Never eat *less* than ten calories per pound of your ideal weight each day and do not skip meals.

5. If you are stuffing yourself for emotional reasons, follow the guidelines on page 200.

There is no limit on portion size or the number of portions you eat during the day. The only exception is for people who often eat when their bodies really do not want food and use food to fill an emotional void. Only about 15 percent of people with weight problems are in that category and that problem can be solved, too, as we will see shortly.

Many people find it hard to believe that they do not need to eat skimpy portions in order to lose weight. They may have been buying tiny dietetic frozen dinners containing two hundred or three hundred calories and essentially starving themselves for years. But that kind of diet does not help your metabolism. It makes it even more sluggish.

Let's try a very different approach. If you wanted to build up the flame on an old potbelly stove, what would you do? Would you throw on a few tiny twigs? Of course not. You would pile on the fuel and fan the flames until it was burning red hot. A human potbelly works the same way. If you give your body tiny amounts of food, you will never fan your biological flame. You will never help your body burn calories quickly.

FAT-BURNING FOODS

Dieters read labels. Before they buy anything, they check how many calories it has. If they have been at it for a while, they have often memorized the exact calorie content of dozens, if not hundreds, of foods.

Most diets were designed with the idea that it really does not make any difference what food you eat so long as you do not go over a set calorie limit. One hundred calories worth of rice or pasta was thought to be just as fattening as one hundred calories of chicken or beef.

But a calorie is not a calorie anymore. Numerous scientific studies have shown that calories coming from potatoes, rice, pasta, or other high-carbohydrate foods do not have the same effect as the very same number of calories from chicken, beef, or salad dressing. The high-carbohydrate foods have much less of a tendency to promote weight gain. In fact, they can promote aggressive weight loss. That is, unless they are prepared with added oils or fats, which neutralizes their advantage, as we will see shortly.

Complex carbohydrates are simply the "starchy" part of foods: the white insides of a potato, pasta, rice, bread, beans, lentils, and most vegetables. They have three powerful features that help you lose weight.

Carbohydrates Are Low in Calories. Did you grow up, as I did, with the idea that carbohydrates were fattening? A whole generation ended up believing that bread and potatoes were the reason for overweight. Well, we were wrong. Carbohydrates are actually very modest in calories. Ounce for ounce, they have less than half the calories of any fat or oil, which keeps carbohydrate-rich foods much lower on the calorie chart than fatty foods. Compare two plates: One has six ounces of spaghetti noodles on it, and the other has six ounces of skinless chicken breast meat. The spaghetti noodles have only 193 calories, while the chicken has nearly 300 calories.

Carbohydrates have only four calories per gram (a gram is 1/28 ounce) while fats have more than double that number, at nine calories per gram. So where did we get the idea that carbohydrates were fattening? It apparently all got started from the fact that people tend to top potatoes with butter and sour cream, spread butter or margarine on their bread, and smother pasta in meat or cheese sauce or olive oil. The fattening, calorie-dense part is the greasy toppings, not the carbohydrates themselves.

Carbohydrates Cannot Go Straight to Fat. Not only are carbohydrates naturally low in calories; *they cannot add directly to your body fat.* There are no little pouches of carbohydrate on your thighs or hips. If you were to eat an enormous quantity of rice, pasta, or potatoes and your body tried to store it as fat, your cells would have to break the carbohydrate molecules apart and build fat molecules out of them. This task uses up fully 23 percent of the calories in the carbohydrate and adds to the negative calorie effect. In contrast, fat or oils in the foods you eat can go to your body fat with the loss of only 3 percent of their calories in the process.

Carbohydrates are also part of the signal mechanism that switches off your appetite. Your brain actually monitors the nutrients you are consuming, and carbohydrates help signal the brain that you have had enough to eat.

Carbohydrates Are Metabolism Boosters. Finally—and most importantly—carbohydrates increase your metabolism. Underneath your Adam's apple at the base of your neck is your thyroid gland. It makes T_4, a weak thyroid hormone that circulates in the blood. The name T_4 refers to the fact that it carries four iodine atoms. Foods that are rich in complex carbohydrates activate T_4 by removing one of these iodine atoms. The resulting active hormone, now called T_3, steps up the calorie burning of your cells just as the thermostat in your living room clicks on your furnace. You may actually feel the difference as increased body heat.[1]

When you take a plate full of fresh pasta and cover it with a crisp tomato sauce, the pasta's complex carbs will step up your metabolism. If you had Mexican beans with Spanish rice or an Indian vegetable curry on saffron rice, your cells will burn calories faster for hours after the meal. To turn this effect on, your body is looking for complex carbohydrates—not protein, not fat, and not anything else. The carbohydrates work by activating thyroid hormone and by other mechanisms, as you'll see shortly.

If you are a chronic dieter, you may find this all a bit shocking. The solution to weight problems is not a diet or anything even resembling a diet. Just the opposite. You need to eat to lose weight permanently. The vital factor is *what* you eat.

Certain foods let you down. They are completely lacking in complex carbohydrate. Take chicken, for example. Many dieters eat skinless chicken breast to reduce their fat intake. They are right to try to cut the fat, but chicken is one of the worst possible choices. Not only does chicken meat hold a substantial amount of fat even without the skin, but chicken contains no complex carbohydrate at all. If you look up chicken in any nutrition reference book, you will see a big zero in the carbohydrate column. Chicken contains protein and fat (fat makes up about 20 percent or more of its calories, even with the skin removed), but not a scrap of carbohydrate. In fact, the only way to get chicken with carbohydrate is to buy it breaded and fried. The tiny shreds of bread would have been much healthier than the greasy chicken they are stuck to. Obviously, this is not the answer. As many frustrated dieters have learned, chicken is certainly no magic food.

The same is true of fish, turkey, beef, pork, or any other meat. They are all just muscles. Muscles contain lots of protein and fat, but never a speck of carbohydrate. Muscles can move animals' legs, flap their wings, or wiggle their tails, but they will not turn on your metabolism and they do not solve weight problems. They cause them.

The chicken and fish routine is not just unhelpful; it can actually be harmful. Because when your diet is low in carbohydrate, more of the T_4 is turned into an inactive hormone called reverse T_3, slowing down your metabolism and short-circuiting your chance for success.

If you are eating fish, chicken, or beef for protein, you should know that a varied menu of plant foods easily provides more than enough protein, even without carefully combining them in any particular way, and gives you the powerful benefits of complex carbs.

Now, if you were worried that increasing thyroid hormone levels might be dangerous, the carbohydrate effect is not enough to make you hyperthyroid. A little thyroid boost is actually normal for your cells, and if you have been missing it all this time, it is no wonder you gained weight.

The thyroid boost is only the beginning of your increased calorie burning. Another hormone, called noradrenaline, is also stepped up when you eat carbohydrate-rich foods. It is a close relative of adrenaline, and it adds to the negative calorie effect.[2]

Researchers at the University of Rochester measured the metabolic rates of six young men. This is simply a measurement of how many calories they burn per hour and is done by analyzing the amounts of oxygen they breathe in and carbon dioxide they breathe out. They then asked each of them to drink a special carbohydrate solution flavored with a bit of lemon juice. Blood tests showed that the carbohydrate turned on their noradrenaline. Their calorie-burning speed increased as well, peaking between thirty and ninety minutes later. And it stayed high for more than 2½ hours.[3] All the while, the subjects did not exercise a bit. In fact, the experiments were done while they rested in bed.

Noradrenaline is also the reason why smokers are often leaner than nonsmokers. Smokers have long known that cigarettes help them stay slimmer. When they quit, they often gain weight. The reason is that cigarettes happen to increase noradrenaline just as carbohydrates do. When people who quit smoking lament what they see on the bathroom scale, what they are noticing, in large part, is the loss of the noradrenaline boost. The good news is you don't need to smoke to get that slimming effect. It comes to you in a very healthy way, as a natural part of a carbohydrate-rich diet.

While meat eaters' hormones are often set to favor weight gain rather than weight loss, which is particularly evident as they become less active in adulthood, a carbohydrate-rich menu increases both active thyroid hormone and noradrenaline and helps burn off the pounds.

Spaghetti, rice, beans, vegetables, and other complex carbs also contain potassium. Canadian researchers recently found that people with more potassium in their blood have faster calorie-burning speeds.[4] We have already seen how potassium helps keep calcium in the bones and lowers blood pressure. It also helps your weight-loss machinery.

As you can see, this is a radical departure from old-fashioned diets. Imagine eating delicious foods in generous amounts and still being able to watch your success on the bathroom scale week after week. No more minuscule portions. No more battles between discipline and gnawing hunger. Increasing carbohydrate is the first part of a wonderful new method that gets the results you have been waiting for, makes it easy to retain your progress, and is far easier than typical "diets."

The most powerful weight-control menu is a vegetarian one. Grains, vegetables, legumes, and fruits are modest in calories. They cannot add to your fat stores without losing nearly a quarter of their calorie content and in the process they turn on your ability to burn calories. The result is a powerful regimen that burns fat.

FOODS WITH THE NEGATIVE CALORIE EFFECT

All foods contain calories. But foods rich in complex carbohydrates are naturally low in calories, increase your calorie-burning, and reduce fat storage.

Grains	Vegetables	Legumes	Fruits
Rice	Potatoes	Black beans	Apples
Pasta	Broccoli	Pinto beans	Bananas
Oatmeal	Spinach	Kidney beans	Cherries
Cream of wheat	Swiss chard	Vegetarian baked	Grapefruit
Corn	Carrots	beans	Oranges
Pretzels	Sweet potatoes	Chickpeas	Peaches
Air-popped	Green beans	Green peas	Pears
popcorn		Lentils	

These are only examples. Other grains, legumes, vegetables, and fruits have similar effects, and the closer they are to their natural state, the better. That means leaving the fiber intact (e.g., choosing brown rice instead of white rice or whole grain bread instead of white bread) and not adding oils. The primary exceptions in the plant kingdom are nuts, seeds, avocados, soy products, and olives, which are high in fat and low in carbohydrate.

How does it work in practice? You'll have to try it to believe it. When meat eaters switch to vegetarian diets, they find that the more overweight they were, the more weight they lose. If they were markedly overweight, they typically lose a great deal and approach their ideal body weight without paying any attention to calorie counts or portion size.[5] Dr. Dean Ornish's well-known and extraordinary program used a low-fat vegetarian diet, along with modest exercise, stress reduction, and smoking cessation in a program to reverse heart disease. But his patients also lost weight. After a year, the average patient lost twenty-two pounds and one patient lost nearly a hundred pounds—all this with no calorie restriction whatsoever.

And the weight tends to stay off. People who stick to vegetarian diets stay thinner than meat eaters. In one study after another, researchers have found that, on average, people on vegetarian diets are a good 10 percent leaner than omnivores.[6]

A patient of mine was a high school teacher and coach who had been trim and athletic in his youth. But starting in his thirties, he began to gain weight and was now about sixty pounds heavier than when he finished college. He had dieted many times, but his weight problem always came back. It was difficult to convince him that if he paid attention only to the types of food he was eating, he could eat as much as he wanted and still lose weight. He finally agreed to try. He followed a low-fat vegetarian diet for three weeks. That meant no animal products at all and keeping vegetable oils to a minimum, too. Three weeks later, his weight had dropped enough so that his pants fit loosely and he had to break in a new notch on his belt. So he tried it for another three weeks. His weight problem continued to melt away. And his taste buds began to change: He began to prefer pasta, veggie chili, and bean burritos instead of the meat-and-poultry diet that had caused his problem.

That was five years ago. He never went back to the meaty diet that had gotten him into trouble, and his weight problem never returned. He feels better than ever and only wishes he had made the switch earlier.

TURNING THE FLAME EVEN HIGHER

Properly chosen, foods can be powerful metabolism boosters. But they are only half the prescription. The other half is getting your body moving. Working muscles turn the flame even higher. This does not mean exercise in the traditional sense of the word. You can get the "exercise" you need by walking around a park or shopping mall, dancing at a nightclub, playing tennis, or anything else that simply gets your body moving.

Movement burns calories, of course. But, more importantly, when your body is moving, your metabolism changes so calories are burned faster. Researchers have measured the metabolic rates of volunteers and watched how they change from moment to moment. These studies show that physical activity turns up your body's metabolism, not only while you are exercising, but for hours afterward as well. You even retain a bit of that fast calorie burning while you are asleep.

The combination of daily physical activity and the dietary changes described above is extremely powerful. It can give you back that teenager's metabolism that allows kids to eat huge amounts of food and never gain weight. It reminds your cells how to really burn off calories.

THE WORLD'S EASIEST AEROBIC EXERCISE

Complicated exercise programs are fine if you like them. Likewise, many people buy expensive shoes, rock and roll aerobics videos, and all kinds of special equipment. But they are not necessary, even for aggressive slimming down.

What I recommend is a half-hour walk every day. It gives you a good metabolic boost in just a short time. If you find it more convenient, go for an hour three times a week. Where and when you walk is up to you—down the sidewalk on your lunch hour, around your neighborhood in the evening, in a park or, yes, a shopping mall (so long as you can keep going past the distractions).

As for pace, don't dawdle, but don't feel that you have to reach any particular target pulse rate or have your elbows flying. Just walk at a good brisk pace. If it feels like a strain or if you are working so hard that you are unable to carry on a conversation, you are doing too much. Just feel your feet move, get your blood flowing, and enjoy your body.

You are not just dissolving fat. You are also dissolving the stresses of the day. Your eyes are looking out at longer distances, away from papers, books, and indoor activities.

If you have any medical condition, are severely overweight, or have been sedentary for some time, check with your doctor before any substantial increase in your physical activity.

IN THE GROOVE

Bodies in motion tend to stay in motion. Bodies at rest tend to stay at rest. The earth and all the other planets spin on their axes and revolve around the sun, generating the changes of seasons, all through their own momentum.

Momentum and inertia are fundamental to human life, too. We tend to continue whatever we have been doing lately. If you have taken a short walk after dinner every night this week, you are likely to do the same tonight. On the other hand, if you have been physically inactive for days on end, you are likely to stay inactive. These cycles continue day after day, week after week.

Physical activity keeps you in a healthy cycle. It tires your muscles out a bit so you will sleep better. You wake up refreshed and energetic so you are in the mood not only to tackle the events of the day but also to get out into the air and get your body moving again.

The opposite kind of cycle is very common. With too many things going on in our lives, we miss the physical activity our bodies would like. We get less sleep, too, and often need a morning cup of coffee just to wake up. When we get run-down and fatigued, we end up eating things we wish we hadn't and letting ourselves go in other ways. We feel stuck, without the energy to break out of the rut. If we can get momentum working for us instead of against us, we benefit enormously.

In physics there is a concept called activation energy. It simply means that just about any activity needs a little push to get started. A stone on a hillside will roll all the way to the bottom, but not until it gets a little push. Gasoline and oxygen will explode, releasing the enormous energy trapped in their molecular bonds, but they need a tiny spark for it to happen.

You might need a little push, too. If you feel a little reluctance to get on your feet, don't worry. That is simply a clue that you, like all heavenly bodies, respond to the laws of nature.

When you get going, you'll get another reward. Physical activity makes your appetite more regular and predictable. Binges are far less likely. This is especially helpful for people who have lost weight and want to stay slim.[7]

STEER CLEAR OF THE WEIGHT PROMOTERS

If you are serious about staying slim, it is vital not just to bring on the calorie-burning foods but also to avoid the foods that are responsible for added weight.

Your number-one enemy is fat. Whether it comes in red meat, chicken, fish, fried foods, butter, margarine, the oils on salads or pasta, or the grease in baked goods, fat is a serious problem any way you look at it. It is loaded with calories, it does nothing at all to help your metabolic rate, and it easily insinuates itself into whatever fat you already have.

Remember, every gram of fat contains nine calories. Carbohydrates have only four. When the fat you eat slides into your body fat, it loses only about 3 percent of its calories in the process, compared to 23 percent for carbohydrates.[8] And worst of all, that grease adds to your own fat layer without doing anything for your metabolism. Grease gives you no burn at all.[9]

Luckily, you will find very little fat in any vegetables, legumes, grains, or fruits, with very few exceptions. But animal products, even those advertised as being "low fat," usually contain much more of it than you would imagine.

Animal fat was designed by nature for the very purpose of storing calories for animals. Chickens, turkeys, cows, pigs, and fish all make fat to store calories. It is not only under their skin; their muscles are permeated with it. Trimming the fat off the outside will not remove the interior fat, which is much more extensive than what you can actually see. Light meat chicken, even without the skin, is about 20 percent fat (as a percentage of calories). That's a load of fat you do not need. At its very lowest, beef is about 30 percent fat. Fish vary in their fat content. Salmon is loaded with fat, while sole or haddock is lower, but all fish contain fat and never contain any complex carbohydrates or any fiber at all. They do not help you lose weight.

Vegetable oils are fattening, too. Sure, they are cholesterol-free and are usually low in saturated fats, but their calorie content is exactly the same as any other kind of fat, ounce for ounce. Take french fries, for example. A potato holds only about ninety-five calories. But when it is cut into french fries and dropped into hot cooking oil, it comes out with nearly three hundred calories entirely because of the oil that soaks in. Although animal fats and vegetable oils differ greatly in their effect on your cholesterol level, they all have exactly the same effect on your waistline.

To go for the best weight-control program, leave all animal products off your plate. That means no meat, poultry, fish, dairy products, or eggs. And throw out any margarine, salad oils, or frying oils that you find in your refrigerator. You'll soon prefer tomato or basil sauce on your spaghetti instead of meat sauce. You'll find that jam goes fine on toast without any butter in between and that Dijon mustard beats margarine on potatoes. Give it a chance. You'll see what I mean.

If you find yourself temporarily craving greasy foods, you are in good company. Almost everybody who changes his or her diet misses fatty foods for a couple of weeks, which is simply a sign that you have become habituated to them. That will pass, and more quickly than you might think. But grease cravings will continue indefinitely if you give in to the impulse and rekindle your taste buds' love affair with fat.

Check the fat content on baked goods you buy. Most breads, bagels, and pretzels are low in fat, while cookies, snack pastries, and croissants are usually at the other end of the spectrum. Compare the calories from fat and the total calories listed on the label. Fat calories should make up no more than 10 to 15 percent of the total.

Low-fat or no-fat salad dressings taste great and avoid the avalanche of grease that comes from the usual variety. Personally, I like a sprinkle of lemon or lime juice on salads or green vegetables.

Although fats and oils are by far the biggest fat promoters, there are two others worth mentioning. Alcohol is concentrated in calories, with seven calories per gram. In addition, alcohol reduces the body's ability to burn fat.[10] A beer belly is exactly what it sounds like.

Sugar is a bit more complicated. Many people blame their weight problems on sugar. But sugar is the simplest form of carbohydrate and, like any other carbohydrate, it has only four calories per gram. There is, however, one way in which sugar really can lead you astray. It is a Trojan Horse for fat. The sugar lures you to cookies, cakes, and pies, and the shortening or butter in them rearranges your profile. While people have tended to blame the sugar, it was really the fat lurking inside that did them in.

Theoretically, you could gain weight if you were to eat a huge amount of sweets. But if you would like to prove to yourself that it is mainly the fat content of sweet foods that does the damage, try gaining weight by eating oranges, apples, or any other sweet fruit. You will find that these essentially fat-free sweets do not promote weight problems.

This does not mean that sugar has no untoward effects. It can have a profound effect on moods, as we saw in chapter 2. However, it should not divert us from the real causes of weight problems.

BURN YOUR CALORIE CHART

You never need to diet again. Why should you cut calories anyway? For most people, the problem was never food quantity; it was food *type*. There is no need to count calories or to measure portion sizes. If every dieter's food scale were simultaneously run over by a car, the world would not gain an ounce.

Traditional diets are designed to fail. That is not to say that the people who plan them are trying to give you a hard time. But by their very design they cannot succeed over the long run for most people. Those diets are based on the idea that you gained weight from eating too much food and that if you would simply eat less, your body will have to burn fat to keep your body working. That makes sense to your brain, but your body fights it every step of the way.

When you stop eating normal amounts, your body misinterprets the diet as starvation. It knows all about starvation because, during the millions of years humans have been on earth, we have had to put up with food shortages over and over. So hard-wired into your chromosomes are antistarvation mechanisms that kick in *automatically* when you take in less food.

First, your metabolism slows down. A very low food intake causes more of your T_4 thyroid hormone to be converted to useless reverse T_3, signaling your cells to hold onto fat, not to get rid of it. Your metabolic rate can drop to 15 to 20 percent below normal, all as a result of a calorie-restricted diet.[11] And dieters know it. They begin to feel cold, constipated, and out of sorts. Their bodies are literally shutting down biological functions.

The slowed metabolism does not last for just a day or two. It can persist for weeks after the diet stops.[12] Researchers at the University of Pennsylvania put a group of women on a five-hundred-calorie diet for just over a month. Their calorie-burning speed dropped almost immediately, and took roughly another month after the diet ended to come back to normal. That's why diets can be so frustrating and why your weight can climb up to and beyond what it was when you started the diet. If, after a period of discouragement, you were to try another calorie-restricted diet, you may lose a bit of weight, followed by another rise back to your starting weight or even higher. This repeating yo-yo phenomenon simply reflects the body's attempts to fight starvation. Some people find that the more diets they try, the heavier they get. It is as if their bodies are storing a little extra fat just in case starvation returns again.

I do not recommend cutting down on your portions. If you do, here is a vital tip: So long as your daily diet includes at least ten calories per day per pound of your target weight, you are not likely to slow your metabolism. For example, if your ideal weight is 150, you should consume at least 1,500 calories per day. Below that, you will slow your metabolism.

BINGES ARE CAUSED BY DIETS

Binges are not caused by a lack of willpower. If you have come to feel that your willpower is not as strong as the next person's, set that thought aside once and for all. Your willpower is every bit as good as anyone else's. Binges are caused not by weak discipline but by diets. Any unusual restriction on the quantity of foods you consume leads to a strong tendency to overeat later. When you eat a normal amount of food at regular meals, binges are much less likely.

If you focus on the types of foods you eat and forget the quantity, your metabolism will remain active and you will be much less likely to overdo it. Typical diets do just the opposite, and that is why you do not want to go anywhere near them.

COMPULSIVE EATING

Most people with weight problems eat no more than anyone else. Their problem is the type of food they eat, not the quantity. However, about 15 percent of people with weight problems do eat unusually large amounts of food. They turn to food in response to emotions: feeling alone, depressed, or angry. Their eating takes on a compulsive, out-of-control feeling. They may feel ashamed of their eating habits and hide food. They eat differently when they are alone than when with other people.

If this has been your experience, you can conquer this problem for good. The solution is twofold. First, follow a menu that makes portions less important. Vegetarian foods without added fat help you to slim down naturally so you can eat normal quantities without feeling guilty. Do not underestimate the power or importance of this step. It is absolutely decisive.

Second, let other people support you psychologically as you break the food compulsion. Overeaters Anonymous is enormously helpful and highly recommended. Meetings are free and can be found in your local phone directory. With the right kinds of foods going for you and the psychological support of Overeaters Anonymous, you have an unbeatable combination.

THE WORLD'S EASIEST WEIGHT-BEARING EXERCISE

This section is for extra credit. You can ignore it and still get a terrific calorie burn. But it can add another dimension to weight control.

Muscles are your calorie burners. Muscle cells just eat them up. So you want to keep your shoulder and thigh muscles strong. How do you do that? Any kind of regular movement helps—even walking, because walking does not just move your feet. It uses all your leg muscles. Your torso moves with every step and your arms move actively from the shoulders. Your neck muscles work to keep your head in balance, toning themselves in the process.

The largest muscles of the body are in your legs. Starting at your buttocks, your leg muscles move your thigh backward, forward, and out to the side. They flex and straighten your knees and move your ankles and toes. Regular walking and routine use of stairs keep these muscles in great shape.

Modified sit-ups are terrific for your abdomen and back. Lie down on your back and elevate your calves and feet by resting them on a chair seat or bench. Put your hands behind your head. Gently raise your shoulders a few inches from the floor and then lower them back down. As you do these sit-ups, alternate pointing your left elbow toward your right knee and your right elbow toward your left knee to give your abdominal muscles a good even workout. The goal is just to tighten your stomach muscles. Don't try to touch your elbows to your knees or to sit all the way up. Ten repetitions every other day is a good goal. If you find sit-ups uncomfortable, keep your shoulders on the floor and raise your knees instead.

The muscles in the upper body—the shoulders and upper arms— tend to be neglected because, unlike our primate cousins, we do not use our arms to move ourselves around. Any routine lifting and carrying works all the muscles of your arms and shoulders. If you want more, push-ups work the muscles of the upper arms and chest. You can start from your knees, if necessary. If you can do ten every other day, these muscles will stay well toned. If you like, you can find mini-barbells at sporting goods stores. They are not especially necessary, but if you do get a set, start with less weight than you think you'll need. Three to five pounds or so is plenty and increase only when you are comfortable. There are five basic movements for your shoulders and arms. Your upper arm moves forward, backward, and out to the side. Your forearm only goes forward and back at the elbow. That is all it was designed for. You can pump mini-barbells in these five directions while you watch television or while you walk, about ten repetitions in each direction. It is more important that exercise be regular than that it be vigorous.

These simple exercises keep your muscles healthy and active. In return, your muscles will burn calories for you, helping you keep slim.

PERMANENT WEIGHT CONTROL

- Increase high-carbohydrate foods, such as pasta, rice, potatoes, breads, beans, and vegetables. They boost active thyroid hormone and noradrenaline to burn calories faster and cannot go straight to fat.
- A half-hour walk every day (or one hour three times a week) increases your metabolism even further.
- Avoid animal products and added oils. They hold densely packed calories.
- Keep alcohol modest and intermittent.
- Avoid calorie restrictions, especially those below ten calories per day per pound of your target weight.
- Compulsive eating can be conquered by a low-fat vegetarian diet in combination with Overeaters Anonymous.

BEYOND GENETICS

Some of us will always be a little taller, and others will be shorter. Likewise, everyone has a little different body size and shape. Part of that is genetic.[13] But it is easy to overestimate the effect of heredity. If everyone in your family was a bit heavyset, it may be a genetic tendency. But it may also reflect food habits and preferences that are passed from parent to child, generation after generation. Whatever your genetic endowment, the guidelines for food choices and simple physical activity that you have read here can help you slim down to the size that nature had in mind for you.

Some people tend to carry their weight in their hips and buttocks. This fat is the most resistant to any type of weight-loss regimen and luckily is the least likely to contribute to health problems. Weight in the abdomen, however, is a strong contributor to all kinds of health problems: heart disease, high blood pressure, diabetes, and cancer. Health risks are significant if a man's waist measurement is greater than his hips at the widest point or if a woman's waist is more than 80 percent of her hip measurement.

If your measurements come out better than that, weight control is not a medical issue for you. It is only a personal or cosmetic issue.

A low-fat vegetarian diet with regular physical activity will help you get to your goal and keep you there. You are not chained by heredity. Yes, some of us will be a little bigger and some a little smaller. But what really limits most of us is desire. If you really want to take control of your body and give this delightfully simple but powerful program a try, you will soon see just how wonderfully it works.

CHAPTER ELEVEN

HEALTHY SKIN AND HAIR

I t was once believed that wrinkles were caused simply by the passage of
time. They are not, or certainly not by time alone.

The time theory seemed like a reasonable conclusion because the
older people are, the more wrinkles they tend to have. However, older
people are also more likely to have heart disease, high blood pressure, and
diabetes, all of which have turned out not to be due to aging but rather to
specific factors that can be controlled. Each of these conditions is preventable. Is it possible that the skin changes we thought were caused by aging
could be similar?

Wrinkles are not caused by facial expressions either. Children smile,
frown, and grimace all day long. They have no wrinkles because their skin
bounces back like a brand-new sponge. Only when the natural proteins
that keep the skin resilient are destroyed do lines and wrinkles form that
reflect your customary facial expressions.

The main causes of wrinkles and discolorations of the skin are sun
damage and free radicals. And that means that you can shield your skin
with protective nutrients, guard against dangerous exposures, and use
special treatments to further protect and rejuvenate your skin. And, in the
process, you'll make some of that damage bounce right off.

The skin has two layers. The one that really needs protection is the
dermis, the skin's underlayer, which provides strength and support like
an artist's canvas. The strength comes from collagen protein strands,
which spread out in every direction to keep the skin from being stretched
too far. Elastic fibers help the skin spring back after movement. If this

"canvas" is intact, your skin is healthy and resilient. When it is damaged, it sags from your bones like a worn painting drooping off its stretcher. The outer layer, the epidermis, is like artist's paint on a canvas, giving it color and protection. Its keratin proteins toughen and waterproof the skin, and special cells, called melanocytes, produce melanin pigments for skin color and tanning.

The next time you are drying off from a shower, take a look at your skin. Notice that the parts of your body that are exposed to the sun—your face or the backs of your hands—are a bit more weathered than protected areas, such as the inside of your upper arm.

Sunlight damages your skin. The light you can see is not the problem. The damaging part is ultraviolet. With a much shorter wavelength than visible light, it flies through space like a stream of bullets, rather than a long sleepy wave. Ultraviolet C has the shortest wavelength and if it could reach the earth's surface, it would fry us like pancakes. Luckily, oxygen and ozone in the atmosphere screen it out. Ultraviolet B is not so destructive as ultraviolet C, but because of its longer wavelength, the atmosphere lets much of it pass on through. You can blame ultraviolet B for most of the wrinkles or spots you may have on your skin. Ultraviolet A has the longest wavelength and easily penetrates the atmosphere. The long wavelength also makes it somewhat less damaging to the skin. It can still do harm, however, especially when it is intensely concentrated, for example, in tanning bulbs.

Ultraviolet rays can hit you even if you are not in direct sun. They bounce off sand on a beach or concrete in your driveway, just as visible light does, and diffuse across the sky before reaching the earth's surface. Thin clouds are not much protection. They block only 20 to 40 percent of ultraviolet rays.

When sunlight hits your skin, 90 to 95 percent of it penetrates. That is what we need to protect against. We can do that by shielding ourselves against these rays and using foods to protect the skin internally. But first, let's look at what actually happens in the skin.

Damage to the upper epidermis is no problem because this layer is constantly rejuvenated from below. When ultraviolet rays reach the dermis, however, they can destroy skin cells and protein fibers.

Ultraviolet light can damage skin directly. But much of the damage is indirect. Ultraviolet rays spark the production of oxygen-free radicals that, as you know, can attack DNA, proteins, and anything else within their reach.[1] As they knock out the collagen and elastic fibers, the skin loses its resilience. It becomes thin and starts to wrinkle. So the exposed parts of your skin age much faster.[2] Even areas as close together as the skin in front of your ear, which is sun-exposed, and the skin behind your ear, which is more shaded, are as different as day and night in how well they retain their natural resilience.[3]

If you were to pull one or two threads out of a canvas, the difference would be imperceptible. But if you were to remove a few more each day, the painting would eventually start to fall apart. Similarly, it takes a while before you notice the damage to your protein fibers. But most adults have already lost quite a few strands from their dermis because of excess sun exposure as children. It is easy to do. It appears that *any* sun exposure, even modest tanning, sparks the production of free radicals and causes some damage to dermal proteins.

This does not mean that the situation is hopeless—far from it. Let's take a look at how to protect ourselves inside and out.

SKIN-PROTECTING FOODS

Art galleries never put paintings near windows and always use lightbulbs that filter out ultraviolet. And the paintings actually defend themselves, so to speak. Dark pigments, like ferrous oxide or carbon black, screen out light and protect the painting against light-induced damage.

Your skin tries to protect itself in the same way. The melanocytes darken the epidermis to screen out ultraviolet. Like a painter with thirty-six hands, a single melanocyte sends melanin pigment out through finger-like projections to three dozen skin cells, coloring each one.[4] Dark-skinned people have no more melanocytes than light-skinned people, but each one produces more melanin, providing much better protection.

As good as this system is, it can use some help. You can give your skin much more protection with both foods and skin care products.

Antioxidants.   Did you ever wonder how plants can stand the sunlight they soak up hour after hour, day after day? If you or I were to stay out in the sun for that long, our skin would shrivel. But plants use the sun's energy to power the chlorophyll machinery that keeps them alive without showing any signs of damage.

Why are plants not affected by the sun? The fact is, they are. The sun forms destructive free radicals in plants just as it does in human skin. But plants have beta-carotene—lots of it—to neutralize free radicals as they form. In an interesting test, a researcher in Berkeley, California, developed a single-celled plant that could not make beta-carotene. As soon as the plant was exposed to light and air, it died.[5] Beta-carotene is vital protection.

It can protect you, too. If you have carrots, sweet potatoes, or other orange or green vegetables on your plate, their beta-carotene readily passes into your skin and helps protect it. If you get a very large amount, either as carrots and sweet potatoes or as pills, you might even notice a trace of its orange color in your skin, which, by the way, is temporary and harmless.

In the early part of the twentieth century, doctors used vegetable-rich diets to help people with very light complexions tan rather than burn.[6] Indeed, they tolerate sun much longer when their diets are rich in beta-carotene.[7] Boston researcher Micheline Matthews-Roth went to unusual lengths to demonstrate beta-carotene's effect. She fed beta-carotene to prison inmates in Arizona for several weeks and then brought them out into direct sun. As expected, beta-carotene made it harder to burn and easier to tan.[8]

Just two carrots supply twenty to thirty milligrams of beta-carotene, which is equivalent to the amounts used in most scientific studies. Vegetables and other foods from plants also supply a full range of other antioxidants that help protect the body tissues: vitamins C and E, the mineral selenium, and other natural compounds that work as a team to knock out the free radicals sunlight generates.

Skin damage is accumulated very slowly, and over the long term, vegetable-rich diets provide a measure of protection.[9] However, this effect is very mild and can easily be overpowered by intense sun exposure. So the best defense combines a healthful diet with protections against sun exposure, as we will see shortly.

Immune Builders.   To protect against skin discolorations and skin cancer, you can actually build your skin's immune protection. This requires three steps: avoiding ultraviolet light, increasing antioxidant-rich foods, and reducing oils in the diet.

Researchers in Sydney, Australia, sent a group of Caucasian men and women to a tanning salon for twelve half-hour treatments. Afterward, the researchers tested their immunity. The subjects were nicely tanned, but they could not make antibodies as well as they had before. In addition, their T cells were activated to turn immune functions off and they had less natural killer cell activity.[10] In other words, their immune defenses were down. This could affect them in many ways, of course, but, most notably, when ultraviolet light damages immunity, it makes skin cancer more likely.

A word about skin cancer: Basal cell or squamous cell cancers are easily treated in most cases, but malignant melanomas are more serious. They usually start as normal moles but develop into irregular shapes, typically larger than a quarter inch in diameter, with varied coloration. Any mole with these characteristics should be promptly checked by a dermatologist. That is also true for moles that change in size or appearance, become itchy or painful, bleed, or arise after age forty.

Here is an important, if surprising, point: Although excess sun exposure increases the risk of melanomas, when they crop up, they are often on skin that was not sun-exposed. The reason is that immune changes caused by ultraviolet light affect the entire body.[11]

Shielding against ultraviolet light helps protect the skin's immune strength. Foods help, too. Just as beta-carotene protects against free radicals and builds your immunity in general, it also improves your defenses against skin cancer. It gives your skin more immune strength.

More surprising is the effect of reducing fat in the diet. Cutting fat intake in half dramatically reduces the risk of precancerous skin changes.[12] At issue is not just how much fat you eat but also the type. Fats and oils in the diet end up in your cell membranes, and the proportions of monounsaturated, polyunsaturated, or saturated fats in your cells tend to mirror your diet. Researchers have consistently found that people who stay free of skin cancer are more likely to have used monounsaturated oils, such as olive or canola oil. People with skin cancer tend to have consumed more polyunsaturated oils, such as safflower oil.[13]

Both mono- and polyunsaturated oils are popular, of course, because they do not raise blood cholesterol levels as saturated fats do. But polyunsaturated oils are very fragile, so to speak; they are particularly vulnerable to free radical attack. (This is true not only in your body but on the shelf. Pastries made with polyunsaturated oils tend to go rancid quickly, due to free radical oxidation.) When polyunsaturates enter the cell membranes of the skin, your skin cells become more sensitive to sunburn and to other forms of sun damage. Monounsaturates, such as olive oil, are much more stable. Saturated fats, such as animal fat or tropical oils, are quite stable as well, but these waxy substances are a problem from the standpoint of cholesterol, as we saw in chapter 8. The best advice on oils, however, is not to use olive oil, as opposed to soybean oil, but rather to keep all oils to a minimum.

SKIN-PROTECTING FOODS

- Have plenty of vegetables each day. Include orange and yellow varieties (e.g., sweet potatoes, carrots) as well as dark green vegetables. Guidelines for serving numbers and sizes are listed in chapter 12.
- Include whole grains and legumes (beans, peas, and lentils) in your daily menu for vitamin E and selenium.
- Avoid animal products.
- Keep oils to a minimum.

FOUR KINDS OF EXTERNAL PROTECTION

Unlike your arteries, heart, liver, or just about any other part of your body, your skin has direct contact with air, sunlight, and pollutants. So its "aging" process begins early in life. But unlike all your internal organs, you can apply protective balms directly to it. Although this book is mainly about foods, there are four skin treatments that you should know about that can rejuvenate and invigorate your skin. Together, they can actually help the skin recover from the elements.

"Damaged skin can repair itself," said Albert M. Kligman, M.D., Ph.D., of the University of Pennsylvania Department of Dermatology. "Like any other part of the body, the skin has a marvelous capacity to recover from injury. But you first have to remove the cause of the injury. For the skin, that means stopping sun damage." We can help the repair process along with the judicious use of sunblocks, moisturizers, exfoliants, and Retin-A.

Sunblockers. Most of your sun damage occurs not during vacations or tanning sessions but simply in the course of daily life, as you get out of your car, wait for a bus, walk down the street, or chat with friends. You cannot avoid the sun all the time, nor would anyone want to. But avoiding midday sun and taking advantage of the protection supplied by hats, clothing, and sunglasses really helps. Skip the tanning salon. Even though they now use bulbs that deliver ultraviolet A rather than ultraviolet B, the dose of ultraviolet A that is required to tan is so large that it also contributes to skin aging, particularly since ultraviolet A penetrates more deeply than ultraviolet B.

Sunscreens help, particularly for those with light skin. Used daily, sunblocks help prevent wrinkles. They also protect against precancerous skin changes and can sometimes even cause skin lesions to go away on their own.[14] They help prevent other skin problems, such as depigmented areas, telangiectasia (fine red lines caused by ultraviolet damage to tiny blood vessels), and the brown, irregular "age spots" that form on sun-exposed skin.

Look for two things in any sunscreen you buy. It should screen out both ultraviolet A and B and have a sun-protection factor (SPF) of 15 or higher. The SPF rating indicates the increase in the length of time it takes to burn. For example, if you would normally burn in twenty minutes under direct sun, a sunscreen with an SPF of 2 would protect you for forty minutes and one with an SPF of 10 would protect you for two hundred minutes. Do not take these figures too literally, though, because perspiration and swimming can cause sunscreens to wash off.

There is no need to swear off the beach or picnics. People love the sun. A little sunlight on a regular basis is needed for normal vitamin D metabolism, although you do not need very much sun to do the job and it can be on any part of your body. Light is also a part of our mood regulation system, although this works through the eyes, not the skin. But sunscreens help you enjoy the outdoors while protecting your skin. If you want a deep-looking tan without shriveling into a prune, new cosmetic products do the job safely and temporarily without the sun by dyeing the outermost cells. In a few days your tanned cells are sloughed off and normal skin color returns.

Moisturizers. In a shady, tropical jungle, your skin would not have much trouble keeping its natural moisture. But that hardly describes the world most of us live in nowadays. "We are naked animals," said Dr. Kligman. "Our skin takes a beating every day, and not just from the sun. Soaps dry the skin. Chemicals in cosmetic products add to the damage. Many people apply twenty to a hundred different chemicals to their skin every day in the cosmetics they use. Over time, they take a real toll."

Hopeless situation? Not at all. Many products are available to help you fight back, keeping natural moisture in the skin. "Ideally, moisturizers should be used starting in early childhood," said Dr. Kligman. "They really help a great deal. And the best ones are the simplest. The less expensive they are, the fewer ingredients they will contain, and that's better for your skin."

Exfoliants. New skin cells form at the bottom of the epidermis. As they mature, they rise to the skin's surface and eventually die and fall off. Products that help remove dead cells give the skin a smoother appearance and help moisturizers and other treatments to work better. Many are now available for daily or twice-daily use. "I would avoid the ones with scrubbing particles in them," said Dr. Kligman. "They scratch the skin. The new alpha hydroxy exfoliants are preferable." Alpha hydroxy acids are fruit acids that loosen dead cells, allowing them to fall away. You will find many brands of alpha hydroxy acids and detailed instructions for their use at any cosmetic counter.

Retin-A. Of all skin products, Retin-A (tretinoin) has created by far the greatest stir. It slows sun-induced skin aging and even reverses it to an extent. Fine wrinkles disappear and discolorations fade. The skin takes on a rosy appearance, with improved elasticity and firmness. Retin-A is actually a relative of beta-carotene. It works by stimulating cells in the epidermis to divide and by encouraging the growth of new collagen protein.[15]

It is not quick. It usually takes several months to work. Initially, it is used nightly. After the first year, many people can use it just twice a week. Mild skin irritation and dryness can occur, especially at the beginning, so moisturizing creams are helpful in the morning. For people with especially sensitive skin, Retin-A should be used every two to three days instead of daily. The cream also increases the sensitivity to sunburn, so sunscreens are important.

Occasionally, after three to five weeks of treatment, reddish spots temporarily appear on the skin. This is good. These are precancerous areas that were already present and are now being obliterated by the Retin-A.

Who benefits most from Retin-A? "For people who start using Retin-A in their thirties and forties, close to 100 percent will see a noticeable improvement in their skin," said Dr. Kligman. "On the other hand, people who have had severe sun damage for many years will not get much from it."

Although Retin-A is sold by prescription, it does not appear to have serious side effects. Researchers have looked for links with cancer, birth defects, or other dangers of long-term use, but have not found any. "Retin-A does not cause cancer," Dr. Kligman said. "In fact, compounds in this family have been shown to prevent cancer of many types. Some clinicians might be reluctant to give Retin-A—or any other medication—to pregnant women, but it is not well absorbed through the skin and large studies show no evidence of birth defects."

These four treatments are often used together. Moisturizers and sunscreens are used each morning. For convenience, combination creams containing both a moisturizer and a sunscreen are now available. Retin-A is used in the evening. Exfoliants can be used once or twice a day.

ROUTINE FOR EXTERNAL PROTECTION

Morning: Apply alpha hydroxy lotion or cream. Then use a combined moisturizer-sunscreen.

Midday: Reapply sunscreen if in direct sun.

Evening: Apply Retin-A or reapply alpha hydroxy lotion or cream.

OTHER FACTORS

Other factors affect the skin. Tobacco and alcohol both contribute to the production of free radicals, and you can see their effect on the skin. Wrinkling is markedly accelerated, and smokers can also develop a slight yellowing of the skin.

Some people find that dairy products make their skin greasy and that avoiding them helps their skin clear up. I noticed this effect quite strongly in a married couple whom I have known for a long time. They are both physicians and had been vegetarians for years, but they continued to consume cheese and other dairy products. They both had persistent oiliness of their skin, which they figured was due to the climate. One day, after not having seen them for a couple of months, I was invited to their home for dinner. I noticed that they both had very healthy-looking skin, and the oiliness was gone. It turned out that they had stopped using dairy products a few weeks earlier, and the improvement was quite noticeable. Many people find the same thing.

I cannot tell you why this happens. It may be that dairy fat affects the oiliness of the skin directly. Oils in the diet enter into the cells of the body, and the skin is no exception. However, the effect may also be a sensitivity to the dairy protein, which is known to cause a wide variety of reactions.

In women, higher levels of androgens ("male hormones") can increase oil production in the skin, leaving skin noticeably oilier.[16] As we saw in chapter 3, foods have a strong influence over hormone production. Dietary changes, sometimes along with natural progesterone, have been used to restore hormone balance in women (see page 220 and pages 93–95). Increases in testosterone levels do not seem to affect skin oiliness in men, since their hormone-induced oil production tends to be fairly high all the time.

HEALTHY EYES

The eyes are the most specialized part of the body's surface. They are designed to take in light and convert the blues and greens and reds you see into nerve impulses for the brain to interpret and remember. But along with the visible light, they get a whopping dose of ultraviolet, which assaults the eyes just as it does the skin. As ultraviolet light passes through the lens, it encourages free radicals to form. They, in turn, spark damaging chemical reactions that lead to cataracts.[17]

Foods can defend you. If your diet is rich in fruits and vegetables, their beta-carotene, vitamin C, and vitamin E pass into your eyes and neutralize free radicals as they form.[18] Avoiding smoking and excess iron will help, too.[19]

Avoiding milk may help, strange as that may sound. As the milk sugar, lactose, is digested, it produces a simple sugar called galactose, which can enter the lens.[20] Infants who lack the enzymes that normally break down galactose develop cataracts within the first year of life. Adults may be affected, too. Countries where dairy products are commonly used have a much higher incidence of cataracts than those where dairy products are rarely consumed.[21] The problem is in the milk sugar rather than the fat, so all dairy products—even skim milk—are under equal suspicion.

Of course, ophthalmologists are more than happy to replace your natural lenses with spanking new synthetic ones, but with the right foods on your side, you may never need them.

As we saw in chapter 1, green vegetables contain carotenoids, which help protect against macular degeneration, a loss of function of the retina that can occur in older people.

HEALTHY HAIR

In the mid-1960s, the Beatles sparked a new language for the age-old conflicts between parents and kids. On the surface, the argument was about hair. Children who wanted to annoy their parents grew their hair. Parents could humiliate their children by insisting on a trim. Hair became a code for assertiveness or insubordination, depending on which end of the scissors you were on.

It did not begin in the 1960s. Hair has been a symbol of power and sexuality ever since Delilah hacked off Samson's mane. But symbols change. Samson's strength may have been in his hair, but the U.S. Marines' image of disciplined strength is a razor cut. When Michael Jordan was at the top of the basketball world, his bald head symbolized athletic prowess. A mop-top Michael Jordan would have looked silly. Lots of teenagers shaved their heads at the same time, and skinheads somehow arrived at the same hairstyle as Buddhist monks. One group defies authority; the other defies worldliness.

Nowadays, hair can be long, short, or absent, and the color of your hair can change with the color of your socks. Hair has caused so much conflict over the decades that it is remarkable how little acrimony there is at present.

As with every other aspect of our biology, foods play a role in the health of our hair, including whether it grows or falls out, and maybe even when it turns gray.

KEEPING YOUR HAIR

Nature's razor has made us remarkably hairless animals. Our cooling system depends on it. Dogs lose heat by panting, but we lose heat through perspiration, and a hairy coat would get in the way.

All our lives, nature is adjusting its work. It quickly replaces the bald-ness of babies with a full head of hair. At puberty, nature subtracts hair at the temples, both in men and women, and adds it to other parts of the body.

Pubic and underarm hair helps spread our own animal scents, for bet-ter or worse. These parts of human anatomy were omitted from classical paintings from the fifteenth through the nineteenth centuries, an omis-sion that so misled nineteenth-century art critic John Ruskin that, upon marrying, he reportedly believed his new wife was abnormal and sought an annulment.[22]

The average human scalp has about 100,000 hair follicles. Blondes have more; redheads have fewer. As buds and flowers bloom in the spring, hair tends to grow more, too, and it falls out more in autumn.

For just about every adult—man or woman—hair thins a bit with time. A tendency toward early hair loss is genetic. If your family tree gleams with bald heads, it is very likely that, sooner or later, you will have some hair loss. However, *when* that happens is another matter. Evidence suggests that food choices influence the hormones that lead to hair loss. Whether you lose your hair at forty or at sixty may well depend on the foods you choose.

Common hair loss depends on testosterone. Without it, you will not lose your hair even if every last one of your male ancestors was totally bald. This was dramatically demonstrated by James B. Hamilton of Yale University in 1942, who showed that testosterone is like a natural hair remover. Men who had had the misfortune of being castrated before pu-berty never became bald, no matter how old they were. In men who had started losing their hair, castration (done for other medical reasons) abruptly stopped the hair recession. If either of these groups of men re-ceived testosterone injections, however, baldness quickly proceeded to match that of their male relatives. If the testosterone injections were stopped, baldness stopped advancing.[23]

In men, testosterone is made in the testes. It travels in the blood-stream to the hair follicles. But testosterone does not kill off the hair folli-cles directly. Inside the follicle, it is converted to a much more powerful hormone called DHT (dihydrotestosterone). (As we saw in chapter 6,

DHT also affects the prostate.) DHT influences the hair follicles profoundly and does so in entirely different ways in different parts of the body. On the face and chest, DHT stimulates the growth of thick curly hair. On the scalp, however, it makes hair thin out and eventually kills off the follicles altogether.[24] The skin above the forehead and at the temples and crown is quick to turn testosterone into DHT and is especially sensitive to its effects.[25] Compared to Asian men, Americans have more of the enzyme that converts testosterone to DHT and have more body hair and more baldness as a result.[26]

Women make a trace of testosterone in addition to much larger amounts of estrogens and progesterone. The amount of testosterone in a woman's body is far less than that of a man, but if, for some reason, it increases, the hair on her scalp will become thinner. In women who have a strong genetic predisposition, even normal amounts of testosterone can cause hair loss.[27] This is precisely the same phenomenon as occurs in men but is muted by the smaller amounts of testosterone women have.

When hair loss occurs in women, it tends to be fairly even over the top of the head and is rarely total, as it can be in men. Testosterone reveals the genetics of your scalp, and the difference between men and women simply reflects the difference in how much of it is in the blood.

Even keeping genetics constant, rates of baldness seem to be affected by food patterns. For example, in Japan, as the traditional rice-based diet is replaced by meat and other Western influences, dermatologists have noticed that baldness appears to be more common and to occur earlier.[28] As we saw in chapter 3, high-fat foods increase testosterone production[29] and reduce the amount of sex hormone binding globulin[30] that keeps it in check. The result is more free testosterone to enter the hair follicle and to send your hair down the bathroom drain. Low-fat high-fiber foods do the opposite, slowing down hormone production and speeding up hormone elimination.

Are these changes really enough to make a difference? Some evidence suggests that they are. Over the course of the year, hormones change in a natural rhythm. Testosterone levels drop in men each spring, and that drop corresponds with a lower rate of hair loss and more hair growth. In the fall, testosterone levels peak, increasing hair loss in both men and women.[31] The changes in sex hormone levels that can come from diet are similar in strength to the seasonal changes that have a measurable effect on hair growth. A low-fat plant-based diet maintains a springtime hormone level year-round.

This does not mean that dietary changes can forestall baldness forever. However, evidence does suggest that the right food choices may well help you make the most of your genetic endowment. The foods that keep hormone effects at bay are vegetables, fruits, grains, and legumes. When your salad arrives at your table, if you sprinkle it with a little lemon juice, you'll be fine. But if you douse it with oil or top it with grated cheese, you're starting down the road toward increased hormone effects. If your soup is minestrone, you'll get a bit of pasta and fiber-rich vegetables. If you had cream of mushroom, you can just imagine what that grease will do to your basic biology. When your entrée arrives, it is angel hair pasta with a light marinara sauce and vegetables on the side. Luckily, you did not order the chicken, which has plenty of hormone-boosting fat and cholesterol but no hormone-taming fiber at all.

The next question is, at what stage of life do hormones exert their greatest influence? Some have suggested that a "biological clock" is set in motion at puberty, causing physical changes to play themselves out depending on the hormone levels that were present at puberty. This theory has been advanced by cancer researchers who cite evidence that the diet followed at puberty has the greatest influence over breast cancer risk later on and also by dermatologists looking at hormonal influences on hair loss.[32] However, diet clearly influences hormones throughout life, suggesting that, while those who are raised on low-fat vegetarian diets are likely to be healthiest, it is never too late to benefit from changing your diet and restoring hormone balance.

EVALUATING HAIR LOSS OR EXCESS

Men who lose their hair rarely seek (or need) medical help, and women who have very slight hair loss may have nothing more than a modest equivalent of male hair loss. Women with more than mild hair loss or hair loss accompanied by menstrual irregularities, acne, or facial hair growth often benefit from a medical evaluation to test for polycystic ovary syndrome, ovarian tumors, adrenal disorders, or other treatable problems.

Other causes of hair loss in women include thyroid problems, stress, high fever, chemical hair treatments, and hairstyles that persistently tug on the hair. An autoimmune cause is believed to be responsible for a type of patchy or diffuse hair loss called alopecia areata. Obesity contributes to hair loss, too. Overweight women with hormone-related hair changes and menstrual irregularities often find that their symptoms improve with weight loss alone.[33]

Childbirth almost always causes some degree of temporary hair loss, sometimes occurring after a delay of a few months. In other animals, this has a useful function—rabbits, for example, line their nests with shed hairs. Humans have less use for it.

People who are malnourished and/or anemic often find that their hair becomes thinner. In Western countries, the greatest risk is for those on calorie-restricted diets.[34] Even a 1200–calorie diet, which is by no means as severe as some that have been offered, can cause diffuse shedding of hair. Part of the reason may be the reduction in active thyroid hormone that is caused by dieting,[35] as we saw in chapter 10. That chapter presents a much better weight control method that avoids calorie restrictions and has just the opposite effect on thyroid hormone.

Hair loss can be caused by medications, including ibuprofen, birth control pills, cimetidine, clofibrate, colchicine, chemotherapy agents, heparin, coumarin derivatives, propranolol, and antiseizure medications. High doses of vitamin A can cause hair loss, among many other problems. Boric acid, which is commonly used as an urban insecticide and in manufacturing, can cause hair loss if ingested.[36]

Aside from getting our diet in order, what are the current treatments? The best-tested treatment is minoxidil (Rogaine). Used topically, it works in about 30 percent of users, both male and female. It usually takes several months to see results. If it is discontinued, baldness returns. Retin-A (tretinoin) works, too, both alone and in a mixture with minoxidil. Dermatologists occasionally use medications that block testosterone's effects and reverse hair thinning in women, although they are not used in men because they are often feminizing.

When premenopausal women have significant hair loss, natural progesterone cream may be helpful. While it is mainly used to treat premenstrual syndrome and to build bone in postmenopausal women, it also seems to help restore hair lost in premenopausal women who have ovulatory disturbances.[37] When ovulation does not occur, the normal progesterone peak is missed so other hormones are produced in higher quantities in order to supply compounds that would normally be made from progesterone. These hormones have masculinizing effects, causing scalp hair loss and increased facial hair. Natural progesterone can block that effect. The use of natural progesterone cream is discussed on pages 172 to 175.

HAIR COLOR AND TEXTURE

The melanocytes that color your skin do the same for your hair. They are the starving artists of the body, with a palette that holds only two colors. Deep brown eumelanin—the same pigment that provides skin color—makes hair black or brown, depending on how much of it your cells pack into each hair. Pheomelanin makes hair red. Blond hairs contain very little pigment and are thinner. Melanocytes can mix these colors depending on your heredity.

These economical artists make both pigments from just one amino acid called tyrosine. And they do that with just one enzyme called tyrosinase. As clever as they are, their productive lives are tragically short. Eventually, they can no longer produce as much melanin as is needed to keep the hairs colored, and the enzymes that make melanin are lost. When that happens, the hair turns gray and eventually white. Some have suggested that, as hair whitens, the melanocytes are not dead but simply retired.[38] In one case, they went back to work after a few decades off. In a 1981 report in the *British Journal of Dermatology*, a seventy-two-year-old woman who had had white hair for many years developed a chronic scalp infection and her hair fell out. When she was treated, her hair regrew and was jet black as it had been decades earlier. Her doctors called it "postinflammatory pigmentation" but never explained it.[39]

Not much is yet known about links between diet and graying of the hair. However, free radicals have not yet been acquitted of playing a role in the process. First, stress has been observed to accelerate hair graying in accounts that have varied from scientific to fanciful. In the latter category come several reports. When Mumtaz Mahal died in 1631, her husband was so aggrieved that his hair reportedly turned white within two weeks. He built the Taj Mahal in her memory. Marie Antoinette was only thirty-eight at her execution, and reports have it that, as the political clouds darkened, her hair suddenly blanched. The *Boston Medical and Surgical Journal* of 1851 reported the case of a gambler who staked $1,000 on a single card, and under such stress his hair turned white the next morning. The journal did not say whether he won the bet.[40]

Loss of hair color due to stress is not an entirely capricious idea. The sudden hair loss called alopecia areata can be triggered by stress and when it occurs, pigmented hairs fall out, leaving the white hairs behind.[41]

Stress encourages the production of free radicals and depletes antioxidants. One might speculate that under accelerated free radical attack the melanocytes die out earlier than they otherwise might. A role for free radicals is also suggested by the observation that men who have heart attacks before age fifty are more likely than other men to have gone gray in their twenties.[42] This has not been found in women. Free radical attacks encourage heart disease, as we saw in chapter 8, and it would not be surprising to learn that free radicals damage the melanocytes and their enzymes that make hair pigment. Nor would it be surprising to find that the same cholesterol-laden meat-based diet that accelerates heart disease and seems to affect the health of hair follicles also damages the hair's coloring mechanism.

In chapter 8, we briefly looked at homocysteine, an amino acid that encourages heart disease. People with a strong genetic tendency to accumulate homocysteine in their blood have higher rates of heart disease, a shorter life span, and accelerated aging. They also have early graying of the hair, which returns to its earlier color when the elevated homocysteine is reduced.[43] Homocysteine is made from methionine, which is plentiful in meat products. Homocysteine is removed with the help of vitamins B_6, B_{12}, and folate.

So does this mean that a vegetable-rich low-fat diet can actually pre-serve hair color a bit longer? Does a diet that fails to protect against free radicals or that encourages heart disease cause graying to occur earlier? As is the case with hair loss, these questions are intriguing but for now unan-swered.

Just as people notice effects of various foods on their skin, they also notice that foods can affect their hair. Regrettably, these observations have never been studied in an organized way and remain anecdotal. Nonetheless, some of them occur commonly enough that they are worth mentioning.

The first was brought to my attention by a patient who found that her hair texture had changed. It seemed flat and lifeless. She had not changed her shampoo or anything else she could think of, but for several weeks the same problem had continued. Her hair remained dull-looking and also became slightly oily. I had no idea what to make of it. She mentioned the change to an expert in Chinese medicine, who asked her if she drank sodas. She said that, in fact, she had been drinking sodas as a pick-me-up in the morning for the past couple of months. He advised her to avoid them.

This advice seemed rather anemic to me and did not resonate with anything I had ever heard of. Nonetheless, within a week or two of avoid-ing sodas, her hair returned to normal. The problem recurred if she had sodas or other sugary foods for several days in a row. The rapid effect suggests that the problem was not in the hair shaft but in the scalp. As odd as it sounds, it is a repeatable phenomenon and others have reported a similar effect.

When the juicing craze began around 1990, some people noticed that vegetable juices seem to make their hair slightly more wavy and their eye-brows bushier. Many people have noticed the effect; none has an explana-tion.

A final example comes from Ed Huling, the owner of Green City Market and Café, a purveyor of elegant vegetarian foods in Bethesda, Maryland. Ed was about thirty when he found that his hair was thinning noticeably. His father's balding had occurred at about the same age, so Ed figured it was nothing more than genetics tinkering with his scalp. However, he also had a weight problem and needed to lose about forty pounds. So he decided to try a vegetarian diet, particularly favoring raw vegetables and fruits. His extra weight gradually dissolved, and a couple of years later it suddenly hit him—his hair had once again become full and thick. He had completely forgotten about his previous thinning, but there it was—a young man's scalp where a balding crown had started.

These anecdotes suggest that we have only begun to investigate the effects foods have on our skin and hair. It is known that nutrients available to the hair follicle have a strong effect on the chemical structure of hair, and growing hairs avidly bind chemicals that are present in the follicle, which is why smokers often have a yellow tinge in their hair that becomes visible as their hair grays.[44]

Skin is the most visible organ of the body, and hair is its product. If your body is poorly nourished, your skin and hair will reflect that. But the right nutrients can help protect your skin and hair.

GETTING STARTED WITH HEALTHY FOODS

The palette that paints a healthy body is made from seemingly simple, yet elegantly complex and powerful foods that come from the soil: vegetables in all their colors and shapes; the full variety of fruits; grains turned into pasta, breads, cereals, tortillas, and pilafs; and legumes, the pods that provide all manner of beans, peas, and lentils. Every cell in your body knows exactly what to do with the nutrients these foods provide. They extract their antioxidants and use them to blanket your cells in a layer of protection. They use other nutrients to switch on detoxifying enzymes that free you from toxins that would restrain your natural strength and beauty. They calm the waves of hormones, clean away plaques of cholesterol, fat, and debris, and protect your arteries and veins. They keep your bones strong and your calorie-burning fires high.

If your cells are given a load of fat and cholesterol, animal proteins, caffeine, or alcohol instead, they are forced to improvise. And sometimes they do not do so well. They tuck the fat under your belt. Even as it starts to bulge, they have nowhere else to put it. They leave the cholesterol in your arteries, since their ability to cope with it is easily exceeded. They break down animal protein, but your bones lose calcium in the process. They eventually eliminate the caffeine and alcohol, but not before they have exerted their not-so-helpful influences over your bones and brain. Whatever palette you present to your body is the one it will use to paint your figure.

When Michelangelo was commissioned to begin the Sistine Chapel ceiling in 1508, Pope Julius II gave him a design of how it should look. The artist was not satisfied. The plan would not begin to use his talents. The two argued, and Michelangelo ultimately abandoned it.

Julius might have found another artist to put his design to work or deferred the project until Michelangelo came around. But instead the pope made an extraordinary decision. He dropped his own plan and asked Michelangelo to paint on the chapel ceiling whatever he wanted to, using his own knowledge and intuition. He gave him scaffolding, plaster and paint, and several assistants and let him envision his own direction without encumbrance. The result was unveiled four years later. Many consider it the greatest masterpiece of all time.

When Michael Schumacher took the wheel of a Formula One car, the team owners could have dictated exactly how he was to handle every turn. But they knew that this young driver's talent far outstripped that of anyone else on the team, or on any other team for that matter. They gave him a car and a pit crew to equal his ability and let him go. His skill and blinding speed did not disappoint them.

If Martha Graham had stuck to the dance steps that were popular when she began her career, she might have been great in a chorus line, but would never have revolutionized the world of contemporary dance.

Every cell in your body has coded in its DNA the plans for the most perfect body and mind you could possibly have. These cells need you to provide the right materials and to let them work. If you give your body nothing different from the foods that your parents and grandparents ate, you will hold yourself back. You may as well give a black-and-white palette to Michelangelo, fill Michael Schumacher's tank with lawnmower fuel, and put wooden shoes on Martha Graham's feet. You will deny yourself the body that really is yours.

This does not mean that the foods you need are expensive, unusual, or difficult to make. Not at all. They simply have to be the *right* foods. In this chapter, we will put together a menu that takes advantage of all the principles covered in this book.

If you eat this way, what results can you expect? The first thing many people notice is the pleasurable discovery that their belts fit a bit looser and the bathroom scale is more forgiving. That is the calorie-burning effect of complex carbohydrates, plus the natural weight reduction that comes when fats and oils are out of the diet. It starts in the first week. If you stick with it, the results can be profound.

As your immunity improves, you will be better able to fend off the colds and flus that fell so many people, particularly in colder weather. You will also be better protected against more serious illnesses, including cancer.

You cannot feel blockages in your arteries dissolving, but that process starts very quickly, and within a year most people have significant changes that are clearly seen on medical tests. When blood flow is once again restored to long-clogged arteries, the energy increase is indescribable.

Blood pressure tends to fall. And the pressure is taken off hemorrhoids and varicose veins. Premenopausal women often notice that their periods are easier. You cannot feel it, but your bones are better off, too, keeping calcium where it belongs.

My main goal is to help you feel and look great, enjoying a healthy body at any age. But that is only the beginning. For most people, life itself is extended. People who follow vegetarian or near-vegetarian diets and avoid tobacco, alcohol, and caffeine gain a decade or so of life. Your own results may be even better, because past studies were done with people whose diets, while vegetarian, were not perfect; they included dairy products and more vegetable oil than I would recommend and, as a result, squeezed out some of the vegetables and fruits that might have taken the place of those calorie-dense foods. If your diet is not only purely vegetarian, but also very rich in vegetables and fruits with their full range of nutrients and free of oily and highly processed foods and dairy products, your menu is optimal.

How to Get Started

As you change your diet, I suggest thinking about it as an experiment. There is no long-term commitment; you are just trying something new. If you like what it does for you, you can continue with it for as long as you like. Most likely, you will love it, want to continue it, and wish that you had started much earlier. The idea of experimenting also means trying new tastes and new products. Some will be delights; others will be duds. That is what experimenting is all about. During the experimental period, be strict with yourself so you really can see its benefits and can give yourself a respite from old habits.

Let's plan a healthy dinner. Four parts are worth remembering:

1. *Vegetables*. First, pick out some vegetables, and be generous with them. Let them cover a third to a half of your plate. Although these humble foods may be afterthoughts in the cuisine of Western countries, you will find yourself thinking about them quite differently as their nutritional power becomes evident and may feel cheated if your lunch or dinner left them out. They provide natural antioxidant protection for your skin, joints, blood vessels, eyes, and every other part of your body.

Take advantage of orange vegetables (carrots, sweet potatoes, and pumpkins), which are especially high in beta-carotene. But do not limit yourself to these because carotenoids and other vital nutrients are in green and yellow vegetables, too. The cruciferous vegetables, such as broccoli, cauliflower, Brussels sprouts, cabbage, and kale, also deserve special mention. They stimulate your liver to make enzymes that eliminate damaging chemicals such as the hydrocarbons that are common in air pollution. Cruciferous vegetables can begin your protection within just a day or two. Raw vegetables (carrots, tomatoes, cabbage, lettuce, cucumbers, and green peppers) and fruits also help your detoxification enzymes by providing glutathione, the carrier molecule that removes toxins from the body.

It is a good idea to keep some vegetables raw or as near to the raw state as possible. Most of their nutrients survive cooking, but a few are reduced by cooking. However, some vegetables, particularly cruciferous vegetables, spinach, chard, and potatoes, are better cooked than raw. Cooking eliminates toxins that can be present in some plants. Avoid adding butter, margarine, or oily salad dressings to vegetables. Instead, a sprinkle of lemon juice on broccoli or salad greens makes them much more palatable to reluctant vegetable eaters. Organic vegetables are preferable and are now widely available at health food stores.

2. *Legumes.* The legume group includes beans, peas, and lentils. Many people think of legumes as the savory replacement for meat in their diet. Baked beans, lentil soups or curries, bean burritos, chickpeas, or veggie chili are satisfying and substantial. But they are much more than that. They have complex carbohydrates, soluble fiber, omega-3 fatty acids, with no cholesterol and almost no fat. Legumes can make up about a quarter of your dinner plate.

Legumes should always be thoroughly cooked, never al dente. If beans give you gas, reduce the amount and try different varieties. For example, many people find that lentils or black beans, which are popular in Caribbean cuisine, are better tolerated than pinto or navy beans. Give your body a little time to adapt and increase the proportion of rice or other grains in your diet.

3. *Grains.* The last quarter of your plate can come from a grain: pasta, rice, breads, corn bread, or whatever your taste calls for. Legumes and grains provide vitamin E and are a great source of complex carbohydrates with almost no fat. Grains also supply selenium. And none of these foods has a scrap of cholesterol.

4. *Fruits.* Fruits make a great dessert and snack. Citrus fruits are especially high in vitamin C, but enjoy the full range of fruits that are now universally available.

Vegetables, legumes, grains, and fruits are the four groups to remember. They provide the nutrition that keeps your body working right and should be on your menu each day. You do not need to adhere rigidly to the portion sizes mentioned above. Nor do you need to carefully combine various grains and beans or have all four groups at every meal. So long as your overall diet contains all four groups, your meals are well planned.

DAILY NUTRITION

- *Vegetables.* Have 3 or more servings of vegetables each day. A serving is 1 cup raw or ½ cup cooked. Include orange and yellow varieties (e.g., sweet potatoes and carrots) as well as dark green vegetables.
- *Legumes.* Include 2 to 3 servings of legumes (beans, peas, lentils, or bean products) per day. A serving is ½ cup cooked beans, 4 ounces of tofu or tempeh, or 8 ounces of soy milk.
- *Whole Grains.* Have 5 or more servings of whole grains. A serving is ½ cup hot cereal, 1 ounce of dry cereal, or 1 slice of bread.
- *Fruits.* Have 3 or more servings of fruits per day. A serving is 1 medium piece of fruit or ½ cup cooked fruit or juice.

Some of the world's most delightful cuisines have been exploiting all of these foods for centuries. At an Italian restaurant, a bowl of minestrone is made from carrots, grean beans, cabbage, peas, chickpeas, and lima, kidney, and Great Northern beans, along with a bit of pasta. Followed by linguine with a light tomato and basil sauce, a side of broccoli or spinach, and fresh fruit for dessert, this meal presents vegetables, legumes, grains, and fruits in such a delightful way that you won't think of them as health foods. But indeed they are.

This dinner is also noteworthy for what it leaves out. It contains no meat, so it skips the heme iron that defies the body's attempts to limit iron absorption and encourages free radical damage. These foods are zero cholesterol and very low in fat, provided they are made with no more than minimal amounts of added oils, and are high in fiber, so they eliminate the chronic elevations of sex hormones that encourage cancer and menstrual symptoms and that may hasten hair loss. They also moderate the change in hormones at menopause, greatly diminishing menopausal problems. This delicious meal is also dairy-free, with none of the aggravations caused by dairy proteins, lactose, or dairy fat.

Another favorite of mine is a Mexican dinner, starting with a big green salad, followed by a burrito of beans wrapped in a wheat tortilla (to which the adventurous may add a few jalapeño peppers), Spanish rice, and fresh pineapple for dessert. The sample menus in the following section will give you many more ideas.

At restaurants, you will have no trouble finding healthy and delicious meals. In addition to ubiquitous Italian and Mexican restaurants, you can enjoy Chinese vegetables on rice (and if you cannot imagine liking tofu, try the Szechuan or home-style varieties—they are out of this world), Japanese vegetarian sushi, Indian vegetable curries, Thai dishes, and many, many others.

THE VEGETARIAN ADVANTAGE

The health advantages described in this book come from plant-based diets only. I strongly suggest avoiding meats and dairy products completely. They contain so many ingredients that accelerate free radical and chemical attacks, artery deterioration, hormone shifts, bone loss, and weight problems that there is no reason to include them ever. What is worse, they tend to be habituating. People who consume a bit of meat here and there tend to miss it when it is gone and often let it take over a bigger and bigger place on their plate. Like coffee or cigarettes, meat seems to get people hooked for reasons that no one has yet figured out. When you scratch meats and dairy products off the menu, you will miss them a bit at first, but soon you'll wish you had made this switch much earlier.

Many people mistakenly believe that if they simply add vegetables to their diet, they will be healthy even if they do not eliminate meats or dairy products. Others imagine that poultry and fish are as healthy as vegetarian foods. They are wrong. Vegetarian diets are much better than diets including even modest amounts of animal products. The National Cancer Institute adopted a Five-a-Day program, encouraging Americans to consume five servings of vegetables and fruits every day. That is a great start, but we also need a "Zero-a-Day" program to eliminate meats and dairy products.

When you change your diet, it helps to think short-term. For two to three weeks, stick to a vegetarian diet. That means no red meat, poultry, or fish and no eggs or dairy products at all. Keep vegetable oils to a minimum as well. Build your diet from vegetables, fruits, grains, and legumes. The recipes in the next section show easy ways to take advantage of the power of these foods. They were chosen because they are not only delicious, but are also surprisingly easy and quick, using familiar ingredients. Menus for two weeks are presented on pages 250 to 263.

After two to three weeks, see how you feel. If your weight has dropped slightly, or your cholesterol has begun to improve, or you find yourself feeling more energetic, you have just begun to tap the power that comes from giving your body the fuel it was designed for. The next step is to continue with these foods for a bit longer to see what they can really do for you.

COMPLETE NUTRITION

A vegetarian diet provides plenty of protein without any careful planning, provided it is drawn from a variety of foods. The old concept of "protein complementing," which required various food combinations to assure adequate protein, has been discarded as dietitians have found that any varied diet of plant foods provides more than enough protein.[1] Green vegetables and legumes easily meet the body's calcium needs, too, as we saw in chapter 9.

Vitamin B_{12} can be a concern for vegetarians, but one that is easily solved. B_{12} is needed for healthy nerves and healthy blood. It is an unusual nutrient in that it is not made by either plants or animals. It comes from bacteria and other one-celled organisms. Bacteria in the soil can occasionally contribute traces of B_{12} to root vegetables. Breakfast cereals and other packaged foods are sometimes enriched with B_{12}, which may be listed among their ingredients by its chemical name cobalamin or cyanocobalamin. Red Star Nutritional Yeast, which is sometimes used to add a cheeselike flavor to foods, is naturally enriched in B_{12}. All common multivitamins, including vegetarian brands, also contain B_{12}. These are all good sources.

Meats and other animal products contain vitamin B$_{12}$ because bacteria produce it in the animals' intestines and it is then absorbed into their tissues. These foods are obviously not recommended due to their inherent fat and cholesterol and other problems.

There is no reason to include animal products in your diet to get B$_{12}$. But do include a source of B$_{12}$ in your regular diet. The recommended dietary allowance is minuscule—only two micrograms per day, and the body actually needs only about half that amount. At any given time, most people have about a three-year supply stored in their livers. If the healthy foods noted above have not made their way onto your plate, B$_{12}$ is available in any typical multivitamin. Health food stores also sell B$_{12}$ supplements. Spirulina, most brands of yeast, and seaweed do not provide B$_{12}$. An adequate intake of vitamin B$_{12}$ is especially important for children, but it is important at all other phases of life, too.

MAKING IT SIMPLE

Most of us do not spend as much time cooking as our parents' generation did. For some us us, ten minutes in the kitchen is about all we can take. The recipes in the next section are designed to cook without much involvement from you once you get them started. Browse through them and see which ones you like. You'll find them surprisingly easy. If they tempt you to try some more, my previous book, *Food for Life*, contains many more recipes devised by Jennifer Raymond, who is a true genius at combining simplicity, familiarity, and taste. Here are a few more tips for those who do not like to spend time cooking:

- Frozen vegetables retain nearly all the nutrition of fresh vegetables and are quick and convenient.
- Canned beans and soups are a snap to fix. Choose the lower-salt varieties.
- More and more companies are producing ready-made spaghetti sauces that can be heated or simply poured from the jar. Check the labels to make sure they are vegetarian and low in fat.

• Try making a couple of extra portions to freeze or save in your refrigerator.

• Health food stores have a huge array of convenience foods, from fat-free, meatless burgers and hot dogs to vegetable potpies and TV dinners. Keep a variety in the freezer. They also carry instant soups that you can keep in a desk drawer.

I hope you enjoy all these delightful foods. Even more, I hope you enjoy the new body that is waiting for you. As your new health and vitality become clearly evident, please do not keep these things a secret. Share your knowledge with others. And let me know how this program has worked for you. I can be reached at Box 6322, Department A, Washington, DC 20015. I look forward to hearing from you.

MENUS AND RECIPES

Congratulations! Your choice to eat a more healthful diet is one of the most exciting and personally empowering decisions you can make. Not only will you look and feel better, but you'll find that the foods you're eating are delicious, satisfying, and simple to prepare.

This chapter will provide menu-planning ideas, shopping tips, and quick, easy recipes. Along with many familiar favorites, you'll find recipes for new foods that will make your diet more interesting and varied even as it becomes more healthful.

MENU PLANNING

By spending just a bit of time thinking through your menus for the next week, you can save a tremendous amount of time, energy, and money. You can get all the ingredients you'll need in a single shopping trip and minimize preparation time by making a bit of extra food that can be incorporated into future meals. You will spend less money on food since advance planning makes it possible to use less processed, less expensive ingredients and having a shopping list reduces the temptation to purchase impulse items.

In this section, you will find two weeks of menu ideas to get you started. You can simply follow the menus as they are, or you can use parts of them to create your own menus. After deciding which recipes you want to prepare, make a list of all the ingredients you need. You'll also want to check which staples you might need (see Foods to Keep on Hand: Stocking the Pantry, page 236), including breakfast cereal, bread, spices, canned soups, and other ready-to-eat foods. Add some extra fresh fruits and vegetables for snacks and you're ready to head to the store. Plan to shop at a time when you're not hungry to reduce the temptation of impulse items. When you get home, post your menu in a visible location so it can be easily referred to and followed.

You may find that you don't actually need to plan for three meals each day of the week. Breakfast, especially during the week, will probably be much the same from day to day. Lunches can be quickly assembled if you have food from previous meals on hand. Soup (either homemade or commercially prepared) is another quick and nutritious lunch item and bean or grain salads are also excellent lunch foods, especially during the hot weather of summer. For many people, dinner is the only meal that takes any planning and it's easy to keep preparation time to a minimum. One simple trick is to prepare more than is needed for a single meal. Serve the food one way for its first presentation, then modify it slightly for its next appearance. For example, Four Bean Salad (page 281) makes a tasty burrito when it is heated and rolled in a warm flour tortilla with salsa and chopped lettuce. Or add some Simple Peanut Sauce (page 292) and a bit of seasoned rice vinegar to Spicy Indonesian Stir-fry (page 326) for a quick and delicious noontime salad.

Foods that require longer cooking may be prepared in quantity and refrigerated in airtight containers for later use. Brown rice, for example, keeps well in the refrigerator for up to a week and can be served with chili, added to casseroles, or made into Quick Rice Pudding (page 333). Cooked potatoes and yams also keep well and are welcome additions to a variety of meals and recipes. A cooked potato can be diced and topped with fat-free vinaigrette and chopped green onions for the world's quickest potato salad. Or cut cooked potatoes into rounds, sprinkle with an herbal seasoning mix, and place under the broiler until lightly browned. Dried beans are also well suited for quantity cooking and can be added to soups, stews, and salads. For a quick bean salad, simply top cooked (or canned) beans with a fat-free dressing.

Cooked rice and beans can also be frozen. Store in airtight containers in portion sizes that are convenient for reheating. For example, cooked beans can be frozen with some of the cooking liquid in 2-cup portions for use in any recipe that calls for a 15-ounce can of beans. Reheat in a microwave, on the stovetop, or in a conventional oven.

Convenience foods can be as healthy as they are quick. An ever-growing array is available in supermarkets and natural food stores. Canned beans, instant soups, prepared sauces, and complete frozen vegetarian meals come to the rescue when you're especially busy and can easily be incorporated into the menus in this section.

Although you might spend a bit more time preparing food at first, as you become familiar with the recipes and preparation techniques in this book, as well as with healthful convenience foods which meet your needs, you can spend as little or as much time as you like.

MENU-PLANNING TIPS

- Plan and shop for a week's meals to save time and money.
- Make extra portions of foods that can be incorporated into subsequent meals.
- Prepare frequently used foods in large enough quantities to supply several meals.
- Substitute convenience foods in the menus where desired.

FOODS TO KEEP ON HAND: STOCKING THE PANTRY

Keeping frequently used ingredients as well as ready-to-eat convenience foods on hand makes it easy to prepare a healthful meal at a moment's notice.

Grains and Grain Products

cold breakfast cereals without added fat or sugars
hot breakfast cereals
pancake and waffle mixes

egg-free pasta: spaghetti, fettucine, rigatoni, and so on
brown rice
white rice
basmati rice, white and brown
quick-cooking brown rice: Lundberg
bulgur (toasted cracked wheat)
couscous
rolled oats
unbleached flour
whole wheat pastry flour
whole wheat flour
cornmeal
polenta
popcorn (for air popping)

Beans, Lentils, and Peas

dried lentils
dried split peas
dried beans: kidney, garbanzo, black, pinto, and so on
black bean flakes: Fantastic Foods, Taste Adventure
pinto bean flakes: Fantastic Foods, Taste Adventure

Fresh Vegetables and Fruits

yellow onions
red onions
garlic
red potatoes
russet potatoes
green cabbage
carrots, baby carrots
celery
prewashed salad mix
prewashed spinach
broccoli
kale or collard greens
apples

oranges
bananas
raisins

Canned Foods

canned beans: kidney, garbanzo, black, pinto, and so on
canned tomatoes
canned tomato sauce
vegetarian soups: Health Valley, Bearitos
vegetarian baked beans: Bush's, Heinz
vegetarian chili beans: Dennison's, Health Valley, Bearitos
fat-free refried beans: Rosarita, Old El Paso, Bearitos
fat-free refried black beans: Bearitos
vegetarian pasta sauce without added oil: Healthy Choice,
    Millina's Finest, Weight Watcher's
salsa without added oil
roasted red peppers packed in water

Frozen Foods

apple juice concentrate
orange juice concentrate
frozen corn
frozen peas
frozen bananas
frozen berries
frozen chopped onions
frozen diced bell peppers
frozen vegetarian dinners
vegetarian hot dogs
vegetarian burgers

Nuts and Seeds

peanut butter
tahini (sesame seed butter)

Breads, Crackers, and Snack Foods

whole grain bread (may be frozen)

flour tortillas (may be frozen)

corn tortillas (may be frozen)

pita bread (may be frozen)

fat-free crackers: Health Valley, RyeKrisp, FinnKrisp, Fantastic Foods

rice cakes, popcorn cakes: Quaker, Chico San, Lundberg

baked tortilla chips: Guiltless Gourmet, Barbara's, Vera Cruz, Kettle Creek

unsalted sourdough pretzels: Snyder's of Hanover, Laura Scudder's, Granny Goose

Convenience Foods

vegetarian soup cups: Fantastic Foods, Nike Spice, The Spice Hunter

vegetarian ramen soups: Westbrae, Soken

dry soup mixes: Taste Adventure

burger mix: Fantastic Foods, Worthington Foods

falafel mix: Fantastic Foods

silken tofu (keeps unrefrigerated up to 1 year)

vegetarian hot dogs: Smart Dogs, Yves Veggie Weiners

vegetarian burgers: Boca Burger, Yves, The Green Giant Harvest Burger, Lightlife Light Burgers

vegetarian cold cuts: Yves, White Wave, Lightlife

baked tofu

seitan: White Wave, Knox Mountain Foods

texturized vegetable protein

soy milk/rice milk

Seasonings and Condiments

herbs and spices: cinnamon, ginger, cloves, ground cumin, cayenne, red pepper flakes, chili powder, curry powder, basil, oregano, black pepper

salt-free seasonings: Mrs. Dash, Parsley Patch, Schilling
low-sodium soy sauce
seasoned rice vinegar
cider vinegar
unsweetened apple butter
fruit preserves, unsweetened or sweetened with fruit juice
fat-free salad dressing
eggless mayonnaise: Nayonaise
stone-ground mustard
ketchup
unsweetened fruit spread
molasses
maple syrup
sugar
baking soda
low-sodium baking powder: Featherweight
hot beverages: herbal teas, Cafix, Postum, Pero
vegetable broth (powder or cubes)
vegetable oil spray (optional)

SHOPPING TIPS

Today's supermarket is a wonderland. Shelves brimming with attractively packaged foods of every description promise to make meals quick, delicious, and interesting. The following guidelines will help you to make nutritious selections:

• Become a label reader! The ingredient list and nutrition information on food labels can provide you with a tremendous amount of useful information.

• Food labels list ingredients in order of prominence in the food: the ingredient present in the greatest amount is first on the list, and so forth. If fat or sugar appear near the top of the list, the food is high in these ingredients. Also check the label for artificial flavors and colors, preservatives, and other additives. The fewer of these, the better.

• Check the nutrition label to determine the amount of fat, sugar, and sodium in each serving of the food.

• When selecting fruits and vegetables, fresh is the best choice from the standpoint of flavor and nutritional value. It is usually the least expensive as well.

• Frozen vegetables and fruits are comparable to fresh in nutritional value and can be a big time-saver. Be sure to choose vegetables that are frozen without butter, oil, or sauces. Choose fruits that are frozen without added sugar.

• When buying canned fruit, select those that have been packed in their own juice rather than a sugar syrup.

• Whenever possible, choose foods with no added fats or oils.

• Choose food with a minimum of added salt.

• Be aware of the many different forms in which sugar is added to foods. Sucrose, dextrose, fructose, high fructose corn syrup, and malt are just a few of the sugars that find their way into processed foods. In general, watch for ingredients ending in "-ose," a suffix that denotes sugar. If a product lists several different types of sugar, it is likely that sugar is a principal ingredient, even if it isn't first on the ingredient list.

• In choosing breads, the first ingredient should be a whole grain flour, such as "whole wheat flour." Don't be misled by breads containing "wheat flour." This is just another term for white flour.

• Avoid foods containing hydrogenated fats. These are fats that have been processed to make them solid (or saturated) and, like other saturated fats, they can raise blood cholesterol levels.

EQUIPPING YOUR KITCHEN

Having the right tools for the job will greatly increase your enjoyment of food preparation. The equipment required for preparing the recipes in this book is really quite simple and available fairly inexpensively in hardware, department, and cooking supply stores.

• Knives—Good-quality knives are essential and may be purchased at hardware or cutlery stores. Chicago Cutlery makes excellent knives that are very reasonably priced. You will need an 8- or 10-inch chef's knife, a slicing knife, a paring knife, and a serrated bread knife.

- Cutting board—A wooden cutting board is the easiest to work on and the best for your knives. Studies have shown that wooden cutting boards are just as hygienic as plastic. Select a cutting board that is large enough to work on comfortably but small enough to lift easily. A good size is about 12 × 15 inches.
- Nonstick skillet—One of the easiest ways to reduce fat in your diet is to use a nonstick skillet. Many foods can be cooked without any added fat, and other foods can be cooked with much less fat than would otherwise be required. Look for a good-quality, heavy-duty pan. These are available in department, specialty cooking, and restaurant supply stores, and although they are not cheap, they will last a lifetime if cared for properly.
- Pots and pans—You will need a large soup pot and a couple of smaller saucepans. Heavy-gauge stainless steel, enamelware, glass, or high-quality nonstick pans are all excellent choices.
- Measuring cups—A set of stainless steel measuring cups in graduated sizes and a 4-cup glass measuring cup should meet all your needs.
- Measuring spoons
- Rubber spatula—invaluable for scraping bowls and pans
- Metal spatula—for burgers, pancakes, and braised potatoes
- Large wooden or metal spoons for stirring
- Glass or metal baking pans—Convenient sizes are 9 × 9-inch square, 9 × 13-inch rectangular, a 9- or 10-inch pie pan, and a 5 × 9-inch bread pan.
- Mixing bowls—2 or 3 large stainless steel mixing bowls
- Colander—metal or plastic, for draining pasta and rinsing vegetables and fruits
- Vegetable steamer—a metal rack or basket that enables vegetables to be cooked above (rather than in) water

COOKING TECHNIQUES

Several of the recipes in this book use the following quick and easy cooking techniques:

- Braising—Instead of sautéing vegetables in oil, cook them in liquid. Heat approximately ½ cup of water, vegetable stock, or wine (the liquid you use will depend on the recipe) in a large pan or skillet. Add the ingredients to be braised and cook over medium-high heat, stirring occasionally, until tender. This will take about 5 minutes for onions and most other vegetables. Add a bit more liquid if needed.

• Grilling—The high heat seals in the flavors of foods and adds its own distinctive flavor as well. Use a nonstick grill and cut all items to be grilled together to a uniform size for even cooking.

• Roasting—A simple and delicious way to prepare vegetables is to roast them in a hot oven (about 500°F). The heat locks in the flavor without the addition of any fat or oil.

• Steaming—Using a collapsible steamer rack, cook vegetables above a small amount of boiling water in a covered pan. This protects nutrients and flavor.

EASY TIPS FOR HEALTHFUL COOKING

The following cooking tips will enable you to reduce the fat and increase the nutritional value of the foods you cook.

• Use nonstick pots and pans. Most foods can be prepared with no added fat.

• Avoid deep-fried foods. Try oven roasting or grilling foods that are usually deep-fried.

• When it is necessary to sauté or fry in oil, a nonstick vegetable oil spray will enable you to do so with a minimum of fat.

• Save bean cooking liquid and use it in place of oil in salad dressings.

• Bean cooking liquid also makes a flavorful stock for soups.

• Serve cooked vegetables with fat-free salad dressing instead of butter or high-fat sauces.

• Thicken soup by pureeing a portion of it and mixing it with the unpureed portion.

• Cream soups can be thickened with a potato. For soups that will be pureed, simply cook and puree the potato along with the other soup ingredients. For other soups, cook a peeled and diced potato in enough water to cover it. When the potato is fork-tender, puree it in its cooking water in the blender and add it to the soup.

• Avocados, coconut, and other nuts and seeds are high in fat and should be used sparingly. Exceptions are chestnuts and water chestnuts, which are low in fat and can add wonderful taste and texture to many dishes.

• Try pureed frozen fruit as a delicious substitute for ice cream.

• Mashed banana, applesauce, and cooked pumpkin can be substituted for all or part of the oil, butter, or shortening in many baked goods.

• Omitting eggs from baked goods will reduce the fat and calories significantly. Try substituting the following for each egg you leave out:

> 1 ounce (2 tablespoons) soft tofu
> ½ banana, mashed
> ⅓ cup applesauce or canned pumpkin
> 1 tablespoon flax seeds pureed in a blender with ¼ cup water
> 1 heaping tablespoon soy flour mixed with 2 tablespoons water
> 2 tablespoons cornstarch
> Ener-G™ egg replacer. Use according to directions.

• To replace eggs that are used for binding, such as in burgers or loaves, try:

> Mashed potato
> Quick-cooking rolled oats
> Cooked oatmeal
> Fine bread crumbs
> Tomato paste

• Many delicious, low-fat products are available for replacing meat in recipes:

> *Texturized vegetable protein (TVP)* is made from defatted soybeans and is an excellent, cholesterol-free substitute for ground meat in dishes like spaghetti sauce, tacos, or chili. It is available in natural food stores.

Seitan ("say-tan"), which is made from a wheat protein called wheat gluten, has a meaty taste and texture that is delicious wherever strips or chunks of meat would be used. It is high in protein but, unlike meat, it is very low in fat and has no cholesterol. Look for it near the tofu in the refrigerator case of your natural food store.

Seitan mixes. Knox Mountain Farm makes packaged seitan mixes that are delicious and easy to prepare. Three flavors are available: original, chicken flavor, and sausage flavor. All are totally vegetarian. Arrowhead Mills also makes a seitan mix. Look for them in your natural food store.

Vegetarian burgers are widely available under a number of different brand names. Many are fat-free. Some are very meat-like, such as the Boca Burger, The Green Giant Harvest Burger, and Yves Veggie Burger. These can be broiled, grilled, or heated in a toaster oven or microwave. They can be broken into pieces and added to chili, spaghetti, and other sauces. Look for them in supermarkets and natural food stores.

Vegetarian hot dogs are now widely available and very tasty. The Smart Dog made by Lightlife and Yves Veggie Weiners are fat-free and delicious in a bun, baked beans, and chili dogs. Look for them in supermarkets and natural food stores.

Vegetarian cold cuts, including pepperoni, bologna, and ham slices, are made by Yves, White Wave, and Lightlife. These all-vegetarian products are fat-free and available in natural food stores and some supermarkets.

Reduced-fat tofu is being produced by several companies and is available in natural food stores and many supermarkets. Use it in any recipe calling for tofu.

Baked tofu comes in a variety of delicious flavors and makes a substantial and satisfying snack. It can be sliced thinly for sandwiches, chopped or shredded for salads, or added to stir-fried vegetables. It is available in the deli case of natural food stores.

• Milk or cream in recipes can easily be replaced with soy or rice milk.

• Replace buttermilk in recipes with an equal amount of soy milk plus 1 tablespoon vinegar for each cup of soy milk.

• Yogurt can be replaced with one of the nondairy yogurts now available. White Wave Dairyless and Soya Latté are two brands. They are available in a variety of flavors in many natural food stores.

• Yogurt used in baking may be replaced with a mixture of soy milk and vinegar. For each cup of yogurt, substitute ¾ cup soy milk mixed with 1 tablespoon vinegar.

• Nutritional yeast adds a cheeselike flavor to salads, sauces, and spreads. It is high in protein and B vitamins and available in natural food stores. Be sure to purchase *nutritional yeast,* not baking yeast or brewer's yeast. Some varieties, including Red Star Nutritional Yeast, are good sources of vitamin B_{12}.

• Reduce salt used in cooking by replacing it with herbs, spices, and other seasonings. A wide variety of salt-free seasoning mixes is available in supermarkets and natural food stores.

• Most baking powder is high in sodium. A few low-sodium varieties, including Featherweight, are available in natural food stores and some supermarkets.

GLOSSARY OF INGREDIENTS

The majority of ingredients in the recipes are common and widely available in grocery stores. A few that may be unfamiliar are described below:

Arrowroot powder. Used as a substitute for cornstarch by those with allergies to corn or those desiring a less refined product. Available in natural food stores.

Balsamic vinegar. A delightful and mellow-flavored wine vinegar available in most grocery stores.

Lavash bread. A versatile Middle Eastern flatbread, similar to a very large flour tortilla. May be rolled up around a variety of fillings or used for dipping with sauces and stews. Available in some supermarkets, natural food stores, and ethnic food stores.

Low-sodium baking powder. Baking powder made without sodium bicarbonate. Available in natural food stores.

Low-sodium soy sauce. Several companies offer soy sauce with reduced amounts of sodium. Check and compare labels to get the brand that is lowest. Available in most grocery stores.

Mirin. A sweet rice cooking wine that can be used as a flavoring in a variety of recipes. Available in most grocery stores in the ethnic food section.

Miso. A fermented soybean paste that adds robust flavor and a hint of saltiness to a variety of foods. Available in natural food stores.

Nayonaise. An eggless, dairyless (and therefore cholesterol-free) mayonnaise made by Nasoya. Available in natural food stores.

Nondairy yogurt. A naturally cultured soy milk product with a taste and texture similar to cow's milk yogurt. Two brands, White Wave Dairyless and Soya Latté, are available in a variety of flavors from natural food stores.

Reduced-fat tofu. A lower-fat version of tofu, made by a number of producers, available in natural food stores and some supermarkets.

Rice milk. A mild-flavored beverage made from partially fermented rice. May be used in place of dairy milk on cereal and in most recipes. Rice Dream and Eden Rice are two brands available in natural food stores and some supermarkets.

Roasted red peppers. Roasted red peppers add great flavor and color to a variety of dishes. Roast your own or purchase them already roasted, packed in water, in most grocery stores.

Salt-free seasoning. A mixture of herbs and other seasonings that provides flavor without adding sodium. A wide selection of brands and flavors are available in grocery stores.

Seasoned rice vinegar. A mild-flavored vinegar, seasoned with sugar and salt. Great for salad dressings and on cooked vegetables. Available in most grocery stores.

Seitan. A meaty-tasting product, made from wheat, that is very low in fat and high in protein. It is available ready-made in the deli case of many natural food stores. A convenient mix, made by Knox Mountain Farm, comes in several flavors.

Silken tofu. A smooth, delicate tofu that is excellent for sauces, cream soups, and dips. Special convenience packaging enables it to be stored without refrigeration for up to a year. Refrigerate after opening. One popular brand, Mori-Nu, is available in most grocery stores.

Soy milk. A milklike beverage made from soybeans, available in a variety of flavors, as well as in low-fat and vitamin- and mineral-fortified versions. Soy milks vary widely in flavor, so try several to find the ones you like best. Available in natural food stores and in many supermarkets.

Spectrum Naturals Spread. A nonhydrogenated margarine substitute available in natural food stores.

Tahini. Sesame seed butter used in salad dressings, sauces, and dips. Available in natural food stores and the ethnic food section of many supermarkets.

Tempeh. A fermented soy food with a tender meatlike texture. Used for burgers as well as in stews and casseroles. Available in a variety of flavors in natural food stores.

Texturized vegetable protein (TVP). Made from defatted soy flour, TVP has a meaty texture when rehydrated with boiling water. Easy to use and an excellent meat substitute in sauces, chili, and stews. Available in natural food stores.

Unbleached flour. White flour that has not been chemically whitened. Available in most grocery stores.

Whole wheat pastry flour. Milled from soft spring wheat, it retains the bran and germ and at the same time produces lighter-textured baked goods than regular whole wheat flour. Available in natural food stores.

MENUS

Day One

Breakfast

French Toast (page 268)
Maple syrup
Strawberries
Melon

Lunch

Curried Lentil Soup (page 294)
Golden Potatoes (page 308)
Spinach Salad with Orange Sesame Dressing (page 285)
Tropical Delight (page 332)

Dinner

Pasta e Fagioli (page 319)
Crostini with Sun-dried Tomatoes (page 293)
Mixed Greens Salad (page 280)
Balsamic Vinaigrette (page 279)
Carrot Cake (page 339)

Day Two

Breakfast

Applesauce Muffins (page 276)
Apple butter or fruit preserves
Apricot Smoothie (page 272)

Lunch

Autumn Stew (page 301)
Spinach Salad with Orange Sesame Dressing (page 285)
Corn Bread (page 277)
Applesauce (page 274)

Dinner

Pasta with Broccoli and Fresh Tomatoes (page 318)
Garlic Bread (page 292)
Mixed Greens Salad (page 280)
Fat-free Dressing (page 278)
Fresh Apricot Crisp (page 331)

Day Three

Breakfast

Cold cereal
Soy milk, rice milk, or fruit juice
Sliced banana
Melon or orange slices

Lunch

Quick Black Bean Burrito (page 290)
Spanish Bulgur (page 314)
Mixed Greens Salad (page 280)
Piquant Dressing (page 278)

Dinner

Roasted Summer Vegetables and Tofu (page 317)
Risotto (page 312)
Delicata Squash (page 306)
Braised Cabbage (page 304)
Fresh fruit

Day Four

Breakfast

Bagel
Fruit preserves
Nondairy yogurt
Peach Sunrise (page 272)

Lunch

Vegetarian hot dog
Bush's vegetarian beans
Rainbow Salad (page 282)
Chocolate Tofu Pudding (page 334)

Dinner

Winter Squash and Red Lentil Stew (page 302)
Golden Potatoes (page 308)
Steamed Kale (page 303)
Mixed greens with Balsamic Vinaigrette (page 279)

Day Five

Breakfast

Breakfast Teff (page 271)
Soy or rice milk
Applesauce (page 274)

Lunch

Spinach Turnovers (page 320)
Couscous Salad (page 287)
Roasted Yams (page 310)

Dinner

Quick Chili (page 324)
Corn Bread (page 277)
Mixed Greens Salad (page 280) with Piquant Dressing (page 278)
Steamed Kale (page 303)
Fresh Apricot Crisp (page 331)

Day Six

Breakfast

Buckwheat Corncakes (page 265)
Maple syrup
Applesauce (page 274)

Lunch

Spinach and Mushroom Fritatta (page 329)
Quick Confetti Rice (page 312)
Steamed broccoli

Dinner

Autumn Stew (page 301)
Whole grain bread
Spinach Salad with Orange Sesame Dressing (page 285)
Quick Indian Pudding (page 335)

Day Seven

Breakfast

Sunday Morning Tofu (page 269)
English muffin
Apricot preserves
Grapefruit half

Lunch

Lavash Roll with Hummus (page 288)
Couscous Salad (page 287)
Carrot and Red Pepper Soup (page 300)
Watermelon Salad (page 284)

Dinner

Vegetarian Swiss Steak (page 328)
Tomato and basil fettuccine
Green salad with Balsamic Vinaigrette (page 279)
Steamed broccoli
Pumpkin Raisin Cookies (page 340)

Day Eight

Breakfast

Cold cereal
Soy milk, rice milk or fruit juice
Sourdough toast
Strawberry preserves
Banana Pineapple Smoothie (page 273)

Lunch

Vegetarian burger
Roasted Potatoes (page 309)
Corn on the cob
Watermelon

Dinner

Spicy Indonesian Stir-fry (page 326)
Simple Peanut Sauce (page 292)
Carrot and Red Pepper Soup (page 300)
Steamed Kale with Pickled Ginger (page 304)
Quick Rice Pudding (page 333)

Day Nine

Breakfast

Pumpkin Spice Muffin (page 275)
Mango Delight (page 273)
Fresh melon

Lunch

Quickie Quesadilla (page 290)
Spanish Bulgur (page 314)
Fresh fruit

Dinner

Polenta with Hearty Barbecue Sauce (page 321)
Steamed Kale (page 303)
Fresh Tomatoes with Basil (page 282)
Yam Pie (page 336)

Day Ten

Breakfast

Creamy Oatmeal (page 270)
Soy or rice milk
Baked Apple (page 274)
Whole wheat toast
Fruit preserves

Lunch

Creamy Lima Soup (page 295)
Rye bread
Red Potato Salad (page 283)
Pumpkin Raisin Cookies (page 340)

Dinner

Tortilla Casserole (page 323)
Spanish Bulgur (page 314)
Zucchini Mexicana (page 305)
Mixed greens with Piquant Dressing (page 278)
Tropical Delight (page 332)

Day Eleven

Breakfast

Cold cereal
Sliced banana
Melon slices

Lunch

Broccoli Potato Soup (page 299)
Spinach Turnovers (page 320)
Quick Confetti Rice (page 312)

Dinner

Vegetarian Tacos (page 322)
Mexican Corn Pie (page 325)
Four Bean Salad (page 281)
Banana Dream Pie (page 337)

Day Twelve

Breakfast

Creamy Oatmeal (page 270)
Applesauce (page 274)
Whole wheat toast
Berry preserves

Lunch

Spicy Yam Soup (page 298)
Steamed Kale (page 303)
Whole wheat bread or roll

Dinner

Shepherd's Pie (page 327)
Delicata Squash (page 306)
Mixed Greens Salad (page 280)
Fat-free Dressing (page 278)
Apple Crisp (page 332)

Day Thirteen

Breakfast

Whole Wheat Banana Cakes (page 266)
Maple syrup
Melon slices

Lunch

Eat-Your-Greens Soup (page 297)
Whole wheat bread
Thai Noodle Salad (page 286)

Dinner

Roasted Summer Vegetables and Tofu (page 317)
Polenta with Sun-dried Tomatoes (page 316)
Delicata Squash (page 306)
Simple Peanut Sauce (page 292)
Mixed Greens Salad (page 280)
Fat-free Dressing (page 278)

Day Fourteen

Breakfast
_____

Sunday Morning Tofu (page 269)
Braised Potatoes (page 270)
English muffin
Apple butter
Fresh fruit

Lunch
_____

Cabbage and Carrot Cobbler (page 330)
Roasted Yams or Sweet Potatoes (page 310)
Mixed Greens Salad (page 280)
Balsamic Vinaigrette (page 279)

Dinner
_____

Pasta e Fagioli (page 319)
Red Potato Salad (page 283)
Steamed broccoli
Fresh Apricot Crisp (page 331)

BREAKFASTS

When you think about breakfast, think whole grains. Whether in the form of hot or cold cereal or whole grain breads or muffins, grains are the perfect way to start the day. Rolled oats, teff, millet, buckwheat, quinoa, and polenta are all quick-cooking and delicious. Serve them with soy milk, rice milk, fresh fruit, cinnamon, or applesauce. Grains left over from previous meals can also be reheated for a quick hot breakfast. Quick Rice Pudding on page 333 can be a nutritious breakfast as well as a delicious dessert. Select cold cereals that do not contain added fat or excessive sugar. If sugar is the first or second ingredient on the label or if the label lists more than one type of sugar (honey, corn syrup, dextrose, malt, or the like), then sugar is a major ingredient.

Whole grain breads and muffins also make quick, nutritious breakfast fare. For weekends and those occasions when you have more time for breakfast, consider pancakes, waffles, or French toast. Or perhaps you'd enjoy Sunday Morning Tofu (page 269) and Braised Potatoes (page 270).

Making Pancakes. Pancakes can lend a festive air to the morning and make breakfast feel really special. The key to making good pancakes is having the right pan at the right temperature. You'll need a good-quality nonstick skillet or griddle with a thick bottom. Getting it just the right temperature is the key to making light and delicious pancakes. Preheat it so that sprinkles of water dance on it but it's not so hot that it smokes. Even with a nonstick surface, a light mist of vegetable oil spray will insure that the pancakes can be turned easily.

Start by mixing the dry ingredients in one bowl and the wet ingredients in another. Preheat the skillet or griddle, then combine the wet and dry ingredients, stirring just enough to remove the lumps. Pour a small amount of batter for each cake (smaller cakes are easier to turn) and let it cook until the top is bubbly and the edges are dry. Turn the cake and let the second side cook for about a minute. Adjust the heat so the pancakes sizzle and cook quickly. The heat is too high if the pan begins to smoke.

I have included four simple pancake recipes in this section. There are also a number of good commercial mixes available that can be prepared with water, omitting any oil, milk, or eggs specified in the directions.

Pancakes are best when served fresh and hot. Try them with fresh fruit and a nondairy yogurt like White Wave Dairyless. Or serve them with fruit preserves or syrup.

Buckwheat Corncakes

Makes sixteen 3-inch pancakes, 2–3 servings

Buckwheat adds a wonderful, hearty flavor to these easily prepared pancakes. I like to serve them with homemade applesauce and Not-So-Sausage, a vegetarian sausage mix available in most natural food stores.

½ cup buckwheat flour
½ cup cornmeal
½ teaspoon low-sodium baking powder
¼ teaspoon baking soda
½ ripe banana, mashed
1½ tablespoons brown sugar
1 tablespoon vinegar
1–1¼ cups soy milk
maple syrup or fruit preserves for serving

Stir the flours, baking powder, and baking soda together in a mixing bowl. In a separate bowl, combine the mashed banana, sugar, vinegar, and 1 cup of the soy milk. Pour liquid ingredients into the flour mixture and stir just enough to remove lumps and make a pourable batter. If the mixture seems too thick, add extra soy milk.

Preheat a nonstick skillet or griddle. Spray lightly with a nonstick spray. Pour small amounts of the batter onto the heated surface and cook until the tops bubble, about 2 minutes. Turn with a spatula and cook the second side until golden brown. Serve immediately with maple syrup or fruit preserves.

Nutrition information per pancake: 80 calories, 2 g protein, 17 g carbohydrate, 0.5 g fat, 5% of calories from fat, 38 mg sodium

Whole Wheat Pancakes

Makes sixteen 3-inch pancakes, 2–3 servings

Four simple ingredients are all it takes to make nutritious, satisfying pancakes. Serve them with fruit preserves or maple syrup.

1 cup whole wheat pastry flour or whole wheat flour
2 teaspoons low-sodium baking powder
1⅓ cups soy or rice milk
1 tablespoon maple syrup, plus more for serving, or fruit preserves for
    serving

Stir the flour and baking powder together. Add the milk and syrup and stir enough to remove the lumps, but do not overmix.

Pour small amounts of the batter onto a preheated nonstick lightly oil-sprayed griddle or skillet and cook until the tops bubble, 2 to 3 minutes. Turn with a spatula and cook the second side until golden brown. Serve immediately.

Nutrition information per pancake: 37 calories, 1 g protein, 7 g carbohydrate, 0.3 g fat, 7% of calories from fat, 9 mg sodium

Whole Wheat Banana Cakes

Makes sixteen 3-inch pancakes, 2–3 servings

1 ripe banana
1¼ cups soy or rice milk
1 tablespoon maple syrup, plus more for serving
1 cup whole wheat pastry flour or whole wheat flour
2 teaspoons low-sodium baking powder

In a large bowl, mash the banana, then stir in the soy milk and 1 tablespoon maple syrup. Stir the flour and baking powder together, then add to the banana mixture.

Pour small amounts of the batter onto a preheated nonstick lightly oil-sprayed griddle or skillet and cook until the tops bubble, 2 to 3 minutes. Turn with a spatula and cook the second side until golden brown. Serve immediately with maple syrup.

Nutrition information per pancake: 44 calories, 1 g protein, 8 g carbohydrate, 0.3 g fat, 7% of calories from fat, 9 mg sodium

Cornmeal Flapjacks

Makes twenty 3-inch pancakes, 3–4 servings

Serve these delicious, satisfying pancakes with fruit preserves, applesauce, or maple syrup.

1½ cups soy or rice milk
1 tablespoon vinegar
2 tablespoons maple syrup
1 cup cornmeal
1 cup whole wheat pastry flour
¼ teaspoon baking soda
⅛ teaspoon salt

Combine the soy or rice milk, vinegar, and maple syrup. Set aside.

Mix the remaining ingredients in a large bowl, then pour in the milk mixture. Stir to remove the lumps, then pour small amounts of the batter onto a preheated nonstick lightly oil-sprayed griddle or skillet and cook until the tops bubble. Turn with a spatula and cook the second side until golden brown. (Stir the batter each time before pouring.) Serve immediately.

Nutrition information per pancake: 62 calories, 1.5 g protein, 12 g carbohydrate, 1 g fat, 13% of calories from fat, 44 mg sodium

French Toast

Serves 2

French toast is quick and cholesterol-free when you make it without eggs. Try varying the bread you use for different flavors and textures.

½ cup soy milk
3 tablespoons unbleached flour
¼ teaspoon cinnamon
1 teaspoon vanilla extract
4 slices of whole wheat or sourdough bread
Fresh fruit, fruit preserves, or maple syrup, for serving

Whisk together the soy milk, flour, cinnamon, and vanilla. Dip the bread in the batter, turning it to coat both sides, then cook it until golden brown in a nonstick skillet. (If the toast sticks, spray the skillet lightly with a nonstick vegetable spray.) Serve with fresh fruit, fruit preserves, or maple syrup.

Nutrition information per 2 slices: 204 calories, 6 g protein, 39 g carbohydrate, 2 g fat, 9% of calories from fat, 235 mg sodium

Sunday Morning Tofu

Serves 4

This is a recipe for those mornings when you have time to linger over a special breakfast. Be sure to use a nonstick skillet; otherwise you will need to increase the amount of oil to prevent the tofu from sticking.

½ medium onion, chopped
2 tablespoons peanuts or cashews
1 teaspoon toasted sesame oil
2 cups sliced mushrooms
1 pound firm tofu
1½ teaspoons curry powder
2 tablespoons low-sodium soy sauce
2 tablespoons raisins
Toasted English muffins and apple chutney, for serving

In a large nonstick skillet, sauté the onion and nuts in the sesame oil until the onion is soft and translucent, about 3 minutes. Add the mushrooms and tofu, then stir in the curry powder and soy sauce. Continue cooking until the mushrooms are tender, about 7 minutes. Stir in the raisins. Serve with toasted English muffins and apple chutney.

Nutrition information per 1 cup serving: 167 calories, 10 g protein, 14 g carbohydrate, 8 g fat, 42% of calories from fat, 310 mg sodium

Braised Potatoes

Serves 4

Serve these delicious potatoes with black bean chili and spicy salsa for a hearty breakfast that is a real eye-opener. Any variety of potato can be used, though red potatoes are especially good. Be sure to use a nonstick skillet.

4 large red potatoes
1 onion, chopped
½ cup water
4 teaspoons low-sodium soy sauce
1 teaspoon chili powder
Freshly ground black pepper (optional)
1 tomato, diced (optional)

Scrub the potatoes but do not peel. Cut into ¼-inch-thick slices. Steam over boiling water until just tender when pierced with a sharp knife.

In a large nonstick skillet, braise the onion in the water and 2 teaspoons soy sauce until soft, about 3 minutes. Add the potatoes, chili powder, and remaining soy sauce and stir gently to mix. Cook over medium heat, stirring occasionally, for 3 to 5 minutes. Sprinkle with freshly ground black pepper and top with diced tomatoes, if desired.

Nutrition information per 1½-cup serving: 200 calories, 6 g protein, 43 g carbohydrate, 0.3 g fat, 1% of calories from fat, 308 mg sodium

Creamy Oatmeal

Serves 4

Rice Dream Beverage is a nondairy milk made from rice. It is sold in natural food stores and many supermarkets. Once you've tried this delicious, creamy oatmeal, you'll never want it any other way.

1 cup rolled oats
3 cups Vanilla Rice Dream Beverage

Combine rolled oats and Rice Dream in a saucepan over medium heat. Bring to a simmer and cook 1 minute. Cover the pan, turn off the heat, and let stand 3 minutes.

Nutrition information per ¾-cup serving: 145 calories, 6 g protein, 25 g carbohydrate, 3 g fat, 17% of calories from fat, 68 mg sodium

Breakfast Teff

Serves 2

Teff has been a staple grain in northern Africa for centuries and has recently been introduced into the United States, to the delight of chefs and nutritionists. This tiny grain is extremely nutritious and makes a delicious breakfast cereal with a flavor reminiscent of Wheatena. Ask for teff in your natural food store.

½ cup teff
2 cups water
¼ teaspoon salt (optional)
Soy or rice milk, for serving

Combine the teff and water in a saucepan and stir to mix. Cook over low heat, stirring occasionally, until thickened, about 5 minutes. Serve with soy or rice milk.

Nutrition information per 1-cup serving: 200 calories, 8 g protein, 35 g carbohydrate, 3 g fat, 14% of calories from fat, 268 mg sodium

Smoothies

Smoothies are one of my favorite ways to enjoy fruit for breakfast. The fruit is frozen, then blended with a small amount of liquid to make a thick, rich-tasting shake. Try the following smoothies for starters, especially when the various fruits are in season.

Peach Sunrise

Serves 1

1 peach, sliced and frozen
¾ to 1 cup vanilla or plain soy milk
1 teaspoon sugar (optional)

Combine all the ingredients in a blender and process until smooth. Serve immediately.

Nutrition information per serving: 156 calories, 4 g protein, 29 g carbohydrate, 1.5 g fat, 9% of calories from fat, 68 mg sodium

Apricot Smoothie

Serves 2

1 cup frozen banana pieces
1 cup frozen apricots
¼ cup undiluted apple juice concentrate
¾ cup soy or rice milk

Combine all the ingredients in a blender and process until smooth. Serve immediately.

Nutrition information per serving: 181 calories, 3 g protein, 40 g carbohydrate, 1 g fat, 6% of calories from fat, 44 mg sodium

Mango Delight

Serves 2

1 orange, peeled
1 cup frozen banana chunks
1 cup frozen mango chunks
½ to 1 cup soy or rice milk

Cut the orange in half and remove any seeds. Place it in a blender, add the remaining ingredients, and blend until thick and smooth.

Nutrition information per serving: 140 calories, 2 g protein, 31 g carbohydrate, 0.8 g fat, 5% of calories from fat, 24 mg sodium

Banana Pineapple Smoothie

Serves 2

1 orange, peeled
1 cup frozen banana chunks
1 cup frozen pineapple pieces
½ to 1 cup soy or rice milk

Cut the orange in half and remove any seeds. Place it in a blender along with all the remaining ingredients and blend on high speed until thick and smooth.

Nutrition information per serving: 156 calories, 3 g protein, 33 g carbohydrate, 1 g fat, 6% of calories from fat, 35 mg sodium

Baked Apples

Serves 4

These baked apples contain no added sugar or fat, yet are delicious and satisfying. Cook them the night before for a quick breakfast treat.

4 large tart apples
3 to 5 pitted dates, chopped
1 teaspoon cinnamon

Preheat the oven to 350°F. Wash the apples, then remove the core to within ¼ inch of the bottoms. Combine the dates and cinnamon, then distribute equally into the centers of the apples. Place in a baking dish filled with ¼ inch of hot water and bake until apples are soft, 40 to 60 minutes. Serve warm or cold.

Nutrition information per apple: 124 calories, 0.5 g protein, 30 g carbohydrate, 0.4 g fat, 3% of calories from fat, 0 mg sodium

Applesauce

Serves 8

Applesauce is delicious on toast, pancakes, and hot cereal. It is also good all by itself.

6 large tart apples
½ to 1 cup undiluted apple juice concentrate
½ teaspoon cinnamon

Peel the apples, if desired, then core and dice them into a large pan. Add the apple juice concentrate to just cover the bottom of the pan, then cook over low heat until the apples are soft. Mash slightly with a fork, if desired, then stir in the cinnamon. Serve hot or cold.

Nutrition information per ¾-cup serving: 90 calories, 0.3 g protein, 21 g carbohydrate, 0.2 g fat, 2% of calories from fat, 5 mg sodium

Pumpkin Spice Muffins

Makes 12 muffins

2 cups whole wheat pastry flour
1 tablespoon low-sodium baking powder
½ teaspoon baking soda
½ teaspoon salt
½ teaspoon cinnamon
¼ teaspoon nutmeg
½ cup sugar
1 15-ounce can solid-pack pumpkin
½ cup water
½ cup raisins

Preheat the oven to 375°F.

Mix together the dry ingredients. Add the pumpkin, water, and raisins and stir until just mixed. Lightly spray muffin cups with nonstick spray and fill to the top. Bake 25 to 30 minutes, until the tops of the muffins bounce back when pressed lightly. Remove from the oven and let stand 1 to 2 minutes, then remove the muffins from the pan. When the muffins are cool, store in an airtight container.

Nutrition information per muffin: 137 calories, 3 g protein, 26 g carbohydrate, 0.1 g fat, 0.4% of calories from fat, 128 mg sodium

Applesauce Muffins

Makes 12 muffins

2 cups whole wheat pastry flour
1 tablespoon low-sodium baking powder
½ teaspoon baking soda
½ teaspoon salt
½ teaspoon cinnamon
½ cup sugar
1 15-ounce can applesauce
½ cup water
½ cup raisins

Preheat the oven to 375°F.

Mix together the dry ingredients. Add the applesauce, water, and raisins and stir until just mixed. Lightly spray muffin cups with nonstick spray and fill to the top. Bake 25 to 30 minutes, until the tops of the muffins bounce back when pressed lightly. Remove from the oven and let stand 1 to 2 minutes, then remove the muffins from the pan. When the muffins are cool, store in an airtight container.

Nutrition information per muffin: 140 calories, 3 g protein, 27 g carbohydrate, 0 g fat, 0% of calories from fat, 127 mg sodium

Corn Bread

Serves 8

This corn bread is quick and easy to prepare and contains no eggs, cholesterol, or added fat.

1½ cups soy milk
1½ tablespoons vinegar
1 cup cornmeal
1 cup unbleached or whole wheat pastry flour
2 teaspoons low-sodium baking powder
½ teaspoon baking soda
½ teaspoon salt

Preheat the oven to 425°F.

Combine the soy milk and vinegar and set aside. Stir the dry ingredients together in a large bowl, then add the soy milk mixture and mix until just blended. Spread evenly in a 9 × 9-inch baking dish that has been lightly sprayed with a nonstick spray and bake for 25 to 30 minutes. Serve hot.

Nutrition information per 3 × 3-inch slice: 124 calories, 3 g protein, 26 g carbohydrate, 0.6 g fat, 4% of calories from fat, 180 mg sodium

SALADS, SANDWICHES, AND SAUCES

Fat-free salad dressings are quick and easy to make. Simply replace the oil in traditional recipes with water, vegetable stock, bean cooking liquid, or seasoned rice vinegar. This section contains recipes for delicious fat-free dressings as well as several fat-free salads.

Fat-free Dressing

Makes ½ cup

Seasoned rice vinegar makes a simple, delicious dressing for salads and cooked vegetables. It will keep in the refrigerator for 2 to 3 weeks.

½ cup seasoned rice vinegar
1 to 2 teaspoons stone-ground or Dijon-style mustard
1 garlic clove, pressed

Whisk all the ingredients together.

Nutrition information per tablespoon: 14 calories, 0 g protein, 3 g carbohydrate, 0 g fat, 0% of calories from fat, 310 mg sodium

Piquant Dressing

Makes ⅓ cup

This dressing is slightly spicy with a south-of-the-border flair.

¼ cup seasoned rice vinegar
2 tablespoons tomato ketchup

1 teaspoon stone-ground mustard
1 garlic clove, minced
½ teaspoon paprika
¼ teaspoon oregano
⅛ teaspoon ground cumin

Whisk all the ingredients together.

Nutrition information per tablespoon: 12 calories, 0 g protein, 3 g carbohydrate, 0 g fat, 0% of calories from fat, 210 mg sodium

Balsamic Vinaigrette

Makes ⅓ cup

Balsamic vinegar is a delicious wine vinegar from Italy with a mellow flavor that is perfect for salads.

2 tablespoons balsamic vinegar
2 tablespoons seasoned rice vinegar
2 tablespoons water
1 to 2 garlic cloves, crushed

Whisk all the ingredients together.

Nutrition information per tablespoon: 6 calories, 0 g protein, 1.5 g carbohydrate, 0 g fat, 0% of calories from fat, 99 mg sodium

Curry Dressing

Makes ½ cup

3 tablespoons seasoned rice vinegar
3 tablespoons water
2 teaspoons stone-ground or Dijon-style mustard
1 teaspoon soy sauce
1 teaspoon sugar or other sweetener
½ teaspoon curry powder
¼ teaspoon black pepper

Whisk all the ingredients together.

Nutrition information per tablespoon: 9 calories, 0 g protein, 2 g carbohydrate, 0 g fat, 0% of calories from fat, 151 mg sodium

Mixed Greens Salad

Serves 6

Prewashed mixtures of salad greens are available in most supermarkets and natural food stores. These mixes are as flavorful as they are attractive and stand well on their own with just a touch of dressing. Other vegetables can be added for additional flavor and nutrition.

½ red or yellow bell pepper, seeded and sliced
1 red or yellow tomato, sliced
½ cup peeled and sliced jicama
6 cups prewashed salad mix
3 tablespoons fat-free dressing

Combine all the ingredients and toss gently to mix.

Nutrition information per 1½-cup serving: 20 calories, 0.2 g protein, 4 g carbohydrate, 0.1 g fat, 3% of calories from fat, 160 mg sodium

Four Bean Salad

Serves 10

This colorful salad is quick to prepare and contains no added fat. It will keep well in the refrigerator for several days.

1 15-ounce can dark kidney beans, drained
1 15-ounce can black-eyed peas, drained
1 10-ounce package frozen lima beans, thawed
1 15-ounce can S&W Pinquitos or other vegetarian chili beans
1 large red bell pepper, diced
½ cup finely chopped onion
2 cups fresh or frozen corn
¼ cup seasoned rice vinegar
2 tablespoons apple cider or distilled vinegar
1 lemon, juiced
2 teaspoons cumin
1 teaspoon coriander
⅛ teaspoon cayenne

Drain the kidney beans, black-eyed peas, and lima beans and combine in a large bowl. Add the pinquitos or chili beans along with their sauce. Stir in the bell pepper, onion, and corn.

Whisk the remaining ingredients together and pour over the salad. Toss gently to mix. Chill at least 1 hour before serving, if possible.

Nutrition information per 1-cup serving: 216 calories, 11 g protein, 41 g carbohydrate, 0.5 g fat, 2% of calories from fat, 104 mg sodium

Rainbow Salad

Serves 6 to 8

In addition to its delicious taste, this colorful salad is a rich source of beta-carotene and other protective nutrients. Nayonaise is an eggless, dairy-free mayonnaise substitute available from natural food stores.

3 cups shredded green cabbage
1½ cups shredded purple cabbage
2 carrots, grated
3 green onions, sliced
2 celery stalks, thinly sliced
¼ cup Nayonaise
2 teaspoons lemon juice

Combine the cabbage, carrots, onions, and celery in a large bowl. Add the Nayonaise and lemon juice and toss to mix.

Nutrition information per ¾-cup serving: 38 calories, .5 g protein, 5 g carbohydrate, 1.4 g fat, 33% of calories from fat, 71 mg sodium

Fresh Tomatoes with Basil

Serves 6

This beautiful salad is one of the best ways I know to enjoy the deep red, vine-ripened tomatoes of summertime.

2 to 3 ripe red tomatoes
¼ cup thinly sliced red onion
1 teaspoon finely chopped fresh basil
2 teaspoons balsamic vinegar
Freshly ground black pepper

Slice the tomatoes and put them in a serving dish along with the onion and basil. Sprinkle with the vinegar and freshly ground black pepper and toss gently to mix.

Nutrition information per ½-cup serving: 25 calories, 1 g protein, 5 g carbohydrate, 0.1 g fat, 3.5% of calories from fat, 8 mg sodium

Red Potato Salad

Serves 8

Red potatoes make a beautiful and delicious fat-free potato salad.

4 large red potatoes, scrubbed
1 small red onion, thinly sliced
1 red or yellow bell pepper, seeded and sliced
¼ cup finely chopped fresh parsley
¼ cup cider vinegar
¼ cup fresh lemon juice
2 tablespoons seasoned rice vinegar
2 garlic cloves, crushed
2 teaspoons stone-ground or Dijon-style mustard
¼ to ½ teaspoon black pepper

Cut the potatoes into ½-inch cubes and steam over boiling water until just tender, 10 to 15 minutes. Rinse with cold water, then place in a large bowl to cool. Rinse the sliced onion under cold water and add it to the cooled potatoes along with the bell pepper and parsley.

Mix together the remaining ingredients, then add to the vegetables and toss gently.

Variation: Substitute Yukon Gold potatoes, available in many supermarkets, for the red potatoes.

Nutrition information per 1-cup serving: 90 calories, 2 g protein, 20 g carbohydrate, 0.2 g fat, 2% of calories from fat, 124 mg sodium

Watermelon Salad

Serves 4 to 6

Watermelon and onions in the same dish? The combination is wonderful! This recipe was created by Jean Marc Fulsack, chef for Dr. Dean Ornish's lifestyle-change program.

3 cups seedless watermelon, peeled and diced
½ cup finely diced red onion, rinsed in cold water
2 tablespoons balsamic vinegar
1 tablespoon seasoned rice vinegar
2 tablespoons finely chopped fresh mint, or ½ teaspoon dried
¼ teaspoon freshly ground black pepper

Combine all the ingredients in a salad bowl and toss to mix. If possible, chill before serving.

Nutrition information per ½-cup serving: 41 calories, 0.6 g protein, 8.5 g carbohydrate, 0.2 g fat, 5% of calories from fat, 52 mg sodium

Spinach Salad with Orange Sesame Dressing

Serves 4 to 6

Toasted sesame seeds add wonderful flavor to this salad.

1 bunch fresh spinach (about 6 cups of leaves)
1 red or yellow bell pepper, cut into strips
¼ to ½ cup thinly sliced red onion
1 orange, peeled and sliced into thin rounds
1 tablespoon sesame seeds
2 tablespoons seasoned rice vinegar
1 tablespoon orange juice concentrate
1 tablespoon water

Trim off the spinach stems and carefully wash the leaves. Dry, then tear any large leaves into bite-size pieces. Place in a salad bowl along with the pepper, onion, and orange slices.

Toast the sesame seeds in a 400°F toaster oven or regular oven for 10 minutes. Transfer to a blender and grind into a powder. Add the vinegar, orange juice concentrate, and water and blend to mix. Pour over the salad and toss just before serving.

Nutrition information per 1-cup serving: 45 calories, 2 g protein, 7 g carbohydrate, 0.7 g fat, 14% of calories from fat, 144 mg sodium

Thai Noodle Salad

Serves 10

This salad is colorful and very satisfying. Udon is a Japanese pasta similar to spaghetti, which is available in many supermarkets and natural food stores. If you cannot find it, use spaghetti instead.

6 ounces udon or spaghetti
1 teaspoon toasted sesame oil
3 tablespoons peanut butter
3 tablespoons seasoned rice vinegar
2 tablespoons dry sherry
2 teaspoons low-sodium soy sauce
2 teaspoons finely minced fresh ginger
1 large garlic clove, minced
⅛ teaspoon cayenne
½ pound asparagus (about 2 cups)
½ bunch broccoli (about 2 cups)
3 green onions
1 red bell pepper, cut into julienne strips
1 cup fresh bean sprouts (optional)
½ cup chopped fresh cilantro (optional)

Bring a large pot of water to a boil. Add the pasta and cook according to package instructions until it is just tender. While the pasta is cooking, combine the sesame oil, peanut butter, rice vinegar, sherry, soy sauce, ginger, garlic, and cayenne to make the dressing. Drain and rinse the cooked pasta under cold water, then toss with the dressing.

Snap the tough ends off the asparagus, then cut or break it into inch-long pieces. Bring a pot of water to a boil, add the asparagus, and cook for 1 minute. Do not overcook! Transfer to a bowl of ice water and chill, then drain. Save the pot of boiling water for cooking the broccoli.

Cut or break the broccoli into bite-size florets. Peel the stems and cut into ½-inch pieces. Cook in boiling water until just barely tender, 1 to 2 minutes. Chill in ice water and drain.

Chop the green onions, including some of the green tops.

Add the vegetables to the pasta and toss to mix. Top with the bean sprouts and chopped cilantro, if desired.

Nutrition information per 1-cup serving: 211 calories, 8 g protein, 33 g carbohydrate, 5 g fat, 20% of calories from fat, 227 mg sodium

Couscous Salad

Serves 6

Couscous has origins in northern Africa and is the world's smallest pasta. It cooks almost instantly and makes a beautiful and flavorful salad.

1 cup couscous
1 cup boiling water
½ small red onion, finely chopped
1 red bell pepper, diced
1 carrot, grated
½ cup finely shredded red cabbage
½ cup fresh or frozen green peas
½ cup currants or raisins
1 tablespoon balsamic vinegar
2 tablespoons seasoned rice vinegar
1 teaspoon toasted sesame oil
1 teaspoon low-sodium soy sauce
1 teaspoon Dijon mustard
1 teaspoon curry powder

Place the couscous in a large bowl and pour the boiling water over it. Stir to mix, then cover and let stand until cooled. Fluff with a fork.

Prepare all the vegetables as directed, then add to the couscous along with the raisins.

Combine the vinegars and the remaining ingredients and mix well. Pour over the salad and toss to mix.

Nutrition information per 1-cup serving: 135 calories, 3.5 g protein, 28 g carbohydrate, 1 g fat, 6% of calories from fat, 152 mg sodium

Lavash Roll with Hummus

Serves 2 to 4

Soft lavash is a Middle Eastern flatbread similar to a very large flour tortilla. It can be spread with a variety of fillings and rolled up like a burrito or
jelly roll. The roll can be cut in half for 2 large servings or into half-inch
slices and served as appetizers. Lavash rolls can be prepared in advance if
tightly wrapped and refrigerated. Look for soft lavash in the deli section
of your supermarket or ethnic food stores. Hummus is a creamy Middle
Eastern pâté made with garbanzo beans. It may be purchased in many
food stores or prepared according to the recipe below.

1 piece soft lavash bread
1 to 2 cups Hummus (recipe follows)
1 to 2 cups leaf lettuce, spinach, or sprouts
1 to 2 carrots, grated
1 cucumber, peeled and sliced
1 tomato, sliced
½ cup chopped green onions

Lavash is usually oblong-shaped, with a wide end and a narrow end.
Turn it so that the wide end is nearest you. Spread a thin layer of hummus evenly over the entire surface. Arrange the lettuce, spinach, or
sprouts in a row across the wide end of the lavash. Cover this with thin
layers of grated carrot, sliced cucumber and tomato, and chopped green
onions. Keep the amount of these vegetables modest, otherwise the roll
will be too large and bulky. Beginning with the wide end, roll the lavash
up tightly around the filling. Cut the roll in half or into ½-inch slices.

Nutrition information per ¼-roll serving: 182 calories, 7 g protein, 31 g carbohydrate, 3 g
fat, 16% of calories from fat, 128 mg sodium

Hummus

Makes about 2 cups, 8 ¼-cup servings

Serve Hummus with crackers, wedges of pita bread, or as a filling in lavash rolls.

1 15-ounce can garbanzo beans
3 tablespoons tahini (sesame seed butter)
2 tablespoons lemon juice
1 to 2 garlic cloves, minced
1 tablespoon finely chopped parsley
¼ teaspoon each cumin and paprika
¼ teaspoon salt

Drain the beans and reserve the liquid. Process the beans until smooth in a food processor using the steel knife or mash them well with a potato masher or fork. Add the remaining ingredients and mix well. The mixture should be moist and spreadable. If it is too dry, add enough of the reserved bean liquid to achieve the desired consistency.

Nutrition information per ¼-cup serving: 101 calories, 4 g protein, 13.5 g carbohydrate, 3 g fat, 28% of calories from fat, 74 mg sodium

Quick Black Bean Burritos

Serves 4

Burritos are one of the quickest, tastiest meals I know. Look for dehydrated black bean flakes or canned refried black beans in natural food stores.

4 flour tortillas
1 cup black bean flakes mixed with 1 cup boiling water or 1 15-ounce
 can fat-free refried black beans
1 to 2 cups shredded lettuce
2 to 3 tomatoes, sliced
3 green onions, sliced
½ cup salsa

Heat a tortilla in a large, ungreased skillet until it is warm and soft. Spread a line of black beans down the center of the tortilla, then top with lettuce, tomatoes, onions, and salsa. Fold the bottom end toward the center, then roll the tortilla around the filling. Repeat with the remaining tortillas.

Nutrition information per 1 burrito serving: 300 calories, 12 g protein, 55 g carbohydrate, 3 g fat, 10% of calories from fat, 196 mg sodium

Quickie Quesadillas

Makes 12 quesadillas, 6 servings

These quesadillas are made with Cheezy Garbanzo Spread. If you make the spread in advance, the quesadillas can be prepared in a jiffy.

1 recipe Cheezy Garbanzo Spread (recipe follows)
12 corn tortillas
3 to 4 green onions, sliced
1 bell pepper, seeded and diced (optional)
2 cups diced tomatoes (optional)
1 cup salsa

Spread 2 to 3 tablespoons of the garbanzo spread on a tortilla and place it, spread side up, in a large heated skillet. As soon as it is warm and soft, fold it in half, then cook it another minute. Remove it from the pan and carefully open it. Sprinkle on some green onions, bell pepper, tomatoes, and salsa. Repeat with the remaining tortillas.

Nutrition information per quesadilla: 142 calories, 4.5 g protein, 24 g carbohydrate, 3 g fat, 18% of calories from fat, 115 mg sodium

Cheezy Garbanzo Spread

Makes about 2 cups, 8 ¼-cup servings

This delicious spread has the look and taste of spreadable cheese and takes only seconds to prepare. Try it on bread and crackers, in casseroles (page 323), and as a filling for quesadillas (page 290). Look for jars of water-packed roasted red peppers near the pickles and olives in your supermarket. Tahini is available in the ethnic food section of many supermarkets and in most natural food stores.

1 15-ounce can garbanzo beans
½ cup roasted red peppers
3 tablespoons tahini (sesame seed butter)
3 tablespoons lemon juice

Drain the garbanzo beans, reserving the liquid, and place them in a food processor or blender with the remaining ingredients. Process until very smooth. If using a blender, you will have to stop it occasionally and push everything down into the blades with a rubber spatula. The mixture should be quite thick, but if it really seems too thick to blend, add a tablespoon or two of the reserved bean liquid.

Nutrition information per ¼-cup serving: 125 calories, 5 g protein, 18 g carbohydrate, 3.5 g fat, 25% of calories from fat, 75 mg sodium

Simple Peanut Sauce

Makes 1 cup

This quick sauce is delicious with cooked vegetables or pasta.

⅓ cup peanut butter
½ cup hot water
1 tablespoon soy sauce
1 tablespoon vinegar (white wine vinegar works well)
2 teaspoons sugar
2 garlic cloves, minced
¼ teaspoon ginger
⅛ teaspoon cayenne

Whisk all the ingredients together in a small saucepan, then heat gently until the sauce is smooth and slightly thickened. Add more water if the sauce becomes too thick.

Nutrition information per tablespoon: 38 calories, 1 g protein, 2 g carbohydrate, 3 g fat, 62% of calories from fat, 38 mg sodium

Garlic Bread

Makes 1 loaf

The mellow, slightly sweet flavor of roasted garlic is perfect for making delicious, fat-free garlic bread.

1 large head garlic
1 to 2 teaspoons Italian seasoning (optional)
1 baguette or loaf of French bread, sliced

Roast the garlic by baking the whole, unpeeled head in a 400°F oven or toaster oven until it feels soft when gently squeezed, about 30 minutes. Peel the cloves or squeeze them out of their skin, then mash them into a paste with a fork. Mix in the herbs, if desired, then spread onto the sliced bread. Wrap tightly in foil and bake at 350°F for 20 minutes.

Nutrition information per 1-inch-slice serving: 91 calories, 3 g protein, 18.5 g carbohydrate, 0.1 g fat, 1% of calories from fat, 179 mg sodium

Crostini with Sun-dried Tomatoes

Serves 10

In this fat-free version of crostini, thin slices of toasted bread are topped with a flavorful blend of tomatoes and roasted red peppers.

6 sun-dried tomato halves
⅓ cup roasted red peppers (about 2 peppers)
4 roasted garlic cloves, chopped or mashed
1 tablespoon finely chopped fresh basil, or 1 teaspoon dried
⅛ teaspoon black pepper
1 sweet baguette or Italian loaf, cut into ½-inch-thick slices

Pour boiling water over sun-dried tomatoes and set aside until softened, about 30 minutes. Pour off the water (it can be saved and used in place of vegetable stock in other recipes) and coarsely chop the tomatoes. Chop the roasted red peppers and add to the tomatoes along with the garlic, basil, and pepper. Let stand 30 minutes.

Place the bread on a baking sheet and toast in a 350°F oven until the outside is crisp, 10 to 15 minutes. Remove from the oven and cool slightly, then spread each piece with the tomato mixture.

Nutrition information per 1-inch-slice serving: 93 calories, 3 g protein, 18.5 g carbohydrate, 0.1 g fat, 1% of calories from fat, 179 mg sodium

SOUPS

Soups can be wonderfully nutritious and convenient. Homemade soups are easy to make and even easier to reheat. They can be prepared without fat and practically cook themselves, whether on the stovetop or in a crockpot.

A wide array of healthful, commercially prepared soup is also available. Instant vegetarian soup cups, which come in a wide assortment of delicious flavors, are so simple: All you add is hot water. Keep them handy in a desk drawer at work or carry them along when you travel. Several companies also make canned soups without added fat and with a minimum of salt. Check your local natural food store.

Curried Lentil Soup

Serves 8

This simple soup is made in a single pot. Serve it with cooked greens and fresh bread or chapatis.

1 cup lentils, rinsed
1 onion, chopped
2 celery stalks, sliced
4 garlic cloves, minced
1 teaspoon whole cumin seed
8 cups water
½ cup couscous or white basmati rice
1 cup chopped tomatoes
1½ teaspoons curry powder
⅛ teaspoon black pepper
1 teaspoon salt

Bring the lentils, onion, celery, garlic, cumin seed, and water to a simmer in a large pot over medium heat. Cover and cook until the lentils are tender, about 50 minutes.

Stir in the couscous or rice, chopped tomatoes, curry powder, and pepper. Continue cooking until the couscous is tender, about 10 minutes. Add salt to taste.

Nutrition information per 1-cup serving: 111 calories, 6 g protein, 21 g carbohydrate, 0.2 g fat, 2% of calories from fat, 327 mg sodium

Creamy Lima Soup

Serves 4 to 6

This soup is quick and satisfying. Use fresh basil and parsley if possible—they really make the soup.

1 onion, chopped
1 large garlic clove, minced
2½ cups water or vegetable stock
1 cup crushed tomatoes
2 cups shredded cabbage
1 tablespoon chopped fresh basil, or 1 teaspoon dried
1 15-ounce can lima beans, drained (or 2 cups frozen lima beans)
⅛ teaspoon black pepper
1 cup soy milk
2 tablespoons chopped fresh parsley
½ teaspoon salt

In a large soup pot, braise the onion and garlic in ½ cup water or stock until soft, about 5 minutes. Add the tomatoes, cabbage, basil, lima beans, pepper, and remaining water or stock. Simmer for 15 minutes.

Ladle about 3 cups of the soup into a blender, add the soy milk and fresh parsley, and blend until smooth, using a low speed and holding the lid on tightly. Stir back into the rest of the soup, add the salt, and heat until very hot and steamy.

Nutrition information per 1½-cup serving: 145 calories, 6 g protein, 28 g carbohydrate, 0.8 g fat, 5% of calories from fat, 308 mg sodium

Quick Vegetable Ramen

Serves 2

Ramen soups contain dried noodles that cook in 2 to 3 minutes and a packet of flavorful seasoning broth. By adding your own fresh vegetables, you can quickly make a tasty, nutritious meal. You can purchase ramen in a variety of flavors from natural food stores and many supermarkets. Be sure to select those brands that are made without animal products or added oil. Two good brands are Westbrae and Soken.

1 package ramen soup
1 cup chopped broccoli
1 green onion, sliced

Follow the package instructions for cooking ramen. Add the broccoli to the boiling water along with the noodles. Stir in the sliced green onion just before serving.

Nutrition information per 1½-cup serving: 85 calories, 3 g protein, 17 g carbohydrate, 0.8 g fat, 8.5% of calories from fat, 381 mg sodium

Eat-Your-Greens Soup

Serves 8

This soup is a beautiful and delicious way to eat green vegetables.

1 onion, chopped
2 celery stalks, sliced
2 potatoes, scrubbed and diced
¾ cup split peas, rinsed
2 bay leaves
6 cups water or stock
2 medium zucchini, diced
1 medium broccoli stalk, chopped
1 bunch fresh spinach, washed and chopped
½ teaspoon dried basil
¼ teaspoon black pepper
⅛ teaspoon cayenne
1½ teaspoons salt

Place the onion, celery, potatoes, split peas, and bay leaves in a large pot with the water or stock and bring to a boil. Lower the heat, cover, and simmer 1 hour. Remove the bay leaves.

Add the zucchini, broccoli, spinach, basil, black pepper, and cayenne and simmer 20 minutes. Transfer to a blender in several small batches and blend until completely smooth, holding the lid on tightly. Return to the pot and heat until steamy. Add salt to taste.

Nutrition information per 1½-cup serving: 142 calories, 6 g protein, 28 g carbohydrate, 0.2 g fat, 1% of calories from fat, 435 mg sodium

Spicy Yam Soup

Serves 8

Yams take on a whole different character in this spicy, slightly sweet soup.

2 medium yams
½ cup water
1 onion, chopped
½ teaspoon each mustard seeds, turmeric, ginger, and cumin
¼ teaspoon cinnamon
⅛ teaspoon cayenne
¾ teaspoon salt
2 cups water
1 tablespoon lemon juice
2 cups soy milk

Peel the yams and cut them into chunks. Steam over boiling water until tender when pierced with a fork, about 40 minutes. Mash (you should have about 2 cups) and set aside.

Braise the onion in ½ cup water until soft, then add the spices and salt. Cook 2 minutes over low heat, stirring constantly, then whisk in 2 cups water, the lemon juice, and the mashed yams. Simmer 10 minutes. Add the soy milk and puree the soup in a blender in 2 to 3 batches until very smooth. Return to the pan and heat over a medium flame until hot and steamy, about 10 minutes.

Nutrition information per 1-cup serving: 82 calories, 2 g protein, 18 g carbohydrate, 0.5 g fat, 6% of calories from fat, 226 mg of sodium

Broccoli Potato Soup

Serves 6

Broccoli is a nutritional powerhouse and makes an absolutely delicious soup.

 1 yellow onion, chopped
 2 garlic cloves, minced
 2½ cups water or vegetable stock
 2 potatoes, diced
 4 cups coarsely chopped broccoli
 ½ teaspoon cumin
 ½ teaspoon salt
 ¼ teaspoon black pepper
 2 cups soy milk
 1 tablespoon tahini (sesame seed butter)

In a large pot, braise the onion and garlic in ½ cup water or stock until the onion is translucent. Add the diced potato and remaining 2 cups water or stock, cover the pot, and simmer until the potatoes are tender, about 15 minutes. Add the chopped broccoli and continue to simmer until the broccoli is tender, about 5 minutes. Stir in the seasonings and tahini. Puree in a blender in small batches until the soup is very smooth. Add some of the soy milk to each batch to facilitate blending. Be sure to fill the blender no more than half full, start on low speed, and hold the lid on tightly. Pour the soup back into the pot and warm it over low heat until steamy.

Nutrition information per 1½-cup serving: 178 calories, 5.5 g protein, 32 g carbohydrate, 3 g fat, 15% of calories from fat, 229 mg sodium

Carrot and Red Pepper Soup

Serves 4

This creamy soup has a subtle, delicious flavor and a rich orange color.

1 onion, chopped
6 carrots, thinly sliced
2 cups water or vegetable stock
2 red bell peppers, roasted
2 cups soy milk
2 teaspoons lemon juice
2 teaspoons balsamic vinegar
½ teaspoon salt
¼ teaspoon freshly ground black pepper

Place the chopped onion and carrots into a pot with the water and simmer, covered, over medium heat until the carrots can be easily pierced with a fork, about 20 minutes.

Roast the peppers by placing them over an open gas flame or directly under the broiler until the skin is completely blackened. Place in a bowl, cover, and let stand about 15 minutes. Slip the charred skin off with your fingers, then cut the peppers in half and remove the seeds.

Blend the carrot mixture along with the peppers in several small batches. Add some of the soy milk to each batch to facilitate blending. Return to the pot and add the lemon juice, vinegar, salt, and pepper. Heat until steamy.

Nutrition information per 1½-cup serving: 122 calories, 4 g protein, 24 g carbohydrate, 1 g fat, 8% of calories from fat, 352 mg sodium

Autumn Stew

Serves 6

Based on traditional Native American foods—squash, corn, and beans—this stew is perfect for an autumn feast. Serve it with warm bread and a crisp green salad. The recipe calls for kabocha squash, which is particularly sweet and flavorful. If you are unable to find this variety, substitute butternut, delicata, or any other winter squash.

1½ cups water or vegetable stock
1 tablespoon low-sodium soy sauce
1 onion, chopped
1 red bell pepper, diced
4 large garlic cloves, minced
1 pound (about 4 cups) kabocha squash or other winter squash
1 15-ounce can chopped tomatoes
1½ teaspoons dried oregano
1 teaspoon chili powder
½ teaspoon cumin
¼ teaspoon black pepper
1 15-ounce can kidney beans
1½ cups fresh or frozen corn

Heat ½ cup water and soy sauce in a large pot, then add the onion, bell pepper, and garlic and cook over medium heat until the onion is translucent and most of the water is evaporated.

Cut the squash in half and remove the seeds, then peel and cut it into ½-inch cubes. Add to the onion mixture along with the chopped tomatoes, remaining 1 cup water, oregano, chili powder, cumin, and pepper. Cover and simmer until the squash is just tender when pierced with a fork, about 20 minutes, then add the kidney beans with their liquid and the corn. Cook 5 minutes longer.

Nutrition information per 1½-cup serving: 185 calories, 6 g protein, 38 g carbohydrate, 0.8 g fat, 4% of calories from fat, 314 mg sodium

Winter Squash and Red Lentil Stew

Serves 8

Try to find kabocha, buttercup, or one of the other sweet winter squashes for this stew. Serve this thick stew over couscous or basmati rice. Add some steamed broccoli or kale for a delicious, satisfying meal.

1 cup red lentils (masoor dal) or yellow split peas
4 cups water
1 onion, chopped
½ teaspoon each mustard seeds, turmeric, ginger, and cumin
¼ teaspoon cinnamon
⅛ teaspoon cayenne
4 cups peeled and diced winter squash (about 2 pounds)
1 tablespoon lemon juice
½ teaspoon salt

Place the lentils and 2 cups water in a pot and bring to a simmer. Cover loosely and cook until the lentils are tender, about 20 minutes.

Braise the onion in ½ cup water until soft and translucent, then add the spices, the remaining 1½ cups water, and the diced squash. Cover and cook over medium heat until the squash is tender when pierced with a fork, about 15 minutes. Stir in the lemon juice, cooked lentils, and salt to taste.

Nutrition information per 1¼-cup serving: 122 calories, 6 g protein, 23 g carbohydrate, 0.5 g fat, 4% of calories from fat, 136 mg sodium

VEGETABLES

Steamed Kale

Serves 2 to 4

Kale is an excellent source of calcium and beta-carotene and simply delicious when prepared according to the recipe below. Try to purchase young, tender greens, as these have the best flavor and texture.

1 bunch (about 1 pound) kale
½ cup water
1 teaspoon low-sodium soy sauce
2 to 3 garlic cloves, minced

Wash the kale, remove the stems, and chop the leaves into ½-inch-wide strips. Heat the water and soy sauce in a large pot or skillet and add the garlic. Cook 30 seconds, then add the greens, toss to mix, cover, and cook over medium-low heat for 3 to 5 minutes. Add water, 1 tablespoon at a time, if necessary to keep the greens from sticking.

Nutrition information per ½-cup serving: 61 calories, 3 g protein, 11 g carbohydrate, 0.4 g fat, 6% of calories from fat, 101 mg sodium

Steamed Kale with Pickled Ginger

Serves 2 to 4

Look for pickled ginger in the Asian food section of your food store.

1 bunch (about 1 pound) kale
½ cup water
1 teaspoon low-sodium soy sauce
2 to 3 garlic cloves, minced
2 teaspoons pickled ginger

Wash the kale, then remove the stems and chop the leaves. Heat the water and soy sauce in a large pot or skillet and add the garlic. Cook 30 seconds, then stir in the greens and pickled ginger. Cover and cook over medium-low heat until the kale is tender, 3 to 5 minutes.

Nutrition information per ½-cup serving: 61 calories, 3 g protein, 11 g carbohydrate, 0.4 g fat, 6% of calories from fat, 101 mg sodium

Braised Cabbage

Serves 2 to 3

This simple cooking technique brings out the delicious, sweet flavor of cabbage.

½ cup water
2 cups coarsely chopped cabbage
Salt and freshly ground black pepper

Bring the water to a boil in a skillet or saucepan. Stir in the cabbage, cover, and cook until it is just tender, about 5 minutes. Sprinkle with salt and pepper to taste.

Nutrition information per ½-cup serving: 16 calories, 0.5 g protein, 4 g carbohydrate, 0 g fat, 0% of calories from fat, 13 mg sodium

Zucchini Mexicana

Serves 6

¼ cup water
2 teaspoons low-sodium soy sauce
1 onion, chopped
3 garlic cloves, minced
3 cups diced zucchini
1 red bell pepper, diced
1 cup frozen or fresh corn kernels
1 teaspoon cumin
1 teaspoon chili powder

Heat the water and soy sauce in a large skillet. Add the onion and garlic and cook until soft. Add the zucchini and bell pepper and cook until the zucchini is just tender, about 5 minutes. Stir in the corn, cumin, and chili powder, and cook 2 minutes longer.

Nutrition information per 1-cup serving: 52 calories, 2 g protein, 11 g carbohydrate, 0.1 g fat, 1% of calories from fat, 76 mg sodium

Delicata Squash

Serves 6

This winter squash is so sweet and flavorful that it really doesn't need any dressing up. Simply steam or bake it until tender. If you want to add some additional flavor, try the simple recipe below. Mirin is a rice wine that is available in most grocery stores in the ethnic foods section.

3 delicata squashes
1 to 2 tablespoons seasoned rice vinegar or mirin
¼ teaspoon freshly ground black pepper

Cut the squashes in half lengthwise and remove the seeds. Place in a vegetable steamer over boiling water and steam until tender, about 15 minutes.

Preheat the oven to 350°F.

Remove the squashes from the steamer and pour off any liquid that has accumulated, then place in an ovenproof dish. Sprinkle with seasoned rice vinegar or mirin and freshly ground black pepper. Bake for 10 minutes.

Nutrition information per 1-cup serving: 92 calories, 2 g protein, 21 g carbohydrate, 0 g fat, 0% of calories from fat, 9 mg of sodium

Mashed Potatoes and Kale

Serves 6

4 russet potatoes
½ to 1 cup soy milk
½ to 1 teaspoon salt
⅛ teaspoon black pepper
1 bunch kale (about 4 cups)
½ cup water
1 teaspoon low-sodium soy sauce
2 to 3 garlic cloves, minced

Scrub the potatoes, peel if desired, and cut into chunks. Place in a large pot with about 1 cup of water and cook, covered, over medium heat until tender when pierced with a fork. Mash them with the water, then add the soy milk and salt and pepper to taste.

Wash the kale, remove the stems, and chop the leaves into small pieces. In a large pot or skillet, heat the water and soy sauce, add the garlic, and cook 30 seconds. Add the greens and toss to mix, then cover and cook over medium heat until tender, about 5 minutes. Add water, 1 tablespoon at a time, if necessary to keep the greens from sticking. Mix the cooked kale with the mashed potatoes and serve.

Nutrition information per 1½-cup serving: 174 calories, 3 g protein, 39 g carbohydrate, 0.4 g fat, 2% of calories from fat, 245 mg sodium

Golden Potatoes

Serves 6

Top these colorful, spicy potatoes with chutney and serve them with lentil or bean soups.

4 large red potatoes
2 teaspoons whole mustard seed
½ teaspoon turmeric
½ teaspoon cumin
¼ teaspoon ginger
⅛ teaspoon cayenne
⅛ teaspoon black pepper
1 cup water
1 onion, chopped
1½ teaspoons soy sauce

Scrub the potatoes, then steam them over boiling water until tender when pierced with a fork, 40 to 50 minutes. Cool completely, then cut them into ½-inch cubes.

Toast the spices in a large nonstick skillet for 1 to 2 minutes, then carefully pour in ½ cup of the water. Add the chopped onion and cook, stirring frequently, until the onion is soft and most of the liquid has evaporated, about 5 minutes. Add the potatoes along with the remaining water and the soy sauce. Stir to mix, then cover and cook over medium heat for 5 minutes. Stir before serving.

Nutrition information per 1-cup serving: 161 calories, 3 g protein, 37 g carbohydrate, 0.1 g fat, 1% of calories from fat, 62 mg sodium

Roasted Potatoes

Serves 6

Be sure to try this simple fat-free version of french fries!

4 medium-large potatoes
2 teaspoons Schilling Garlic and Herb Seasoning or other seasoning
      mix
¼ teaspoon salt
Freshly ground black pepper

Preheat the oven to 500°F.

Scrub the potatoes and cut them into strips. Lightly spray a 9 × 13-inch baking dish with nonstick spray and spread the potatoes in it. Sprinkle with the seasonings and toss to mix. Bake until tender when pierced with a fork, about 30 minutes.

Nutrition information per 1-cup serving: 147 calories, 2 g protein, 34 g carbohydrate, 0.1 g fat, 1% of calories from fat, 100 mg sodium

Roasted Yams or Sweet Potatoes

Serves 6

4 yams or sweet potatoes
2 teaspoons Schilling Garlic and Herb Seasoning or other seasoning
    mix
¼ teaspoon salt
Freshly ground black pepper

Preheat the oven to 500°F.

Scrub the sweet potatoes or yams and cut them into chunks. Spray a 9 × 13-inch baking dish with nonstick spray. Spread the yams in the dish, sprinkle with the seasonings, and toss to mix. Bake until tender when pierced with a fork, 25 to 30 minutes.

Nutrition information per 1-cup serving: 158 calories, 1.5 g protein, 38 g carbohydrate, 0 g fat, 0% of calories from fat, 145 mg sodium

GRAINS

Brown Rice

Makes 3 cups of cooked rice, 6 servings

Cooking brown rice in extra water ensures perfect rice every time and actually reduces the cooking time.

    1 cup short-grain brown rice
    4 cups water
    ¼ teaspoon salt (optional)

Rinse and drain the rice. In a saucepan, bring the water to a boil, then add the rice and salt, if desired. Once the water returns to a boil, lower the heat slightly, then cover and simmer about 40 minutes until the rice is soft but still retains a hint of crunchiness. Pour off any excess water.

Nutrition information per ½-cup serving: 115 calories, 2.5 g protein, 25 g carbohydrate, 0.5 g fat, 4% of calories from fat, 88 mg sodium

Risotto

Makes 2½ cups, 6 servings

Risotto is made with arborio rice, which is available in specialty food stores and a growing number of supermarkets. The secret to making a wonderful, creamy risotto is adding the liquid in small amounts and stirring constantly.

1 onion, finely chopped
½ cup water or vegetable stock
½ teaspoon salt
1 cup arborio rice
4 to 5 cups boiling water or vegetable stock

Braise the onion in ½ cup water until it is soft and translucent, then stir in the salt and rice. Add ½ cup boiling water, stirring constantly, until it is completely absorbed. Continue adding boiling water, ½ cup at a time, stirring constantly, until the rice is tender and all the water is absorbed.

Nutrition information per ½-cup serving: 122 calories, 2 g protein, 27 g carbohydrate, 0.2 g fat, 1.5% of calories from fat, 179 mg sodium

Quick Confetti Rice

Serves 4 to 6

This colorful rice pilaf has no added fat, so be sure to use a nonstick skillet.

2 tablespoons water or stock
2 cups cooked brown rice
½ cup frozen corn

½ cup frozen peas
½ cup diced red bell pepper, fresh or canned
½ teaspoon curry powder
¼ cup raisins (optional)
Salt

Add the water to a skillet along with the cooked rice. Using a spatula or the back of a wooden spoon, separate the rice kernels. Add the remaining ingredients and heat until steamy hot. Add salt to taste.

Nutrition information per ¾-cup serving: 139 calories, 4 g protein, 30 g carbohydrate, 0.5 g fat, 3% of calories from fat, 184 mg sodium

Bulgur

Makes about 2½ cups, 5 servings

Bulgur is cracked wheat that has been toasted to give it a delicious, nutty flavor. It cooks in about 15 minutes and is an excellent accompaniment to a wide variety of foods, from chili to roasted vegetables.

2 cups water
1 cup bulgur
¼ teaspoon salt

Bring the water to a boil in a saucepan, then stir in the bulgur and salt. Reduce the heat to a simmer, then cover and cook until the bulgur is tender, about 15 minutes.

Nutrition information per ½-cup serving: 113 calories, 4 g protein, 24 g carbohydrate, 0.2 g fat, 2% of calories from fat, 110 mg sodium

Spanish Bulgur

Serves 8

Cracked and toasted wheat makes a quick and delicious Spanish pilaf. Serve it with chili or refried beans.

2 cups bulgur
3½ cups boiling water
2 garlic cloves, minced
2 teaspoons olive oil
4 to 6 teaspoons chili powder
1 teaspoon ground cumin
½ teaspoon salt

Place the bulgur in a large bowl and pour the boiling water over it. Cover the bowl and let stand 20 minutes, until the bulgur is tender. Drain off any excess water.

In a large skillet, sauté the garlic in oil for a few seconds over medium heat. Do not let it brown. With the pan still on the heat, stir in the soaked bulgur and add the chili powder, cumin, and salt. Turn with a spatula to mix in the spices and continue cooking until the mixture is very hot. Serve immediately.

Nutrition information per ¾-cup serving: 158 calories, 5.5 g protein, 31 g carbohydrate, 1.3 g fat, 8% of calories from fat, 154 mg sodium

Couscous

Makes 3 cups, 6 servings

Couscous cooks in minutes and makes a delicious side dish or salad.

½ teaspoon salt
1½ cups boiling water
1 cup couscous

Bring the salted water to a boil in a small pan. Stir in the couscous, then remove the pan from heat and cover it. Let stand 10 to 15 minutes, then fluff with a fork and serve.

Nutrition information per ½-cup serving: 91 calories, 3 g protein, 20 g carbohydrate, 0 g fat, 0% of calories from fat, 182 mg sodium

Polenta

Makes 4 cups, 8 servings

Polenta, or coarsely ground cornmeal, has long been a staple grain in northern Italy. It cooks easily and is delicious with marinara or any other spicy sauce. Pour the cooked polenta onto a platter and top it with sauce or spoon it into a bread pan and chill it, then slice and grill it.

1 cup polenta
1 cup cold water
½ to 1 teaspoon salt
4 cups boiling water

Stir the polenta and cold water together in a saucepan. Stir in the salt and boiling water and simmer, stirring frequently, until thickened, about 15 minutes.

Nutrition information per ½-cup serving: 62 calories, 1.5 g protein, 14 g carbohydrate, 0.2 g fat, 3% of calories from fat, 133 to 267 mg sodium

Polenta with Sun-dried Tomatoes

Makes 4 cups, 8 servings

Sun-dried tomatoes add a subtle flavor and beautiful color.

    12 sun-dried tomatoes
    1 cup polenta
    ½ to 1 teaspoon salt
    1 cup cold water
    4 cups boiling water

Cut sun-dried tomatoes into small pieces using a sharp knife or kitchen shears. In a large pot, combine the tomato pieces, polenta, salt, and 1 cup cold water. Stir to mix, then add 4 cups boiling water and simmer, stirring frequently, until thickened, about 15 minutes.

Nutrition information per ½-cup serving: 95 calories, 2 g protein, 20 g carbohydrate, 0.3 g fat, 3% of calories from fat, 137 to 270 mg sodium

ENTRÉES

Roasted Summer Vegetables and Tofu

Serves 8

Grilling or oven-roasting vegetables is so easy and brings out their best flavors. For this recipe you should have a total of about 6 cups of chopped vegetables.

2 to 3 cups cubed summer squash (zucchini, crookneck, or scallop)
1 onion, cut into chunks
1 red bell pepper, seeded and cut into large pieces
2 cups small mushrooms
½ pound very firm tofu, cut into 1-inch cubes
1 tablespoon Spike, Schilling Garlic and Herb, or other seasoning mix
2 tomatoes, cut into wedges

Preheat the oven to 500°F.

Prepare the vegetables as directed and mix them with the tofu cubes. Divide between two 9 × 13-inch baking dishes and sprinkle with the seasoning. Toss to mix, then spread evenly in the dishes. Bake until the vegetables are tender and the edges just begin to darken, 15 to 20 minutes. Spread the cooked vegetables over Risotto (page 312), Polenta (page 315), or pasta and top with fresh tomato wedges.

Nutrition information per 1-cup serving: 55 calories, 4 g protein, 7 g carbohydrate, 1 g fat, 14% of calories from fat, 7 mg sodium

Pasta with Broccoli and Fresh Tomatoes

Serves 6 to 8

This dish features tender broccoli in a spicy tomato sauce served over pasta.

    12 ounces pasta (rigatoni, rotelle, or the like)
    1 15-ounce can garbanzo beans, drained (reserve liquid)
    ½ cup roasted red peppers
    3 tablespoons tahini (sesame seed butter)
    3 tablespoons lemon juice
    4 large garlic cloves, finely chopped
    ¼ teaspoon hot red pepper flakes
    1 tablespoon olive oil
    4 large tomatoes, diced
    1 bunch broccoli (about 1½ pounds), broken into florets
    ¼ teaspoon salt (optional)
    ¼ teaspoon freshly ground black pepper

Cook the pasta in a large pot of boiling water until just tender. Rinse quickly with cold water and drain.

Puree the drained garbanzo beans, red peppers, tahini, and lemon juice in a blender or food processor until very smooth. If the mixture is too thick to blend, add a tablespoon or two of the reserved bean liquid.

In a large skillet, sauté the garlic and red pepper flakes in olive oil for 1 minute, then add the diced tomatoes, cover, and cook over medium heat for 5 minutes. Add the broccoli florets, cover, and cook until the broccoli is bright green and just tender. This should only take 3 to 5 minutes. Add salt, if desired.

Gently stir the garbanzo mixture into the cooked pasta and spread it on a platter. Sprinkle with freshly ground black pepper and top with the broccoli-tomato mixture. Serve immediately.

Nutrition information per 1½-cup serving: 243 calories, 8.5 g protein, 39 g carbohydrate, 5 g fat, 19% of calories from fat, 96 mg sodium

Pasta e Fagioli

Serves 10

Pasta and beans, an Italian favorite, is simple and satisfying!

½ cup water or vegetable stock
2 onions, chopped
1 large bell pepper, diced
2 carrots, sliced
2 celery stalks, sliced
½ pound (about 2 cups) mushrooms, sliced
1 15-ounce can chopped tomatoes
1 15-ounce can kidney beans, drained
½ teaspoon paprika
½ teaspoon black pepper
2 tablespoons low-sodium soy sauce
8 ounces rigatoni (or similar pasta)

In a large pot, heat the water or stock. Braise the onions for 3 minutes, then add the pepper, carrots, and celery and cook for 5 minutes over medium heat. Add the mushrooms, then cover the pan and cook an additional 7 minutes, stirring occasionally. Add the tomatoes, kidney beans, paprika, pepper, and soy sauce, then cover and cook 10 to 15 minutes.

Cook the pasta in a large pot of boiling water until just tender. Rinse and drain, then add it to the vegetable mixture.

Nutrition information per 1½-cup serving: 147 calories, 6.5 g protein, 29 g carbohydrate, 0.4 g fat, 2% of calories from fat, 137 mg sodium

Spinach Turnovers

Makes 12 turnovers, 6 servings

These are quite quick to assemble and keep well for several days in the refrigerator.

    1 pound fresh spinach leaves
    1 cup chopped red onion
    ¼ cup water
    ¼ cup chopped fresh parsley
    1½ teaspoons dried dill
    ½ teaspoon salt
    ¼ teaspoon black pepper
    2 tablespoons lemon juice
    6 flour tortillas
    1 to 2 tablespoons olive oil

Remove the stems from the spinach and wash the leaves. Chop coarsely and set aside.

In a large pot, cook the onion in water until soft, then stir in the parsley, dill, salt, pepper, and chopped spinach. Cook over medium heat, stirring often, until the spinach is wilted and the mixture is dry. Stir in the lemon juice.

Preheat the oven to 375°F.

To assemble the turnovers, cut a tortilla in half. Using your fingers or a pastry brush, wet the edges with water. Place about 2 tablespoons of filling in the center of the tortilla. Now imagine the tortilla divided into thirds. Fold one edge over, matching the curves, and press the edge firmly to seal. Fold the remaining edge over and press the edges firmly to seal. Brush lightly with olive oil. Place the turnovers on a baking sheet and bake until lightly browned, about 25 minutes.

Nutrition information per turnover: 177 calories, 6 g protein, 24 g carbohydrate, 5 g fat, 27% of calories from fat, 324 mg sodium

Polenta with Hearty Barbecue Sauce

Serves 4 to 6

Seitan adds a meaty taste and texture to this savory barbecue sauce. In this recipe it is served over hot polenta. For a variation, try it with pasta or as a topping on burger buns for Sloppy Joes. Look for seitan in the deli case of your natural food store.

1½ cups water
3 teaspoons low-sodium soy sauce
1 large onion, finely chopped
1 bell pepper, finely diced
3 large garlic cloves, minced
1 15-ounce can tomato sauce
1 tablespoon sugar
1 teaspoon chili powder
2 tablespoons cider vinegar
1 tablespoon peanut butter
1 teaspoon stone-ground or Dijon-style mustard
8 ounces coarsely chopped or grated seitan
4 cups cooked polenta (page 315)

Heat ½ cup water and 1 teaspoon soy sauce in a large pot. Add the chopped onion, bell pepper, and garlic and cook until the onion is soft and translucent. Add the remaining ingredients and cook over medium heat, stirring frequently, for 10 minutes. Spread the cooked polenta onto a serving bowl or platter, then top with the sauce and serve.

Nutrition information per 1½-cup serving: 136 calories, 11 g protein, 22 g carbohydrate, 0.3 g fat, 2% of calories from fat, 430 mg sodium

Variation: Rehydrate 1 cup of texturized vegetable protein in 1 cup of boiling water and substitute it for the seitan.

Nutrition information per 1½-cup serving: 134 calories, 8 g protein, 24 g carbohydrate, 0.4 g fat, 3% of calories from fat, 373 mg sodium

Vegetarian Tacos

Makes 10 to 12 tacos

Texturized vegetable protein (TVP) is made from soybeans and makes a quick and delicious taco filling. It is available at natural food stores and in some supermarkets.

1 cup water
1 small onion, chopped
2 garlic cloves, crushed
1 small green bell pepper, diced
¾ cup texturized vegetable protein
½ cup tomato sauce
2 teaspoons chili powder
½ teaspoon cumin
¼ teaspoon oregano
1 tablespoon nutritional yeast (optional)
1 tablespoon low-sodium soy sauce
12 corn tortillas
4 green onions, sliced
1 cup shredded leaf lettuce
1 medium tomato, diced
½ cup salsa or taco sauce

Heat ½ cup of the water in a large skillet and cook the onion, garlic, and bell pepper over medium heat until the onion is soft, about 5 minutes. Add the TVP, tomato sauce, chili powder, cumin, oregano, nutritional yeast, soy sauce, and remaining water. Cook over medium heat until the mixture is fairly dry, about 3 minutes.

Spread a small amount of the filling mixture on a tortilla and place it in a heated, ungreased skillet. When it is warm and pliable, fold the tortilla in half and cook each side for 30 to 60 seconds. Garnish with onions, lettuce, tomatoes, and salsa.

Variation: For Seitan Tacos, substitute 1½ cups of ground seitan for the rehydrated texturized vegetable protein.

Nutrition information per taco (with TVP): 130 calories, 7 g protein, 21 g carbohydrate, 1 g fat, 10% of calories from fat, 75 mg sodium

Nutrition information per taco (with seitan): 160 calories, 10 g protein, 25 g carbohydrate, 1.5 g fat, 9% of calories from fat, 137 mg sodium

Tortilla Casserole

Serves 12

1 cup water
1 large onion, chopped
1 tablespoon minced garlic (about 4 large cloves)
1 28-ounce can crushed tomatoes
4 teaspoons chili powder
2 teaspoons cumin
⅔ cup texturized vegetable protein (TVP)
⅔ cup water
1 15-ounce can garbanzo beans, drained
½ cup roasted red peppers (about 2 peppers)
3 tablespoons lemon juice
3 tablespoons tahini (sesame seed butter)
12 corn tortillas, torn in half
2 15-ounce cans vegetarian chili beans
1 cup chopped green onions
1–2 cups corn, fresh or frozen

Braise the onion and garlic in ½ cup water until onion is soft, about 5 minutes. Add the tomatoes, chili powder, cumin, TVP, and the remaining ½ cup water and simmer over medium heat 5 minutes.

Puree the garbanzo beans, roasted peppers, tahini, and lemon juice in a food processor or blender until very smooth. Set aside.

Preheat the oven to 350°F.

Spread about ½ cup of the tomato sauce in the bottom of a 9 × 13-inch baking dish. Cover with a layer of tortillas, then spread with a third of the garbanzo bean mixture. Sprinkle a third of the undrained chili beans, the green onions, and the corn. Spread about 1 cup of sauce over this. Repeat the layers twice, ending with sauce. Make sure all the tortillas are covered. Bake for 25 minutes, until hot and bubbly.

Nutrition information per 3 × 3-inch serving: 246 calories, 11 g protein, 42 g carbohydrate, 3.5 g fat, 13% of calories from fat, 290 mg sodium

Quick Chili

Serves 8

There's nothing quite like a bowl of steaming hot chili to warm a cold winter day. Texturized vegetable protein adds flavor and texture and is available in natural food stores.

½ cup boiling water
½ cup texturized vegetable protein
1 onion, chopped
1 green bell pepper, diced
2 large garlic cloves, minced
½ cup water or vegetable stock
2 15-ounce cans pinto beans
1 15-ounce can tomato sauce
1 cup fresh or frozen corn
1 to 2 teaspoons chili powder
1 teaspoon dried oregano
½ teaspoon ground cumin
⅛ teaspoon cayenne (more for spicier beans)

Pour the boiling water over the texturized vegetable protein and let stand until softened.

Braise the onion, bell pepper, and garlic in water until the onion is soft, then add the remaining ingredients, including the texturized vegetable protein. Simmer at least 30 minutes.

Nutrition information per 1-cup serving: 164 calories, 10 g protein, 30 g carbohydrate, 0.4 g fat, 2% of calories from fat, 158 mg sodium

Mexican Corn Pie

Serves 8 to 10

Serve this spicy rice and corn pie with Quick Chili (page 324) or Quick Black Bean Burritos (page 290).

2½ cups water
1 cup brown basmati rice (or other long-grain brown rice)
1 large onion, chopped
2 large garlic cloves, crushed
1 red bell pepper, diced
2 cups fresh or frozen corn
1 4-ounce can diced chilies
1 cup cornmeal
1 teaspoon salt
1 teaspoon cumin
2 tablespoons nutritional yeast (optional)
3 cups soy milk

Bring 2 cups water to a boil and add the rice. Adjust the heat so the water simmers, then cover and cook until the rice is tender, about 50 minutes.

Preheat the oven to 350°F.

In a large ovenproof skillet (see Note below), braise the onion, garlic, and bell pepper in the remaining ½ cup water until the onion is soft and translucent, about 5 minutes. Remove from the heat and stir in the remaining ingredients, including the cooked rice. Bake for 45 minutes.

Note: If you don't have an ovenproof skillet, bake the pie in a 9 × 13-inch casserole dish.

Nutrition information per 1-cup serving: 156 calories, 4 g protein, 32 g carbohydrate, 1 g fat, 6% of calories from fat, 305 mg sodium

Spicy Indonesian Stir-fry

Serves 8

Once the vegetables are all prepared, this dish cooks in a flash. Udon is a Japanese pasta available in many supermarkets and natural food stores. If you cannot find it, use spaghetti.

8 ounces udon or spaghetti
2 teaspoons toasted sesame oil
1 teaspoon turmeric
½ teaspoon cumin
¼ teaspoon red pepper flakes
1 onion, sliced
2 cups sliced mushrooms
½ pound firm tofu, cut into cubes
2 celery stalks, sliced
2 cups shredded green cabbage
1 red bell pepper, seeded and cut into strips
2 cups bean sprouts (optional)
2 tablespoons low-sodium soy sauce

Cook the noodles in a large pot of boiling water until just tender. Drain and rinse quickly with cold water.

Add the oil to a large nonstick wok or skillet, then add the spices and onion and cook over high heat until the onion is soft, about 3 minutes. Add the mushrooms, tofu, and celery and cook another 3 minutes. Add the cabbage and bell pepper, then cover and cook 4 minutes, stirring occasionally. Add the cooked noodles, bean sprouts, if desired, and soy sauce and toss gently to mix. Serve immediately, with Simple Peanut Sauce (page 292), if desired.

Nutrition information per 1½-cup serving: 136 calories, 8 g protein, 21 g carbohydrate, 2 g fat, 14% of calories from fat, 185 mg sodium

Shepherd's Pie

Serves 10

This is a hearty and satisfying vegetable stew with a top "crust" of fluffy mashed potatoes.

4 large russet potatoes, diced
½ to 1 cup soy milk
½ teaspoon salt
½ cup water or vegetable stock
2 onions, chopped
1 large bell pepper, diced
2 carrots, sliced
2 celery stalks, sliced
½ pound (about 2 cups) mushrooms, sliced
1 15-ounce can chopped tomatoes
1 15-ounce can kidney beans, drained
½ teaspoon paprika
½ teaspoon black pepper
2 tablespoons low-sodium soy sauce

Dice the potatoes and steam them until tender. Mash, adding enough soy milk to make them smooth and spreadable. Add salt to taste. Set aside.

In a large pot, heat the water or stock and cook the onions for 3 minutes. Add the pepper, carrots, and celery and cook for 5 minutes over medium heat. Add the mushrooms, then cover the pan and cook an additional 7 minutes, stirring occasionally. Add the tomatoes, kidney beans, paprika, pepper, and soy sauce, then cover and cook 10 to 15 minutes.

Preheat the oven to 350°F.

Put the vegetables into a 9 × 13-inch baking dish and spread the mashed potatoes evenly over the top. Sprinkle with paprika. Bake for 25 minutes, until hot and bubbly.

Nutrition information per 1½-cup serving: 217 calories, 6 g protein, 47 g carbohydrate, 0.4 g fat, 2% of calories from fat, 257 mg sodium

Vegetarian Swiss Steak

Serves 8

Seitan is made from wheat and has a taste and texture hearty enough to satisfy any meat eater. Serve this dish over pasta or rice with a crisp green salad.

1 large onion
½ cup white wine or water
3 cups sliced mushrooms
1 large green bell pepper, diced
1 red bell pepper, diced (optional)
2 tablespoons minced garlic (about 8 large cloves)
2 tablespoons chopped fresh basil, or 2 teaspoons dried
¼ cup light miso dissolved in ½ cup water
1 28-ounce can chopped tomatoes
¼ teaspoon black pepper
16 ounces seitan, cut into thick slices

Cut the onion in half, then into thin slices. Heat the wine or water in a large skillet or pot and braise the onion until it is soft, about 5 minutes. Add the sliced mushrooms, bell peppers, garlic, and basil. Continue cooking over medium heat for 8 to 10 minutes, then stir in the dissolved miso, tomatoes, and pepper. Simmer 5 minutes.

Preheat the oven to 350°F.

Spread ½ cup of sauce evenly in the bottom of a large casserole dish. Arrange the seitan slices in the dish, then cover with the rest of the sauce. Cover the dish and bake for 20 to 25 minutes.

Nutrition information per 1-cup serving: 144 calories, 18 g protein, 14 g carbohydrate, 0.5 g fat, 3% of calories from fat, 448 mg sodium

Spinach and Mushroom Fritatta

Serves 8

This fritatta is like a crustless quiche. It is made with silken tofu, which is available in most grocery stores.

½ cup water
1 onion, chopped
2 garlic cloves, minced
2 cups sliced mushrooms
1 10-ounce package frozen spinach, thawed and squeezed dry
1 10.5-ounce package firm silken tofu
1 tablespoon tahini (sesame seed butter)
2 teaspoons dried basil
½ teaspoon salt
¼ teaspoon black pepper
¼ teaspoon nutmeg
¼ teaspoon celery seed
2 tablespoons couscous
¼ cup soy milk, rice milk, or water
1 ripe tomato, thinly sliced

Heat the water in a large pot or skillet and cook the onion and garlic until soft, about 3 minutes. Add the mushrooms and cook another 5 minutes. Stir in the spinach and cook until the mixture is very dry.

Preheat the oven to 350°F.

In a food processor or blender, process the tofu and tahini until very smooth. Rub the basil between the palms of your hands to crush it, then mix it into the tofu along with the salt, pepper, nutmeg, celery seed, couscous, and soy milk. Add to the spinach mixture and stir to mix.

Pour into a 10-inch pie pan that has been sprayed with a nonstick spray. Bake for 15 minutes. Arrange the sliced tomatoes around the edge, then bake another 10 minutes. Let stand 10 minutes before serving.

Variation: For Spinach and Mushroom Quiche, pour into a partially baked 10-inch pie shell and bake as above. Let stand 10 minutes before serving.

Nutrition information per 2-inch slice: 86 calories, 6 g protein, 11 g carbohydrate, 2 g fat, 19% of calories from fat, 269 mg sodium

Cabbage and Carrot Cobbler

Serves 10

Shredded cabbage and grated carrots make a hearty and colorful vegetable pie. White Wave Dairyless is a soy yogurt available in many natural food stores.

1 cup water
4 cups shredded green cabbage
1 cup grated carrot
2 onions, sliced
1¼ cups plain White Wave Dairyless
¼ teaspoon salt
⅛ teaspoon black pepper
2 cups whole wheat pastry flour
2 teaspoons low-sodium baking powder
¼ teaspoon salt
1 cup soy or rice milk
2 tablespoons olive oil

Preheat the oven to 375°F.

Place the water, cabbage, carrots, and onion in a large pot. Cover and cook over medium heat for 5 minutes. Uncover and continue cooking an additional 5 minutes. Stir in 1 cup Dairyless, salt, and pepper. Set aside.

Stir the flour, baking powder, and salt together in a mixing bowl. Add the remaining ¼ cup Dairyless, milk, and olive oil and stir just to mix. The batter will be quite thick. Spread in a greased 9 × 13-inch baking dish. Spread the cabbage mixture evenly over the top and bake for 35 minutes.

Nutrition information per 1-cup serving: 164 calories, 6 g protein, 26 g carbohydrate, 4 g fat, 22% of calories from fat, 143 mg sodium

DESSERTS

Fresh Apricot Crisp

Serves 8

4 cups pitted apricots, coarsely chopped
2 tablespoons lemon juice
2 cups rolled oats
¼ cup sugar or other sweetener
¼ cup Spectrum Naturals Spread or margarine
2 tablespoons water

Preheat the oven to 350°F.

Toss the chopped apricots with the lemon juice and set aside. Combine the rolled oats, sugar, and Spectrum Naturals Spread (see Note below) and mix thoroughly. Remove 1 cup and set aside. Add the water to the remainder and mix until crumbly.

Spray a 9-inch square baking pan lightly with a nonstick spray. Pat the oat mixture into the pan. Spread the apricots evenly over this and top with the reserved crumb mixture. Bake for 35 to 40 minutes, until the top crust is lightly browned.

Note: Spectrum Naturals Spread is like margarine in flavor and consistency but is made without hydrogenated fats.

Nutrition information per ¾-cup serving: 153 calories, 4 g protein, 25 g carbohydrate, 4 g fat, 23% of calories from fat, 48 mg sodium

Apple Crisp

Serves 10

4 large tart apples
¾ cup sugar or other sweetener
½ cup flour
1 teaspoon cinnamon
1½ cups rolled oats
⅓ cup Spectrum Naturals Spread or margarine

Preheat the oven to 350°F.

Peel the apples, if desired, then core and slice them thinly. Toss with ½ cup sugar, 1 tablespoon flour, and cinnamon. Spread evenly in a 9 × 13-inch baking dish.

Mix the rolled oats with the remaining flour and sugar. Add the Spectrum Naturals Spread (or margarine) and work the mixture until it is uniformly crumbly. Sprinkle evenly over the fruit.

Bake for 45 minutes, until lightly browned. Let stand 10 minutes before serving.

Nutrition information per ¾-cup serving: 189 calories, 3 g protein, 35 g carbohydrate, 4 g fat, 20% of calories from fat, 61 mg sodium

Tropical Delight

Serves 3

Pureed frozen fruit makes a wonderful dessert without the fat or refined sugar of ice cream. Many supermarkets carry frozen pineapple and mango or you can make your own by freezing canned pineapple chunks and fresh mango. To freeze bananas, peel and break into chunks. Freeze in a single layer on a tray, then store in an airtight container.

1 orange, peeled
½ cup frozen banana chunks
1 cup frozen pineapple chunks
1 cup frozen mango chunks
½ to 1 cup soy milk

Cut the orange in half and remove any seeds, then place in a blender with the remaining ingredients and process until thick and very smooth.

Nutrition information per 1-cup serving: 141 calories, 2 g protein, 31 g carbohydrate, 1 g fat, 4.5% of calories from fat, 17 mg sodium

Quick Rice Pudding

Serves 3 to 4

1½ cups soy milk (vanilla or plain)
1 tablespoon cornstarch or arrowroot
2 cups cooked rice (white or brown)
¼ cup maple syrup
⅓ cup raisins
¼ teaspoon cinnamon
1 teaspoon vanilla extract
½ teaspoon almond extract

Pour the soy milk into a medium-sized saucepan and stir in the cornstarch. Add the rice, maple syrup, raisins, and cinnamon and bring to a simmer over medium heat. Cook 3 minutes, then remove from the heat and stir in the vanilla and almond extracts. Serve hot or cold.

Nutrition information per 1-cup serving: 151 calories, 2.5 g protein, 34 g carbohydrate, 1 g fat, 6% of calories from fat, 28 mg sodium

Chocolate Tofu Pudding

Serves 4

Silken tofu makes a wonderful, creamy pudding. Look for it in your grocery store.

  1 pound silken tofu
  2 tablespoons cocoa
  ¼ teaspoon salt
  ⅓ to ½ cup maple syrup (use larger amount if using firm tofu)
  1 teaspoon vanilla extract

Place all the ingredients into a blender and process until completely smooth. Spoon into small bowls and chill before serving.

Nutrition information per ½-cup serving: 213 calories, 13 g protein, 33 g carbohydrate, 3.4 g fat, 14% of calories from fat, 145 mg sodium

Quick Indian Pudding

Serves 4

You'll love this quick, delicious version of Indian pudding, which bakes for just 30 minutes.

½ cup cornmeal
4 cups soy milk
1 tablespoon canola oil
1 tablespoon molasses
¼ cup maple syrup
¼ teaspoon salt
1 teaspoon ginger
½ teaspoon cinnamon

In a heavy saucepan, stir the cornmeal into 2 cups soy milk and bring to a simmer. Cook over medium heat, stirring often, for 5 minutes. Stir in the oil, molasses, maple syrup, salt, and spices. Stir in 1 additional cup soy milk and continue cooking for 10 minutes, stirring often.

Preheat the oven to 350°F.

Pour into a 1½-quart baking dish, then pour in the remaining cup of milk. Stir a few strokes to just barely mix. Bake for 30 minutes. Turn off the oven. Leave the pudding in the oven with door closed until the oven is cool. Serve the pudding warm or cold.

Nutrition information per 1-cup serving: 167 calories, 4 g protein, 30 g carbohydrate, 4 g fat, 20% of calories from fat, 155 mg sodium

Yam Pie

Serves 8

Similar in flavor to pumpkin pie, this tasty dessert is a rich source of beta-carotene.

2 medium yams
⅓ cup sugar
3 tablespoons cornstarch or arrowroot powder
½ teaspoon cinnamon
¼ teaspoon ginger
⅛ teaspoon cloves
⅛ teaspoon salt
1½ cups soy milk
1 Fat-free Piecrust (recipe page 338)

Peel the yams and cut them into 1-inch chunks. Steam in a covered pot over boiling water until tender when pierced with a fork, about 40 minutes. Mash, leaving some chunks. You should have about 2 cups.

Preheat the oven to 350°F.

In a mixing bowl, whisk together the sugar, cornstarch, spices, and salt, then stir in the soy milk and the mashed yams. Pour into the pre-baked fat-free crust or an unbaked 9- or 10-inch standard piecrust and bake for 35 minutes. Cool before cutting.

Nutrition information per 2-inch slice (with fat-free crust): 158 calories, 3 g protein, 36 g carbohydrate, 0.5 g fat, 3% of calories from fat, 152 mg sodium

Nutrition information per 2-inch slice (with conventional crust): 261 calories, 4 g protein, 42 g carbohydrate, 8 g fat, 28% of calories from fat, 155 mg sodium

Banana Dream Pie

Serves 8

This fabulous, rich-tasting pie contains no eggs or cream. For a completely fat-free version, omit the almonds and use the fat-free crust, which follows. Either way, it is simply heavenly.

 1 Tender Almond Piecrust (recipe page 338) or 1 Fat-free Piecrust
   (recipe page 338)
 ½ cup sugar or other sweetener
 5 tablespoons cornstarch
 2 cups rice or soy milk
 ½ teaspoon salt
 1 teaspoon vanilla extract
 ½ pound firm tofu
 2 ripe bananas
 2 tablespoons coarsely chopped almonds

Prepare the crust according to directions. Cool.

Mix the sugar and cornstarch in a saucepan, then stir in the milk and salt. Cook over medium heat, stirring constantly, until very thick. Remove from the heat and stir in the vanilla. Drain the tofu and blend it in a food processor until it is totally smooth, then add the pudding and blend until smooth.

Slice the bananas into thin rounds over the cooled crust. Spread the tofu mixture on top.

Toast the chopped almonds in a 375°F. oven until lightly browned, about 10 minutes, then sprinkle evenly over the pie. Refrigerate until completely chilled, at least 2 hours.

Nutrition information per 2-inch slice (with almond crust): 206 calories, 6 g protein, 30 g carbohydrate, 6.5 g fat, 28% of calories from fat, 180 mg sodium

Nutrition information per 2-inch slice (with fat-free crust): 162 calories, 4 g protein, 33 g carbohydrate, 1.6 g fat, 9% of calories from fat, 204 mg sodium

Fat-free Piecrust

Makes one 9-inch crust

This tasty crust is quick and easy to prepare.

1 cup Grape-Nuts cereal
¼ cup apple juice concentrate (undiluted)

Preheat the oven to 350°F.

Mix together the Grape-Nuts and apple juice concentrate. Pat into a thin layer on the bottom and sides of a 9-inch pie pan. Don't worry if there are some gaps. Bake for 8 minutes. Cool before filling.

Nutrition information per 2-inch slice: 68 calories, 2 g protein, 15 g carbohydrate, 0.1 g fat, 1% of calories from fat, 97 mg sodium

Tender Almond Piecrust

Makes 1 crust

The next best thing to a fat-free piecrust is a crust made with no refined fats or oils. This easy crust is made with almonds, which add wonderful flavor to any pie.

⅔ cup almonds
⅔ cup whole wheat pastry flour
¼ teaspoon salt
1 tablespoon sugar
2 tablespoons water

Toast the almonds in a 400°F. oven for 15 minutes. Cool. Turn the oven temperature down to 350°F.

Grind the almonds into fine pieces in a food processor, then mix in the flour, salt, and sugar. Add the water and mix thoroughly. The mixture should be just moist enough to hold together. Press into a 10-inch pie pan. Bake for 12 minutes. Cool before filling.

Nutrition information per 2-inch slice: 90 calories, 3 g protein, 9 g carbohydrate, 5 g fat, 49% of calories from fat, 55 mg sodium

Carrot Cake

Serves 9

This delicious carrot cake is made without eggs or oil.

    2 cups grated carrots
    1½ cups raisins
    2 cups water
    1½ teaspoons cinnamon
    1½ teaspoons allspice
    ½ teaspoon cloves
    1 cup sugar
    ½ teaspoon salt
    3 cups unbleached or whole wheat pastry flour
    1½ teaspoons baking soda
    1 cup soy milk
    Tofu Cream Frosting (recipe follows)

Simmer the grated carrots, raisins, water, and spices in a saucepan for 10 minutes. Stir in the sugar and salt and simmer for 2 more minutes. Cool completely.

Preheat the oven to 350°F.

In a large bowl, stir the flour and soda together. Add the cooled carrot mixture along with the soy milk and stir just to mix. Spray a 9 × 9-inch pan with nonstick spray and spread the batter in it. Bake for 1 hour. A toothpick inserted into the center should come out clean. Serve plain or frost with Tofu Cream Frosting when completely cooled.

Nutrition information per serving (without frosting): 318 calories, 6 g protein, 73 g carbohydrate, 3 g fat, 8% of calories from fat, 283 mg sodium

Nutrition information per 3 × 3-inch slice (with frosting): 388 calories, 9 g protein, 80 g carbohydrate, 4 g fat, 9% of calories from fat, 354 mg sodium

Tofu Cream Frosting

Makes 1⅓ cups, enough to frost one 9 × 9-inch cake

1 cup firm tofu (½ pound)
2 tablespoons oil
2 tablespoons fresh lemon juice
3 to 4 tablespoons maple syrup
¼ teaspoon salt
½ teaspoon vanilla extract

Combine all the ingredients in a blender and blend until very smooth. Scrape the sides of blender often with a rubber spatula to get the frosting completely smooth.

Nutrition information per 2½-tablespoon serving: 70 calories, 3 g protein, 7 g carbohydrate, 4 g fat, 46% of calories from fat, 71 mg sodium

Pumpkin Raisin Cookies

Makes thirty-six 3-inch cookies

Children love these plump, moist cookies because they taste so good. You'll love them because they're loaded with beta-carotene and other nutrients.

3 cups whole wheat pastry flour
4 teaspoons baking powder
1 teaspoon salt
1 teaspoon baking soda
1 teaspoon cinnamon
½ teaspoon nutmeg
¾ cup sugar or other sweetener
1 15-ounce can solid-pack pumpkin

1 ripe banana, mashed
1 cup soy milk or water
1 cup raisins

Preheat the oven to 350°F.

Mix the dry ingredients together and set aside. Add the pumpkin, mashed banana, soy milk or water, and raisins. Mix until just combined.

Drop by tablespoonfuls onto a baking sheet that has been sprayed with a nonstick spray. Bake for 15 minutes, until lightly browned. Remove from the baking sheet with a spatula and place on a rack to cool. Store in an airtight container.

Nutrition information per cookie: 72 calories, 1.5 g protein, 16 g carbohydrate, 0 g fat, 0.4% of calories from fat, 132 mg sodium

NOTES

ONE. PROTECTING EVERY CELL

1. Krinsky, N. I. 1992. Mechanism of action of biological antioxidants. *Proceedings of the Society for Experimental Biology and Medicine* 200:248–54; Flenley, D. C. 1987. What should an ideal antioxidant do (and not do)? *Bulletin Européen de Physiopathologie Respiratoire (Oxford)* 23:279–85.

2. Januszczak, W. 1990. *Sayonara Michelangelo: the Sistine Chapel restored and repackaged.* Reading, MA: Addison-Wesley.

3. Krinsky, Mechanism of action.

4. National Research Council. 1989. *Recommended dietary allowances.* Washington, DC: National Academy Press.

5. Ibid.

6. Krinsky, Mechanism of action; Sinclair, A. J., A. H. Barnett, and J. Lunec. 1990. Free radicals and antioxidant systems in health and disease. *British Journal of Hospital Medicine* 43:334–44.

7. Murphy, S. P., A. F. Subar, and G. Block. 1990. Vitamin E intakes and sources in the United States. *American Journal of Clinical Nutrition* 52:361–67.

8. Krinsky, Mechanism of action; Burton, G. W., and K. U. Ingold. 1984. Beta-carotene: an unusual type of lipid antioxidant. *Science* 224:569–73.

9. Canfield, I. M., J. W. Forage, and J. G. Valenzuela. 1992. Carotenoids as cellular antioxidants. *Proceedings of the Society for Experimental Biology and Medicine* 200:260–65.

10. Krinsky, Mechanism of action; Olson, J. A., and R. E. Hodges. 1987. Recommended dietary intakes (RDI) of vitamin C in humans. *American Journal of Clinical Nutrition* 45:693–703.

11. Sinclair, Free Radicals and antioxidant systems.

12. Kinsman, R. A., and J. Hood. 1971. Some behavioral effects of ascorbic acid deficiency. *American Journal of Clinical Nutrition* 24:455–64.

13. Block, G. 1991. Epidemiologic evidence regarding vitamin C and cancer. *American Journal of Clinical Nutrition* 54:1310S–14S.

14. Olson and Hodges, RDI of vitamin C in humans.

15. Krinsky, Mechanism of action.

16. Becker, B. F. 1993. Towards the physiological function of uric acid. *Free Radical Biology and Medicine* 14:615–31.

17. Sevanian, A., K. J. A. Davies, and P. Hochstein. 1991. Serum urate as an antioxidant for ascorbic acid. *American Journal of Clinical Nutrition* 54:1129S–34S.

18. Beck, J., and M. Daley. 1993. *Art restoration: the culture, the business and the scandal.* London: John Murray Ltd., 90–91.

19. Ibid., 64.

20. Rosenfeld, W., and L. Concepcion. 1986. Endogenous antioxidant defenses in neonates. *Free Radical Biology and Medicine* 2:295–98.

21. Johnson, L., F. Bowen, S. Abbasi, et al. 1985. Relationship of prolonged pharmacologic serum levels of vitamin E to incidence of sepsis and necrotizing enterocolitis in infants with birth weight 1,500 grams or less. *Pediatrics* 75:619–38; Arrowsmith, J. B., G. A. Faich, D. K. Tomita, J. N. Kuritsky, and F. W. Rosa. 1989. Morbidity and mortality among low birth weight infants exposed to an intravenous vitamin E product, E-Ferol. *Pediatrics* 83:244–49; and Mino, M. 1992. Clinical uses and abuses of vitamin E in children. *Proceedings of the Society for Experimental Biology and Medicine* 200:266–70.

22. Flenley, What should an ideal antioxidant do.

23. Ibid.; Rosenfeld and Concepcion, Endogenous antioxidant defenses.

24. Flenley, What should an ideal antioxidant do.

25. Ibid.

26. Ibid.

27. Prasad, J. S. 1980. Effect of vitamin E supplementation on leukocyte function. *American Journal of Clinical Nutrition* 33:606–608; Baehner, R. L., L. A. Boxer, L. M. Ingraham, C. Butterick, and R. A. Haak. 1981. The influence of vitamin E on human polymorphonuclear cell metabolism and function. *Annals of the New York Academy of Sciences* 393:237–49; and Engle, W. A., M. C. Yoder, J. L. Baurley, and Y. U. Poa-Lo. 1988. Vitamin E decreases superoxide anion production by polymorphonuclear leukocytes. *Pediatric Research* 23:245–48.

28. Vitamin E Research and Information Service. 1994. *Vitamin E fact book*. La Grange, IL: VERIS, 28.

29. Seddon, J. M., U. A. Ajani, R. D. Sperduto, et al. 1994. Dietary carotenoids, vitamins A, C, and E, and advanced age-related macular degeneration. *Journal of the American Medical Association* 272:1413–20; Hankinson, S. E., and M. J. Stampfer. 1994. All that glitters is not beta-carotene. *Journal of the American Medical Association* 272:1455–56.

30. Seddon et al., Dietary carotenoids.

31. Willett, W. C., M. J. Stampfer, B. A. Underwood, J. O. Taylor, and C. H. Hennekens. 1983. Vitamins A, E, and carotene: effects of supplementation on their plasma levels. *American Journal of Clinical Nutrition* 38:559–66.

32. Meyskens, F. L., Jr. 1990. Coming of age—the chemoprevention of cancer. *New England Journal of Medicine* 323:825–28.

33. Flenley, What should an ideal antioxidant do?

34. Lauffer, R. B. 1991. *Iron balance*. New York: St. Martin's Press.

35. Olson, RDI of vitamin C in humans; Nienhuis, A. W. 1981. Vitamin C and iron. *New England Journal of Medicine* 304:170–71.

36. Lauffer, *Iron balance*.

37. Ibid.

38. Nordmann, R., C. Ribiere, and H. Rouach. 1992. Implication of free radical mechanisms in ethanol-induced cellular injury. *Free Radical Biology and Medicine* 12:219–40.

39. Ibid.; Girre, C., E. Hispard, P. Therond, S. Guedj, R. Bourdon, and S. Dally. 1990. Effect of abstinence from alcohol on the depression of glutathione peroxidase activity and selenium and vitamin E levels in chronic alcoholic patients. *Alcoholism: Clinical and Experimental Research* 14:909–12.

TWO. CLEAN BLOOD, STRONG IMMUNITY

1. Van Vleet, E. S., V. U. Fossato, M. R. Sherwin, H. B. Lovett, and F. Dolci. 1988. Distribution of coprostanol, petroleum hydrocarbons, and chlorinated hydrocarbons in sediments from canals and coastal waters of Venice, Italy. *Organic Geochemistry* 13:757–63.

2. Munzner, R. 1986. Modifying action of vegetable juice on the mutagenicity of beef extract and nitrosated beef extract. *Food and Chemical Toxicology* 24:847–49.

3. Zhang, Y., P. Talalay, C. G. Cho, and G. H. Posner. 1992. A major inducer of anticarcinogenic protective enzymes from broccoli: isolation and elucidation of structure. *Proceedings of the National Academy of Sciences* 89:- 2399–403; Prochaska, H. J., A. B. Santamaria, and P. Talalay. 1992. Rapid detection of inducers of enzymes that protect against carcinogens. *Proceedings of the National Academy of Sciences* 89:2394–98.

4. Coles, B., and B. Ketterer. 1990. The role of glutathione and glutathione transferases in chemical carcinogenesis. *Critical Reviews in Biochemistry and Molecular Biology* 25:47–70.

5. Pantuck, E. J., C. B. Pantuck, W. A. Garland, et al. 1979. Stimulatory effect of Brussels sprouts and cabbage on human drug metabolism. *Clinical Pharmacology and Therapeutics* 25:88–95.

6. Flagg, E. W., R. J. Coates, and D. P. Jones. 1994. Dietary glutathione intake and the risk of oral and pharyngeal cancer. *American Journal of Epidemiology* 139:453–65.

7. Neher, J. O., and J. Q. Koenig. 1994. Health effects of outdoor air pollution. *American Family Physician* 49:1397–1404.

8. *Consumer Reports.* February 1992. Is our fish fit to eat? 103–14.

9. Committee on Evaluation of the Safety of Fishery Products, Institute of Medicine. 1991. *Seafood safety.* Washington, DC: National Academy Press.

10. General Accounting Office. 1990. *Food safety and quality: FDA surveys not adequate to demonstrate safety of milk supply.* Washington, DC: U.S. General Accounting Office.

11. Hergenrather, J., G. Hlady, B. Wallace, and E. Savage. 1981. Pollutants in breast milk of vegetarians. *New England Journal of Medicine* 304:792.

12. Sachdev, P. 1993. The neuropsychiatry of brain iron. *Journal of Neuropsychiatry* 5:18–29; Bodovitz, S., M. T. Falduto, D. E. Frail, and W. L. Klein. 1995. Iron levels modulate alpha-secretase cleavage of amyloid precursor protein. *Journal of Neurochemistry* 64:307–15.

13. Bartzokis, G., D. Sultzer, J. Mintz, et al. 1994. In vivo evaluation of brain iron in Alzheimer's disease and normal subjects using MRI. *Biological Psychiatry* 35:480–87.

14. Bush, A. L., W. H. Pettingell, G. Multhaup, et al. 1994. Rapid induction of Alzheimer A-beta amyloid formation by zinc. *Science* 265:1464–67.

15. Harrington, C. R., C. M. Wischik, F. K. McArthur, G. A. Taylor, J. A. Edwardson, and J. M. Candy. 1994. Alzheimer's-disease-like changes in tau

protein processing: association with aluminum accumulation in brains of renal dialysis patients. *The Lancet* 343:993–97.

16. Crapper McLachlan, D. R. 1994. Aluminum and Alzheimer's disease. *Canadian Medical Association Journal* 151:268–69.

17. Doll, R. 1993. Review: Alzheimer's disease and environmental aluminum. *Age and Ageing* 22:138–53.

18. Benditt, E. P. 1977. The origin of atherosclerosis. *Scientific American* 236:74–85.

19. Sherwin, M. R., E. S. Van Vleet, V. U. Fossato, and F. Dolci. 1993. Coprostanol in lagoonal sediments and mussels of Venice, Italy. *Marine Pollution Bulletin* 26:501–7.

20. Simmons, K. 1984. Physicians continue to study cause(s) of "bubble boy's" death. *Journal of the American Medical Association* 251:1929–31.

21. Tada, T. 1992. Nutrition and the immune system in aging: an overview. *Nutrition Reviews* 50:360.

22. Wick, G., I. A. Huber, X. Qing-Bo, E. Jarosch, D. Schonitzer, and G. Jurgens. 1990. The decline of the immune response during aging: the role of an altered lipid metabolism. *Annals of the New York Academy of Sciences* 621: 277–90.

23. Makinodan, T., J. Lubinski, and T. C. Fong. 1987. Cellular, biochemical, and molecular basis of T-cell senescence. *Archives of Pathology and Laboratory Medicine* 111:910–14.

24. Wick et al., The decline of the immune response during aging.

25. Cuthbert, J. A., and P. E. Lipsky. 1984. Immunoregulation by low density lipoproteins in man. *Journal of Clinical Investigation* 73:992–1003; Pepe, M. G., and L. K. Curtiss. 1986. Apolipoprotein E is a biologically active constituent of the normal immunoregulatory lipoprotein, LDL-In. *Journal of Immunology* 136:3716–23; and Traill, K. N., L. A. Huber, G. Wick, and G. Jurgens. 1990. Lipoprotein interactions with T cells: an update. *Immunology Today* 11:411–17.

26. Hawley, H. P., and G. B. Gordon. 1976. The effects of long chain free fatty acids on human neutrophil function and structure. *Laboratory Investigation* 34:216–22.

27. Barone, J., J. R. Hebert, and M. M. Reddy. 1989. Dietary fat and natural-killer-cell activity. *American Journal of Clinical Nutrition* 50:861–67.

28. Nordenstrom, J., C. Jarstrand, and A. Wiernik. 1979. Decreased chem-

otactic and random migration of leukocytes during intralipid infusion. *American Journal of Clinical Nutrition* 32:2416–22.

29. Endres, S., R. Ghorbani, V. E. Kelley, et al. 1989. The effect of dietary supplementation with n-3 polyunsaturated fatty acids on the synthesis of inter-leukin-1 and tumor necrosis factor by mononuclear cells. *New England Journal of Medicine* 320:265–71; Kelley, D. S., L. B. Branch, J. E. Love, P. C. Taylor, Y. M. Rivera, and J. M. Iacono. 1991. Dietary alpha-linoleic acid and immunocompetence in humans. *American Journal of Clinical Nutrition* 53: 40–46; and Von Schacky, C., S. Fischer, P. C. Weber. 1985. Long-term effect of dietary marine omega-3 fatty acids upon plasma and cellular lipids, platelet function, and eicosanoid formation in humans. *Journal of Clinical Investigation* 76:1626–31.

30. Guthrie, H. A., and J. C. Scheer. 1981. Nutritional adequacy of self-selected diets that satisfy the four food groups guide. *Journal of Nutrition Education* 13:46–49.

31. Louria, D. B. 1990. Effect of supplementation with zinc and other micronutrients on cellular immunity of the elderly. *Journal of the American College of Nutrition* 9:363–64; Bogden, J. D., J. M. Oleske, M. A. Lavenhar, et al. Effects of one year of supplementation with zinc and other micronutrients on cellular immunity in the elderly. *Journal of the American College of Nutrition* 1990;9:214–25.

32. Bogden et al., Effects of one year of supplementation.

33. Ibid.

34. Schlesinger, L., M. Arevalo, S. Arredondo, B. Lonnerdal, and A. Stekel. 1993. Zinc supplementation impairs monocyte function. *Acta Paediatrica* 82: 734–38.

35. Makinodan et al., Cellular, biochemical, and molecular basis of T-cell senescence; Watson, R. R., R. H. Prabhala, P. M. Plezia, D. S. Alberts. 1991. Effect of beta-carotene on lymphocyte subpopulations in elderly humans: evidence for a dose-response relationship. *American Journal of Clinical Nutrition* 53:90–4; and Bendich, A. 1989. Carotenoids and the immune response. *Journal of Nutrition* 119:112–15.

36. Watson et al., Effect of beta-carotene.

37. Bendich, Carotenoids and the immune response.

38. Beisel, W. R. 1982. Single nutrients and immunity. *American Journal of Clinical Nutrition* 35:Feb. Suppl:417–68; Watson, R. R. 1986. Immunological

enhancement by fat-soluble vitamins, minerals, and trace metals: a factor in cancer prevention. *Cancer Detection and Prevention* 9:67–77; and Chandra, S., and R. K. Chandra. 1986. Nutrition, immune response, and outcome. *Progress in Food and Nutrition Science* 10:1–65.

39. Tengerdy, R. P. 1989. Vitamin E, immune response, and disease resistance. *Annals of the New York Academy of Sciences* 570:335–44.

40. Meydani, S. N., M. Meydani, P. M. Barklund, et al. 1989. Effect of vitamin E supplementation on immune responsiveness of the aged. *Annals of the New York Academy of Sciences* 570:283–90.

41. Malter, M., G. Schriever, and U. Eilber. 1989. Natural killer cells, vitamins, and other blood components of vegetarian and omnivorous men. *Nutrition and Cancer* 12:271–78.

42. Meydani et al., Effect of vitamin E supplementation on immune responsiveness of the aged.

43. Benowitz, N. L. 1990. Clinical pharmacology of caffeine. *Annual Review of Medicine* 41:277–88; Chou, T. 1992. Wake up and smell the coffee: caffeine, coffee, and the medical consequences. 157:544–53.

44. Al-Hachim, G. M. 1989. Teratogenicity of caffeine; a review. *European Journal of Obstetrics, Gynecology, and Reproductive Biology* 31:237–47.

45. Benowitz, Clinical pharmacology of caffeine; Chou, Wake up and smell the coffee.

46. Dlugosz, L., and M. B. Bracken. 1992. Reproductive effects of caffeine: a review and theoretical analysis. *Epidemiologic Reviews* 14:83–100.

47. Stavric, B. 1992. An update on research with coffee/caffeine. *Food and Chemical Toxicology* 30:533–55.

48. Chou, Wake up and smell the coffee.

49. Ibid.

50. Ibid.

51. Superko, H. R., W. Bortz, Jr., P. T. Williams, J. J. Albers, and P. D. Wood. 1991. Caffeinated and decaffeinated coffee effects on plasma lipoprotein cholesterol, apolipoproteins, and lipase activity: a controlled, randomized trial. *American Journal of Clinical Nutrition* 54:599–605.

52. Chou, Wake up and smell the coffee.

53. Barnard, R. J., L. Lattimore, R. A. Holly, S. Cherny, and N. Pritikin. 1982. Response of non-insulin-dependent diabetic patients to an intensive program of diet and exercise. *Diabetes Care* 5:370–74; Barnard, R. J., M. R. Mas-

sey, S. Cherny, L. T. O'Brien, and N. Pritikin. 1983. Long-term use of a high-complex-carbohydrate, high-fiber, low-fat diet and exercise in the treatment of NIDDM patients. *Diabetes Care* 6:268–73.

54. Anderson, J. W. 1983. Plant fiber and blood pressure. *Annals of International Medicine* 98 (Part 2):842; Dodson, P. M., P. J. Pacey, P. Bal, A. J. Kubicki, R. F. Fletcher, and K. G. Taylor. 1984. A controlled trial of a high-fiber, low-fat, and low-sodium diet for mild hypertension in type 2 (non-insulin-dependent) diabetic patients. *Diabetologia* 27:522; and Roy, M. S., G. Stables, B. Collier, A. Roy, and E. Bou. 1989. Nutritional factors in diabetics with and without retinopathy. *American Journal of Clinical Nutrition* 50: 728–30.

55. Crane, M. G., and C. Sample. 1994. Regression of diabetic neuropathy with total vegetarian diet. *Journal of Nutritional Medicine.* In press.

56. Karjalainen, J., J. M. Martin, M. Knip, et al. 1992. A bovine albumin peptide as a possible trigger of insulin-dependent diabetes mellitus. *New England Journal of Medicine* 327:302–7.

57. Hjollund, E., O. Pederson, B. Richelsen, H. Beck-Nielsen, and N. S. Sorensen. 1983. Increased insulin binding to adipocytes and monocytes and increased insulin sensitivity of glucose transport and metabolism in adipocytes from non-insulin-dependent diabetics after a low-fat/high-starch/high-fiber diet. *Metabolism* 32:1067; Ward, G. M., R. W. Simpson, H. C. R. Simpson, B. A. Naylor, J. I. Mann, and R. C. Turner. 1982. Insulin receptor binding increased by high-carbohydrate, low-fat diet in non-insulin-dependent diabetics. *European Journal of Clinical Investigation* 12:93.

58. AMA Council on Scientific Affairs Dietary Fiber and Health, 1989. *Journal of the American Medical Association* 262:542–46; Jenkins, D. J. A., T. M. S. Wolever, R. H. Taylor, H. Barker, and H. Fielden. 1982. Exceptionally low blood glucose response to dried beans: comparison with other carbohydrate foods. *British Medical Journal* 2:578–80; and Jenkins, D. J. A., T. M. S. Wolever, R. H. Taylor, et al. 1982. Slow release carbohydrate improves second meal tolerance. *American Journal of Clinical Nutrition* 35:1339–46.

59. American Diabetes Association. 1991. Nutritional recommendations and principles for individuals with diabetes mellitus. *Diabetes Care* 14:20–27.

THREE. HOW TO CALM THE HORMONE STORMS

1. Prentice, R., D. Thompson, C. Clifford, S. Gorbach, B. Goldin, and D. Byar. 1990. Dietary fat reduction and plasma estradiol concentration in healthy postmenopausal women. *Journal of the National Cancer Institute* 82: 129–34; National Cancer Institute. 1994. *Measures of progress against cancer: cancer prevention.* Bethesda, MD: National Institutes of Health.

2. Hamalainen, E., H. Adlercreutz, P. Puska, and P. Pietinen. 1983. Decrease of serum total and free testosterone during a low-fat, high-fiber diet. *Journal of Steroid Biochemistry* 18:369–70; Hamalainen, E., H. Adlercreutz, P. Puska, and P. Pietinen. 1984. Diet and serum sex hormones in healthy men. *Journal of Steroid Biochemistry* 20:459–64; Ingram, D. M., F. C. Bennett, D. Willcox, and N. de Klerk. 1987. Effect of low-fat diet on female sex hormone levels. *Journal of the National Cancer Institute* 79:1225–29; and Rose, D. P., A. P. Boyar, C. Cohen, and L. E. Strong. 1987. Effect of a low-fat diet on hormone levels in women with cystic breast disease. I. Serum steroids and gonadotropins. *Journal of the National Cancer Institute* 78:623–26.

3. Adlercreutz, H. 1990. Western diet and Western diseases: some hormonal and biochemical mechanisms and associations. *Scandinavian Journal of Clinical Laboratory Investigation* 50, Suppl 201:3–23.

4. De Ridder, C. M., J. H. H. Thijssen, P. Van't Veer, et al. 1991. Dietary habits, sexual maturation, and plasma hormones in pubertal girls: a longitudinal study. *American Journal of Clinical Nutrition* 54:805–13.

5. Adlercreutz, Western diet and Western diseases; Belanger, A., A. Locong, C. Noel, et al. 1989. Influence of diet on plasma steroid and sex hormone binding globulin levels in adult men. *Journal of Steroid Biochemistry* 32:829–33.

6. Gray, A., D. N. Jackson, and J. B. McKinlay. 1991. The relation between dominance, anger, and hormones in normally aging men: results from the Massachusetts Male Aging Study. *Psychosomatic Medicine* 53:375–85.

7. Adlercreutz, Western diet and Western diseases.

8. Adlercreutz, Western diet and Western diseases; Goldin, B. R., H. Adlercreutz, J. T. Dwyer, L. Swenson, J. H. Warram, and S. L. Gorbach. 1981. Effect of diet on excretion of estrogens in pre- and postmenopausal women. *Cancer Research* 41:3771–73; Goldin, B. R., and S. L. Gorbach. 1988. Effect of diet on the plasma levels, metabolism, and excretion of estrogens. *American Journal of*

Clinical Nutrition 48:787–90; Shultz, T. D., and J. E. Leklem. 1983. Nutrient intake and hormonal status of premenopausal vegetarian Seventh-Day Adventists and premenopausal nonvegetarians. *Nutrition and Cancer* 4:247–59; and Barbosa, J. C., T. D. Shultz, S. J. Filley, and D. C. Nieman. 1990. The relationship among adiposity, diet, and hormone concentrations in vegetarian and nonvegetarian postmenopausal women. *American Journal of Clinical Nutrition* 51:798–803.

9. Osborne, M. P., H. L. Bradlow, G. Y. C. Wong, and N. T. Telang. 1993. Upregulation of estradiol C16-hydroxylation in human breast tissue: a potential biomarker of breast cancer risk. *Journal of the National Cancer Institute* 85:1917–20.

10. Reichman, M. E., J. T. Judd, C. Longcope, et al. 1993. The effects of alcohol consumption on plasma and urinary hormone concentrations in premenopausal women. *Journal of the National Cancer Institute* 85:722–27.

11. Willett, W. C., M. J. Stampfer, G. A. Colditz, B. A. Rosner, C. H. Hennekens, and F. E. Speizer. 1987. Moderate alcohol consumption; and the risk of breast cancer. *New England Journal of Medicine* 316:1174–80.

12. Symons, J. M., T. A. Bellar, J. K. Carswell, et al. 1975. National organics reconnaissance survey for halogenated organics (NORS). *Journal of the American Water Works Association* 67:634–47; Cantor, K. P., F. I. Hoover, T. J. Mason, and I. J. McCabe. 1978. Association of cancer mortality with halomethanes. *Journal of the National Cancer Institute* 61:979–85; Hogan, M. D., P. Y. Chi, T. J. Mitchell, and D. G. Hoel. 1979. Association between chloroform levels in finished drinking water supplies and various site-specific cancer mortality rates. *Journal of Environmental Pathology and Toxicology* 2:873–87; and Crump, K. S., and H. A. Guess. 1982. Drinking water and cancer: review of recent epidemiological findings and assessment of risks. *Annual Review of Public Health* 3:339–57.

13. Davis, D. L., H. L. Bradlow, M. Wolff, T. Woodruff, D. G. Hoel, and H. Anton-Culver. 1993. Medical hypothesis: xenoestrogens as preventable causes of breast cancer. *Environmental Health Perspectives* 101:372–77.

14. Wolff, M. S., P. G. Toniolo, E. W. Lee, M. Rivera, and N. Dubin. 1993. Blood levels of organochlorine residues and risk of breast cancer. *Journal of the National Cancer Institute* 85:648–52.

15. Walrath, J., F. Li, et al. 1985. Causes of death among female chemists. *American Journal of Public Health* 75:883–85.

16. Westin, J., and E. Richter. 1990. The Israeli breast cancer anomaly. *Annals of the New York Academy of Sciences* 609:269–70.

17. Grodin, J. M., P. K. Siiteri, and P. C. MacDonald. 1973. Source of estrogen production in postmenopausal women. *Journal of Clinical Endocrinology and Metabolism* 36:207–14; MacDonald, P. C., C. D. Edman, D. L. Hemsell, et al. 1978. Effect of obesity on conversion of plasma androstenedione to estrone in postmenopausal women with and without endometrial cancer. *American Journal of Obstetrics and Gynecology* 130:448–55.

18. Armstrong, B., and R. Doll. 1975. Environmental factors and cancer incidence and mortality in different countries, with special reference to dietary practices. *International Journal of Cancer* 15:617–31; Rose, D. P., A. P. Boyar, and E. L. Wynder. 1986. International comparisons of mortality rates for cancer of the breast, ovary, prostate, and colon, and per capita food consumption. *Cancer* 58:2363–71; Gregorio, D. I., L. J. Emrich, S. Graham, J. R. Marshall, and T. Nemoto. 1985. Dietary fat consumption and survival among women with breast cancer. *Journal of the National Cancer Institute* 75:37–41; and Verreault, R., J. Brisson, L. Deschenes, F. Naud, F. Meyer, and L. Belanger. 1988. Dietary fat in relation to prognostic indicators in breast cancer. *Journal of the National Cancer Institute* 80:819–25.

19. Sharpe, R. M., and N. E. Skakkebaek. 1993. Are oestrogens involved in falling sperm counts and disorders of the male reproductive tract? *The Lancet* 341:1392–95.

20. Seth, R., P. Samarajeewa, and W. F. Coulson. Production and utilisation of antibodies directed against oestrone sulphate using specific hapten synthesis. *Journal of Immunoassay* (U.S.) 1992;13:297–314; Hawkins, R. A., M. L. Thomson, and E. Killen. 1985. Oestrone sulphate, adipose tissue, and breast cancer. *Breast Cancer Research and Treatment* 6:75–87; Holdsworth, R. J., R. B. Heap, J. M. Booth, and M. Hamon. 1982. A rapid direct radioimmunoassay for the measurement of oestrone sulphate in the milk of dairy cows and its use in pregnancy diagnosis. *Journal of Endocrinology* 95:7–12; Velle, W. 1976. Endogenous anabolic agents in farm animals. *Environmental Quality and Safety Supplement* (5):159–70; Monk, E. L., R. E. Erb, and T. A. Mollett. 1975. Relationships between immunoreactive estrone and estradiol in milk, blood, and urine of dairy cows. *Journal of Dairy Science* 58:34–40.

21. Armstrong and Doll, Environmental factors and cancer incidence; Hirayama, T. 1978. Epidemiology of breast cancer with special reference to the

role of diet. *Preventive Medicine* 7:173–95; Stocks, P. 1970. Breast cancer anomalies. *British Journal of Cancer* 24:633–43; and Gaskill, S. P., W. L. McGuire, C. K. Osborne, and M. P. Stern. 1979. Breast cancer mortality and diet in the United States. *Cancer Research* 39:3628–37.

22. General Accounting Office. November 1990. *Food safety and quality: FDA surveys not adequate to demonstrate safety of milk supply.* Washington, DC: U.S. General Accounting Office.

23. Daughaday, W. H., and D. M. Barbano. 1990. Bovine somatotropin supplementation of dairy cows: Is the milk safe? *Journal of the American Medical Association* 264:1003–5.

24. Arteaga, C. L., and C. K. Osborne. 1989. Growth inhibition of human breast cancer cells in vitro with an antibody against the type I somatomedin receptor. *Cancer Research* 49:6237–41; Pollak, M., J. Costantino, C. Polychronakos, et al. 1990. Effect of tamoxifen on serum insulin-like growth factor I levels in stage I breast cancer patients. *Journal of the National Cancer Institute* 82:1693–97.

25. Daughaday and Barbano, Is the milk safe?

26. Clyne, P. S., and A. Kulczycki. 1991. Human breast milk contains bovine IgG. Relationship to infant colic? *Pediatrics* 87:439–44.

27. Colditz, G. A., M. J. Stampfer, W. C. Willett, C. H. Hennekens, B. Rosner, and F. E. Speizer. 1990. Prospective study of estrogen replacement therapy and risk of breast cancer in postmenopausal women. *Journal of the American Medical Association* 264:2648–53.

Four. Staying Young Sexually

1. Bernstein, C., and V. Johns. 1989. Sexual reproduction as a response to H^2O^2 damage in schizosaccharomyces pombe. *Journal of Bacteriology* 171: 1893–97.

2. Bernstein, C. 1993. Sex as a response to oxidative DNA damage. In Halliwell, B., and O. I. Aruoma, eds. *DNA and free radicals.* 1993. Chichester, UK: Simon and Schuster.

3. Diokno, A. C., M. B. Brown, and A. R. Herzog. 1990. Sexual function in the elderly. *Archives of Internal Medicine* 150:197–200.

4. Bachmann, G. A., S. R. Leiblum, B. Sandler, et al. 1985. Correlates of sexual desire in postmenopausal women. *Maturitas* 7:211–16.

5. Schiavi, R. C., J. Mandeli, and P. Schreiner-Engel. 1994. Sexual satisfaction in healthy aging men. *Journal of Sex and Marital Therapy* 20:3–13; McKin-

lay, J. B., and H. A. Feldman. 1993. Age-related variation in sexual activity and interest in normal men: results from the Massachusetts Male Aging Study. In A. Rossi, ed. *Sexuality across the life course.* Chicago: University of Chicago Press; and Mulligan, T., and C. R. Moss. 1991. Sexuality and aging in male veterans: a cross-sectional study of interest, ability, and activity. *Archives of Sexual Behavior* 20:17–25.

6. Nankin, H. R. 1985. Fertility in aging men. *Maturitas* 7:259–65.

7. Swerdloff, R. S., and C. Wang. 1993. Androgen deficiency and aging in men. *Western Journal of Medicine* 159:579–85.

8. Ibid.

9. Kaplan, H. S., and T. Owett. 1993. The female androgen deficiency syndrome. *Journal of Sex and Marital Therapy* 19:3–24.

10. Ibid.

11. Eriksson, C. J. P., T. Fukunaga, and R. Lindman. 1994. Sex hormone response to alcohol. *Nature* 369:711.

12. Lee, J. R. Personal communication. 1994.

13. Kaplan, The female androgen deficiency syndrome; Smith, P. J., and R. L. Talbert. 1986. Sexual dysfunction with antihypertensive and antipsychotic agents. *Clinical Pharmacy* 5:373–84.

14. Lauffer, R. B. 1991. *Iron balance.* New York: St. Martin's Press.

15. Diokno et al., Sexual function in the elderly.

16. Kaplan, The female androgen deficiency syndrome.

17. Stuart, F. M., D. C. Hammond, and M. A. Pett. 1987. Inhibited sexual desire in women. *Archives of Sexual Behavior* 16:91–106.

18. Ibid.

FIVE. SPECIAL INFORMATION FOR WOMEN: MENOPAUSE, MENSTRUAL SYMPTOMS, AND CANCER

1. De Mille, A. 1991. *Martha: the life and work of Martha Graham.* New York: Vintage: 47.

2. Graham, M. 1991. *Blood memory.* New York: Simon and Schuster: 37.

3. Barnard, N. D. 1990. *The power of your plate.* Summertown, TN: Book Publishing Co.: 120.

4. Stumpf, P. G. 1990. Pharmacokinetics of estrogen. *Obstetrics and Gynecology* 75:9S–14S.

5. Huppert, L. C. 1987. Hormonal replacement therapy: benefits, risks, doses. *Medical Clinics of North America* 71:23–39.

6. Ibid.

7. Colditz, G. A., M. J. Stampfer, W. C. Willett, et al. 1992. Type of postmenopausal hormone use and risk of breast cancer: 12-year follow-up from the Nurses' Health Study. *Cancer Causes and Control* 3:433–39; Yang, C. P., J. R. Daling, P. R. Band, R. P. Gallagher, E. White, and N. S. Weiss. 1992. Noncontraceptive hormone use and risk of breast cancer. *Cancer Causes and Control* 3:475–79; and Bergkvist, L., H. O. Adami, I. Persson, R. Hoover, and C. Schairer. 1989. The risk of breast cancer after estrogen and estrogen-progestin replacement. *New England Journal of Medicine* 321:293–97.

8. Colditz et al., Type of postmenopausal hormone use; Bergkvist et al., Risk of breast cancer after estrogen.

9. Huppert, Hormonal replacement therapy.

10. Ibid.; Matthews, K. A., R. R. Wing, L. H. Kuller, et al. 1990. Influences of natural menopause on psychological characteristics and symptoms of middle-aged healthy women. *Journal of Consulting and Clinical Psychology* 58: 345–51.

11. Ross, R. K., A. Paganini-Hill, T. M. Mack, M. Arthur, and B. E. Henderson. 1981. Menopausal oestrogen therapy and protection from death from ischaemic heart disease. *The Lancet* 1:858–60; Stampfer, M. J., W. C. Willett, G. A. Colditz, B. Rosner, F. E. Speizer, and C. H. Hennekens. 1985. A prospective study of postmenopausal estrogen therapy and coronary heart disease. *New England Journal of Medicine* 313:1044–49; and Bush, T. L., E. Barrett-Connor, L. D. Cowan, et al. 1987. Cardiovascular mortality and noncontraceptive use of estrogen in women: results from the Lipid Research Clinics Program follow-up study. *Circulation* 75:1102–9.

12. Matthews et al., Influences of natural menopause.

13. Leidy, L. E. 1990. Early age at menopause among left-handed women. *Obstetrics and Gynecology* 76:1111–14.

14. Huppert, Hormonal replacement therapy.

15. Swartzman, L. C., R. Edelberg, and E. Kemmann. 1990. Impact of stress on objectively recorded menopausal hot flushes and on flush report bias. *Health Psychology* 9:529–45.

16. Lock, M. 1991. Contested meanings of the menopause. *The Lancet* 337:1270–72.

17. Beyene, Y. 1986. Cultural significance and physiological manifesta-

tions of menopause: a biocultural analysis. *Culture, Medicine, and Psychiatry* 10:47–71.

18. Follingstad, A. H. 1978. Estriol, the forgotten estrogen? *Journal of the American Medical Association* 239:29–30; Heimer, G. M. 1987. Estriol in the postmenopause. *Acta Obstetrica et Gynecologica Scandinavica* Suppl 139:3–23; Molander, U., I. Milsom, P. Ekelund, D. Mellstrom, and O. Eriksson. 1990. Effect of oral oestriol on vaginal flora and cytology and urogenital symptoms in the postmenopause. *Maturitas* 12:113–20; and Gerbaldo, D., A. Ferraiolo, S. Croce, M. Truini, and G. L. Capitanio. 1991. Endometrial morphology after 12 months of vaginal oestriol therapy in postmenopausal women. *Maturitas* 13:269–74.

19. Semmens, J. P., and G. Wagner. 1982. Estrogen deprivation and vaginal function in postmenopausal women. *Journal of the American Medical Association* 248:445–48; Dennerstein, L. 1985. Sexuality in the climacteric years. *Maturitas* 7:191–92.

20. Smith, P. J., and R. L. Talbert. 1986. Sexual dysfunction with antihypertensive and antipsychotic agents. *Clinical Pharmacy* 5:373–84.

21. Adlercreutz, H., E. Hamalainen, S. Gorbach, and B. Goldin. 1992. Dietary phyto-oestrogens and the menopause in Japan. *The Lancet* 339:1233.

22. Beard, M. K. 1992. Atrophic vaginitis. *Postgraduate Medicine* 91:257–60.

23. DiRaimondo, C. V., A. C. Roach, and C. K. Meador. 1980. Gynecomastia from exposure to vaginal estrogen cream. *New England Journal of Medicine* 302:1089–90.

24. Ware, M. D., E. K. Thomas, and M. Notelovitz. 1985. Serum hormone levels in men exposed to vaginal oestrogen cream: a preliminary report. *Maturitas* 7:373–76.

25. Beard, Atrophic vaginitis.

26. Beyene, Cultural significance and physiological manifestations of menopause.

27. Chou, T. 1992. Wake up and smell the coffee: caffeine, coffee, and the medical consequences. *Western Journal of Medicine* 157:544–53.

28. Dennerstein, L., C. Spencer-Gardner, G. Gotts, J. B. Brown, M. A. Smith, and G. D. Burrows. 1985. Progesterone and the premenstrual syndrome: a double blind crossover trial. *British Medical Journal* 290:1617–21.

29. Lee, J. R. 1993. *Natural progesterone.* Sebastopol, CA: BLL Publishing.

30. Hirayama, T. Epidemiology of breast cancer with special reference to the role of diet. *Preventive Medicine* 1978. 7:173–95.

31. Toniolo, P., E. Riboli, F. Protta, M. Charrel, and A. P. Cappa. 1989. Calorie-providing nutrients and risk of breast cancer. *Journal of the National Cancer Institute* 81:278.

32. Willet, W. C. 1987. Dietary fat and risk of breast cancer. *New England Journal of Medicine* 316:22–28.

33. Howe, G. R., T. Hirohata, T. Hislop, et al. 1990. Dietary factors and risk of breast cancer: combined analysis of 12 case-control studies. *Journal of the National Cancer Institute* 82:561–69; Willett, W. C., B. F. Polk, M. J. Morris, et al. 1983. Prediagnostic serum selenium levels and risk of cancer. *The Lancet* 2:130–34.

34. Messina, M. J., and S. Barnes. 1991. The role of soy products in reducing cancer. *Journal of the National Cancer Institute* 83:541–46.

35. Willett, W. C., M. J. Stampfer, F. A. Colditz, et al. 1987. Moderate alcohol consumption and the risk of breast cancer. *New England Journal of Medicine* 316:1174–80.

36. Miller, D. R., L. Rosenberg, D. W. Kaufman, et al. 1989. Breast cancer before age 45 and oral contraceptive use: new findings. *American Journal of Epidemiology* 129:269.

37. Lubin, F., A. M. Ruder, Y. Wax, and B. Modan. 1985. Overweight and changes in weight throughout adult life in breast cancer etiology. *American Journal of Epidemiology* 122:579–88.

38. Miller, F. A., L. H. Hempelmann, A. M. Dutton, J. W. Pifer, E. T. Toyooka, and W. R. Ames. 1969. Breast neoplasms in women treated with X rays for acute postpartum mastitis. A pilot study. *Journal of the National Cancer Institute* 43:803–11.

39. Lynch, H. T., W. A. Albano, J. J. Heieck, et al. 1984. Genetics, biomarkers, and control of breast cancer: a review. *Cancer, Genetics, and Cytogenetics* 13:43–92.

40. Goldman, B. A. 1991. *The truth about where you live.* New York: Random House.

41. Bernstein, L., B. E. Henderson, R. Hanisch, J. Sullivan-Halley, and R. K. Ross. 1994. Physical exercise and reduced risk of breast cancer in young women. *Journal of the National Cancer Institute* 86:1403–8.

42. Wynder, E. L., T. Kajitani, J. Kuno, J. C. Lucas, Jr., A. DePalo, and J. Farrow. 1963. A comparison of survival rates between American and Japanese patients with breast cancer. *Surgery, Gynecology, and Obstetrics* 117:196–200; Linden, G. 1973. Letter to the editor. In *Journal of Cancer* 12:543; Gregorio,

D. I., L. J. Emrich, S. Graham, J. R. Marshall, and T. Nemoto. 1985. Dietary fat consumption and survival among women with breast cancer. *Journal of the National Cancer Institute* 75:37–41; LeMarchand, L., L. N. Kolonel, and A. M. Y. Nomura. 1985. Ethnic differences in survival after diagnosis of breast cancer—Hawaii. *Journal of the American Medical Association* 254:2728; and Verreault, R., J. Brisson, L. Deschenes, F. Naud, F. Meyer, and L. Belanger. 1988. Dietary fat in relation to prognostic indicators in breast cancer. *Journal of the National Cancer Institute* 80:819–25.

    43. Gregorio et al., Dietary fat consumption.

    44. Holm, L. E., E. Callmer, M. L. Hjalmar, E. Lidbrink, B. Nilsson, and L. Skoog. 1989. Dietary habits and prognostic factors in breast cancer. *Journal of the National Cancer Institute* 81:1218–23.

    45. Verreault et al., Dietary fat in relation to prognostic indicators in breast cancer; Donegan, W. L., A. J. Hartz, and A. A. Rimm. 1978. The association of body weight with recurrent cancer of the breast. *Cancer* 41:1590–94; Newman, S. C., A. B. Miller, and G. R. Howe. 1986. A study of the effect of weight and dietary fat on breast cancer survival time. *American Journal of Epidemiology* 123:767–74; and Schapira, D. V., N. B. Kumar, G. H. Lyman, and C. E. Cox. 1991. Obesity and body fat distribution and breast cancer prognosis. *Cancer* 67:523–28.

    46. Wynder, E. L., G. C. Escher, and N. Mantel. 1966. An epidemiological investigation of cancer of the endometrium. *Cancer* 19:489–520; Armstrong, B., and R. Doll. 1975. Environmental factors and cancer incidence and mortality in different countries, with special reference to dietary practices. *International Journal of Cancer* 15:617–31; and Elwood, J. M., P. Cole, K. J. Rothman, and S. D. Kaplan. 1977. Epidemiology of endometrial cancer. *Journal of the National Cancer Institute* 59:1055–60.

    47. Armstrong and Doll, Environmental factors and cancer incidence; Lingeman, C. H. 1974. Etiology of cancer of the human ovary: A review. *Journal of the National Cancer Institute* 53:1603–18; and Risch, H. A., M. Jain, I. D. Marrett, and G. R. Howe. 1994. Dietary fat intake and risk of epithelial ovarian cancer. *Journal of the National Cancer Institute* 86:1409–15.

    48. Risch et al., Dietary fat intake and risk.

    49. Cramer, D. W., W. C. Willett, D. A. Bell, et al. 1989. Galactose consumption and metabolism in relation to the risk of ovarian cancer. *The Lancet* 2:66–71.

    50. Cramer, D. W., H. Xu, and T. Sahi. 1994. Adult hypolactasia, milk

consumption, and age specific fertility. *American Journal of Epidemiology* 139: 282–89.

51. De Mille, *Martha,* 103.

52. Graham, *Blood memory,* 29.

53. Ibid., 102.

SIX. SPECIAL INFORMATION FOR MEN: IMPOTENCE AND PROSTATE PROBLEMS

1. Feldman, H. A., I. Goldstein, D. G. Hatzichristou, R. J. Krane, and J. B. McKinlay. 1994. Impotence and its medical and psychosocial correlates: results of the Massachusetts Male Aging Study. *Journal of Urology* 151:54–61.

2. Michal, V. 1982. Arterial disease as a cause of impotence. *Clinics in Endocrinology and Metabolism* 11:725–48.

3. Diokno, A. C., M. B. Brown, and A. R. Herzog. 1990. Sexual function in the elderly. *Archives of Internal Medicine* 150:197–200.

4. Michal, Arterial disease as cause of impotence; Wabrek, A. J., and R. C. Burchell. 1980. Male sexual dysfunction associated with coronary heart disease. *Archives of Sexual Behavior* 9:69–75.

5. Morley, J. E., S. G. Korenman, F. E. Kaiser, A. D. Mooradian, and S. P. Viosca. 1988. Relationship of penile brachial pressure index to myocardial infarction and cerebrovascular accidents in older men. *American Journal of Medicine* 84:445–48.

6. Michal, Arterial disease as cause of impotence.

7. Feldman et al., Impotence and medical and psychosocial correlates.

8. Carroll, J. L., D. Ellis, and D. H. Bagley. 1992. Impotence in the elderly. *Urology* 39:226–30.

9. Bulpitt, C. J., C. T. Dollery, and S. Carne. 1976. Change in symptoms of hypertensive patients after referral to hospital clinic. *British Heart Journal* 38: 121–28.

10. Morley, J. E., and F. E. Kaiser. 1992. Impotence in elderly men. *Drugs and Aging* 2:330–44.

11. Muller, S. C., H. El-Damanhoury, J. Ruth, and T. F. Lue. 1991. Hypertension and impotence. *European Urology* 19:29–34.

12. Kaiser, F. E., S. P. Viosca, J. E. Morley, A. D. Mooradian, S .S. Davis, and S. G. Korenman. 1988. Impotence and aging: clinical and hormonal factors. *Journal of the American Gerontological Society* 36:511–19.

13. Antoniou, L. D., R. J. Shalhoub, T. Sudhakar, and J. C. Smith. 1977. Reversal of uraemic impotence by zinc. *The Lancet* 2:895–900.

14. Morley and Kaiser, Impotence in elderly men; Smith, P. J., and R. L. Talbert. 1986. Sexual dysfunction with antihypertensive and antipsychotic agents. *Clinical Pharmacy* 5:373–84.

15. Diokno et al., Sexual function in the elderly; Morley and Kaiser, Impotence in elderly men; and Isaacs, J. T. 1994. Etiology of benign prostatic hyperplasia. *European Urology* 25 (suppl 1):6–9.

16. Feldman et al., Impotence and medical and psychosocial correlates; Morley and Kaiser, Impotence in elderly men.

17. Morley and Kaiser, Impotence in elderly men.

18. Ibid.

19. Michal, Arterial disease as cause of impotence.

20. Isaacs, Etiology of benign prostatic hyperplasia.

21. Ibid.

22. Ball, A. J., R. C. Feneley, and P. H. Abrams. 1981. The natural history of untreated "prostatism." *British Journal of Urology* 53:613–16.

23. Jonler, M., M. Riehmann and R. C. Bruskewitz. 1994. Benign prostatic hyperplasia: current pharmacological treatment. *Drugs* 47:66–81.

24. Wasserman, N. F., and P. K. Reddy. 1994. Therapeutic alternatives to surgery for benign prostatic hyperplasia. *Investigative Radiology* 29:224–37.

25. Ibid.; Hald, T. 1994. Review of current treatment of benign prostatic hyperplasia. *European Urology* 25 (suppl 1):15–19.

26. Araki, H., H. Watanabe, T. Mishina, and M. Nakao. 1983. High-risk group for benign prostatic hypertrophy. *Prostate* 4:253–64.

27. Ibid.

28. Jonler et al., Benign prostatic hyperplasia.

29. Chirillo-Marucco, E., et al. Extract of Serenoa repens (Permixon R) in the treatment of prostatic hypertrophy. 1983. *Urologia* 5:1269–77; Walker, M. Feb.-Mar. 1991. Serenoa repens extract (Saw palmetto) relief for benign prostatic hypertrophy (BPH). *Townsend Letter for Doctors:* 107–110; and Perlmutter, D. 1994. *LifeGuide.* Naples, FL: LifeGuide Press.

30. Sakr, W. A., G. P. Haas, B. F. Cassin, J. E. Pontes, and J. D. Crissman.

1993. The frequency of carcinoma and intraepithelial neoplasia of the prostate in young males. *Journal of Urology* 150:379–85.

31. Thompson, I. A. 1994. Observation alone in the management of localized prostate cancer: the natural history of untreated disease. *Urology* 43 (suppl):41–46.

32. Breslow, N., C. W. Chan, G. Dhom, et al. 1977. Latent carcinoma of prostate at autopsy in seven areas. *International Journal of Cancer* 20:680–88.

33. Armstrong, B., and R. Doll. 1975. Environmental factors and cancer incidence and mortality in different countries, with special reference to dietary practices. *International Journal of Cancer* 15:617–31; Howell, M. A. 1974. Factor analysis of international cancer mortality data and per capita food consumption. *British Journal of Cancer* 29:328–36; Rotkin, I. D. 1977. Studies in the epidemiology of prostatic cancer: expanded sampling. *Cancer Treatment Report* 61:173–80; Blair, A., and J. F. Fraumeni, Jr. 1978. Geographic patterns of prostate cancer in the United States. *Journal of the National Cancer Institute* 61: 1379–84; Kolonel, L. N., J. H. Hankin, J. Lee, S. Y. Chu, A. M. Y. Nomura, and M. W. Hinds. 1981. Nutrient intakes in relation to cancer incidence in Hawaii. *British Journal of Cancer* 44:332–39; Schuman, L. M., J. S. Mandel, A. Radke, U. Seal, and F. Halberg. 1982. Some selected features of the epidemiology of prostatic cancer: Minneapolis-St. Paul, Minnesota case control study, 1976–1979. In Magnus, K., ed. *Trends in cancer incidence: causes and practical implications.* Washington, DC: Hemisphere Publishing Corp.; Graham, S, et al. 1983. Diet in the epidemiology of carcinoma of the prostate gland. *Journal of the National Cancer Institute* 70:687–92; Ross, R. K., H. Shimizu, A. Paganini-Hill, G. Honda, and B. E. Henderson. 1987. Case-control studies of prostate cancer in blacks and whites in Southern California. *Journal of the National Cancer Institute* 78:869–74; Oishi, K., K. Okada, O. Yoshida, et al. 1988. A case-control study of prostatic cancer with reference to dietary habits. *Prostate* 12:179–90; Severson, R. K., A. M. Nomura, J. S. Grove, and G. N. Stemmermann. 1989. A prospective study of demographics, diet, and prostate cancer among men of Japanese ancestry in Hawaii. *Cancer Research* 49:1857–60; and Mettlin, C., S. Selenskas, N. Natarajan, and R. Huben. 1989. Beta-carotene and animal fats and their relationship to prostate cancer risk: A case-control study. *Cancer* 64:605–12.

34. Breslow et al., Latent carcinoma of prostate; Howell, Factor analysis of international cancer mortality data; Severson et al., Prospective study of demographics, diet, and prostate cancer; Hirayama, T. Changing patterns of cancer in

Japan with special reference to the decrease in stomach cancer mortality. In Hiatt, H. H., J. D. Watson, and J. A. Winstein, eds. 1977. *Origins of human cancer. Book A, Incidence of cancer in humans.* Cold Spring Harbor, NY: Cold Spring Harbor Laboratory; Hirayama, T. 1979. Epidemiology of prostate cancer with special reference to the role of diet. *National Cancer Institute Monographs* 53:149–54; Phillips, R. L. 1975. Role of life-style and dietary habits in risk of cancer among Seventh-Day Adventists. *Cancer Research* 35:3513–22; and Mills, P., W. L. Beeson, R. L. Phillips, and G. E. Fraser. 1989. Cohort study of diet, lifestyle, and prostate cancer in Adventist men. *Cancer* 64:598–604.

35. Hautmann, R. E., T. W. Sauter, and U. K. Wenderoth. 1994. Radical retropubic prostatectomy: morbidity and urinary continence in 418 consecutive cases. *Urology* 43 (suppl):47–51.

36. Hauri, D., H. Knonagel, and K. Konstantinidis. 1989. Radical prostatectomy in cases of prostatic carcinoma: the problem concerning erectile impotence. *Urologia Internationalis* 44:272–78.

37. Thompson, Observation in management of localized prostate cancer.

38. Ibid.

39. Ploch, N. R., and M. K. Brawer. 1994. How to use prostate-specific antigen. *Urology* 43 (suppl):27–35.

SEVEN. SURGE-PROTECTING YOUR VEINS AND ARTERIES

1. Ghetti, A., and M. Batisse. 1983. The overall protection of Venice and its lagoon. *Nature and Resources* 19:7–19.

2. Burkitt, D. P. 1976. Varicose veins: facts and fantasy. *Archives of Surgery* 111:1327–32.

3. Callam, M. J. 1994. Epidemiology of varicose veins. *British Journal of Surgery* 81:167–73.

4. Cornu-Thenard, A., P. Boivin, J. M. Baud, I. de Vincenzi, and P. H. Carpentier. 1994. Importance of the familial factor in varicose disease. *Journal of Dermatologic Surgery and Oncology* 20:318–26.

5. Callam, Epidemiology of varicose veins.

6. Burkitt, Varicose veins.

7. Pollack, A. A., and E. H. Wood. 1949. Venous pressure in the saphenous vein at the ankle in man during exercise and changes in posture. *Journal of Applied Physiology* 1:649–62.

8. Negus, D. 1993. Recurrent varicose veins: a national problem. *British Journal of Surgery* 80:823–24; Neglen, P., E. Einarsson, and B. Eklof. 1993. The functional long-term value of different types of treatment for saphenous vein incompetence. *Journal of Cardiovascular Surgery* 34:295–301.

9. Fligelstone L., G. Carolan, N. Pugh, A. Shandall, and I. Lane. 1993. An assessment of the long saphenous vein for potential use as a vascular conduit after varicose vein surgery. *Journal of Vascular Surgery* 18:836–40.

10. Burkitt, D. P., C. Latto, S. B. Janvrin, and B. Mayou. 1977. Pelvic phleboliths: epidemiology and postulated etiology. *New England Journal of Medicine* 296:1387–90.

11. Mitropoulos, K. A., G. J. Miller, J. C. Martin, B. E. A. Reeves, and J. Cooper. 1994. Dietary fat induces changes in factor VII coagulant activity through effects on plasma stearic acid concentration. *Arteriosclerosis and Thrombosis* 14:214–22.

12. Burkitt, D. P. 1975. Hemorrhoids, varicose veins, and deep vein thrombosis: epidemiologic features and suggested causative factors. *Canadian Journal of Surgery* 18:483–88.

13. Ibid.

14. Ibid.

15. Johanson, J. F., and A. Sonnenberg. 1990. The prevalence of hemorrhoids and chronic constipation: an epidemiologic study. *Gastroenterology* 98:380–86; Smith, L. E. 1992. Hemorrhoidectomy with lasers and other contemporary modalities. *Surgical Clinics of North America* 72:665–79.

16. Smith, Hemorrhoidectomy with lasers; Dennison, A. R., D. C. Wherry, and D. L. Morris. 1988. Hemorrhoids: nonoperative management. *Surgical Clinics of North America* 68:1401–9.

17. American Heart Association. 1991. *1992 heart and stroke facts.* Dallas: American Heart Association.

18. Grimm, R. H., Jr., A. S. Leon, D. B. Hunninghake, K. Lenz, P. Hannan, and H. Blackburn. 1981. Effects of thiazide diuretics on plasma lipids and lipoproteins in mildly hypertensive patients. *Annals of Internal Medicine* 94:7–11; Freis, E. D., and B. J. Materson. 1984. Short-term versus long-term changes in serum cholesterol with thiazide diuretics alone. *The Lancet* 1:1414–15; Johnson, B. F. 1986. The effects of thiazide diuretics upon plasma lipoproteins. *Journal of Hypertension* 4:235–39; and McCarron, D. A. 1984. Diuretic therapy for mild hypertension: the "real" cost of treatment. *American Journal of Cardiology* 53:9A–11A.

19. Weinberger, M. H. 1993. Salt sensitivity. In Izzo, J. L., and H. R. Black, eds. *Hypertension primer.* Washington, DC: American Heart Association.

20. Ophir, O., G. Peer, J. Gilad, M. Blum, and A. Aviram. 1983. Low blood pressure in vegetarians: the possible role of potassium. *American Journal of Clinical Nutrition* 37:755–62; Melby, C. L., G. C. Hyner, and B. Zoog. 1985. Blood pressure in vegetarians and nonvegetarians: a cross-sectional analysis. *Nutrition Research* 5:1077–82; and Melby, C. L., D. G. Goldflies, G. C. Hyner, and R. M. Lyle. 1989. Relation between vegetarian/nonvegetarian diets and blood pressure in black and white adults. *American Journal of Public Health* 79: 1283–88.

21. Rouse, I. L., and L. J. Beilin. 1984. Editorial review: vegetarian diet and blood pressure. *Journal of Hypertension* 2:231–40; Anderson, J. W. 1983. Plant fiber and blood pressure. *Annals of Internal Medicine* 98 (Part 2):842.

22. Rouse, I. L., B. K. Armstrong, L. J. Beilin, and R. Vandongen. 1983. Blood-pressure-lowering effect of a vegetarian diet: controlled trial in normotensive subjects. *The Lancet* 1:5–10; Rouse, I. L., L. J. Beilin, D. P. Mahoney, et al. 1986. Nutrient intake, blood pressure, serum and urinary prostaglandins and serum thromboxane B2 in a controlled trial with a lacto-ovo-vegetarian diet. *Journal of Hypertension* 4:241–50; Margetts, B. M., L. J. Beilin, B. K. Armstrong, and R. Vandongen. 1985. A randomized controlled trial of a vegetarian diet in the treatment of mild hypertension. *Clinical and Experimental Pharmacology and Physiology* 12:263–66; and Margetts, B. M., L. J. Beilin, R. Vandongen, and B. K. Armstrong. 1986. Vegetarian diet in mild hypertension: a randomised controlled trial. *British Medical Journal* 293:1468–71.

23. Rouse and Beilin, Editorial review; Sacks, F. M., and E. H. Kass. 1988. Low blood pressure in vegetarians: effects of specific foods and nutrients. *American Journal of Clinical Nutrition* 48:795–800; and Armstrong, B., H. Clarke, C. Martin, W. Ward, N. Norman, and J. Masarei. 1979. Urinary sodium and blood pressure in vegetarians. *American Journal of Clinical Nutrition* 32: 2472–76.

24. Trout, D. L. 1991. Vitamin C and cardiovascular risk factors. *American Journal of Clinical Nutrition* 53:322S–5S.

25. Ernst, E., L. Pietsch, A. Matrai, and J. Eisenberg. 1986. Blood rheology in vegetarians. *British Journal of Nutrition* 56:555–60; Ernst, E., A. Matrai, and L. Pietsch. 1987. Vegetarian diet in mild hypertension. *British Medical Journal* 294:180.

26. Lindahl, O., L. Lindwall, A. Spangberg, A. Stenram, and P. A. Ocker-

man. 1984. A vegan regimen with reduced medication in the treatment of hypertension. *British Journal of Nutrition* 52:11–20.

EIGHT. CLEANING YOUR ARTERIES

1. Esterbauer, H., G. Striegl, H. Puhl, et al. 1989. The role of vitamin E and carotenoids in preventing oxidation of low-density lipoproteins. *Annals of the New York Academy of Sciences* 570:254–67.

2. Esterbauer, The role of vitamin E; Esterbauer, H., M. Dieber-Rotheneder, G. Striegl, and G. Waeg. 1991. Role of vitamin E in preventing the oxidation of low-density lipoprotein. *American Journal of Clinical Nutrition* 53:314S–21S; Gey, K. F., P. Pushak, P. Jordan, and U. K. Moser. 1991. Inverse correlation between plasma vitamin E and mortality from ischemic heart disease in cross-cultural epidemiology. *American Journal of Clinical Nutrition* 53:1–9; Stampfer, M. J., C. H. Hennekens, J. E. Manson, G. A. Colditz, B. Rosner, and W. C. Willet. 1993. Vitamin E consumption and the risk of coronary disease in women. *New England Journal of Medicine* 328:1444–49; Rimm, E. B., M. J. Stampfer, A. Asherio, E. Giovannucci, G. A. Colditz, and W. C. Willet. 1993. Vitamin E consumption and the risk of coronary disease in men. *New England Journal of Medicine* 328:1450–56; Jialal, I., and S. M. Grundy. 1993. Effect of combined supplementation with alpha-tocopherol, ascorbate, and beta-carotene on low-density lipoprotein oxidation. *Circulation* 88:2780–86; Frei, B. 1991. Ascorbic acid protects lipids in human plasma and low-density lipoprotein against oxidative damage. *American Journal of Clinical Nutrition* 54:1113S–18S; Niki, E. 1991. Action of ascorbic acid as a scavenger of active and stable oxygen radicals. *American Journal of Clinical Nutrition* 54:1119S–24S; and Hennekins, C. November 1990. Presentation to the American Heart Association. Beta-Carotene Therapy for Chronic Stable Angina, Dallas, Texas, November 13, 1990.

3. Hunter, J. E. 1990. N-3 Fatty acids from vegetable oils. *American Journal of Clinical Nutrition* 51:809–14; Renaud, S., F. Godsey, E. Dumont, C. Thevenon, E. Ortchanian, and J. L. Martin. 1986. Influence of long-term diet modification on platelet function and composition in Moselle farmers. *American Journal of Clinical Nutrition* 43:136–50; and Emken, E. A., R. O. Adlof, H. Rakoff, and W. K. Rohwedder. 1989. Metabolism of deuterium-labeled linolenic, lineolic, oleic, stearic, and palmitic acid in human subjects. In Baillie, T. A., and J. R. Jones, eds. Synthesis and applications of isotopically

labelled compounds. 1988. Amsterdam: Elsevier Science Publishers BV: 713–16.

4. Salonen, J. T., R. Salonen, K. Nyyssonen, and H. Korpela. 1992. Iron sufficiency is associated with hypertension and excess risk of myocardial infarction: the Kuopio Ischaemic Heart Disease Risk Factor Study (KIHD). *Circulation* 85:864.

5. Ascherio, A., W. C. Willett, E. B. Rimm, E. L. Giovannucci, and M. J. Stampfer. 1994. Dietary iron intake and risk of coronary disease among men. *Circulation* 89:969–74.

6. Belcher, J. D., J. Balla, G. Balla, et al. 1993. Vitamin E, LDL, and endothelium. Brief oral vitamin supplementation prevents oxidized LDL-mediated vascular injury in vitro. *Arteriosclerosis and Thrombosis* 13:1779–89.

7. Lipid Research Clinics Program. 1984. The lipid research clinics coronary primary prevention trial results, II. *Journal of the American Medical Association* 251:365–74.

8. Trout, D. L. 1991. Vitamin C and cardiovascular risk factors. *American Journal of Clinical Nutrition* 53:322S–25S.

9. Castelli, W. P. 1984. Epidemiology of coronary heart disease. *American Journal of Medicine* 76:4–12.

10. Austin, M. A., and J. E. Hokanson. 1994. Epidemiology of triglycerides, small dense low-density lipoprotein, and lipoprotein(a) as risk factors for coronary heart disease. *Medical Clinics of North America* 78:99–115.

11. Melish, J., N. A. Le, H. Ginsberg, D. Steinberg, and W. V. Brown. 1980. Dissociation of apopprotein B and triglyceride production in very low-density lipoproteins. *American Journal of Physiology* 239:E354–62.

12. Anderson, J. W., N. J. Gustafson, D. B. Spencer, J. Tietyen, and C. A. Bryant. 1990. Serum lipid response of hypercholesterolemic men to single and divided doses of canned beans. *American Journal of Clinical Nutrition* 51:1013–19; Wood, P. D., M. L. Stefanick, D. M. Dreon, et al. 1988. Changes in plasma lipids and lipoproteins in overweight men during weight loss through dieting as compared with exercise. *New England Journal of Medicine* 319:1173–79.

13. Von Eckardstein, A., M. R. Malinow, B. Upson, et al. 1994. Effects of age, lipoproteins, and hemostatic parameters on the role of homocyst(e)inemia as a cardiovascular risk factor in men. *Arteriosclerosis and Thrombosis* 14:460–64.

14. Stampfer, M. J., M. R. Malinow, W. C. Willett, et al. 1992. A prospective study of plasma homocyst(e)ine and risk of myocardial infarction in U.S. physicians. *Journal of the American Medical Association* 268:877–81.

15. Selhub, J., P. F. Jacques, P. W. F. Wilson, D. Rush, and I. H. Rosenberg. 1993. Vitamin status and intake as primary determinants of homocysteinemia in an elderly population. *Journal of the American Medical Association* 270:2693–98.

16. Austin and Hokanson, Epidemiology of triglycerides; Simons, L. A. 1993. Lipoprotein(a): important risk factor or passing fashion? *Medical Journal of Australia* 158:512–14; and Wade, D. P., J. G. Clarke, G. E. Lindahl, et al. 1993. Genetic influences on lipoprotein(a) concentration. *Biochemical Society Transactions* 21:499–502.

17. Austin and Hokanson, Epidemiology of triglycerides.

18. Fruchart, J. C., G. Ailhaud, and J. M. Bard. 1993. Heterogeneity of high-density lipoprotein particles. *Circulation* 87 (suppl III): 22–27.

19. Lichtenstein, A. H., L. M. Ausman, W. Carrasco, J. L. Jenner, J. M. Ordovas, and E. J. Schaefer. 1994. Hypercholesterolemic effect of dietary cholesterol in diets enriched in polyunsaturated and saturated fat. *Arteriosclerosis and Thrombosis* 14:168–75; Vuoristo, M., and T. A. Miettinen. 1994. Absorption, metabolism, and serum concentrations of cholesterol in vegetarians: effects of cholesterol feeding. *American Journal of Clinical Nutrition* 59:1325–31.

20. Shekelle, R. B., and J. Stamler. 1989. Dietary cholesterol and ischemic heart disease. *The Lancet* 1:1177–79.

21. Ibid.

22. Moncada, S., J. F. Martin, and A. Higgs. 1993. Symposium on regression of atherosclerosis. *European Journal of Clinical Investigation* 23:385–98.

23. Willett, W., and F. M. Sacks. 1991. Chewing the fat—how much and what kind. *New England Journal of Medicine* 324:121–23.

24. Hunninghake, D. B., E. A. Stein, and C. A. Dujovne. 1993. The efficacy of intensive dietary therapy alone or combined with lovastatin in outpatients with hypercholesterolemia. *New England Journal of Medicine* 328: 1213–19.

25. Messina, M., and V. Messina. 1994. *The simple soybean and your health.* Garden City Park, NY: Avery Publishing Group.

26. Ornish, D., S. E. Brown, L. W. Scherwitz, et al. 1990. Can lifestyle changes reverse coronary heart disease? *The Lancet* 336:129–33; Blankenhorn, D. H., S. A. Nessim, R. L. Johnson, M. E. Sanmarco, S. P. Azen, and L. Cashin-Hemphill. 1987. Beneficial effects of combined colestipol-niacin therapy on coronary atherosclerosis and coronary venous bypass grafts. *Journal of the American Medical Association* 257:3233–40; and Brown, G. B., J. J. Albers, L. D.

Fisher, et al. 1990. Niacin or lovastatin combined with colestipol regresses coronary atherosclerosis and prevents clinical events in men with elevated apolipoprotein B. *New England Journal of Medicine* 323:1289–98.

27. Mensink, R. P., and M. B. Katan. 1990. Effect of dietary trans fatty acids on high-density and low-density lipoprotein cholesterol levels in healthy subjects. *New England Journal of Medicine* 323:439–45; Willett, W. C., M. J. Stampfer, J. E. Manson, et al. 1993. Intake of trans fatty acids and risk of coronary heart disease among women. *The Lancet* 341:581–85; and Siguel, E. N., and R. H. Lerman. 1993. Trans-fatty acid patterns in patients with angiographically documented coronary artery disease. *American Journal of Cardiology* 71: 916–20.

28. Willett et al. Intake of trans fatty acids.

29. Ouart, M. D., B. L. Damron, F. G. Martin, R. B. Christmas, and D. R. Sloan. 1992. *Poultry Science* 71:821–28.

30. Subcommittee on Poultry Nutrition, National Research Council. 1984. *Nutrient requirements of poultry.* Washington, DC: National Academy Press.

31. Hay, J. D., and W. R. Morrison. 1970. Isomeric monoenoic fatty acids in bovine milk fat. *Biochimica et Biophysica Acta* 202:237–43; Parodi, P. W. 1976. Distribution of isomeric octadecenoic fatty acids in milk fat. *Journal of Dairy Science* 59:1870–73.

32. Willett et al., Intake of trans fatty acids; Enig, M. G., R. J. Munn, and M. Keeney. Dietary fat and cancer trends—a critique. *Federation Proceedings* 37:2215–20.

33. Van Horn, L. V., K. Liu, D. Parker, et al. 1986. Serum lipid response to oat product intake with a fat-modified diet. *Journal of the American Dietetic Association* 86:759–64; Anderson, J. W., N. H. Gilinsky, D. A. Deakins, S. F. Smith, D. S. O'Neal, D. W. Dillon, and P. R. Oeltgen. 1991. Lipid responses of hypercholesterolemic men to oat-bran and wheat-bran intake. *American Journal of Clinical Nutrition* 54:678–83; and Kesaniemi, Y. A., S. Tarpila, and R. A. Miettinen. 1990. Low vs. high dietary fiber and serum, biliary, and fecal lipids in middle-aged men. *American Journal of Clinical Nutrition* 51:1007–12.

34. Anderson et al., Serum lipid response; Anderson, J. W. 1987. Dietary fiber, lipids, and atherosclerosis. *American Journal of Cardiology* 60:17G–22G.

35. Anderson et al., Serum lipid response; Mathur, K. S., M. A. Khan, R. D. Sharma. 1968. Hypocholesterolemic effect of Bengal gram: a long-term study in man. *British Medical Journal* 1:30–31; Grande, F., J. T. Anderson, and

A. Keys. 1965. Effect of carbohydrates of leguminous seeds, wheat and potatoes on serum cholesterol concentration in man. *Journal of Nutrition* 86:313–17; Bingwen, L., W. Zhaofeny, L. Wahshen, and Z. Rongjue. 1981. Effects of bean meal on serum cholesterol and triglycerides. *Chinese Medical Journal* 94:455–58; Hellendoorn, E. W. 1976. Beneficial physiologic action of beans. *Journal of the American Dietetic Association* 69:248–53; Jenkins, D. J. A., G. S. Wong, R. Patten, et al. 1983. Leguminous seeds in the dietary management of hyperlipidemia. *American Journal of Clinical Nutrition* 38:567–73; and Jenkins, D. J. A., T. M. S. Wolever, J. Kalmusky, et al. 1987. Low-glycemic index diet in hyperlipidemia: use of traditional starchy foods. *American Journal of Clinical Nutrition* 46:66–71.

36. Anderson et al. Serum lipid response.

37. Life Sciences Research Office, Federation of American Societies for Experimental Biology. 1987. *Physiological effects and health consequences of dietary fiber.* Washington, DC, American Heart Association. 1988. Dietary guidelines for healthy Americans: a statement for physicians and health professionals by the Nutrition Committee. *Arteriosclerosis* 8:218A–21A.

38. Sabate, J., G. E. Fraser, K. Burke, S. F. Knutsen, H. Bennett, and K. D. Lindsted. 1993. Effects of walnuts on serum lipid levels and blood pressure in normal men. *New England Journal of Medicine* 328:603–7.

39. Bordia, A. 1981. Effect of garlic on blood lipids in patients with coronary heart disease. *American Journal of Clinical Nutrition* 34:2100–103.

40. Castelli, Epidemiology of coronary heart disease.

41. Wood et al., Changes in plasma lipids.

42. Enos, W. F., R. H. Holmes, and J. Beyer. 1953. Coronary disease among United States soldiers killed in action in Korea. *Journal of the American Medical Association* 152:1090–93.

43. Schnall, P. L., C. Pieper, J. E. Schwartz, et al. 1990. The relationship between "job strain," workplace diastolic blood pressure, and left ventricular mass index. *Journal of the American Medical Association* 263:1929–35.

44. Castelli, Epidemiology of coronary heart disease.

45. Sibai, A. M., H. K. Armenian, and S. Alam. 1989. Wartime determinants of arteriographically confirmed coronary artery disease in Beirut. *American Journal of Epidemiology* 130:623–31.

46. Rozanski, A., C. N. Bairey, D. S. Krantz, et al. 1988. Mental stress and the induction of silent myocardial ischemia in patients with coronary artery disease. *New England Journal of Medicine* 318:1005–12.

47. Ornish et al., Can lifestyle changes reverse coronary heart disease?; Blankenhorn et al., Beneficial effects; and Brown et al., Niacin or lovastatin.

48. Ornish et al., Can lifestyle changes reverse coronary heart disease?

49. Moncada et al., Symposium on regression of atherosclerosis.

50. Colditz, G. A., R. Bonita, M. J. Stampfer, et al. 1988. Cigarette smoking and risk of stroke in middle-aged women. *New England Journal of Medicine* 318:937–41.

NINE. STRONG BONES AND HEALTHY JOINTS

1. Abelow, B. J., T. R. Holford, and K. L. Insogna. 1992. Cross-cultural association between dietary animal protein and hip fracture: a hypothesis. *Calcified Tissue International* 50:14–18.

2. Remer, T., and F. Manz. 1994. Estimation of the renal net acid excretion by adults consuming diets containing variable amounts of protein. *American Journal of Clinical Nutrition* 59:1356–61.

3. Ibid.

4. Marsh, A. G., T. V. Sanchez, O. Mickelsen, J. Keiser, and G. Mayor. 1980. Cortical bone density of adult lacto-ovo-vegetarian and omnivorous women. *Journal of the American Dietetic Association* 76:148–51; Calvo, M. S. 1993. Dietary phosphorus, calcium metabolism, and bone. *Journal of Nutrition* 123:1627–33.

5. Massey, L. K., and S. J. Whiting. 1993. Caffeine, urinary calcium, calcium metabolism, and bone. *Journal of Nutrition* 123:1611–14.

6. Nordin, B. E. C., A. G. Need, H. A. Morris, and M. Horowitz. 1993. The nature and significance of the relationship between urinary sodium and urinary calcium in women. *Journal of Nutrition* 123:1615–22.

7. Ibid.

8. Lemann, J., Jr., J. A. Pleuss, and R. W. Gray. 1993. Potassium causes calcium retention in healthy adults. *Journal of Nutrition* 123:1623–26.

9. Hopper, J. L., and E. Seeman. 1994. The bone density of female twins discordant for tobacco use. *New England Journal of Medicine* 330:387–92.

10. Riggs, B. L., H. W. Wahner, J. Melton, L. S. Richelson, H. L. Judd, and M. O'Fallon. 1987. Dietary calcium intake and rates on bone loss in women. *Journal of Clinical Investigation* 80:979–82; Dawson-Hughes, B. 1991. Calcium supplementation and bone loss: a review of controlled clinical trials.

American Journal of Clinical Nutrition 54:274S–80S; and Mazess, R. B., and H. S. Barden. 1991. Bone density in premenopausal women: effects of age, dietary intake, physical activity, smoking, and birth-control pills. *American Journal of Clinical Nutrition* 53:132–42.

11. Abelow et al., Cross-cultural association between dietary animal protein and hip fracture.

12. Mazess and Barden, Bone density in premenopausal women; Dawson-Hughes, B., P. Jacques, and C. Shipp. 1987. Dietary calcium intake and bone loss from the spine in healthy postmenopausal women. *American Journal of Clinical Nutrition* 46:685–87.

13. Heaney, R. P., and C. M. Weaver. 1990. Calcium absorption from kale. *American Journal of Clinical Nutrition* 51:656–57.

14. Nicar, M. J., and C. Y. C. Pak. 1985. Calcium bioavailability from calcium carbonate and calcium citrate. *Journal of Clinical Endocrinology and Metabolism* 61:391–93.

15. Nelson, M. E., E. C. Fisher, F. A. Dilmanian, G. E. Dallal, and W. J. Evans. 1991. A 1-y walking program and increased dietary calcium in postmenopausal women: effect on bone. *American Journal of Clinical Nutrition* 53: 1304–11.

16. Holick, M. F. 1994. Importance of an adequate source of vitamin D for calcium metabolism. NIH Consensus Development Conference on Optimal Calcium Intake. Bethesda, MD: National Institutes of Health.

17. Broadus, A. E. 1981. Mineral metabolism. In Felig, P., J. D. Baxter, A. E. Broadus, and L. A. Frohman. *Endocrinology and metabolism.* New York: McGraw-Hill.

18. Chapuy, M. C., M. E. Arlot, F. Duboeuf, et al. 1992. Vitamin D_3 and calcium to prevent hip fractures in elderly women. *New England Journal of Medicine* 327:1637–42.

19. Jacobus, C. H., M. F. Holick, Q. Shao, et al. 1992. Hypervitaminosis D associated with drinking milk. *New England Journal of Medicine* 326: 1173–77.

20. Holick, M. F., Q. Shao, W. W. Liu, and T. C. Chen. 1992. The vitamin D content of fortified milk and infant formula. *New England Journal of Medicine,* 326:1178–81.

21. Holick, Importance of an adequate source of vitamin D for calcium metabolism.

22. Felson, D. T., Y. Zhang, and M. T. Hannan. 1993. The effect of post-

menopausal estrogen therapy on bone density in elderly women. *New England Journal of Medicine* 329:1141–46.

23. Lee, J. R. 1990. Osteoporosis reversal; the role of progesterone. *International Clinical Nutrition Review* 10:384–91.

24. Prior, J. C. 1990. Progesterone as a bone-trophic hormone. *Endocrine Review* 11:386–98; Prior, J. C., Y. Vigna, and N. Alojado. 1991. Progesterone and the prevention of osteoporosis. *Canadian Journal of Obstetrics/Gynecology* 3:178.

25. Beasley, R. P., P. H. Bennett, and C. C. Lin. 1993. Low prevalence of rheumatoid arthritis in Chinese. *Journal of Rheumatology* Suppl. 10:11–15.

26. Skoldstam, L., L. Larsson, and F. D. Lindstrom. 1979. Effects of fasting and lactovegetarian diet on rheumatoid arthritis. *Scandinavian Journal of Rheumatology* 8:249–55; Skoldstam, L. 1986. Fasting and vegan diet in rheumatoid arthritis. *Scandinavian Journal of Rheumatology* 15:219–23; Kremer, J. M., J. Bigauoette, A. V. Michalek, et al. 1985. Effects of manipulation of dietary fatty acids on clinical manifestations of rheumatoid arthritis. *The Lancet* 1:184–87.

27. Kjeldsen-Kragh, J., M. Haugen, C. F. Borchgrevink, et al. 1991. Controlled trial of fasting and one-year vegetarian diet in rheumatoid arthritis. *The Lancet* 338:899–902.

28. Kremer et al., Effects of manipulation of dietary fatty acids.

29. Darlington, L. G., and N. W. Ramsey. 1993. Review of dietary therapy for rheumatoid arthritis. *British Journal of Rheumatology* 32:507–14.

30. Sobel, D. 1989. *Arthritis: what works.* New York: St. Martin's Press.

31. Chang, N. C. 1993. Rheumatic diseases in China. *Journal of Rheumatology* Suppl. 10:41–45.

32. Merry, P., M. Grootveld, J. Lunec, and D. R. Blake. 1991. Oxidative damage to lipids within the inflamed human joint provides evidence of radical-medicated hypoxic-reperfusion injury. *American Journal of Clinical Nutrition* 53:362S–69S.

33. Bland, J. H. 1983. The reversibility of osteoarthritis: a review. *American Journal of Medicine* 74(6A):16–26.

34. Hochberg, M. C. 1991. Epidemiologic considerations in the primary prevention of osteoarthritis. *Journal of Rheumatology* 18:1438–40; Hart, D. J., and T. D. Spector. 1993. The relationship of obesity, fat distribution, and osteoarthritis in women in the general population: the Chingford Study. *Journal of Rheumatology* 20:331–35.

35. Hart and Spector, The relationship of obesity, fat distribution, and osteoarthritis in women; Carman, W. J., M. F. Sowers, V. M. Hawthorne, and L. A. Weissfeld. 1994. Obesity as a risk factor for osteoarthritis of the hand and wrist: a prospective study. *American Journal of Epidemiology* 139:119–29.

36. Cauley, J. A., C. K. Kwoh, G. Egeland, et al. 1993. Serum sex hormones and severity of osteoarthritis of the hand. *Journal of Rheumatology* 20: 1170–75.

37. Spector, T. D., D. J. Hart, P. Brown, et al. 1991. Frequency of osteoarthritis in hysterectomized women. *Journal of Rheumatology* 18:1877–83.

38. Cauley et al., Serum sex hormones; Spector et al., Frequency of osteoarthritis in hysterectomized women; and Samantha, A., A. Jones, M. Regan, S. Wilson, and M. Doherty. 1993. Is osteoarthritis in women affected by hormonal changes or smoking? *British Journal of Rheumatology* 32:366–70.

39. Peyron, J. G. 1991. Is osteoarthritis a preventable disease? *Journal of Rheumatology* 18 (Suppl. 27):2–3.

40. Hochberg, Epidemiologic considerations.

41. Felson, D. T., M. T. Hannan, A. Naimark, et al. 1991. Occupational physical demands, knee bending, and knee osteoarthritis, results from the Framingham study. *Journal of Rheumatology* 18:1587–92; Cooper, C., T. McAlindon, D. Coggon, P. Egger, and P. Dieppe. 1994. Occupational activity and osteoarthritis of the knee. *Annals of the Rheumatic Diseases* 53:90–93.

42. Lane, N. E., B. Michel, A. Bjorkengren, et al. 1993. The risk of osteoarthritis with running and aging: a 5-year longitudinal study. *Journal of Rheumatology* 20:461–68.

43. Gibson, T., A. V. Rodgers, H. A. Simmonds, F. Court-Brown, E. Todd, and V. Meilton. 1983. A controlled study of diet in patients with gout. *Annals of the Rheumatic Diseases* 42:123–27.

44. McCarty, D. J. 1994. Crystals and arthritis. *Disease-a-Month* 40: 259–99.

TEN. HOW TO DISSOLVE FAT PERMANENTLY

1. Danforth, E., Jr., E. A. H. Sims, E. S. Horton, and R. F. Goldman. 1975. Correlation of serum triiodothyronine concentrations (T3) with dietary composition, gain in weight, and thermogenesis in man. *Diabetes* 24:406; Spaulding, S. W., I. J. Chopra, R. S. Sherwin, and S. S. Lyall. 1976. Effect of caloric restriction and dietary composition on serum T3 and reverse T3 in man.

Journal of Clinical Endocrinology and Metabolism 42:197–200; and Mathieson, R. A., J. L. Walberg, F. C. Gwazdauskas, D. E. Hinkle, and J. M. Gregg. 1986. The effect of varying carbohydrate content of a very-low-caloric diet on resting metabolic rate and thyroid hormones. *Metabolism* 35:394–98.

2. Welle, S., U. Lilavivathana, and R. G. Campbell. 1980. Increased plasma norepinephrine concentrations and metabolic rates following glucose ingestion in man. *Metabolism* 29:806–9.

3. Ibid.

4. Deriaz, O., G. Theriault, N. Lavallee, G. Fournier, A. Nadeau, and C. Bouchard. 1991. Human resting energy expenditure in relation to dietary potassium. *American Journal of Clinical Nutrition* 54:628–34.

5. Ornish, D., S. E. Brown, L. W. Scherwitz, et al. 1990. Can lifestyle changes reverse coronary heart disease? *The Lancet* 336:129–33; Dwyer, J. T., L. D. V. H. Mayer, R. F. Kandel, and F. Mayer. 1973. The new vegetarians. *Journal of the American Dietetic Association* 62:503–9.

6. Melby, C. L., G. C. Hyner, and B. Zoog. 1985. Blood pressure in vegetarians and nonvegetarians: a cross-sectional analysis. *Nutrition Research* 5:1077–82; Melby, C. L., D. G. Goldflies, G. C. Hyner, and R. M. Lyle. 1989. Relation between vegetarian/nonvegetarian diets and blood pressure in black and white adults. *American Journal of Public Health* 79:1283–88; Sacks, F. M., D. Ornish, B. Rosner, S. McLanahan, W. P. Castelli, and E. H. Kass. 1985. Plasma lipoprotein levels in vegetarians: the effect of ingestion of fats from dairy products. *Journal of the American Medical Association.* 254:1337–41; Pixley, F., D. Wilson, K. McPherson, and J. Mann. 1985. Effect of vegetarianism on development of gallstones in women. *British Medical Journal* 291:11–12; Burr, M. L., J. Batese, A. M. Fehily, and A. S. Leger. 1981. Plasma cholesterol and blood pressure in vegetarians. *Journal of Human Nutrition* 35:437–41; Rouse, I. L., B. K. Armstrong, L. J. Beilin, and R. Vandongen. 1984. Vegetarian diet, blood pressure, and cardiovascular risk. *Australian and New Zealand Journal of Medicine* 14:439–43; and Frentzel-Beyme, R., J. Claude, and U. Eilber. 1988. Mortality among German vegetarians: first results after five years of follow-up. *Nutrition and Cancer* 11:117–26.

7. Kissileff, H. R., F. X. Pi-Sunyer, K. Segal, S. Meltzer, and P. A. Foelsch. 1990. Acute effects of exercise on food intake in obese and nonobese women. *American Journal of Clinical Nutrition* 52:240–45.

8. Some calories count more than others. 1988. *Tufts University Diet and Nutrition Letter* 6:2.

9. Schutz, Y., J. P. Flatt, and E. Jequier. 1989. Failure of dietary fat intake to promote fat oxidation: a factor favoring the development of obesity. *American Journal of Clinical Nutrition* 50:307–14.

10. Suter, P. M., Y. Schutz, and E. Jequier. 1992. The effect of ethanol on fat storage in healthy subjects. *New England Journal of Medicine* 326:983–87; de Castro, J. M., and S. Orozco. 1990. Moderate alcohol intake and spontaneous eating patterns of humans: evidence of unregulated supplementation. *American Journal of Clinical Nutrition* 52:246–53.

11. Wadden, T. A., G. D. Foster, K. A. Letizia, and J. L. Mullen. 1990. Long-term effects of dieting on resting metabolic rate in obese outpatients. *Journal of the American Medical Association* 264:707–11; Foster, G. D., et al. 1990. Controlled trial of the metabolic effects of a very-low-calorie diet: short- and long-term effects. *American Journal of Clinical Nutrition* 51:167–72.

12. Foster et al., Controlled trial of the metabolic effects of a very-low-calorie diet.

13. Stunkard, A. J., J. R. Harris, N. L. Pedersen, and G. E. McClearn. 1990. The body-mass index of twins who have been reared apart. *New England Journal of Medicine* 322:1483–87.

ELEVEN. HEALTHY SKIN AND HAIR

1. Sanford, K. K., R. Parshad, and R. Gantt. Responses of human cells in culture to hydrogen peroxide and related free radicals generated by visible light: relationship to cancer susceptibility. In Johnson, J. E., R. Walford, D. Harman, and J. Miquel, eds. 1986. *Free radicals, aging, and degenerative diseases.* New York: Alan R. Liss.

2. Stanulis-Praeger, B. M., and B. A. Gilchrest. 1989. Effect of donor age and prior sun exposure on growth inhibition of cultured human dermal fibroblasts by all trans-retinoic acid. *Journal of Cell Physiology* 139:116–24.

3. Gilchrest, B. A., G. Szabo, E. Flynn, and R. M. Goldwyn. 1983. Chronologic and actinically induced aging in human facial skin. *Journal of Investigative Dermatology* 80:81s–85s.

4. Ortonne, J. P., D. B. Mosher, and T. B. Fitzpatrick. 1983. *Vitiligo and other hypomelanoses of hair and skin.* New York: Plenum.

5. Sistrom, W. R., M. Griffiths, and R. Y. Stanier. 1956. The biology of a photosynthetic bacterium which lacks colored carotenoids. *Journal of Cellular and Comparative Physiology* 48:473–515.

6. Bendes, J. H. 1926. Heliotherapy in tuberculosis. *Minnesota Medicine* 9:112.

7. Matthews-Roth, M. M., M. A. Pathak, T. B. Fitzpatrick, et al. 1970. Beta-carotene as a photoprotective agent in erythropoietic protoporphyria. *New England Journal of Medicine* 282(22):1231–34; Matthews-Roth, M. M., M. A. Pathak, T. B. Fitzpatrick, et al. 1977. Beta-carotene therapy for erythropoietic protoporphyria and other photosensitivity diseases. *Archives of Dermatology* 113:1229–32.

8. Matthews-Roth, M. M., M. A. Pathak, J. Parris, T. B. Fitzpatrick, E. H. Kass, K. Toda, and W. Clemens. 1972. A clinical trial of the effects of oral beta-carotene on the responses of human skin to solar radiation. *Journal of Investigative Dermatology* 59(4):349–53.

9. Vahlquist, A., and B. Berne. 1986. Sunlight, vitamin A, and the skin. *Photodermatology* 3:203–5.

10. Hersey, P., M. Bradley, E. Hasic, G. Haran, A. Edwards, and W. H. McCarthy. 1983. Immunological effects of solarium exposure. *The Lancet* 1:545–48.

11. O'Dell, B. L., T. Jessen, L. E. Becker, R. T. Jackson, and E. B. Smith. 1980. Diminished immune response in sun-damaged skin. *Archives of Dermatology* 116:559–61.

12. Black, H. S., J. A. Herd, L. H. Goldberg, et al. 1994. Effect of a low-fat diet on the incidence of actinic keratosis. *New England Journal of Medicine* 330:1272–75.

13. Mackie, B. S., L. E. Mackie, L. D. Curtin, and D. J. Bourne. 1987. Melanoma and dietary lipids. *Nutrition and Cancer* 9:219–26.

14. Thompson, S. C., D. Jolley, and R. Marks. 1993. Reduction of solar keratoses by regular sunscreen use. *New England Journal of Medicine* 329:1147–51.

15. Kligman, A. M. 1989. The treatment of photoaged human skin by topical tretinoin. *Drugs* 38:1–8; Goldfarb, M. T., C. N. Ellis, and J. J. Voorhees. 1990. Topical tretinoin: its use in daily practice to reverse photoageing. *British Journal of Dermatology* 122:Suppl 35:87–91.

16. Simpson, N. B., and J. H. Barth. Hair patterns: hirsuities and baldness. In Rook, A., and R. Dawber, eds. 1991. *Diseases of the hair and scalp*. London: Blackwell Scientific Publications.

17. Varma, S. D. 1991. Scientific basis for medical therapy of cataracts by antioxidants. *American Journal of Clinical Nutrition* 53:335S–45S.

18. Jacques, P. F., and L. T. Chylack, Jr. 1991. Epidemiologic evidence of a role for the antioxidant vitamins and carotenoids in cataract prevention. *American Journal of Clinical Nutrition* 53:352S–5S; Robertson, J. M., A. P. Donner, and J. R. Trevithick. 1991. A possible role for vitamins C and E in cataract prevention. *American Journal of Clinical Nutrition* 53:346S–51S.

19. Garland, D. 1990. Role of site-specific, metal-catalyzed oxidation in lens aging and cataract: a hypothesis. *Experimental Eye Research* 50:677–82.

20. Couet, C., P. Jan, and G. Debry. 1991. Lactose and cataract in humans: a review. *Journal of the American College of Nutrition* 10(1):79–86.

21. Simoons, F. J. 1982. A geographic approach to senile cataracts: possible links with milk consumption, lactase activity, and galactose metabolism. *Digestive Diseases and Sciences* 27(3):257–64.

22. Wojnarowska, F. T. Psychological factors and disorders of the hair. In Rook, A., and R. Dawber, ed. 1991. *Diseases of the hair and scalp.* London: Blackwell Scientific Publications.

23. Hamilton, J. B. 1942. Male hormone stimulation is prerequisite and an incitant in common baldness. *American Journal of Anatomy* 71:451–80.

24. Adachi, K., and K. Motonari. 1970. Adenyl cyclase in human hair follicles: its inhibition by dihydrotestosterone. *Biochemical and Biophysical Research Communications* 41:884–90; Burke, K. E. 1989. Hair loss: what causes it and what can be done about it. *Postgraduate Medicine* 85:52–77.

25. Bingham, K. D. 1981. The metabolism of androgens in male pattern alopecia: a review. *International Journal of Cosmetic Science* 3:1–8; Sawaya, M. E., L. S. Honig, L. D. Garland, and S. L. Hsia. 1988. Hydroxysteroid dehydrogenase activity in sebaceous glands of scalp in male-pattern baldness. *Journal of Investigative Dermatology* 91:101–5.

26. Lookingbill, D. P., L. M. Demers, C. Wang, A. Leung, R. S. Rittmaster, and R. J. Santen. 1991. Clinical and biochemical parameters of androgen action in normal healthy Caucasian versus Chinese subjects. *Journal of Clinical Endocrinology and Metabolism* 72:1242–48.

27. Simpson and Barth, Hair patterns.

28. Inaba, M. 1985. *Can human hair grow again?* Tokyo: Azabu Shokan, Inc.

29. Hamalainen, E. K., H. Adlercreutz, P. Puska, and P. Pietinen. 1983. Decrease of serum total and free testosterone during a low-fat high-fiber diet. *Journal of Steroid Biochemistry* 18:369–70; Hamalainen, E. K., H. Adlercreutz, P. Puska, and P. Pietinen. 1984. Diet and serum sex hormones in healthy men.

Journal of Steroid Biochemistry 20:459–64; Adlercreutz, H. 1990. Western diet and Western diseases: some hormonal and biochemical mechanisms and associations. *Scandinavian Journal of Clinical Laboratory Investigation* 50, Suppl 201:3–23; Hill, P. B., E. L. Wynder, L. Garbaczewski, H. Garnes, and A. R. P. Walker. 1979a. Diet and urinary steroids in black and white North American men and black South African men. *Cancer Research* 39:5101–5; Hill, P. B., and E. L. Wynder. 1979b. Effect of a vegetarian diet and dexamethasone on plasma prolactin, testosterone and dehydroepiandrosterone in men and women. *Cancer Letters* 7:273–82; Hill, P., E. Wynder, L. Garbaczewski, H. Garnes, A. R. P. Walker, and P. Helman. 1980. Plasma hormones and lipids in men at different risk for coronary heart disease. *American Journal of Clinical Nutrition* 33:1010–18; and Howie, B. J., and T. D. Shultz. 1985. Dietary and hormonal interrelationships among vegetarian Seventh-Day Adventists and nonvegetarian men. *American Journal of Clinical Nutrition* 42:127–34.

30. Reed, M. J., R. W. Cheng, M. Simmonds, W. Richmond, and V. H. T. James. 1987. Dietary lipids: an additional regulator of plasma levels of sex hormone binding globulin. *Journal of Clinical Endocrinology and Metabolism* 64: 1083–85.

31. Reinberg, A., M. Lagoguey, J-M. Chauffournier, and F. Cesselin. 1975. Circannual and circadian rhythms in plasma testosterone in five healthy young Parisian males. *Acta Endocrinologica* 80:732–43; Reinberg, A., M. Lagoguey, F. Cesselin, et al. 1978. Circadian and circannual rhythms in plasma hormones and other variables of five healthy young human males. *Acta Endocrinologica* 88:417–27; Smals, A. G. H., P. W. C. Kloppenborg, and Th. J. Benraad. 1976. Circannual cycle in plasma testosterone levels in man. *Journal of Clinical Endocrinology and Metabolism* 42:979–82; Bellastella, A., T. Criscuolo, A. Mango, et al. 1983. Circannual rhythms of plasma luteinizing hormone, follicle-stimulating hormone, testosterone, prolactin, and cortisol in prepuberty. *Clinical Endocrinology* 19:453–59; and Randall, V. A., and F. J. G. Ebling. 1991. Seasonal changes in human hair growth. *British Journal of Dermatology* 124:146–51.

32. Simpson and Barth, Hair patterns.

33. Ibid.

34. Fiedler, V. C., and A. Hafeez. Diffuse alopecia: telogen hair loss. In Olsen, E. A. 1994. *Disorders of hair growth: diagnosis and treatment.* New York: McGraw-Hill.

35. Ibid.

36. Ibid.; Simpson, N. B. Diffuse alopecia: endocrine, metabolic, and

chemical influences on the follicular cycle. In Rook, A., and R. Dawber. eds. 1991. *Diseases of the hair and scalp.* London: Blackwell Scientific Publications.

37. Lee, J. R. 1993. *Natural progesterone.* Sebastopol, CA: BLL Publishing.

38. Ortonne, J. P., and G. Prota. 1993. Hair melanins and hair color: ultra-structural and biochemical aspects. *Journal of Investigative Dermatology* 101: 82S–89S.

39. Verbov, J. 1981. Erosive candidiasis of the scalp, followed by the reappearance of black hair after 40 years. *British Journal of Dermatology* 105:595–98.

40. Jelinek, J. E. 1972. Sudden whitening of the hair. *Bulletin of the New York Academy of Medicine* 48:1003–13.

41. Ibid.

42. Gould, L., C. V. R. Reddy, K. C. Oh, S. G. Kim, and W. Becker. 1978. Premature hair graying: a probable coronary risk factor. *Angiology* 29:800–3.

43. Olszewski, A. J., and K. S. McCully. 1993. Homocysteine metabolism and the oxidative modification of proteins and lipids. *Free Radical Biology and Medicine* 14:683–93.

44. Rook, A. J., and R. P. R. Dawber. The colour of hair. In Rook, A., and R. Dawber, eds. 1991. *Diseases of the hair and scalp.* London: Blackwell Scientific Publications.

TWELVE. GETTING STARTED WITH HEALTHY FOODS

1. American Dietetic Association. 1993. Position of the American Dietetic Association on vegetarian diets. *Journal of the American Dietetic Association* 93: 1317–19.

FOR FURTHER READING

COOKBOOKS

Diamond, Marilyn. *The American Vegetarian Cookbook.* New York: Warner Books, 1990.

Havala, Suzanne, and Mary Clifford. *Simple, Lowfat, & Vegetarian.* Baltimore: The Vegetarian Resource Group, 1994.

McDougall, John, and Mary McDougall. *The New McDougall Cookbook.* New York: Dutton, 1993.

Messina, Mark, and Virginia Messina. *The Simple Soybean and Your Health.* New York: Avery Publishing Group, 1994.

People for the Ethical Treatment of Animals and Ingrid Newkirk. *The Compassionate Cook.* New York: Warner Books, 1993.

Raymond, Jennifer. *The Peaceful Palate.* Palo Alto, CA: Sun Ray Press, 1992.

Sass, Lorna. *Recipes from an Ecological Kitchen.* New York: William Morrow & Co., 1982.

————. *Great Vegetarian Cooking Under Pressure.* New York: William Morrow & Co., 1994.

Stepaniak, Joanne. *The Uncheese Cookbook.* Summertown, TN: The Book Publishing Company, 1994.

Stepaniak, Joanne, and Kathy Hecker. *Ecological Cooking.* Summertown, TN: The Book Publishing Company, 1991.

Wagner, Lindsay, and Ariane Spade. *The High Road to Health.* New York: Prentice Hall Press, 1990.

Wasserman, Debra, and Reed Mangels. *Simply Vegan.* Baltimore: The Vegetarian Resource Group, 1991.

NUTRITION INFORMATION

Attwood, Charles. *Dr. Attwood's Low-Fat Prescription for Kids.* New York: Viking, 1995.

Barnard, Neal. *Food For Life.* New York: Harmony Books, 1993.

————. *The Power of Your Plate.* Summertown, TN: The Book Publishing Company, 1994.

Kradjian, Bob, M.D. *Save Yourself from Breast Cancer.* New York: Berkley Publishing Group, 1994.

Kushi, Michio. *The Cancer Prevention Diet.* New York: St. Martin's Press, 1993.

Lauffer, Randall. *Iron Balance.* New York: St. Martin's Press, 1991.

Ludington, Aileen, and Hans Diehl. *Lifestyle Capsules.* Santa Barbara, CA: Woodbridge Press, 1991.

McDougall, John. *The McDougall Program.* New York: Plume Books, 1991.

Moran, Victoria. *Get the Fat Out: 501 Simple Ways.* New York: Crown Trade Paperbacks.

Moran, Victoria. *The Love-Powered Diet.* San Rafael, CA: New World Library, 1992.

Ornish, Dean. *Dr. Dean Ornish's Program for Reversing Heart Disease.* New York: Random House, 1990.

————. *Eat More, Weigh Less.* New York: HarperCollins, 1993.

Perlmutter, David. *LifeGuide.* Naples, FL: LifeGuide Press, 1994.

Robbins, John. *May All Be Fed.* New York: William Morrow and Co., 1992.

INDEX

Jennifer Raymond, M.S., is a popular cooking and nutrition instructor from Palo Alto, California. She works as a nutrition consultant with Dean Ornish, M.D., in his "Open Your Heart" program for the prevention and reversal of heart disease and has worked with the federal government's Nutrition Education Training Project to improve the nutritional quality of the national school lunch program. Her first cookbook, *The Best of Jenny's Kitchen,* was published in 1981, and was followed closely by her television series, *Cooking—Naturally!* Her most recent cookbook, *The Peaceful Palate,* features a wide selection of low-fat, easily prepared recipes.

CONVERSION CHART

EQUIVALENT IMPERIAL AND METRIC MEASUREMENTS

American cooks use standard containers, the 8-ounce cup and a tablespoon that takes exactly 16 level fillings to fill that cup level. Measuring by cup makes it very difficult to give weight equivalents, as a cup of densely packed butter will weigh considerably more than a cup of flour. The easiest way therefore to deal with cup measurements in recipes is to take the amount by volume rather than by weight. Thus the equation reads:

1 cup = 240 ml = 8 fl. oz.   ½ cup = 120 ml = 4 fl. oz.

It is possible to buy a set of American cup measures in major stores around the world.

In the States, butter is often measured in sticks. One stick is the equivalent of 8 tablespoons. One tablespoon of butter is therefore the equivalent to ½ ounce/15 grams.

LIQUID MEASURES

Fluid ounces	U.S.	Imperial	Milliliters
	1 tsp	1 tsp	5
¼	2 tsp	1 dessertspoon	10
½	1 tbs	1 tbs	15
1	2 tbs	2 tbs	28
2	¼ cup	4 tbs	56
4	½ cup		110
5		¼ pint or 1 gill	140
6	¾ cup		170
8	1 cup		225
9			250, ¼ liter
10	1¼ cups	½ pint	280
12	1½ cups		340
15		¾ pint	420
16	2 cups		450
18	2¼ cups		500, ½ liter
20	2½ cups	1 pint	560
24	3 cups		675
25		1¼ pints	700
27	3½ cups		750
30	3¾ cups	1½ pints	840
32	4 cups		900
35		1¾ pints	980
36	4½ cups		1000, 1 liter
40	5 cups	2 pints	1120
48	6 cups		1350
50		2½ pints	1400
60	7½ cups	3 pints	1680
64	8 cups		1800
72	9 cups		2000, 2 liters

SOLID MEASURES

U.S. and Imperial Measures		Metric Measures	
ounces	pounds	grams	kilos
1		28	
2		56	
3½		100	
4	¼	112	
5		140	
6		168	
8	½	225	
9		250	¼
12	¾	340	
16	1	450	
18		500	½
20	1¼	560	
24	1½	675	
27		750	¾
28	1¾	780	
32	2	900	
36	2¼	1000	1
40	2½	1100	
48	3	1350	
54		1500	1½
64	4	1800	
72	4½	2000	2
80	5	2250	2¼
90		2500	2½
100	6	2800	2¾

OVEN TEMPERATURE EQUIVALENTS

Fahrenheit	Celsius	Gas Mark	Description
225	110	¼	Cool
250	130	½	
275	140	1	Very Slow
300	150	2	
325	170	3	Slow
350	180	4	Moderate
375	190	5	
400	200	6	Moderately Hot
425	220	7	Fairly Hot
450	230	8	Hot
475	240	9	Very Hot
500	250	10	Extremely Hot

Any broiling recipes can be used with the grill of the oven, but beware of high-temperature grills.

SUGGESTED EQUIVALENTS AND SUBSTITUTES FOR INGREDIENTS

all-purpose flour—plain flour
baking sheet—oven tray
buttermilk—ordinary milk
cheesecloth—muslin
coarse salt—kitchen salt
confectioner's sugar—icing sugar
cornstarch—cornflour
granulated sugar—caster sugar

half and half—12% fat milk
heavy cream—double cream
plastic wrap—cling film
shortening—white fat
unbleached flour—strong, white flour
vanilla bean—vanilla pod
zest—rind
zucchini—courgettes or marrow